Implementing Cisco Networking Solutions

Configure, implement, and manage complex network designs

Harpreet Singh

BIRMINGHAM - MUMBAI

Implementing Cisco Networking Solutions

First published: September 2017

Production reference: 1260917

Published by Packt Publishing Ltd.
Livery Place
35 Livery Street
Birmingham
B3 2PB, UK.
ISBN 978-1-78712-178-2

www.packtpub.com

Credits

Author
Harpreet Singh

Reviewer
Amir Roknifard

Commissioning Editor
Pratik Shah

Acquisition Editor
Prachi Bisht

Content Development Editor
Dattatraya More

Technical Editor
Sneha Hanchate

Copy Editors
Laxmi Subramanian
Ulka Manjrekar

Project Coordinator
Shweta H Birwatkar

Proofreader
Safis Editing

Indexer
Pratik Shirodkar

Graphics
Tania Dutta

Production Coordinator
Deepti Naik

About the Author

Harpreet Singh has more than 20 years of experience in the data domain and has been designing and implementing networks and solutions across technologies from X.25, FR, ATM, TCP/IP, and MPLS-based networks. Harpreet is a gold medalist and earned his bachelor of engineering degree before completing his postgraduate diploma in business administration. He has been a part of the faculty at the Advanced Level Telecom Training Center, a premier institute under the UNDP program for the training of telecom officers, where he conducted training on data networks, including technologies such as X.25, Frame Relay, ATM, Siemens Switches, and IP/ MPLS networks.

Harpreet has been a part of the core team for multiple pan-India network rollouts ranging from plain IP to Carrier Ethernet and MPLS. He has been involved with all major service providers in India. He was the network architect for the first pan-India IP network in 1997, the first MPLS network rollout in India in 2002, and the largest MetroE deployment in the world at the time in 2004. He was the technical director for the largest ever mobile backhaul IP network based on an IP/MPLS network. He is currently a technology consultant at Cisco Systems, engaged in large and complex cross-technology projects for strategic customers, advising them on network design, operations, and digital transformations.

Harpreet has been a speaker at forums such as APRICOT, IETE, and other international conferences. He can be reached at `harpreet_singh_2000@yahoo.com`.

About the Reviewer

Amir Roknifard is a self-educated cyber security Solutions Architect with a focus on web application, network, and mobile security. He leads research, development, and innovation at KPMG Malaysia and is a hobby coder and programmer that enjoy spending his time educating people about privacy and security, so that ordinary people have the knowledge to protect themselves. He likes automation and developed an integrated platform for Cyber Defense teams that could take care of their day-to-day workflow from request tickets to final reports.

He has completed many projects in the governmental, military and public sectors in different countries, and worked for banks and other financial institutions, oil and gas and telecommunication companies. He also has hours of lecturing on IT and information security topics on his resume, and reviewed several books in realm of information technology and security.

Amir also founded the Academician Journal, which aims to narrow the gap between academia and the information security industry. It tries to identify the reasons this gap occurs, analyse them and address them. He picks up new ideas that may be able to solve the problems of tomorrow and develops them. That is why like-minded people are always welcome to suggest their ideas for publication or co-authoring a piece of research through handle: @roknifard.

www.PacktPub.com

For support files and downloads related to your book, please visit www.PacktPub.com.

Did you know that Packt offers eBook versions of every book published, with PDF and ePub files available? You can upgrade to the eBook version at www.PacktPub.com and as a print book customer, you are entitled to a discount on the eBook copy. Get in touch with us at service@packtpub.com for more details.

At www.PacktPub.com, you can also read a collection of free technical articles, sign up for a range of free newsletters and receive exclusive discounts and offers on Packt books and eBooks.

https://www.packtpub.com/mapt

Get the most in-demand software skills with Mapt. Mapt gives you full access to all Packt books and video courses, as well as industry-leading tools to help you plan your personal development and advance your career.

Why subscribe?

- Fully searchable across every book published by Packt
- Copy and paste, print, and bookmark content
- On demand and accessible via a web browser

Customer Feedback

Thanks for purchasing this Packt book. At Packt, quality is at the heart of our editorial process. To help us improve, please leave us an honest review on this book's Amazon page at https://www.amazon.com/dp/178712178X.

If you'd like to join our team of regular reviewers, you can e-mail us at customerreviews@packtpub.com. We award our regular reviewers with free eBooks and videos in exchange for their valuable feedback. Help us be relentless in improving our products!

As I started on the journey of writing this book and sharing what I have learned over the years with a wider audience, I was both excited and nervous. Excited because I was sharing something I have learned with others, and nervous because of the feeling of responsibility that I don't want to tell the wrong story, even by mistake. Now that I have finished writing the drafts, I pause to think and look at what worked and what did not.

I wouldn't have been able to complete this work without a few people supporting me without asking any questions, and tolerating my moodiness when the deadlines were near. Thankfully, they really do have a lot of faith in me... and a high level of endurance. For that, I have to thank my parents, teachers, seniors, and colleagues, who made me capable of writing this book.

I would also like to thank my wife, Vandana, has always been a source of strength and encouragement in whatever I do in life. If I have truly learned anything from this experience, it is that writing a book needs a lot of prodding (believe me, I know) and that tough love, however annoying it may be, actually works.

My kids, Preetika and Pranav, who held on to their questions and riddles when I was writing, deserve a special mention. More so because they tell me that they had to tolerate me during this time, as I was always half concentrating, the other half thinking about the book. Although I think that may be true to a large extent, one can never truly be sure with teenagers. Even so, if I choose to write another one, I promise to be with them both in body and mind.

They say the best way to learn is to teach. And I learned so many things during the writing of this book. So, how can I forget my friend, Vikas Sharma, who got me the opportunity to work on this book, and the publishers, the editors Dattatraya More and Sneha Hanchate, and the technical reviewer Amir Rocknifard, who worked with me and kept me on a high through constant encouragement and feedback.

Finally, I would also like to mention the friendships I have built over the years. Friends across ages, from school, college, and previous organizations, have all contributed in some way or the other in shaping this book, because of the things I have learned from them and I am truly grateful.

Even though this book is on IP networking, and it may be hypocritical of me to say so, I would like to end this by saying what I would probably preach to my children:
Computer networking is useless. Make friends instead.

Table of Contents

Preface

Most enterprises use Cisco networking equipment to design and implement their networks. However, some networks outperform the networks in other enterprises in terms of performance and meeting new business demands, because they were designed for the present, keeping the future in mind. This book talks about how to design and implement enterprise networks for small-to-midsize organizations efficiently and effectively, so that the network design can accommodate the newer demands from the users in a seamless manner from adding more branches/users, to adding new services, and evaluating and implementing new technologies to optimize costs or enhance user experience.

What this book covers

We divided the book into three broad sections as follows:

- Network design fundamentals, where we review the fundamentals of TCP/ IP and discuss the network life cycle. We will also cover the business relevance of the network, and how networks are keeping up with the challenges of evolving businesses.
- The second part focuses on the various functional areas in the enterprise network, and covers the technologies and design choices within each functional area.
- The third section discusses an approach on managing and operating the network, and provide best practices for network management, and finally provide tips on troubleshooting the network.

Chapter 1, *Network Building Essentials*, provides a quick review the OSI and the TCP/IP stack, talks about the network life cycle, and covers the various life stages of the network from preparing to build the network, planning the network, designing the network, implementing the network, operating it, and finally optimizing the network.

Chapter 2, *Networks for Digital Enterprises*, talks about the emerging trends in enterprise IT networks, and talks about how changing business models are changing network designs. We will discuss desirable network traits in this section, which will then be used in the design sections.

Chapter 3, *Components of the Enterprise Network*, discusses the different parts of the enterprise network and lays down the reference architecture to be used throughout the book. This section consists of outlining the different parts of the network, for example, LAN, WAN, DC, and a internet connectivity, and defines the functional requirements from each part of the network. This chapter also introduces the reader to the various networking equipment such as switches and routers, and introduce IOS.

Chapter 4, *Understanding and Configuring Campus Network Technologies*, reviews IP addressing and basic layer 2 and layer 3 protocols, and discusses the complete design of the local area network in a floor of the building and extends it to the campus. The chapter discusses the design choices for a layer 2/layer 3 boundary, the various protocols used at layer 2, and the various routing protocols.

Chapter 5, *Understanding and Configuring Wireless Access Technologies,*discusses the various terminologies used in wireless networks, and provides a quick overview of the various wireless standards. The chapter then details on how to configure a wireless network within the enterprise in centralized and flexconnect modes of operation.

Chapter 6, *Understanding and Configuring WAN Technologies*, discusses the various types of options available for connecting different networks over wide area networks. The chapter describes technologies such as packet switched networks, leased lines, and MPLS VPNs, covering the pros and cons of each approach, and provides guidelines on how to use public networks to build overlay WAN using tunnels.

Chapter 7, *Understanding and Configuring Data Center Technologies*, describes the functions of a data center, and presents a sample design for how to segment the data center into various segments to ensure the security of the network.

Chapter 8, *Understanding and Configuring Network Security*, deals with the security aspects of the network infrastructure and provides guidelines on securing the control plane, the management plane, and the data plane in the network. This chapter also provides an overview of technologies involved in securing the network beyond routers and switches.

Chapter 9, *Understanding and Configuring Quality of Service*, talks about the importance of Quality of Service (QoS), discusses the impact of network degradation on various types of applications, and provides guidance on how to deploy QoS on the network to prioritize business-critical applications.

Chapter 10, *A Systematic Approach to Network Operations*, provides an introduction to the various models used for network life cycle and discusses an approach that helps to manage the network in a structured manner. The chapter also provides guidelines and best practices for network management.

Chapter 11, *Basic Troubleshooting Skills and Techniques*, provides an overview of the various issues on the network and provides an approach to troubleshooting the IP network.

What you need for this book

You will need an open mind and a lot of discussions with stakeholders to capture the user requirements, after which the technologies and design choices in this book will help you build a robust network. Most of the configurations shown in this book are for iOS release 15.

Who this book is for

This book is meant for network designers and IT engineers who are involved in designing the enterprise network and are involved in taking decisions to make network changes in order to meet newer business needs, such as evaluating new technology choices, enterprise growth, and adding new services on the network. The reader is expected to have a general understanding of the fundamentals of networking, including the OSI stack and IP addressing. This book will build upon these basic concepts and talk about the entire network life cycle, from designing the network to configuring the various Cisco devices to be used on the network.

Conventions

In this book, you will find a number of styles of text that distinguish between different kinds of information. Here are some examples of these styles, and an explanation of their meaning.

Code words in text, database table names, folder names, filenames, file extensions, pathnames, dummy URLs, user input, and Twitter handles are shown as follows:

"To save or write an image, we can use the `imsave()` function."

A block of code is set as follows:

```
Router(config)# interface GigabitEthernet 0/1
Router(config-if)# description To_Switch_Gig_0/1
Router(config-if)# ip addr 10.1.1.1 255.255.255.0
Router(config-if)# ip local-proxy arp
```

When we wish to draw your attention to a particular part of a code block, the relevant lines or items are set in bold:

```
Switch(config)# interface GigabitEthernet 0/1
Switch(config-if)# description User_facing_port
Switch(config-if)# storm-control broadcast level 5.00
Switch(config-if)# storm-control unicast level 80.00
Switch(config-if)# storm-control action trap
```

New terms and **important words** are shown in bold. Words that you see on the screen, in menus or dialog boxes, for example, appear in the text like this: "Clicking the **Next** button moves you to the next screen."

Warnings or important notes appear in a box like this.

Tips and tricks appear like this.

Reader feedback

Feedback from our readers is always welcome. Let us know what you think about this book-what you liked or disliked. Reader feedback is important to us as it helps us develop titles that you will really get the most out of. To send us general feedback, simply email feedback@packtpub.com, and mention the book's title in the subject of your message. If there is a topic that you have expertise in and you are interested in either writing or contributing to a book, see our author guide at www.packtpub.com/authors.

Customer support

Now that you are the proud owner of a Packt book, we have a number of things to help you to get the most from your purchase.

Downloading the example code

You can download the example code files for this book from your account at `http://www.packtpub.com`. If you purchased this book elsewhere, you can visit `http://www.packtpub.com/support` and register to have the files emailed directly to you.

You can download the code files by following these steps:

1. Log in or register to our website using your email address and password.
2. Hover the mouse pointer on the **SUPPORT** tab at the top.
3. Click on **Code Downloads & Errata**.
4. Enter the name of the book in the **Search** box.
5. Select the book for which you're looking to download the code files.
6. Choose from the drop-down menu where you purchased this book from.
7. Click on **Code Download**.

Once the file is downloaded, please make sure that you unzip or extract the folder using the latest version of:

- WinRAR / 7-Zip for Windows
- Zipeg / iZip / UnRarX for Mac
- 7-Zip / PeaZip for Linux

The code bundle for the book is also hosted on GitHub at `https://github.com/PacktPublishing/Implementing-Cisco-Networking-Solutions`. We also have other code bundles from our rich catalog of books and videos available at `https://github.com/PacktPublishing/`. Check them out!

Downloading the color images of this book

We also provide you with a PDF file that has color images of the screenshots/diagrams used in this book. The color images will help you better understand the changes in the output. You can download this file from `https://www.packtpub.com/sites/default/files/downloads/ImplementingCiscoNetworkingSolutions_ColorImages.pdf`.

Errata

Although we have taken every care to ensure the accuracy of our content, mistakes do happen. If you find a mistake in one of our books-maybe a mistake in the text or the code-we would be grateful if you could report this to us. By doing so, you can save other readers from frustration and help us improve subsequent versions of this book. If you find any errata, please report them by visiting http://www.packtpub.com/submit-errata, selecting your book, clicking on the **Errata Submission Form** link, and entering the details of your errata. Once your errata are verified, your submission will be accepted and the errata will be uploaded to our website or added to any list of existing errata under the Errata section of that title.

To view the previously submitted errata, go to https://www.packtpub.com/books/content/support and enter the name of the book in the search field. The required information will appear under the **Errata** section.

Piracy

Piracy of copyrighted material on the internet is an ongoing problem across all media. At Packt, we take the protection of our copyright and licenses very seriously. If you come across any illegal copies of our works in any form on the internet, please provide us with the location address or website name immediately so that we can pursue a remedy.

Please contact us at copyright@packtpub.com with a link to the suspected pirated material.

We appreciate your help in protecting our authors and our ability to bring you valuable content.

Questions

If you have a problem with any aspect of this book, you can contact us at questions@packtpub.com, and we will do our best to address the problem.

1
Network Building Essentials

"Alone we can do so little; together we can do so much."

- Helen Keller

Information technology (IT) has become an integral part of any modern business. This reliance on the use of technology has led to a lot of successful new businesses, and even a small delay in adopting new technology, not to mention alack of willingness to adopt new technologies, has led to the elimination of so many businesses around the world.

Networks are the foundation for IT, as they help connect multiple elements in the technological landscape of any organization. In this chapter, we will discuss the basic concepts that the reader will find useful in their goal of learning how to build IT networks. We will cover the following topics in this chapter:

- The need for networking and an introduction to IT networks
- A standard reference model for a network called the Open Systems Interconnection (OSI) model
- The TCP/IP protocol stack
- The various stages in building a network

Introduction to networks

The advent of computers has had a profound impact on society. These mechanical brains can carry out most jobs today in almost all sectors from medicine, education, aviation, retail, manufacturing, entertainment, communication, science and technology, research, aerospace, banking, space exploration, weather forecasting, and business transactions—the list is endless.

Computers have evolved a long way from the machine that Charles Babbage invented to the machines we see today. Much of it has been possible by the technological advances in semiconductor technology, which has made computers sleek, faster, and cost-effective. However, computers would not be as useful as they are today, if they were *"egoist machines"* not talking to one another, creating islands of excellence.

Businesses felt the need to leverage computing power across domains, and had a strong desire to automate the process to reduce manual dependencies. This acted as the driver for the evolution of communication networks that would enable communication between standalone computers. This ability to network computers has made them much more effective and acceptable in modern business.

As businesses evolved, and became more competitive, information and communication were regarded as among the most important factors that define the success of an organization, and hence the channels of carrying this information and communication became the lifelines of the organization. With the ever-increasing use of computers for carrying out most of the tasks in an organization, the information flow and communication between computers is becoming as important, if not more so, than between humans.

Early computer networks used different protocols such as DECnet, SNA, NetBIOS, and IPX to make computers communicate with each other. Although this facilitated networking, most of the protocols were proprietary, thereby limiting connectivity between machines from different vendors. Computer networking was fraught with cost inefficiencies, and interoperability issues because of the lack of a standard networking protocol that could be used across all vendors. Fortunately, the success of the ARPANET and the internet gave a big impetus to TCP/IP protocol, and the wide acceptance of the TCP/IP protocol stack among home and enterprise users forced many vendors to implement the stack on their devices. This changed computer networking and brought it to the levels of standardization and plug and play nature that exists today.

The OSI model and the TCP/IP stack

"A common language is a first step towards communication across cultural boundaries."

- Ethan Zuckerman

In communication, it is critical to have a common language and semantics that both parties can understand for the communication to be effective. This can be thought of as having a common language when talking of human communication, and as a protocol while talking of computer networking/communications. As discussed in the previous section, with the advent of computer networking, many vendors came out with their own proprietary protocols for computers to talk to each other, leading to interoperability issues between computer systems and networking was limited to devices from the same vendor. You can't get a person who knows only Chinese to effectively communicate with a person who knows only Russian!

International bodies involved in standardization were making efforts to evolve an open common framework, which could be used by all devices that needed to communicate with each other. These efforts led to the development of a framework called the **Basic Reference Model** for **Open Systems Interconnections** (**OSI**) reference model. This was jointly developed by the **International Organization for Standardization** (**ISO**) and **International Telegraph and Telephone Consultative Committee** (**CCITT**) (abbreviated from the Comité Consultatif International Téléphonique et Télégraphique), which later became the ITU-T.

We will broadly define the OSI model in the subsequent section, and then dive deeper into the TCP/IP model that will help clarify some of the concepts that might appear vague in the OSI discussion, as the OSI model is only a reference model without any standardization of interfaces or protocols, and was developed before the TCP/IP protocols were developed.

OSI had two major components as defined in the ISO/IEC 7498-1 standard:

- An abstract model of networking, called the Basic Reference Model or seven-layer model
- A set of specific protocols defined by other specifications within ISO

Basic OSI reference model

The communication entities perform a variety of different functions during the communication process. These functions range from creating a message, formatting the message, adding information that can help detect errors during transmission, sending the data on the physical medium, and so on.

The OSI reference model defines a layered model for interconnecting systems, with seven layers. The layered approach allows the model to group similar functions within a single layer, and provides standard interfaces allowing the various layers to talk to each other.

Figure 1 shows the seven layers of the OSI model. It is important to note that the reference model defines only the functions of each layer, and the interfaces with the adjoining layers. The OSI model neither standardizes the interfaces between the various layers within the system (subsequently standardized by other protocol standards) nor delves into the internals of the layer, as to how the functions are implemented in each layer.

The OSI model describes the communication flow between two entities as follows:

- The layers have a strict peering relationship, which means that layers at a particular level would communicate with its peer layers on the other nodes through a peering protocol, for example, data generated at layer 3 of one node would be received by the layer 3 at the other node, with which it has a peering relationship.
- The peering relationship can be between two adjacent devices, or across multiple hops. As an example, the intermediate node in figure 1, that has only layers 1 through 3, the peering relationship at layer 7 will be between the layer 7 at the transmitting and receiving nodes, which are not directly connected but are multiple hops away.
- The data to be transmitted is composed at the application layer of the transmitting node and will be received at the application layer of the receiving node.
- The data will flow down the OSI-layered hierarchy from layer 7 to layer 1 at the transmitting node, traverse the intermediate network, and flow up the layered hierarchy from layer 1 to layer 7 at the receiving node. This implies that within a node, the data can be handed over by a layer to its adjacent layer only. Each layer will perform its designated functions and then pass on the processed data to the next layer:

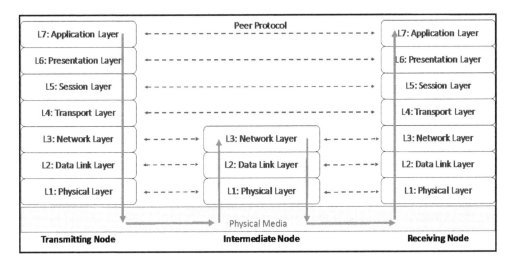

Figure 1: The OSI reference model

The high-level functions of each layer are described as follows:

Layer 1 - The physical layer

The primary function of this layer is to convert the bit stream onto the physical medium by converting it into electrical/optical impulses or radio signals. This layer provides the physical connection to the underlying medium and also provides the hardware means to activate, maintain, and de-activate physical connections between data link entities. This includes sequencing of the bit stream, identifying channels on the underlying medium, and optionally multiplexing. This should not be confused with the actual medium itself.

Some of the protocols that have a layer 1 component are Ethernet, G.703, FDDI, V.35, RJ45, RS232, SDH, DWDM, OTN, and so on.

Layer 2 - The data link layer

The data link layer acts as the driver of the physical layer and controls its functioning. The data link layer sends data to the physical layer at the transmitting end and receives data from the physical layer at the receiving node. It also provides error detection and correction that might have occurred during transmission/reception at the physical medium, and also defines the process for flow control between the two nodes to avoid any buffer overruns on either side of the data link connection. This can happen using PAUSE frames in Ethernet, and should not be confused with flow control in higher layers.

Some of the protocols that operate at the data link layer are LAPB, 802.3 Ethernet, 802.11 WiFi and 802.15.4 ZigBee, X.25, **Point to Point** (**PPP**) protocol, HDLC, SLIP, ATM, Frame Relay, and so on.

Layer 3 - The network layer

The basic service of the network layer is to provide the transparent transfer of datagrams between the transport layers at the two nodes. This layer is also responsible for finding the right intermediate nodes that might be required to send data to the destination node, if the destination node is not on the same network as the source node. This layer also breaks down datagrams into smaller fragments, if the underlying datalink layer is not capable of handling the datagram that is offered to the network layer for transport on the network.

A fundamental concept in the OSI stack is that data should be passed to a higher layer at the receiving node as it was handed over to the lower layers by the transmitting peer. As an example, the TCP layer passes TCP segments to the IP layer, and the IP layer might use the services of the lower layers, leading to fragment packets on the way to the destination, but when the IP layer passes the data to the TCP layer at the receiving node, the data should be in the form of TCP segments that were handed down to the IP layer at the transmitting end. To ensure this transparent transfer of datagrams to the receiving node TCP layer, the network layer at the receiving node reassembles all the fragments of a single datagram before handing it over to the transport layer.

The OSI model describes both connection-oriented and connectionless modes of the OSI network layer.

Connection- oriented and **connectionless modes** are used to describe the readiness of the communicating nodes before the process of actual data transfer between the two nodes. In the connection-oriented mode, a connection is established between the source and the destination, and a path is defined along the network through which actual data transfer would happen. A telephone call is a typical example of this mode, where you cannot talk until a connection has been established between the calling number and the called number.

In the connectionless mode of data transfer, the transmitting node just sends the data on the network without first establishing a connection, or verifying whether the receiving end is ready to accept data, or even if the receiving node is up or not. In this mode, there is no connection or path established between the source and the destination, and data generally flows in a hop by hop manner, with a decision being taken on the best path towards the destination at every hop. Since, data is sent without any validation of the receiving node status, there is no acknowledgement of data in a connectionless mode of data transfer. This is unlike the connection-oriented mode, where the path is defined the moment a connection is established, and all data flows along that path, with the data transfer being acknowledged between the two communicating nodes.

Since data packets in a connection-oriented mode follow a fixed path to the destination, the packets arrive in the same sequence at the receiver in which they were transmitted. On the other hand, packets in the case of a connectionless network might reach the receiver out of sequence if the packets are routed on different links on the network, as decisions are taken at every hop.

The OSI standard defined the network layer to provide both modes. However, most of the services were implemented in practice as the connectionless mode at layer 3, and the connection-oriented aspects were left to layer 4. We will discuss this further during our discussion on TCP/IP.

Some of the protocols that operate at the network layer are AppleTalk, DDP, IP, IPX, CLNP, IS-IS, and so on.

Layer 4 - The transport layer

The transport layer provides the functional and procedural means of transferring variable-length data sequences from a source to a destination host via one or more networks. This layer has end-to-end significance and provides a connectionless or connection-oriented service to the session layer. This layer is responsible for connection establishment, management, and release.

The transport layer controls the reliability of a given link through end-to-end flow control, segmentation/de-segmentation, and error control. This layer also provides multiplexing functions of multiplexing various data connections over a single network layer.

Some protocols operating at the transport layer are TCP, UDP, SCTP, NBF, and so on.

Layer 5 - The session layer

The primary purpose of the session layer is to coordinate and synchronize the dialog between the presentation layers at the two end points and to manage their data exchange. This layer establishes, manages, and terminates connections between applications. The session layer sets up, coordinates, and terminates conversations, exchanges, and dialogues between the applications at each end.

Some of the protocols operating at the session layer are sockets, NetBIOS, SAP, SOCKS, RPC, and so on.

Layer 6 - The presentation layer

The presentation layer provides a common representation of the data transferred between application entities, and provides independence from differences in data representation/syntax. This layer is also sometimes referred to as the syntax layer. The presentation layer works to transform data into the form that the application layer can accept. This layer is also responsible for encryption and decryption for the application data.

Some examples of protocols at the presentation layer are MIME, ASCII, GIF, JPEG, MPEG, MIDI, SSL, and so on.

Layer 7 - The application layer

The application layer is the topmost layer of the OSI model, and has no upper-layer protocols. The software applications that need communication with other systems interact directly with the OSI application layer. This layer is not to be confused with the application software, which is the program that implements the software; for example, HTTP is an application layer protocol, while Google Chrome is a software application.

The application layer provides services directly to user applications. It enables the users and software applications to access the network and provides user interfaces and support for services such as email, remote file access and transfer, shared database management, and other types of distributed information services.

Some examples of application layer protocols are HTTP, SMTP, SNMP, FTP, DNS, LDAP, Telnet, and so on.

The TCP/IP model

The **Advanced Research Projects Agency Network** (**ARPANET**), which was initially funded by the US **Department of Defense** (**DoD**) was an early packet-switching network and the first network to implement the protocol suite TCP/IP. ARPANET was the test bed of the TCP/IP protocol suite which resulted in the TCP/IP model also known as the DoD model.

The TCP/IP model is a simplified model of the OSI model and has only four broad layers instead of the seven layers of the OSI model. *Figure 2* shows the comparison between the two models. As can be seen from the following figure, the TCP/IP model is a much more simplified model, where the top three layers of the OSI model have been combined into a single application layer, and the physical and data link layers have been combined into a network access layer:

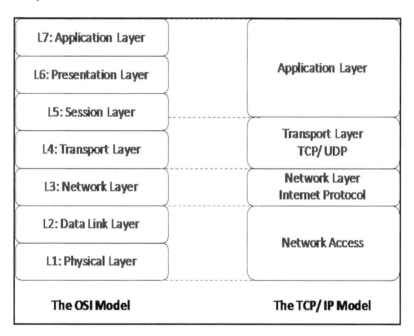

Figure 2: Comparing the OSI model with TCP/IP model

Some of the major differences between the two models are as follows:

- The functions of the application layer in the TCP/IP model include the functions of the application, presentation and session layer of the OSI model

- The OSI session layer function of graceful close/end-to-end connection setup, management, and release is taken over by the TCP/IP transport layer (**Transmission Control Protocol**)
- The network access layer combines the functions of the OSI data link and the physical layers
- The network layer in the OSI mode can be connection oriented or connectionless, while the **Internet Protocol** (**IP**) is a connectionless protocol
- The transport layer in the OSI model is connection oriented, whereas, different protocols at the transport layer in the TCP/IP model provide different types of services; for example, TCP provides a connection oriented service, while UDP provides a connectionless service

Let's explore what happens when data moves from one layer to another in the TCP/IP model taking *Figure 3* as an example. When data is given to the software application, for example, a web browser, the browser sends this data to the application layer, which adds a HTTP header to the data. This is known as application data. This application data is then passed on to the TCP layer, which adds a TCP header to it, thus creating a TCP segment. This segment is then passed on to the network layer (IP layer) where the IP header is added to the segment creating an IP packet or IP datagram. This IP header is then encapsulated by the data link adding a data link header and trailer, creating a Frame. This frame is then transmitted onto the transmission medium as a bit stream in the form of electrical/optical/radio signals depending upon the physical media used for communication:

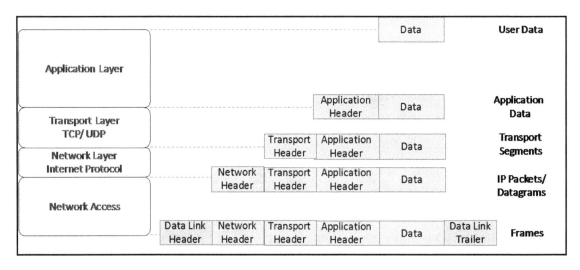

Figure 3: Data flow across the TCP/IP layers

A simplified stack showing some protocols in the TCP/ IP stack is shown in the following figure:

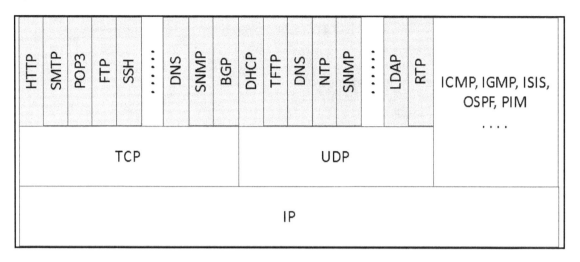

Figure 4: Common protocols in the TCP/IP stack

Let's delve deeper into the TCP/IP model by looking at the TCP/IP headers in some more detail.

Internet Protocol (IP)

Internet Protocol (**IP**) as it is commonly known, was developed by Bob Kahn and Vinton Cerf, and is a protocol operating at layer 3 (network layer) of the OSI model. The primary function of the IP is to transfer datagrams from source to destination and provide a network transport service. As noted in the preceding section, IP as defined in the TCP/IP model operates in a connectionless mode, and hence is sometimes referred to as Send and Pray protocol, as there is no acknowledgement/guarantee that the IP datagrams sent by the source have been received by the destination. This function is left to the upper layers of the protocol stack.

Figure 5 shows the structure and fields of an IPv4 header. The IPv4 header is defined in the IETF standard, RFC 791. The header is appended by the network layer to the TCP/UDP segments handed to the network layer. The length of the header is always a multiple of 4 bytes. The section consists of multiple fields that are outlined in the following figure.

The length of each part of the IPv4 header in bits is highlighted in *Figure 5* within parenthesis after the name of the field:

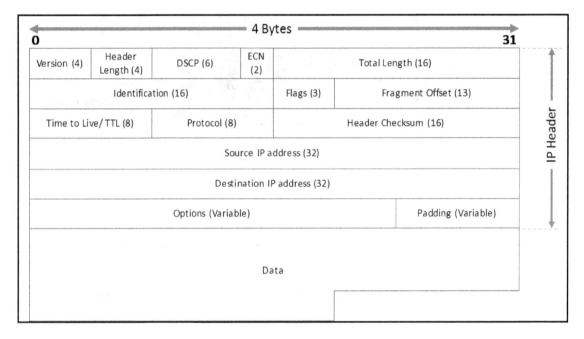

Figure 5: IPv4 packet format

We will now talk about the fields in brief:

- **Version (4)**: This is a 4-bit field and is used to decode the IP address version being used by the IP system. The version for the header depicted in *Figure 5* is version 4. There is a newer version of IP called IP version 6 or IPv6, which has a different header format and is discussed later.
- **Header Length**: This is again a 4-bit field, and encodes the length of the IP header in 4-byte words. This means that if the IPv4 header has no options, the header would be 20 bytes long, and hence would consist of five 4-byte words. Hence, the value of the header length field in the IP header would be 5. This field cannot have a value less than 5 as the fields in the first 20 bytes of the IPv4 header are mandatory.

- **DSCP**: **Differentiated Services Code Point** (**DSCP**) is a 6-bit field in the IPv4 header and is used to encode the **Quality of Service** (**QoS**) required by the IP datagram on the network. This field will define if the packet will be treated as a priority packet on the network, or should be discarded if there is congestion on the network. This field was not in the original RFC for IP, but was added later by RFC 2474 to support differentiated models for QoS on IP networks. We will discuss this in detail in the chapter on QoS implementation.

- **ECN**: **Explicit Congestion Notification** (**ECN**) is a 2-bit field defined by RFC 2481, and the latest standard for this at the time of writing is RFC3168. This field is used to explicitly notify the end hosts if the intermediate devices have encountered congestion so that the end devices can slow down the traffic being sent on the network, by lowering the TCP window. This helps in managing congestion on the network even before the intermediate devices start to drop packets due to queue overruns.

- **Total Length**: This is a 16-bit field that encodes the total length of the IP datagram in bytes. The total length of the IP datagram is the length of the TCP segment plus the length of the IP header. Since this is a 16-bit field, the total length of a single IP datagram can be 65535 bytes (216-1). The most commonly used length for the IP datagram on the network is 1500 bytes. We will delve deeper into the impact of the IP datagram size in the later chapters while discussing the impact on the WAN.

- **Identification (ID)**: This 16-bit value uniquely identifies an IP datagram for a given source address, destination address, and protocol, such that it does not repeat within the maximum datagram lifetime, which is set to 2 minutes by the TCP specification (RFC 793). RFC 6864 has made some changes to the original fields that are relevant only at high data rates, and in networks that undergo fragmentation. These issues will be discussed in the later chapters.

- **Flags**: These are three different flags in the IPv4 header as shown in *Figure 6*. Each flag is one bit in length. The flags are used when the IP layer needs to send a datagram of a length that cannot be handled by the underlying data link layer. In this case, the intermediate nodes can fragment the datagram into smaller ones, which are reassembled by the IP layer at the receiving node, before passing on to the TCP layer. The flags are meant to control the fragmentation behavior:

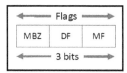

Figure 6: Flags in IPv4 header

- **MBZ**: This stands for **Must be Zero** (**MBZ**), where bits are always sent as 0 on the network.
- **DF**: This stands for **Do Not Fragment** (**DF**) bit, which if set to 1 means that this packet should not be fragmented by the intermediate nodes. Such packets are discarded by the intermediate nodes, if there is a need to fragment these packets, and an error message is sent to the transmitting node using **Internet Control Message Protocol** (**ICMP**).
- **MF**: This stands for **More Fragments** (**MF**) bit, which if set to 1 signifies that this is a fragmented packet and there are more fragments of the original datagram. The last fragment and an unfragmented packet will have the MF bit as 0:
    - **Fragment Offset**: This field is 13 bits long and is used only by the fragmented packets to denote where in the original datagram the fragment belongs. The first fragment will have the offset as 0 and the subsequent fragments will have the fragment offset value that defines the length of all fragments before this fragment in the original datagram as a number, where each number is 8 bytes.
    - **Time To Live/TTL**: This 8-bit field is used to denote the maximum number of intermediate nodes that can process the packet at the IP layer. Each intermediate node decrements the value by 1 to ensure that the IP packet does not get caught in an infinite routing loop and keeps on going back and forth between nodes. The packet is discarded when the field reaches a zero value, and is discarded by the node, and an error message sent to the source of the datagram as an ICMP message.
    - **Protocol**: This 8-bit field is used to denote what upper layer protocol is being encapsulated in the IP packet. Since the IP layer multiplexes multiple transport layers, for example, UDP, TCP, OSPF, ICMP, IGMP, and so on, this field acts as a demultiplexing identifier to identify which upper layer should the payload be handed to at the receiving node. The values for this field were originally defined in RFC 1700, which is now obsolete, and is replaced by an online database. Some of the common values for the protocol field are shown in the following figure:

Protocol Number	Hex	Keyword	Protocol
1	0x01	ICMP	Internet Control Message Protocol
2	0x02	IGMP	Internet Group Management Protocol
6	0x06	TCP	Transmission Control Protocol
17	0x11	UDP	User Datagram Protocol
88	0x58	EIGRP	EIGRP
89	0x59	OSPF	Open Shortest Path First

Figure 7: Some common IP protocol numbers

- **Header Checksum**: This 16-byte field is used for checking the integrity of the received IP datagram. This value is calculated using an algorithm covering all the fields in the header (assuming this field to be zero for the purposes of calculating the header checksum). This value is calculated and stored in the header when the IP datagram is sent from source to destination and at the destination side this checksum is again calculated and verified against the checksum present in header. If the value is the same, then the datagram was not corrupted, else it's assumed that datagram was received corrupted.

- **Source IP address and Destination IP address**: These 32-bit fields contain the source and destination IP addresses respectively. Since the length of an IPv4 address is 32 bits, this field length was set to 32 bits. With the introduction of IPv6, which has a 128-bit address, this cannot fit in this format, and there is a different format for an IPv6 header.

- **Options**: This optional, variable-length field contains certain options that can be used by IP protocol. Some of these options can be used for Strict Source routing, Loose Source routing, Record route options, and so on that are used for troubleshooting and other protocols.

- **Padding**: This is a field that is used to pad the IP header to make the IPv4 header length a multiple of 4 bytes, as the definition of the Header Length field mandates that the IPv4 header length is a multiple of 4 bytes.

- **Data**: This variable length field contains the actual payload that is encapsulated at the IP layer, and consists of the data that is passed onto the upper layer transport protocols to the IP layer. The upper layer protocols attach their own headers as the data traverses down the protocol stack, as we saw in *Figure 3: Data flow across the TCP/IP layers*.

Transmission Control Protocol (TCP)

"The single biggest problem with communication is the illusion that it has taken place."

- George Bernard Shaw

As discussed in the previous section, IP provides a connectionless service. There is no acknowledgement mechanism in the IP layer, and the IP packets are routed at every hop from the source to the destination. Hence, it is possible that some packets sent by the transmitting node are lost on the network due to errors, or are discarded by the intermediate devices due to congestion on the network. Hence the receiving node will never receive the lost packets in the absence of a feedback mechanism.

Further, if there are multiple paths on the network to reach the destination from the source, it is possible that packets will take different paths to reach the destination, depending upon the routing topology at a given time. This implies that packets can reach the receiving node out of sequence with respect to the sequence in which they were transmitted.

The TCP layer ensures that whatever was transmitted is correctly received. The purpose of the TCP layer is to ensure that the receiving host application layer sees a continuous stream of data as was transmitted by the transmitting node as though the two were connected through a direct wire. Since TCP provides that service to the application layer using the underlying services of the IP layer, TCP is called a connection-oriented protocol.

A typical TCP segment is shown in *Figure 8*, where the different fields of the TCP header are shown along with their lengths in bits in parentheses. A brief description of the functions of the various fields is shown in the following figure:

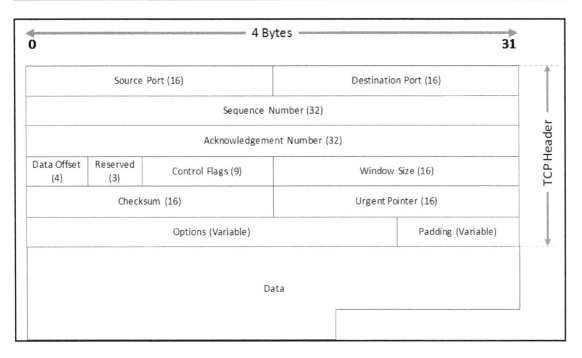

Figure 8: Transmission Control Protocol (TCP) segment structure

- **Source Port/Destination Port**: As discussed in the earlier sections, the transport layer provides the multiplexing function of multiplexing various data connections over a single network layer. The source port and destination port fields are 16-bit identifiers that are used to distinguish the upper layer protocols. Some of the common TCP port numbers are shown in the following figure:

TCP Port	Hex	Keyword	Protocol
20	0x14	FTP	File Transfer Protocol, Data
21	0x15	FTP	File Transfer Protocol, Control
22	0x16	SSH	Secure Shell
25	0x19	SMTP	Simple Mail Transfer Protocol
80	0x50	HTTP	Hyper Text Transfer Protocol
110	0x6E	POP	Post Office Protocol

Figure 9: Common TCP Port Numbers

- **Sequence Number**: This 16-bit field is used to number the starting byte of the payload data in this TCP segment with relation to the overall data stream that is being transmitted as a part of the TCP session.
- **Acknowledgement Number**: This 16-bit field is a part of the feedback mechanism to the sender and is used to acknowledge to the sender how many bytes of the stream have been received successfully, and in sequence. The acknowledgement number identifies the next byte that the receiving node is expecting on this TCP session.
- **Data Offset**: This 4-bit field is used to convey how far from the start of the TCP header the actual message starts. Hence, this value indicates the length of the TCP header in multiples of 32-bit words. The minimum value of this field is 5.
- **Reserved**: These are bits that are not to be used, and will be reserved for future use.
- **Control flags**: There are 9 bits reserved in the TCP header for control flags and there are 9 one-bit flags as shown in *Figure 10*. Although these flags are carried from left to right, we will describe them in the random order for ease of understanding:

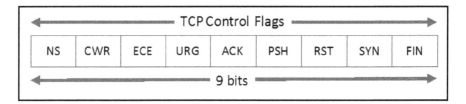

Figure 10: TCP control Flags

- **SYN**: This 1-bit flag is used to initiate a TCP connection during the three-way handshake process.
- **FIN**: This 1-bit flag is used to signify that there is no more data to be sent on this TCP connection, and can be used to terminate the TCP session.
- **RST**: This 1-bit flag is used to reject the connection to maintain synchronization of the TCP session between two hosts.
- **PSH**: Push (**PSH**) is a 1-bit flag that tells the TCP receiver not to wait for the buffer to be full, but to send the data gathered so far to the upper layers.
- **ACK**: This 1-bit flag is used to signify that the Acknowledgement field in the header is significant.
- **URG**: Urgent (**URG**) is also a 1-bit flag, and when set signifies that this segment contains Urgent data and the urgent pointer defines the location of that urgent data.

- **ECE**: This 1-bit flag (ECN Echo) signals to the network layer that the host is capable of using Explicit Congestion techniques as defined in the ECN bit section of the IP header. This flag is not a part of the original TCP specification, but is added by RFC 3168.
- **CWR**: This is also a 1-bit flag added by RFC 3168. The Congestion Window Reduced (CWR) flag is set by the sending host to indicate that it received a TCP segment with the ECE flag set.
- **NS** (1 bit): This 1-bit flag is defined by an experimental RFC 3540, with the primary intention that the sender can verify the correct behavior of the ECN receiver.
        - **Window Size**: This 16-bit field indicates the number of data octets beginning with the one indicated in the acknowledgment field, which the sender of this segment is willing to accept. This is used to prevent the buffer overruns at the receiving node.
        - **Checksum**: This 16-byte field is used for checking the integrity of the received TCP segment.
        - **Urgent Pointer**: The urgent pointer field is often set to zero and ignored, but in conjunction with the URG control flags, it can be used as a data offset to identify a subset of a message that requires priority processing.
        - **Options**: These are used to carry additional TCP options such as **Maximum Segment Size** (**MSS**) that the sender of the segment is willing to accept.
        - **Padding**: This is a field that is used to pad the TCP header to make the header length a multiple of 4 bytes, as the definition of the data offset field mandates that the TCP header length be a multiple of 4 bytes.
        - **Data**: This is the data that is being carried in the TCP segment and includes the application layer headers.

Most of the traffic that we see on the internet today is TCP traffic. TCP ensures that application data is sent from the source to the destination in the sequence that it was transmitted, thus providing a connection oriented service to the application. To this end, TCP uses acknowledgement and congestion control mechanisms using the various header fields described earlier. At a very high level, if the segments are received at the receiver TCP layer that are out of sequence, the TCP layer buffers these segments and waits for the missing segments, asking the source to resend the data if required. This buffering, and the need to sequence datagrams, needs processing resources, and also causes unnecessary delay for the receiver.

We live in a world where data/information is time sensitive, and loses value if delivered later in time. Consider seeing the previous day's newspaper at your doorstep one morning. Similarly, there are certain types of traffic that lose their value if the traffic is delayed. This type of traffic is usually voice and video traffic when encapsulated in IP. Such traffic is time sensitive and there is no point in providing acknowledgements, and adding to delays. Hence, this type of traffic is carried in a **User Datagram Protocol** (**UDP**) that is a connectionless protocol and does not use any retransmission mechanism. We will explore this more during our discussions on designing and implementing QoS.

User Datagram Protocol (UDP)

UDP is a protocol that provides connectionless service to the application, and sends data to the application layer as received, without worrying about lost parts of the application data stream or some parts being received out of order. A UDP packet is shown in *Figure 11*:

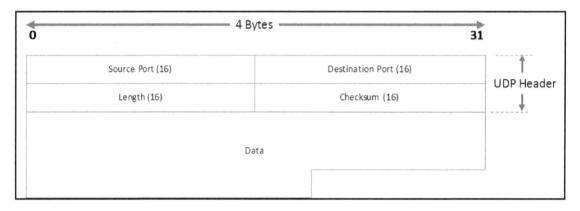

Figure 11: UDP packet structure

Since UDP provides lesser services compared to TCP, the packet has fewer fields and is much simpler. The UDP datagram can be of any length as can be encapsulated in the IP packets as follows, and has a header that is of fixed 8-byte length. The different fields in the UDP packet are discussed as follows:

- **Source Port/Destination Port**: Like TCP, UDP also serves multiple applications and hence has to provide the multiplexing function to cater to multiple applications that might want to use the services of the UDP layer. The source port/destination port fields are 16-bit identifiers that are used to distinguish the upper layer protocols. Some of the common UDP port numbers are shown in the following figure:

UDP Port	Hex	Keyword	Protocol
49	0x31	TACACS	Terminal Access Controller Access-Control System
53	0x35	DNS	Domain Name System
67	0x43	BOOTP	Bootstrap Protocol, Server
68	0x44	BOOTP	Bootstrap Protocol, Client
69	0x45	TFTP	Trivial File Transfer Protocol
123	0x7B	NTP	Network Time Protocol

Figure 12: Common UDP port numbers

- **Length**: This 16-bit field represents the total size of each UDP datagram, including both header and data. The values range from a minimum of 8 bytes (the required header size) to sizes above 65,000 bytes.
- **Checksum**: Similar to TCP, this 16-bit field is used for checking the integrity of the received UDP datagram.
- **Data**: This is the data that is being carried in the UDP packet and includes the application layer headers.

IP version 6

IPv6 is a new version of the IP protocol. The current version IPv4 had a limited number of IP addresses (2^{32} addresses), and there was a need to connect more hosts. Hence IPv6 allows for a 128-bit address field compared to a 32-bit address field in IPv4. Hence, IPv6 can have 2^{128} unique IP addresses. IPv6 also provides some new features and does away with some features of the IPv4 packet such as fragmentation and Header checksum. *Figure 13* shows the IPv6 header and shows the various fields of the IPv6 header:

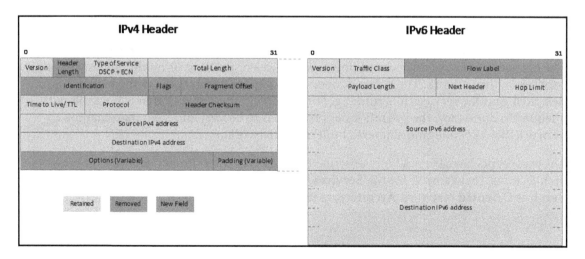

Figure 13: IPv6 header

We will not go into the details of IPv6 in this book, but will cover it as and when required during the discussion on design and implementation.

Building a network

Now that we have reviewed the basics of the networking protocols that would be fundamental to build an Enterprise network, let's discuss the considerations for building an IP network.

Purpose of networks

We see so many networks around us. Each network has a specific purpose for which it is built. For example, the primary purpose of the networks that we see in computer labs is to provide access to shared resources, most notably printers and data storage. The networks in the manufacturing plant are meant to carry control signals for the various plant machinery that are connected on the network. The military and defense networks have a totally different purpose.

Since the networks are supposed to deliver different services to the end users, the design of the network will be different, and will be defined by the characteristics of the services to a large extent. Hence, the starting point for planning a network is to define the services that the network will offer, so that the network can be built accordingly.

Once the network is built, and starts offering services to the end users, it needs to be operated, and changes need to be made on the network on a day-to-day basis. The operations include monitoring the network for critical network parameters, and taking corrective action in case of network incidents such as outages/performance degradations. The changes might also include adding new services or deleting or modifying any existing services on the network. The network operations depend upon the way the network is designed, and the services it is running. For example, for a network that is not built with adequate redundancy, the operations approach has to be very different than that for a network that has enough resiliencies built in the network.

These concepts have been widely described and used in the frameworks used for network architectures, for example, for the **Services, Network, Operations** (**SNO**) approach, or the **Services Oriented Network Architecture** (**SONA**) framework proposed by Cisco.

Network lifecycle

As discussed in the previous section, the network is built for a specific purpose. Operating the network involves making changes to the network parameters, and sometimes design, to meet new business/application requirements, and finally the network is either replaced by a new design or incorporates a new technology. Since the network is dynamic, it is important to have a systematic approach based on the different phases of the network. Different approaches have been proposed by different vendors, but almost all of them are essentially overlapping and similar. In this section, we will cover Cisco's PPDIOO approach for network lifecycle, as it is the most comprehensive approach, and is a superset of other approaches within the scope of the network lifecycle. **PPDIOO** is an acronym for **Prepare, Plan, Design, Implement, Operate, and Optimize**.

Other forms of the lifecycle approach that are simplified versions of the PPDIOO approach are the **Plan, Build, Manage** (**PBM**) approach where some of the stages of the PPDIOO approach are combined into the three phases of the PBM approach.

Advantages of network lifecycle approach

The network lifecycle approach provides several key benefits aside from keeping the design process organized. Some of the benefits of using a structured lifecycle approach to network design are as follows:

- **Lowering the total cost of network ownership**: Businesses have always used the **total cost of ownership** (**TCO**) approach to take decisions. With IT becoming more and more relevant to business today, their IT decisions have to follow the approach of TCO rather than a pure **capital expenditure** (**CAPEX**) approach. This means that the **operational expenses** (**OPEX**) that have to be incurred while running and maintaining the network are also an important factor in the overall network approach. The network lifecycle approach helps in lowering the TCO by:
  - Identifying, evaluating, and choosing the right technology options.
  - Developing and documenting a design that is aligned with the business/service requirements.
  - Building implementation plans that can minimize the risk of implementation, thus avoiding cost and time overruns.
  - Planning for the operations as an integral part of network design so as to improve the operational efficiency by choosing the right set of tools, and operational skills required.

- **Increasing services uptime**: Downtime or outages are the most dreaded terms in network operations, as they causes service disruption resulting in loss of revenue and goodwill. A network lifecycle approach can help reduce downtime by:
    - Identifying the network elements that need to be highly available for service availability, and designing the network for redundancy of such elements.
    - Planning the operational skills required for the network, and ensuring that the **Network Operations Center** (**NOC**) staff has the right skills.

- **Improving business agility**: As businesses are faced with dynamic market trends, IT needs to be able to support business quickly and efficiently. This agility means that the network should have the ability to make changes to the way existing services are delivered on the network, or the ability to quickly add new services to the network based on the business requirements. A lifecycle approach helps provide this agility to the network by:
    - Capturing the business and technology requirements and their dependencies.
    - Developing detailed designs for each service at a block level and at a configuration level such that new services can be added without impacting the existing services.
    - Defining the horizontal and vertical scaling options for the network design during the design phase itself so that capacity can be quickly added to the network when required by the applications.
    - Creating operational run books and bringing in operational efficiencies through the proper use of tools and the right resource skills.

The PPDIOO approach consists of six phases as depicted in *Figure 14*, which are described as shown in the following diagram:

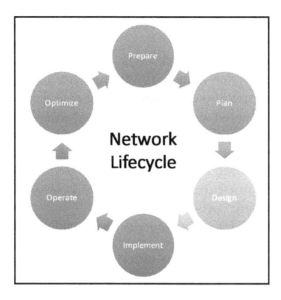

Figure14: The PPDIOO approach

Prepare phase

"Planning is bringing the future into the present so that you can do something about it now."

- Alan Lakein

It is said with reference to the OSI layers that there is an eighth layer that rides preceding the application layer, and that is the business layer, as this is the layer that will define what applications are to be used on the network. The prepare phase tries to capture the business layer and the technological requirements of the underlying network infrastructure.

The prepare and the plan phases of the network lifecycle talk about the future and then hand it over to the next phases, which are concerned with how to build the present network so that it can meet the future requirements.

The prepare phase involves establishing the organizational requirements from a business perspective, and developing an appropriate technology strategy. The following are some examples of questions to be answered in this stage:

- What is the vision of the company?

- What are the business goals of the company today, and anticipating the goals and IT requirements in the future?
- What is the cloud strategy for the organization?
- Would the organization want to own the network assets and build a data center, or just host the applications in an outsourced data center?
- What will be the model of the DC outsourcing? Infrastructure as a Service or Platform, or Software as a Service?
- What is the communications strategy of the company? Would the company want to move to cloud-based models for its internal communications?
- What will be the WAN strategy for the network? Would the WAN links be owned or on a shared network?
- What is the Operations strategy for the organization?

The end goal of this stage is to develop a network strategy by comparing the different options and to propose an architectural view that identifies the various technologies to be used in the network, and the interdependencies between the various technologies. This phase also covers a lot of financial analysis, and building business cases for the decisions as all decisions have to be backed by sound financial reasoning.

By preparing for the network rollout in this manner, the company has a fair view of the budgetary requirements for the project in terms of time, money, and resources, and a long-term roadmap that can be leveraged as the business requirements change with time.

Most of these decisions are taken by the senior management and have already been taken by the time a network is being designed and implemented. Hence, we will not delve any further into these aspects in this book, but focus on the implications of the various technologies and how they impact the operational and business models in subsequent chapters.

Plan phase

This is the phase where the job of an actual network architect starts. This phase involves getting the right stakeholders together and documenting the network requirements with respect to the network goals, services, user needs, and so on. The plan phase involves identifying the sites, classifying them, and evaluating the existing network infrastructure if any to understand if the existing assets can be reused and redesigned for the new network. This phase also involves finalizing the hardware requirements for the network infrastructure devices.

Some of the questions that need to be answered at this stage are as follows:

- Who are the users of this network and what is the level of segmentation required between the various users?
- What are the services required by each group of users?
- Where are the users located?
- What is the hardware required to meet the user requirements?
- Where will the new hardware be installed?
- What are the power and space requirements at the locations?
- What are the existing services/network if any that need to be integrated/replaced by the new network?
- Where would the network be connected to the internet?
- What is the current security state of the company?
- What operational skills will be required to design/implement and operate the network?

Two important documents that are created during this phase are the **Customer Requirement Document** (**CRD**) that contains the detailed technical specifications of the network to be built, and the **Site Requirement Specification** (**SRS**) document that contains the physical, electrical, and environmental specifications for each site, where the equipment will be deployed. Site audits are done based upon the SRS documents to ensure that the sites are ready for the equipment to be installed, and any gaps/corrective action required is identified.

We will cover some of these topics in `Chapter 2`, *Networks for Digital Enterprises*, where we will describe the network requirements for a modern enterprise.

Design phase

The business requirements have been drilled down into technical requirements until the planning phase. Now is the time to convert the technical requirements into the actual protocol-level details that will ensure that the network delivers the technical, functional, and performance requirements that the network is being designed for. In this phase of the network lifecycle, some of the most technical decisions are made such as:

- What should be the physical topology of the network?
- What should be the logical topology of the network?
- How should we plan for redundancy at the node level, site level, and at a service level?

- What should be the IP addressing schema for the network?
- What protocols should run on the network?
- How do we prioritize the different types of applications on the network?
- How do we segment the users on the network?
- How do we ensure security of the network devices?
- What management protocols should be run on the network?
- How would the different services be deployed on the network?
- How would we ensure that adding a new service does not impact any existing service?

It is in the design phase of the network lifecycle that the documents called the **High-level design** (**HLD**) and **Low-level design** (**LLD**) documents are made. The high-level design talks about the network design at a protocol level, and the low-level design talks about how to implement the design on the network devices and arriving at configuration templates. These design documents detail the design to meet the requirements of availability, reliability, flexibility, security, scalability, and performance.

The detailed design can also help in chalking out the day-to-day operational activities and network management processes, thereby simplifying network operations and helping to reduce OPEX and TCO. The design phase is also the phase when the design is validated on a staged network in the lab and configuration templates are fine-tuned.

Another important activity in the design phase is to define the test cases that will be executed on the network to ensure that the network is built as designed. The test case document is generally called an **Acceptance Test Plan** (**ATP**) document or a **Network Ready for Use** (**NRFU**) test plan. Having a documented test plan down to the details on how to execute the tests and what commands to run to validate the network implementation is crucial to ensure that the network will run as per the required specifications. A typical NRFU will have two parts: one covering the test cases that can be carried out on a standalone basis at each site, and the other part covering the end-to-end service testing across the entire network. The NRFU document can also add additional parts specific to network integration/service migration if the new network has to be integrated with any existing assets, or any existing services need to be migrated on the network that is being built.

We will cover these activities like choosing the right protocols and building the configuration templates based on these protocol choices in Chapters 3 to 9.

Implement phase

In the implement phase, the goal is to integrate devices and new capabilities in accordance with the design and without compromising network availability or performance. The implementation phase is where the actual implementation of the design starts. This phase includes deploying the network equipment and configuring it.

Site audits are reviewed and the actual implementation of the devices, including rack and stack power on testing is done in this stage. Some of the documents required for this stage include detailed installation documents for each type of equipment and the test process for each device type. Further, **Network Implementation Plan** (**NIP**) documents are created that are detailed documents for each site that is a part of the network. These documents lay down the list of equipment to be deployed at the site, the rack layouts, port connectivity diagrams, and the actual device configurations, along with the IP addressing and other variable parameters for each device at the site. The configurations are derived based on the configuration templates that were created and tested in the design phase. This document becomes the reference document for the implementation engineer who has to simply download the configuration onto the new devices and conduct the tests that are specific to the site.

Once all sites are up and ready, and the WAN connectivity is established, end-to-end service testing is conducted based on the NRFU test cases.

Any migration of existing services or any integration of networks with the existing network infrastructure is also carried out in this phase and the success validated against the test cases as defined in the NRFU document.

Operate phase

The operation phase of the network is when the actual users start using the network and the operations staff starts monitoring the network and services delivered on the network. It is important to have a multifaceted approach to network operations, that would include the domains of people, processes, and tools. The primary goal in the network operations phase is to maintain network and service uptime, at minimal cost. This can be done only if the organization has the right skills in the resources tasked with network operations, a structured process for the day-to-day activities so that the tasks are not dependent on individuals, but every single person carries a job in the same way as the others would. The tools aspect is essential to improve efficiencies, as mundane and routine tasks can be automated, thereby allowing the NOC resources to focus on actual problems and reducing the chances of manual error.

It is important to add at this point, that nearly 67% of the IT budget is operational and only 33% of the expense is of a capital nature. Since the operations involve a large expense, any advances in the process to improve availability or to bring down cost are of great value to an organization.

The network operations involve monitoring the vital parameters of the network to increase service availability uptime, improve service quality and mitigate outages, and monitor performance of the network devices for any potential signs that can cause an outage or security issues on the network. We will cover operations in more detail in Chapter 10, *A Systematic Approach to Network Operations* and Chapter 11, *Basic Troubleshooting Skills and Techniques* later in this book.

Optimize phase

One needs to constantly evolve and improve to maintain a competitive advantage. A **continual/continuous improvement process** (**CIP**) is an ongoing effort to improve products, services, or processes. It is this desire of the organization to continuously evolve and improve that is addressed in the optimization phase.

This process is closely tied to the operations phase as the results of the operations phase are analyzed to detect recurring problems and to see if there are any design discrepancies, or enhancements that can be made to the network to improve service availability or performance. The goal of the optimize phase is to identify and resolve problems before they actually start to manifest themselves on the network resulting in service disruptions.

The optimize phase of the network lifecycle can cause changes to the network design to meet the service specifications with respect to functionality, performance, security, availability, and so on. In such cases, the network engineers go back to the drawing board to evaluate new alternatives and propose new approaches to meet the changing needs. Some of the things might need minor tweaks to the design, and hence can be handled by going back to the design phase of the network lifecycle, followed by implementation and testing. However, optimization can also be triggered by the maturity of a new technology in the market, and hence that needs a much broader scope, and the organization needs to start at the plan phase, and follow the complete cycle all over again. Whatever be the case, it is important to document the reasons for change, the proposed solution, and then follow it up with the rigor of the complete lifecycle in order for the network to be capable of meeting new requirements in a sustainable manner.

Summary

We discussed the basics of networking in this chapter, delving deep into the TCP and IP protocols, as these are fundamental protocols that will enable all services in a modern enterprise.

We also looked at the network lifecycle approach and the various stages of the network as it is built, with stress upon the need for the multiple activities required for building a network.

We will apply these concepts in the next chapters to discuss the various parts of an IT network and the design considerations for each of these parts of the network. This will cover the campus local area network, the wireless networks, the wide area networks, and data center. We will discuss the various characteristics of the network as a whole in Chapter 2, *Networks for Digital Enterprises* and Chapter 3, *Components of the Enterprise Network* and delve deep into the different domains in the later chapters.

2
Networks for Digital Enterprises

"The world is changing very fast. Big will not beat small anymore. It will be the fast beating the slow."

- Rupert Murdoch

We all live in a world today where the boundaries between the physical world and the digital world are blurred. Today's world is more digital than physical, where even the machines have networking requirements. This digitization has helped create opportunities and has great promise to change our everyday lives.

In this chapter, we will discuss the following topics:

- The requirements for changing business models on the underlying network infrastructure
- The enabling technologies for digitization
- Cisco's architectural framework (Digital Network Architecture)
- Different aspects of the network infrastructure

The impact of technology on business

The world is changing, and changing fast. We have seen so much technological innovation in the last decade that we might not have witnessed in the previous century. This rapid growth has impacted all spheres of our lives, and has changed the way we communicate and interact with other people, even machines; it has changed the way we conduct business with our partners and customers; it has changed our lifestyles, changing the definition of luxury and necessity.

We have seen conventional business models being toppled by new innovative business models; for example, Uber is changing the way we have recognized the taxi industry for centuries. We have seen an evolution of highly profitable new companies that own minimal assets, for example, online shopping giants such as Alibaba, Amazon, e-bay, and Airbnb. There has also been a change in the way new customers are being acquired through targeted marketing in near real-time, by analyzing their preferences and historical choices.

The driver for all of these successes has been one or all of the three following factors:

- Enhancing customer experience
- Improving workforce productivity
- Bringing efficiency into business operations

Most of these successes have been achieved by effectively collecting and analyzing the available data from multiple sources, processing the data at the speed at which the data is being generated, adding contextual information to the available data, and taking meaningful decisions and communicating back effectively and efficiently with their customers and partners. It is evident that Information Technology has played a crucial role in the success of these giants. It should not come as a surprise then that most CEOs have started to consider IT as a critical success factor rather than a cost center.

Digitization as the key enabler

"Digitization has created opportunities for everybody to accumulate information in a way they were never able to, and analyse it with the speed that just wasn't there."

- Ken Moelis

The demand for digital technologies in an always connected world from the Gen-Y and more so, Gen-Z consumers, who are willing to share and consume data and live in a connected world where social networks are trusted more than well-known brands has been a big pull factor for the digitization initiatives. On the other side, there has been a tremendous push for digitization from enabling technologies such as IoT, cloud, and pervasive connectivity. To top it all, digitization made business sense because of the innovative thought and disruptive business models, which challenged the status quo.

If data has to be analyzed using computing power, data has to be digitized, and that is where IoT technologies and sensors play a critical role. It generates the information in a format that is a critical input to the business decision making process, and can be processed easily. This data could be the GPS location of a taxi/customer, in the case of Uber, or the environmental data from machine sensors or video feeds from different cameras.

Data is being generated by machines, devices, sensors, wearables, social media, live streams, connected devices, and smart cars. The list is endless. **International Data Corporation** (**IDC**), a global provider of market intelligence and a premier research firm on consumer technology markets, estimates that we have more than 11 billion devices connected to the internet today, and that is growing at 4800 devices per minute. The amount of data that is being generated is astonishing. As an example, it was reported that Ford's new Ferrari-fighting supercar, the Ford-GT, has more than 50 sensors and 28 microprocessors built-in, and a single car is capable of generating more than 100 GB of data per hour. It is not only about the location where the data is being generated, but also about the volume that is being generated.

According to some studies from IDC, IBM, and other venture capital organizations such as DN Capital, 2.5 Exabytes (1 Exabyte = 10^{18} bytes) of data is being generated per day, and all of this data needs to be processed to get meaningful information that can be used to take decisions. Hence, it is important to transfer data to where it can be processed. Thus, the network to transport the data becomes a critical part of the digital foundation.

The data being created is so huge in volume that processing it in near real-time needs massive computing resources. This means much bigger data centers and a lot more storage and computers. However, another trait of the data is that it is not continuous but comes in spikes, and organizations might want to have a lot more data to process on a given day, week, season, and a lot less data to process during the next. Building a data center to do everything on its own premises would mean building the infrastructure to its peak capacity, bringing down the utilization levels, leading to inefficiencies and hence higher costs. In today's ever-so-competitive world, no business can afford to bear these costs upfront, tolerate any under-utilization of assets. This has led to the rise in cloud models that use these resources in a pool that can be paid-per-use rather than paying for full-time deployment.

Like any planning process, digitization also starts with the preparation phase where organizations need to have a clearly defined digital strategy outlining the areas they want to focus on for competitive advantage, and what digital capabilities they want to build along the value chain. Since the focus areas evolve in accordance with the changing market environment while the underlying infrastructure exists today, or has to be built today, it is imperative that the underlying infrastructure meets the needs of the digital wave when new use cases are to be incorporated.

The next section talks about the evolving technologies at the infrastructure layer that would enable the success of the digitization trend in an organization.

A digital-ready infrastructure

"It is not the beauty of a building you should look at; it's the construction of the foundation that will stand the test of time."

- David Allan Coe

Enterprises need to build on a foundation that can help innovate at speed, keep up with change, and prepare them for what can come in the future. Digital transformation requires a digital-ready infrastructure, which is simple, intelligent, automated, and secure. There are multiple elements of the digitization infrastructure of an organization as we will see in *Figure 1* next. We can broadly classify the infrastructure into three parts:

- A host of input and output systems that interact with the human world. This would include IoT systems (such as wearable sensors, the sensors in vehicles, homes, and manufacturing plants), mobile systems, CCTV cameras, and environmental sensors.
- The underlying network infrastructure that carries the data from the I/O systems to the processing centers and back to the I/O ecosystem. This would typically include the wireless networks in the IoT access domain (for example, IoT technologies such as LoRa, 6LowPAN, and Fog Area Network), mobile networks, Wi-Fi networks, and wired connectivity for higher data rates.
- Processing centers that process the inputs generated from the I/O ecosystem. This would typically be the **data center** (**DC**) in the organization. However, with the demand being very dynamic within the DC, cloud providers are becoming increasingly relevant as a part of this block. Some processing can also be done closer to the edge and that is where the Edge computing platforms become relevant, for example, a computing blade within a router, or a Linux-like computing platform that is available within a router/switch as in a Cisco IOx application environment.

This entire infrastructure has to be simple, highly secure, and automated so as to be flexible enough to meet any changing requirements. We will cover these requirements in detail in subsequent sections of this chapter:

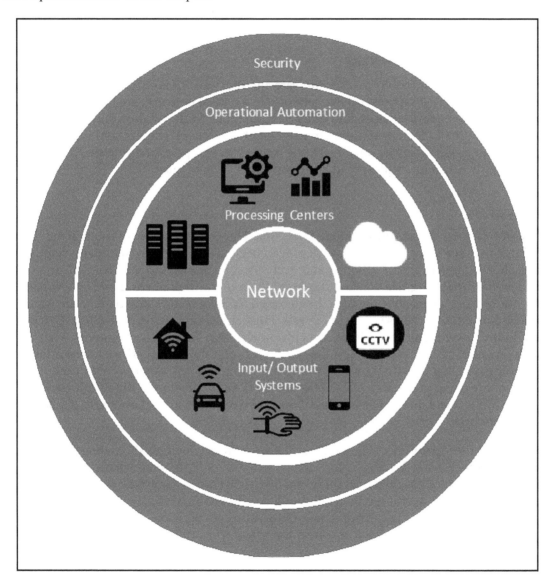

Figure 1: Digitization infrastructure

Enabling technologies

In the previous section we discussed the three major areas of a digital infrastructure. This section discusses some of the enabling technologies in these areas.

Input/output systems

The real need is for endpoints to communicate and the network is only a medium of communication. The endpoints on the network, in a typical network, are the computers, servers, printers, mobile devices, and other IT equipment. In the modern enterprise, these endpoints could also include building management devices, RF readers, and fire management systems, and so on. Of late, the number of end points has increased tremendously due to the widespread adoption of IoT technologies.

IoT systems

IoT, as a concept, has been around for a long time. This technology was visible in the form of a large number of sensors that were deployed in control systems in manufacturing plants, home gadgets, mobile phones, and even virtual gaming consoles. The sensors could take real-life inputs, digitize them, and present them to the digital world and vice versa. Since the sensors were active devices, they needed a power source, and battery life was limited, thus limiting the use of these devices. Further, the sensors were isolated devices with limited networking capabilities, which would further limit their usefulness. The development of battery-efficient, low-power devices and the introduction of networking protocols gave a big push to the use of these technologies. These devices could now communicate using protocols such as **Low Range (LoRa**), Bluetooth, **Bluetooth Low Energy (BLE)**, **IPv6 Low-power wireless Personal Area Network (6LowPAN)**, ZigBee, and mobile networks.

The range of these networks is generally limited, and these devices talk to their gateways using the protocols listed earlier, which then connect over IP to other networks across the WAN. This provides the ability for these small sensors spread across the physical world, to create meaningful data that can then allbecollated and analyzed at a central location to help in providing a cohesive view, helping take better business decisions. We will cover only the IP networks as a part of this book and treat the gateways to the other networks as users of the IP network.

Network

The data that has been generated now needs to be carried to the processing centres where it will be processed. The networks could be wired or wireless, and low-speed to very-high speednetworks. The type of network depends upon the type of traffic to be transported.

With IP becoming the de facto standard of communications, the networks are typically IP networks, while smaller localized networks could use some of the IoT protocols described earlier, and connect to the IP network through gateways.

The IP network will consist of switches and routers, and other devices such as firewalls, load balancers, and DC switches from different vendors. Each of these devices is a package of hardware and software: hardware that forwards the packets and provides the interfaces and software that provides the logic and protocols that would be used on the network.

Software-defined networking

Software-defined networking (**SDN**) has emerged as a concept to decouple the hardware and software components within networking devices with the intention of using commodity hardware for networking equipment. While there are advantages to this decoupling in terms of being able to use commodity hardware, that also means taking the wheel back in time with respect to innovation. Most of the innovation in the networking domain has been made possible through an optimal mix of hardware and software, and designing hardware that can run the software efficiently. It is for this reason that **Application Specific Integrated Circuits** (**ASICs**) were developed, that could make the networking devices operate efficiently at high speeds. If software and hardware were to be totally decoupled, the benefits of ASICs would have to go away, and commodity hardware would lead to no differentiation as far as packet forwarding is concerned. It is for this reason that some companies, including Cisco, have taken a hybrid approach to SDN, and have developed a controller that brings some parts of the software into the controller, while retaining the other network-centric software components in the underlying hardware. We will cover this in detail in the section on *Cisco's Digital Network Architecture*:

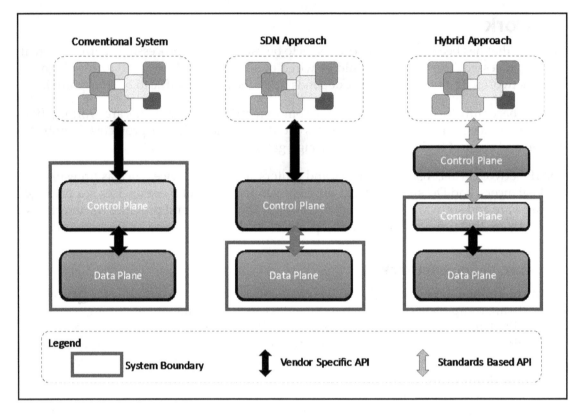

Figure 2: Software-defined networking

Network function virtualization

SDN has decoupling of hardware and software as its core principle. This has manifested itself as a concept called **network function virtualization** (**NFV**), where a specific network function, for example, **Network Address Translation** (**NAT**) or a Firewall function is virtualized and taken out on external hardware or even a standard x86 processor as a virtual machine. NFV has emerged as a technology that can help scale up the network in a more agile manner. For example, if the traffic at a branch has increased, and there is a need to add more firewalling capacity to the network, additional network functions can be turned on, and cascaded to add capacity to meet the enhanced demand. NFV treats network functions such as virtual machines/applications, and hence can be moved around the network and turned on and off on demand.

Network programmability

SDN allows the network to be managed/configured by a controller, and NFV enables adding, deleting, and moving network functions on demand. This entire thing, when put together has immense potential to change the conventional way of networking and make the networks more agile and flexible.

By taking inputs from the network with respect to traffic loads, congestion, and routing behavior and running advanced analytics, network operators can take decisions on the changes they require on the network at a given instant. These changes can then be deployed on the network in runtime by making routing changes, topology changes, or even augmenting network capacity with respect to network functions. All this is possible because of the open interfaces and standard based APIs that would allow any programmer to use these APIs and operate the network efficiently.

An example of this is seen in terms of **Software Defined Wide Area Networks (SD-WAN)**. Imagine a network topology in which certain traffic has two paths from source to destination. This traffic can also be of multiple types, for examples, delay sensitive, loss sensitive, or loss and latency tolerant traffic. By analyzing the performance of the two paths from source to destination, the network operator can force certain traffic to take a path that would provide better performance for a specific traffic type.

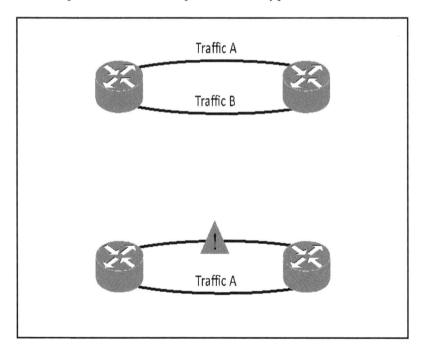

Figure 3: Software Defined WAN failure

Processing centres

The data from the endpoints needs to be processed and analyzed. Data, if not analyzed, is of no practical use. The processing of data can be done at the edges of the network or within a central location where all data is collected and then processed.

Edge computing

As IoT systems proliferate, and send more and more data, this data needs to be sent to the servers where it can be processed over the network infrastructure. This means that the data consumes bandwidth on the WAN links all the way up to the data center where the processing happens. More importantly, the data being sent from the edge to the DC takes a finite amount of time to be transported. Some data is time sensitive, and hence needs to be processed and reactive action taken with minimal latency.

As an example, consider that we are measuring the temperature of a hot furnace using a temperature sensor that is connected to the network using IoT protocols. This sensor would send the temperature of the furnace periodically to the central site. However, this means that a lot of data has to travel from the edge to the data center where the data can be processed. This has to traverse the WAN, and hence cause congestion on the network. If the application that monitors the temperature can be brought closer to the source of data, multiple problems can be addressed. First, the WAN bandwidth is conserved, as the data travels only until the server that is now not hosted in the DC, but is much closer to the source. Secondly, the latency is much less, and action can be taken quickly for time sensitive data. Thirdly, it helps the application to scale, by having a distributed model, where small modules of applications run closer to the source, enabling the overall application to handle much more data, and the central application can control the edge applications, and poll only processed data, which is much lower in volume.

This has led to the growth of edge computing, where small compute resources are placed closer to the edge, or source of data. Placing compute resources requires a controlled environment, and rack space, thereby adding to the operational problems, while the compute power required is not too large. Hence, newer ways of addressing these compute requirements have evolved, called edge computing. Some of the examples of these edge computing platforms are server blades on Cisco routers, or for even smaller compute requirements, the IOx application environment, where a Linux platform is provided natively on certain Cisco routers and switches without even using conventional Cisco computing hardware such as the UCS blades.

Cloud computing

The growing cost pressures on businesses in a highly competitive world forced IT teams within organizations to use every resource to its optimal capacity. This led to a lot of innovations especially in computing space. The average utilization of a compute machine was in the range of 20-30%, which was a big improvement area. Server virtualization as a technology solved this challenge, by abstracting the underlying server hardware, and making multiple computing machines run on them virtually. These machines come to be known as **Virtual Machines** (**VMs**) as the user was using them as he would use a physical machine, but these were not tied to any underlying physical infrastructure.

Cloud computing is the term used to describe the environments that provide shared computing resources on demand. These *clouds* can be private if they are hosted within the data center within the organization's premises, or public where the infrastructure is not built, but taken as a service from a service provider such as AWS.

Cloud computing can move the application workloads from one physical machine to another at the click of a button using automation software that can move these workloads or VMs from one physical server to another. In a private cloud, these workloads remain within the organization's DC, while in a public cloud, these machines remain within the provider's data centers. In a hybrid cloud environment, the workloads can move between the on-premise DC, and the service provider's DC.

This flexibility from a computing perspective brings its own set of challenges of moving VMs across data centers, both on-premise and to the cloud data centers. At the same time, there are challenges on the networking side to provide secure connectivity between the private and public clouds, which needs to be addressed.

We will cover the networking implications of cloud computing in Chapter 7, *Understanding and Configuring Data Center Technologies*.

Analytics

Analytics is processing data to discover and interpret meaningful patterns therein. Analytics is a combination of the fields of databases, statistics, and data sciences. Companies may apply analytics for a variety of use cases. Imagination is the limit for deciding what you can do with data analytics. Some examples that might sound familiar around data analytics are companies trying to find out what type of products are being bought by users, what destinations are frequently visited by a taxi user, what phone applications are used by a particular user, and so on.

A lot of this lies in the application domain. However, data analytics is being increasingly used in the networking and security domains as well. For example, what is the normal traffic pattern on the network? What are the different protocols on the network? Is there a higher than average traffic on the network for a given protocol/user? Who are the top users on the network? What are the top traffic types on the network?

Some of this is being used in technologies called **Network Behavior Analysis** (**NBA**) using protocols such as NetFlow, to get more visibility into the network, and to detect any indicators of compromise from a security standpoint. We will cover the security aspects in Chapter 8, *Understanding and Configuring Network Security*.

Network as the cornerstone

We have discussed in the preceding section, the various technologies involved in digitization. The essence of digitization is creating new experiences for the customers and getting new insights about customer behavior that can be used to enhance services/generate additional revenues.

Network is becoming ever so important in this digitization wave, as the network serves as the highway for transporting data efficiently and effectively. It is the network allows organizations to make full use of digitization as the data is widespread, and needs to be collected and processed effectively either in the DC or in the cloud. Further, this environment is dynamic and the network has to be able to support all possible scenarios and has to be agile enough to adapt to meet the changing needs.

The network as a standalone entity is now being viewed not only as transport infrastructure for the data being generated, but is also being used to enable new customer experiences, and providing new insights about user patterns. We will discuss these aspects in the upcoming sections.

Network enabling new experiences

The primary role of the network is to transport data from the source to the destination securely and intelligently. Intelligently would imply that the network should be able to differentiate between the data that is business critical or latency sensitive, and make all efforts to transfer that data quickly to the destination, without any loss on the network.

Imagine running an IP video call on a network that is congested, and hence has packet loss. The entire experience of having a video call would be degraded, and the purpose of using video over voice for better collaboration and interactivity will be defeated. But that is the primary job of the network.

Let's look at how the network is enabling new experiences for the end users. The first changed is using wireless instead of a wired connection. Even though we might have an Ethernet port at our desk, and we are sitting close to the port, we will connect to the network over Wi-Fi network if one is available. The idea of having to manage cables and connect to the network on a wired connection is passé.

Wi-Fi connectivity has become the expectation from users these days. We even expect it when we visit a coffee shop or a shopping mall. And people are being offered this connectivity at no incremental cost to the user most of the time.

This is because the network is providing a channel to connect to the customer and engage the customer in more meaningful ways, which can help drive better experience enhancing customer loyalty, and bringing in more business options. This is where location based services come into play.

Wi-Fi is provided to the end users using different Wi-Fi Access points that radiate signals, and the users connect to the nearest AP based on the user credentials and the networks being advertised. Organizations these days can use technologies such as Wi-Fi to detect that a new user has come into the network coverage zone and send him information on how to connect to the network. Once the user is connected, the network can be used to send specific messages to the user that could be promotional offers in the store or other information over the same network.

This can go a step further where advanced analytics can be used to find out where exactly the user is, and send them navigation maps to get to the nearest billing desk, kids play zone, or an area where there is a flash sale offer. The same network technology can be used to locate a person in real time, and hence keep track of where a person is at a given point in time. This could be used for security purposes such as: to track kids in an entertainment park, or to track how many times a user visited a particular region, and whether the user is returning customer or is a first-time customer. The list is endless, and constrained only by imagination, relating to how the user experience can be enhanced by using the information provided by the underlying network infrastructure. We will talk about the technologies that enable the location-based services on a Wi-Fi network in Chapter 5, *Understanding and Configuring Wireless Access Technologies*.

Network providing new Insights

We have discussed the importance of the underlying network in the previous sections. In a way, it is critical for efficient delivery of packets and in enabling new experiences. The network sees all traffic within the organization and knows which users are communicating with whom. We have learned in Chapter 1, *Network Building Essentials*, that the intermediate devices in the network, typically routers, operate at layer 3 of the OSI stack. They see all the IP packets and are sources of a lot of other valuable information with regards to the behavior of the users. By collecting the information about the packets traversing the network, and analyzing the data, we can get deeper insights into the network and user behavior. Note that we are not collecting or snooping on the actual data, but are only looking at the layer 3 information that is available in the IP headers. If we run protocols such as NetFlow, we can also get some layer 4 information about the traffic, for example, TCP port numbers that can be used to identify the type of applications running on the network. Additional telemetry information can be received from the network devices by using protocols such as SNMP.

This analysis of telemetry data to gain insights is called NBA. NBA can be used to get information such as which user groups are talking to which other user groups; what are the top applications that are using the most bandwidth on the network; what are the servers that are sending the most amount of data on the network; and the applications being used by different users/user groups.

By collecting this data over a period of time, the network can be baselined with respect to the normal behavior of the types of traffic on the network and the different user behavior with regards to the applications they use, the servers they access on the network, and the normal traffic volume they send on the network. The data collected can then be correlated to the baseline data to detect any significant deviations of traffic, user behavior, or any new applications that are being transported on the network. This can provide valuable information that can be used by the security teams within the organization to predict any virus/worms, suspicious user behavior with respect to any data leaks, or unauthorized access to a set of network resources and to determine whether the network resources are being used for business critical applications, and take corrective action.

The data analysis can be augmented by providing context to the data in terms of what IP addresses are allocated to which users (for example, from an AD server), and the actionable information can be passed on to specific applications that can be used to take corrective action by reconfiguring the network devices. This complete cycle can be automated in an SDN environment, and shown in the following figure:

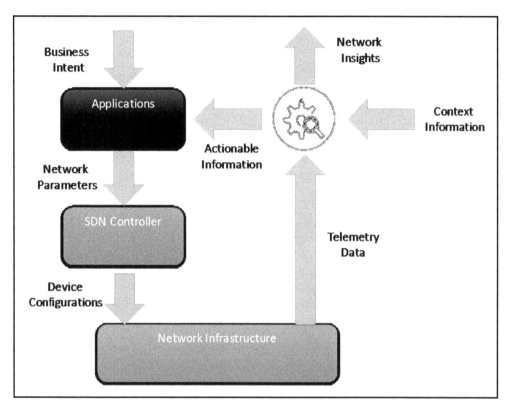

Figure 4: The network data loop

Facets of a digital infrastructure

We have discussed how networks should behave, and the services that a network should deliver for a new age IT infrastructure. This section talks about network design requirements and the various characteristics that should be considered while designing and implementing a network. Most of these have been the basic guiding principles even before the digitization wave, which shows that these principles have stood the test of time. A network that has to meet the requirements of a dynamic organization, however, has new principles that need to be considered such as agility and programmability. This section focuses on the different parameters that can be used to measure the effectiveness of the network design.

Functionality

"The function of design is letting design function."

- Micha Commeren

Functionality is the quality or state of being `functional`. It is the most essential element of network design. The primary function of network design is to meet the requirements of the users, and make the network deliver what was agreed with the users as requirements. If a network does not do what it is designed to do, it is a failed design regardless of whatever else it might have.

If a network was built to carry multiple types of traffic but ended up being capable of carrying only a certain type of traffic while the other types traffic could not be delivered either due to lack of support for the protocols or bandwidth, the network is not functional. Also, if the network can transfer data between the communicating nodes, but with significant delays such that the users cannot complete the business-critical transactions in a seamless manner, we would say that the network has failed the test of functionality. In most scenarios, the user experience is the best test of functionality of the network.

As an example, consider a network built to deliver **high definition (HD)** video to the endpoints, but could deliver only **standard definition (SD)** video due to bandwidth limitations, this network has failed the functionality test.

The network might have all the other properties mentioned hereafter, but those are the icing on the cake. If there is no cake, the icing is useless.

All networks have a specific purpose, and the network design has to ensure that the purpose is catered for the network.

Resiliency

"You may encounter many defeats, but you must not be defeated."

- Dr. Maya Angelou

A network consists of physical components (for example, network devices, physical cables, and transmission links from service providers) and software components that are running within these physical devices. Like everything that is real, the network devices have a specific lifetime and will fail at some time. Further, the software that runs on these devices, even though designed and tested, will have bugs and behave erratically/hang-up at times. Any of these events will lead to a part of the network being nonfunctional. Resiliency is the property of the network that allows the network to be functional regardless of certain parts/components of the networks being out of service.

Resiliency translates to **network availability** and can always be measured as uptime of the network. Uptime is usually represented as a percentage, and is defined as the percentage of time that the network delivers specific services with the contracted performance parameters during a specified interval. It is important to define the parameters that determine whether the service is available or not available. As an example, if a network were designed to deliver HD video service but the users had to fallback to use SD video due to network constraints, the network would be termed unavailable for the HD video service for that duration.

Let's consider the uptime of a network device as an example. A device uptime is typically characterized by the average time between failures of the device. This is also known as its **Mean Time Between Failures** (**MTBF**). Now assume that it takes on an average x time to repair/replace the device. This time is typically referred to as **Mean Time To Repair** (**MTTR**). Hence, for a total duration of **MTBF + MTTR**, the device was up only for **MTBF** time. Hence, the uptime is calculated as follows:

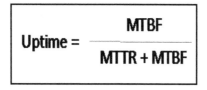

$$Uptime = \frac{MTBF}{MTTR + MTBF}$$

Figure 5: Calculating network uptime

A network uptime of 99.9 percent translates into 0.1 percent outage, which means the network can be down for about 525 minutes in a year. This is more than 8 hours of outage in a year, and could translate to a lot of loss if the network runs revenue generating services. It is not uncommon to find CIOs talking about network uptime of 99.99 percent or 99.999 percent (also called four nines, and five nines, respectively). However, the challenge is that the network is made of components that might not have an uptime as high as the ask. For example, a WAN link might only give us an uptime of 99.5 percent. Hence, the problem statement translates to how do we build a network such that the overall network delivers more uptime than the individual components can deliver.

One way to improve uptime/availability is to use devices that have a high MTBF value. At the same time, uptime can be increased by reducing the time to repair (MTTR) by improving operational practices.

The network is a group of network components and the overall network uptime would be a function of the overall components and the way in which these components are connected together. Consider a network that has two components, that is, **Component A** and **Component B**, that are connected in such a manner that if any single component fails, the service would be down. If the uptime for each individual component is U_a and U_b, then the uptime of the system that has these two devices in series (U_s) is the product of the two uptimes:

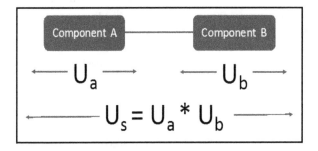

Figure 6: Calculating availability in a series of elements

On the other hand, if the two systems are connected in a manner such that the two components can act as a backup for each other, and where one component fails, there is no outage of the system as the load can be taken by the second system, the uptime of the system in this case is calculated as shown next:

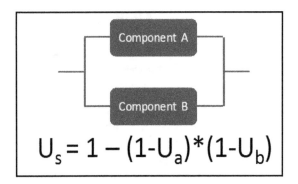

Figure 7: Calculating availability in a redundant combination

It can be seen from the preceding section that if we have system components in parallel/load-sharing mode, then the overall system availability can be improved drastically. However, there is another aspect to adding components in such a redundant mode-cost. Each additional component adds to the cost of the overall system and the additional cost has to be justified to the additional uptime that would be achieved by virtue of the additional component. The following table shows the uptime of a system of N components, where all components are in parallel with the uptime of each component being 98 percent. As can be seen from the table, the incremental gain of adding a third component is very small and might not justify the additional investment. Hence, most systems are built with two redundant components, with three components being used in a redundant mode where the outage can lead to a total network outage:

Number of Systems	Uptime of system
1	98.000%
2	99.960%
3	99.999%
4	100.000%

Figure 8: Effect of redundancy in availability

We will build on these concepts of redundancy during the network design and implementation chapters, where we will design a network with redundant options.

Modularity

"Divide each difficulty into as many parts as is feasible and necessary to resolve it."

- Rene Descartes

Modularity refers to creating a network in small building blocks or modules such that each module performs a certain function. The idea is to simplify the design process and create small parts of the network that can be designed independently of each other. The only important thing to define in a modular network design is how would the different modules interact with each other and which would be the interfaces and protocols that would connect the different modules?

Building a modular network provides the flexibility to pull in subject matter experts for different domains to build individual modules and an overall architect who defines the interactions between the various modules so that the network can function cohesively as a whole.

From an operational perspective, modularity simplifies network troubleshooting, as it becomes easier to identify which module is causing a problem or needs optimization. Furthermore, the identified module can be redesigned or optimized independently of the other modules, as long as the functional specifications of the interconnectivity with the other modules do not change. Hence, modularity of network design provides the flexibility to efficiently change the network design at minimal risk to meet the changing business demands.

This approach is very helpful in network design and we will drill down deep into this in the next chapter.

Flexibility

"The measure of intelligence is the ability to change"

- Albert Einstein

Networks were traditionally designed for speed rather than flexibility. But in today's world, where services can be moved from the on-premises data center to a cloud provider in a matter of minutes, the network needs to be able to support the services regardless of where they are being delivered from. In other words, the network needs to change and adapt to ensure optimal service delivery even though the service is now being delivered from the cloud and not the on-premises data center.

Today's networks are converged networks and carry different types of traffic on a converged network infrastructure. This traffic could be operational domain traffic, IT traffic, voice, or even CCTV traffic. Different applications have different demands from the network and the network has to be able to cater to all of these. These requirements include the ability to add new traffic types or even virtual networks on demand without influencing existing traffic/networks, or the ability to temporarily extend a network topology to serve events such as an ad hoc multicast from the CEO to all employees within the organization and the ability to reconfigure the network in real-time for resilience.

This brings us to the discussion that the network needs to be flexible so that it can be changed quickly. An organization using a broadband internet to build a secure connection between two sites until such time as the leasing MPLS circuit from the service provider can be commissioned is a practical example of network flexibility.

Companies that aim for agility and flexibility are transforming from conventional hardware-centric network deployment and are reaping the benefits of technologies such as NFV and SDN to make their networks more agile and flexible.

Furthermore, these organizations are deploying tools that can automate the operational tasks to ensure that the changes are done with speed and security minimizing the chances of human error.

Scalability

"It is not the load that breaks you down, it's the way you carry it."

- Ena Horne

Future-ready enterprise networks should be able to expand on-demand to enable rapid growth of IT services and applications. The traffic patterns and user behavior are changing very fast. Any new trigger can bring a drastic change in the existing traffic patterns and user behavior. To address these needs, the enterprise network must be able to scale efficiently to accommodate capacity needs.

Scalability is the ability of the network to handle more traffic and applies to all domains of the network from the LAN, WAN, IoT, data center, and so on. A scalable network means that you would be able to augment the capacity of the network as the load increases without having to make any changes to the fundamental design of the network.

Scalability could be horizontal or vertical. Vertical scaling means the ability to expand the capacity of the network by augmenting the capacity within the system. Horizontal scaling is the ability to augment the capacity by adding more of the already existing infrastructure and split the load between them, by making them logically look like one entity.

Note that what may be considered horizontal or vertical scalability depends on the user's perspective. For example, adding more servers behind a load balancer in a DC to augment capacity would be considered horizontal scaling with respect to compute scale. However, the same compute capacity addition within the DC would be considered vertical scaling from a DC scaling perspective, and adding another DC and load balancing between the two data centers would be considered horizontal scaling. In general, horizontal scaling takes more planning and effort than vertical scaling.

Security

> *"Most bad behaviour comes from insecurity."*
>
> *- Debra Winger*

Networks are built to be used, not abused. However, there are instances where the networks are put to malicious use, either knowingly or unknowingly. Malicious use could be a sudden burst of traffic on the network causing congestion and degrading the experience for users, directing traffic towards a critical server to overwhelm the server resources and hence make it unavailable, taking control of network nodes/devices to manipulate routing or snoop data sending traffic to spread virus/worms or other malicious code, and so on. If the network is not secured properly, the network is not reliable and cannot be entrusted by users to transport data with confidence.

A secure network means that the data can be sent from source to destination through the network with the performance benchmarks that have been set for the network without the data being spoofed, copied, altered, or rerouted through unnecessary hops, or unauthorized data being injected on the network.

With the fast evolution of ransomware, **advanced persistent threat** (**APT**) attacks and changes in network and security architectures, network security has become increasingly complex yet vital to protecting the business, with no room for compromise. Network security is a big topic in itself and comprises data plane security, control plane security, and management plane security. We will cover these aspects in the chapter on Network Security.

Agility

> *"Speed, agility, and responsiveness are the keys to future success."*
>
> *- Anita Roddick*

This is one of the new tenets of network design that was not talked about a couple of years ago. Networks were designed to be modular and flexible, but agile was a far-fetched thought primarily because the networks were meant to be static, or at least quasi-static. Changes were made to the network but that went through a complete change cycle, a design cycle, and hence was time consuming.

Today's business environment is dynamic, hence the networks need to be able to support these dynamic environments. Networks need to change at the speed of business if they are to be positive contributors to business. Hence, designing networks that are agile is a basic consideration in today's network design rather than an afterthought.

Agility means giving the network the ability to change quickly. The changes may include making routing changes based on the underlying network performance, bringing up new locations and integrating them with the network, making widespread changes on the network to meet new security threats, and so on. The list of use cases is endless.

Agility provides the network the capability of changing the way it handles traffic flows in response to any change in business requirements or network performance. Conventional networks were built using conventional hardware, and provisioned and configured using command-line interfaces. This meant shipping hardware to the remote site of a new office needed to be connected, leading to delays in bringing up new sites. Configuration on a device-by-device basis using the command-line interface meant that all devices had to be configured sequentially by operators leading to delays and often operator errors leading to availability issues. Technologies such as SDN and NFV and features such as Plug and Play have been the real enablers of making the networks agile.

The APIC-EM controller as defined in the DNA section and the applications running on top are examples of how SDN and network programmability are making networks more agile.

Manageability

"Everything should be made as simple as possible. But not simpler."

- Albert Einstein

Networks are like living things that need to be taken care of and often change with time due to new requirements being put on the networks to cater to new services. Network operations is the discipline that involves monitoring the network on a real-time basis to monitor the network performance and to detect any incidents such as link failures, device failures, link congestion, and so on. The network operator needs to be able to monitor the network, detect and analyze any inputs received from the network, and then take corrective action based on the criticality or business impact that the events have on the network.

The network design has a lot of bearing on the correlation of the network events in the case of outages or performance degradations on the network. If the network design is too complex, the events cannot be correlated easily and the time to take a decision on the corrective action to be taken gets prolonged. This can cause network outages, or prolonged business disruptions, that are detrimental to business.

Manageability of the network requires that the network design is simple so that the network operator can intuitively analyze the network events to ensure continuous availability of services and applications for the business.

Manageability can be enhanced using automation and orchestration tools, where standard protocols and tools are used to take care of the repetitive tasks. The evolution of SDN and the availability of a lot of custom applications that use the standard-based APIs of the network devices or the SDN controllers is helping network operators manage the network effectively.

Visibility and analytics

"If you can't measure it, you can't improve it."

- Peter Drucker

Manageability is also being extended in today's networks to include the capability to provide complete visibility about the network. This visibility includes providing information about which users or applications are using the network resources, what the round-trip delays from one part of the network to another are, whether the users on the network are communicating with the network resources they should, whether the network traffic at a given point is conforming to an established network traffic baseline or whether there are significant deviations, and so on.

All of this data can be used by network operators to provide a benchmark, and then use tools and processes to ensure that these benchmarks are being constantly improved.

Cisco Digital Network Architecture

Cisco has been at the leading edge of networking and enabling its customers to adopt technologies that help them prepare for the future. In the wave of digitization, SDN, NFV, cloud adoption, analytics and orchestration, Cisco has come out with an architecture called the Digital Network Architecture.

Cisco's Digital Network Architecture (DNA) is an open, extensible, software-driven architecture that accelerates and simplifies your enterprise network operations. The fundamental principle of DNA is to enable a software-centric network infrastructure that can be changed to meet business needs.

Cisco's DNA delivers the same consistent experience to wired users, wireless users, and remote VPN users, and uses advanced analytics to provide rich insights into the network.

Cisco's DNA is based on the following key pillars:

- **Virtualization**: Cisco brings **Network Function Virtualization** (**NFV**) to the enterprise branch and provides the flexibility to run not only Cisco's network functions such as routers, firewalls, wide area acceleration services, and so on but also third-party services, including standard windows-based services such as DHCP servers on an NFV platform. The goal is to deliver consistent services and user experience regardless of the form factor of the underlying network infrastructure components.

- **Automation**: Cisco used the hybrid mode of SDN and introduced a controller that it calls **Application Policy Infrastructure Controller-Enterprise Module** (**APIC-EM**). This SDN controller abstracts the network and provides a layer that provides open, standard-based APIs that can be used by developers to create applications that can be run on top of the controller to meet specific business goals. Cisco also provides some apps bundled with the controller like the Plug and Play app, that can help configure devices automatically when they are connected to the network by pulling their configuration from a central configuration repository server, significantly reducing the provisioning time and errors.

- **Analytics**: Cisco believes that the network is the source of a lot of useful information that can be used to deliver new experiences and gain insights into the network. Cisco's DNA collects the information from the network devices using telemetry data such as SNMP and Netflow, and uses advanced analytics on the collected data to provide meaningful insights about the network.

- **Cloud Service Management**: Cisco's DNA uses cloud-based service models to reduce the deployment times for critical services for its end customers. Providing cloud-based services also helps customers to scale on-demand thus providing them the flexibility and agility that their business needs.
- **Open, Standards-based APIs**: Cisco's controller is an open and standards-based controller that provides a rich set of northbound APIs that are used by ecosystem partners and developers to build custom applications that can be run on top of the SDN controller.

Cisco's DNA ensures that the network is not only open, flexible, and agile enabling it meeting changing business needs but is also secure, ensuring that the network is able to detect and mitigate any attacks in a structured manner and not be reactive in its approach to security. Enterprises can reap the benefits of automation in terms of reduced operational costs using the APIC-EM controller and the associated applications:

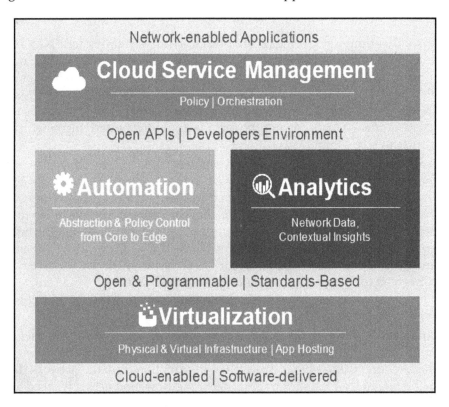

Figure 9: Cisco's Digital Networking Architecture

The DNA services are delivered through the use of Cisco ONE software and does not require a rip and replace approach for the underlying hardware that might have been deployed by the customers, hence ensuring investment protection for the existing customers.

Summary

In this chapter, we discussed the changing role of networks in a digital world, the various challenges faced by networks because of dynamic business environments, and how networks can be adapted to these challenges by using a structured approach to network design.

We looked at the different characteristics of good network design and what they mean from an operations perspective.

In the next chapter, we will delve deeper into how to accommodate the desirable characteristics while designing the network. We will cover the different parts of an organization's IT network and discuss the functions of each part of the network before we drill down into each part individually in later chapters.

3

Components of the Enterprise Network

"The whole is greater than the sum of its parts."

-Aristotle

We have discussed the different traits of a good network design in the previous chapter. In this chapter, we will talk about the different parts of the enterprise network and talk about how the fundamental principles discussed in the previous chapter are applied in the actual design of the network.

We will cover the following topics in this chapter:

- Introduction to networking devices (switches and routers)
- Introduction to Cisco Internetworking Operating System (IOS)
- Functional places in the network

If you have worked on IOS, you can move directly to the third section in the chapter.

Networking devices and their functions

The network is built of many components, including the networking devices such as routers and switches interconnected by links. These links may be local, connecting two devices side by side like a patch cord connecting two switches, or a **Wide Area Network** (**WAN**) link that connects two routers that are in different locations. This section introduces some of the common devices that are used to build the networks and the broad functions of these devices.

Switches

A switch is a device that operates at layer 2 of the OSI stack, and is the most common device that you would find in the network.

Many layer 2 technologies came into existence at different times, to meet user requirements. Some of these layer 2 technologies are X.25, Frame Relay, ATM, and Ethernet. There are switches available for each of these technologies.

Out of the multiple layer 2 competing technologies, Ethernet became the de facto standard at layer 2 of the OSI model, primarily driven by its low cost and the fact that Ethernet scales from 10 Mbps to 40 Gbps and beyond. This book will use the term switch in general for an Ethernet switch.

A typical model of a Cisco catalyst switch with Ethernet ports is shown in the following figure:

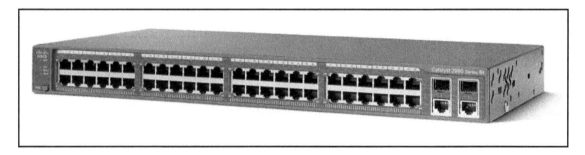

Figure 1: A Cisco Catalyst 2960 Switch; source: www.cisco.com

A switch is a device that works at layer 2 of the OSI model, and switches frames from one port to another. A switch is a device that has multiple hosts connected to it, and hence is the first point of access into the network for wired users. A switch may be thought of as a black box that has Ethernet ports to which hosts are connected using physical cables. The frames from one host is switched to the other hosts connected to the switch based on the layer 2 or data link addresses only. In the case of Ethernet, these addresses are the **Media Access Control** (**MAC**) addresses.

There are some switches that just switch frames between ports and have very limited abilities to implement traffic controls or run any networking protocols. These switches are called unmanaged switches. Some switches have additional management functionality inbuilt that allows them to run networking protocols and implement advanced features, such as filtering traffic based on layer 2 frames. These switches have a data plane for switching frames and a control plane that implements these advanced functions. Such switches are called managed switches. The building blocks of a managed switch are as shown in the following figure:

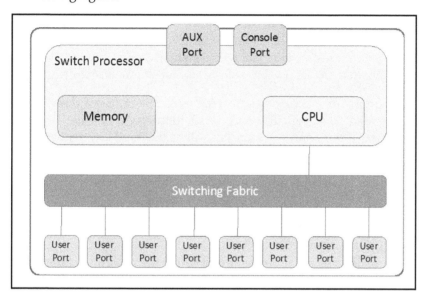

Figure 2: Parts of a managed switch

A switch, in addition to having the physical ports to connect, would also have a **Switch Processor**, which is a mini computer that controls the switch. The switching processor has a **CPU** for processing, **Memory** and **Console Port**, and **AUX Port**. While the **CPU** runs the software that controls the switching functions, the software for the same is stored in the memory.

The memory can be divided into two parts. One part runs the software that controls the various hardware elements in the switch and runs the software that implements the various protocols and features supported by the switch. This software in Cisco is called the **Internetworking Operating System (IOS)**.

The other part of the memory is used to store the transient data that is created, and deleted as the switch starts to perform the switching functions. The most common use of this memory is to save the switching tables. These switching tables essentially contain the MAC address to port mappings, so that when a frame is received to be forwarded to a particular destination MAC address, the same is switched to the relevant port by referring to the switching table.

The ports on the **Switch Processor** are used to get access to the switch for downloading software images, and getting access to the IOS software for configuration and troubleshooting the switch. There is a console port, which is an asynchronous port with a USB port or a RJ45 connector for connecting external devices such as a PC or a laptop to gain access to the command-line interface of the switch. Some switches also have an auxiliary port (AUX) that can be used to connect to the switch remotely using a modem.

Each switch has buffers for each port so that frames can be buffered if there are multiple frames to be forwarded on a particular port for small intervals of time. This helps when there is congestion on a port, and some frames can be buffered and sent after the earlier frames have been transmitted.

 The buffering adds additional latency to the switching time, and hence should be avoided for low latency scenarios.

Switches perform additional functions over and above the basic switching function for the data frames. These include marking traffic received on specific ports as priority traffic, and setting the DSCP bits or 802.1p bits in the IP or Ethernet headers. This classification is then used to provide the right quality of service to the packets when they are being transported over the rest of the network. We will cover these details in Chapter 9, *Understanding and Configuring Quality of Service*.

Additionally, since the switch is the point of access to the network for all wired users, the switch port can be used to group the users and assign them to specific VLANs. These vlans can be used to restrict access for specific users, or can be used to provide access only to certain parts of the network. Ports can be assigned to separate vlans either statically by configuration, or dynamically using specific protocols such as 802.1x, which is a protocol used for **Network Access Control** (**NAC**). We will cover details about network access control in `Chapter 8`, *Understanding and Configuring Network Security*.

Switches are also important sources of information about the traffic flowing on the network. Since the switch is where the users are directly connected, we can get exact information about the traffic on a per port basis, which translates into traffic per user if the user connects directly to a physical port on the switch. This information is generally exported to external systems for analysis in the form of Netflow records.

Switches come in various models depending upon the number of ports, type of ports, and the features supported by the switch. The type of port could be depending upon the physical connectors, for example, copper ports or optical ports. Also, the copper ports could be normal ports or **Power over Ethernet** (**PoE**) ports, which provide power to the devices that are connected to the switch on these ports, such as VoIP phones or **wireless access points** (**WAPs**). Further, switches could be of a fixed form factor or modular. Fixed form factor switches have a fixed number of ports, and, if more ports are needed, you need to add more switches to the network. Modular switches, on the other hand, are switches that are modular and have a chassis that has multiple line cards. There could be one or more processor cards and line cards of different types that can be inserted into the chassis to add more ports to the switch.

Further, some switches may be stackable using a stacking cable. Stacking cables connect to special ports called stacking ports of different switches at the two ends. These cables connect the processors and the switching fabrics between the two switches, thus allowing the two switches to look like an integrated switch that can be managed using a single console through a single switch processor. Different types of switches have different limits on the number of switches that can be stacked together.

You can apply the concepts of resiliency, redundancy, scalability, and modularity that we discussed in the last chapter, to a standalone switch to understand how the network can be designed efficiently. For example, if a network needs to be scalable to address more users at a location, it would be a good idea to use a stackable switch or a modular switch. If the switch is critical, and is required to have a high uptime, the switch should have redundant components such as power supplies and switch processors that can keep the switch up and running even if one of the redundant components goes down.

Cisco has different models of switches for different uses, such as the Catalyst 2k, Catalyst 3k, and Catalyst 4k, Catalyst 6500, and the recently launched Catalyst 9k series at the campus edge, and the Nexus series of switches for the Data Center.

Wireless Access Points

Figure 3: A Cisco Wireless Access Point; source: www.cisco.com

Wireless access has become the de facto standard for connecting devices to the network. This is primarily because of the need to do away with cables, and the ability to connect to the network while on the move. Wireless Infrastructures are becoming more and more common, and Wireless speeds have increased tremendously over the last couple of years.

An **Access Point** (**AP**) is the equivalent of an access switch that converts the electrical signals to the **Radio Frequency** (**RF**) signals and vice versa for communication. Each AP has an RF antenna that is used to radiate the RF signals into the air, and a physical port for connecting the user back to the network. Some APs are also deployed in a mesh mode, where the backhaul or connectivity to the network is via a series of RF hops. However, in typical campus scenarios, the AP would have a wired port to connect back to the core network over an Ethernet port. Some APs also draw power over the same Ethernet port using **Power over Ethernet** (**PoE**) technology defined in the IEEE 802.3af standard, that can provide up to 15W of power over the UTP cables of category 5e (Cat5e) or higher. This was later enhanced to PoE + (IEEE Standard 802.3at), providing 30W, and Cisco proprietary UPOE that provides 60W of power to devices. The upcoming standard 802.3bt would enhance this limit to 90W over an Ethernet cable.

Wi-Fi standards for RF transmission have also evolved from time to time, providing different access speeds over the RF interface:

Standard	Frequency (GHz)	Bandwidth (Mbps) (Not throughput)
802.11	2.4	2
802.11a	5	54

802.11b	2.4	11
802.11g	2.4	54
802.11n	2.4/ 5	600
802.11ac	5	6900

We will compare the technologies used in the Wi-Fi domain in more detail in Chapter 5, *Understanding and Configuring Wireless Access Technologies*.

Routers

Figure 4: A Cisco Router; source: www.cisco.com

A router is a device that works at layer 3 of the OSI model, and hence routes IP packets between different subnets. The hardware architecture at a block level would be similar to that of a switch, with the difference that the switch processor is replaced by a route processor. Since the router operates at a higher OSI layer than that of a switch, all the functions of a layer 2 switch would also be inbuilt into the router.

The route processor is the brain of the router. The routing tables are built by the route processor by running various routing protocols that we will discuss in the next chapter. These routing tables can then be sent to specific ASICs controlling the different ports on a router for faster processing.

A router may have one or more Ethernet ports that connect to different LAN segments, one or more WAN ports that can connect to the WAN links over serial interfaces such as an E1 interface providing 2 Mbps bandwidth, or even ATM interfaces that can connect to legacy ATM backbones. The router will also have the console port and optional AUX ports for connecting to the device for configuration.

Like switches, routers also come in multiple form factors and could be modular or fixed configuration devices. Some of the commonly used routers in the Cisco family are the **Integrated Services Routers (ISR)** 3k & ISR4k series, or the highend ASR 9k series of routers. All of these routers would run a variant of the IOS software that implements the different features within the router, including the different routing protocols. IOS is the most common software, while IOS-XE is a modular build of the IOS software. IOS-XR is a modular software that runs on highend routers.

Firewalls

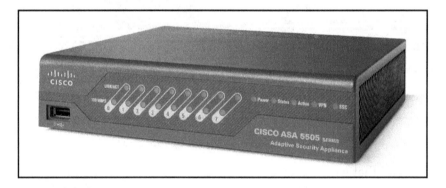

Figure 5: Cisco Firewall; source: www.cisco.com

A firewall is a layer 4 device, which essentially is a device that is used to protect the network from any attacks. The firewall basically inspects and filters packets based on predefined rules on the firewall. These rules might be of the following nature:

- Allow TCP outgoing connections only
- Rate limit TCP connection requests to a specific rate
- Block all TCP traffic on a specific port
- Block all UDP traffic on a specific port

Organizations generally use IP addresses that are not routable on the public internet. This prevents the users within the organization from accessing public internet resources, unless the source addresses in the packets is changed to a globally valid IP address. This is known as address translation, and is also a function that is performed by the firewalls. A firewall can also act like a **Virtual Private Network** (**VPN**) termination device, which helps the remote users to securely connect to the organization.

A new generation of firewalls provide additional information by providing context to the network traffic by integrating with other devices such as Active Directory servers, and correlating IP addresses seen on the network with the actual usernames. Some firewalls also provide deep packet inspection features and can look into the application layer information as well, providing advanced protection against threats. These firewalls with enhanced features and capabilities and the ability to correlate data across devices are called **Next Generation Firewalls** (**NGFW**).

A firewall is typically placed at the network edge to protect the network from any outside attacks or before critical servers to protect the servers from attacks from users. We will discuss the deployment of firewalls in Chapter 7, *Understanding and Configuring Data Center Technologies*.

A Cisco ASA firewall runs software that is different from the IOS, and is called the ASA OS.

Introduction to Cisco IOS

Internetwork Operating System (**IOS**) is the operating system that runs on all Cisco routers and switches. The primary function of the IOS is to manage the hardware resources and ensure that adequate memory and CPU cycles are available for the various processes that would run on the router.

The modern IOS has evolved from the original IOS that used to run on Cisco devices in the early days, and was rewritten to simplify and bring in modularity to the software. However, the basic functions remain unchanged.

The IOS runs a lot of processes on top of the fundamental operating system that manages the hardware and software resources on the router. These processes are the modules that implement the actual routing protocols, and perform tasks such as system configuration, maintenance, and troubleshooting.

The Cisco IOS **command-line interface** (**CLI**) is the primary user interface used for configuring, monitoring, and maintaining Cisco devices. The CLI can be accessed using a router console or terminal, or remotely by a telnet or ssh session into the router. All Cisco IOS commands are run through the CLI.

IOS command modes

The Cisco IOS command-line interface is divided into different command modes. Each command mode has its own set of commands for the configuration, maintenance, and monitoring of the router and network operations. The commands available depend upon the mode of the CLI, and can be queried by entering the question mark symbol (?) at the CLI prompt. CLI commands can be used to navigate from one mode to another within the IOS CLI.

The different modes of the Cisco IOS CLI are described as follows:

- **Setup mode**: This mode is used for the initial setup of the Cisco router/switch and provides an interactive mode for entering the basic parameters required for configuring the Cisco device through the system configuration dialog. If the system does not find any configuration file stored in the NVRAM, it prompts if the user wants to enter the setup mode, and use the system configuration dialog. If the user declines, the router enters the User EXEC mode. The user can use the setup command in the Privileged EXEC mode.
- **User EXEC mode**: This is the mode the router enters upon a normal uninterrupted boot sequence. This mode provides a very limited subset of commands primarily for connectivity and accessing the basic system information. The commands at this level do not change the configuration of the router. The commands available in this mode can be changed through router configuration. On a working device, a user enters this mode when he connects using a console terminal.
- **Privileged EXEC mode**: This mode is entered using the `enable` command at the User EXEC prompt, and requires a password to be accessed. This is the mode where all show commands can be run on the IOS CLI. The user can run debug commands on the router in this mode. However, this mode still does not allow the commands that can make changes to the router configuration, but one can enter the configuration mode using a command at this level. Users can return to the User EXEC mode using the exit command at this prompt.

- **Global configuration mode**: This mode is entered from the Privileged EXEC mode by using the `configure terminal` command. This mode requires an additional password to be accessed. The commands in this mode can be used to change the router configuration. There are multiple hierarchies within the global configuration level, for example, interface configuration mode, subinterface configuration mode, protocol configuration modes, and feature specific configuration modes. The commands available would depend on the feature set available on the router IOS version.

- **ROM monitor mode**: This mode is used when the router cannot boot properly. If the device does not find a valid system image to load when it is booting, the system will enter ROM monitor mode. ROM monitor (ROMMON) mode can also be accessed by interrupting the boot sequence during startup. This mode is primarily used for advanced troubleshooting.

The following figure provides a pictorial view of the main command modes used in the Cisco IOS CLI:

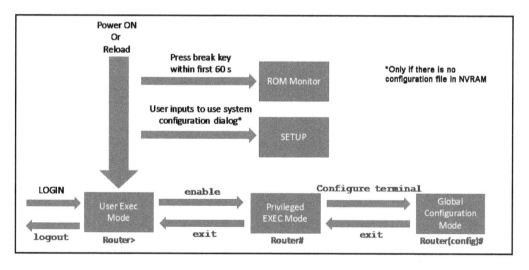

Figure 6: Cisco IOS modes

Configuration files

A networking device has to be customized for use though the definition of specific parameters that define how the device should function. These parameters include the name of the router (hostname), interface IP addresses, the routing protocols and their parameters such as area IDs or autonomous system numbers. These parameters are configured by the network administrators and are stored in the form of configuration files on these devices.

Configuration files contain the Cisco IOS software commands used to customize the functionality of the Cisco device running an IOS image. The commands are translated and executed by the IOS when the system is booted, and parameters from these commands are used to customize the router functionality.

An IOS device on initial boot starts up without any specific parameters. These parameters are configured by the network administrators by entering into the configuration mode of the IOS CLI as described in the preceding section. These changes are generally executed either immediately when they are entered, or when the user exits the configuration mode. Newer platforms and IOS releases also have the feature of a configuration commit, where the configurations are executed only when the commit command is executed. The changes made to the router configuration are stored in the RAM of the device. The configuration being used by the IOS at a given point in time, is called the running configuration.

Since the running configuration is stored in the RAM, the configuration gets deleted when the device is powered off. Hence, a copy of the configuration needs to be stored in a Non-volatile memory such as NVRAM, PCMCIA cards, or the bootflash memory. This copy of the stored configuration is known as the **startup configuration**. The startup configuration file is copied into the RAM during the router boot process, and becomes the running configuration. During the operation of the network, it is possible that the configuration needs some changes. These configuration changes are done through the configuration mode on the router and are made directly to the running configuration. These changes can be lost if the device undergoes a power cycle for any reason. Hence, it is important to save the changes and copy the running configuration file into the startup configuration file. This will ensure that any changes made after the last power on of the device are persistent across power cycles. The command used to copy the running configuration to the startup configuration is `copy running-config startup-config`, which is a Privileged EXEC mode command.

Places in the network

"A place for everything, everything in its place."

- Benjamin Franklin

A network is a collection of interconnected devices performing specific functions. These functions are performed at different places on the network. For example, controlling access to the network based on the user profile and credentials is done at the edge of the network; choosing one link out of multiple options to send traffic across the WAN is done at the WAN Edge; enforcing security policies to protect the server infrastructure of the company is done within the data center, and so on. This segregation of network functions helps to keep the network simple and modular.

Let's take a small organization as an example to discuss this concept in a bit more detail. Let's assume an organization ABC Inc. that starts in a single location. This organization will have a set of users who would be connected to the **Local Area Network** (**LAN**), and will have a farm of servers that will host the applications for the users, for example, email application and any other business applications that have resources that are shared among the users. Let's call this server farm a mini data center (DC). The users also need connectivity to the internet, and the company has an internet link that connects the organization to the internet service provider.

The data center and the user LAN are connected to allow the users to access the servers in the DC. Similarly, the DC and the internet need connectivity to allow the organization to host its website or even exchange emails with the external world. The LAN block needs connectivity to the internet so that the users can access the internet for any research on the internet, or any other activity permitted by the rules of the organization.

The server infrastructure hosts critical information, and delivers business-critical services for the organization. Connecting this server infrastructure or the DC to the internet would require implementing security policies and controls on the connection. Similarly, the user LAN connectivity to the internet would need security policies to ensure that the users do not get infected by any malware on the internet. The following figure depicts the network setup for a very small organization, with the block in between depicting the security controls between the various network parts:

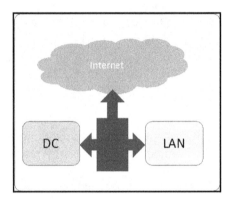

Figure 7: A sample network for a small organization

Hence, the basic organizational network consists of three broad parts, which are the **LAN**, the Data Center (**DC**), and the **Internet**.

Now, let's consider that the organization ABC Inc. grows over time, and sets up multiple branches at different remote locations outside its main office where they initially started. There would be users who would work out of the remote locations, and would need connectivity to the applications that are critical for the business of the organization. These applications are hosted in the DC at the main office and it would not be practical to host these applications at each remote location. This could be for a variety of reasons; for example, there might not be enough space and power at the branches to host the servers, maintaining servers at the remote locations requires dedicated skilled manpower at these locations which is not always possible, the applications use databases that are common for all users and so on. Hence, the remote branches need to connect to the DC at the main office. This can be done by providing connectivity from the branches to the central DC over leased lines taken from a bandwidth service provider, or even shared bandwidth using **Virtual Private Networks** (**VPNs**) from VPN service providers. Some branches might be at locations where there is no service provider available who can offer leased lines or VPN services, and the internet might be the only form of connectivity. These users would connect to the main DC over encrypted tunnels.

There are multiple methods of connectivity, and each method would have its own advantages and disadvantages. We will cover the pros and cons and the various approaches in depth in Chapter 6, *Understanding and Configuring WAN Technologies*. The example organization we have built has evolved to the one shown in the following figure. Note that we still have the connectivity to the internet only from the main site. This is primarily to ensure centralized accounting of resources, and to ensure that the internet access policy and the necessary security controls can be enforced at the central location, rather than proliferating it to all sites that would lead to management overhead.

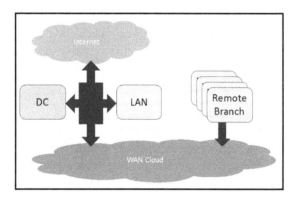

Figure 8: A sample network for a medium organization

Next, let's consider that ABC Inc. has done too well and has grown so big that it sets up another main office and a backup data center at a different location. Some of the branches have grown into large campuses, which have a large number of users. The company has expanded into the cloud and has provided internet connectivity at all branches so that access to cloud-hosted applications can be provided directly from the branches over the local internet connection, rather than the users having to come all the way to the main locations for internet access. The network has evolved into the one shown in the following figure:

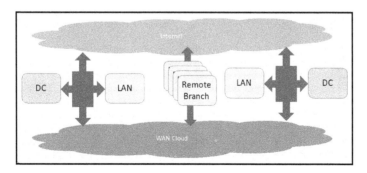

Figure 9: A sample network for a large organization

As we can see from this example, the organization and, hence, the network can grow over time from a handful of users to a couple of hundreds, or, perhaps, thousands of users. A number of branches or remote locations may then need to be integrated into the network. The business model of the company can change from in-house applications to a partly cloud-hosted model. A good network design should ensure that the fundamental network architecture does not change, when the organization expands, or the business models change. All this can happen, only if the network was designed and built, not as a monolithic whole, but a combination of various elements. One can relate this to the modular and flexible approach of the network design.

Building the network as an interconnection of various building blocks ensures that the network is simple with the various network functions clearly defined for each network block. This also ensures that there is a clear demarcation between the different blocks, and a problem in one of the blocks can be easily identified.

Building a network on this approach ensures that traffic flows can be visualized easily as the traffic moves from one block to another though the points of interconnection, leading to a predictable network behavior. Further, since the building blocks are independent entities, several blocks of this sort can be added to the overall network to ensure that the network scales to meet the growing business needs. Adding a backup data center, or multiple branches in the organization described previously are examples of how this can be done.

We have emphasized the need to build the network in a modular manner. Now, we will discuss the various building blocks of the network in the following sections. Each of these building blocks has to adhere to the fundamental design principles of scalability, flexibility, modularity, and individually.

Campus network

A campus network block is the part of the network where the users connect to the network. This can be considered to be the edge of the network, where all users would connect to the network. The primary function of the campus network block is to provide connectivity to the end users.

This connectivity could be over a wired or a wireless infrastructure. A good campus design would ensure that the users get the same experience, regardless of the mode of connectivity, and the design would scale out as the number of users grows. A good campus network would follow a hierarchical network design consisting of the core, distribution, and access tiers. It is not essential to start a network with all three tiers, but the design should enable you to scale up to the three-tier model if the network expands to accommodate more users. An example of a campus network that starts small, but scales to a three-tier design is shown in the following figure:

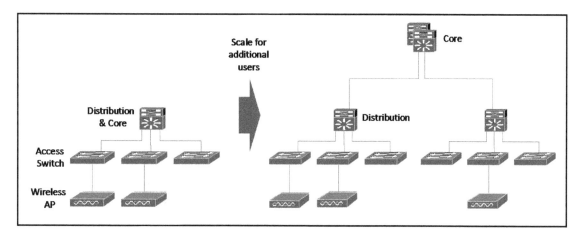

Figure 10: Scalable campus switching topology

The functions of the campus network block include:

- Providing physical ports or wireless connectivity to the IT end point such as laptops, desktops, IP phones, printers and so on
- Providing physical ports or wireless connectivity to any IoT systems, surveillance cameras, sensors, and so on
- Aggregating the traffic from similar users and keeping the traffic from different groups isolated from each other
- Allowing only authorised users to access
- Marking the traffic for prioritization of different types of traffic and prioritizing the traffic as it flows from the edge of the network to the core, or vice versa
- Providing Netflow information that can be used for analytics of traffic

The campus network block can be as small as a local area network consisting of a couple of users, and as large as a campus of a few thousand users spread across multiple buildings in the campus. Hence, there is not a single design that can be applied to all campuses. We will discuss the different design options for the campus in Chapter 4, *Understanding and Configuring Campus Network Technologies*. We will cover the wireless aspects of campus design in Chapter 5, *Understanding and Configuring Wireless Access Technologies*.

Wide Area Network (WAN)

As the network expands to multiple locations, there is a need to connect the multiple campus or branch networks to each other. This connectivity from the campus networks from different locations to the data center might be on dedicated links taken from service providers or over a shared infrastructure of the service provider, who will provide virtual network services over the **Service Provider** (**SP**) infrastructure and isolate traffic of different customers. An alternative way of connecting the branches to the data center could be over the internet over manual tunnels configured using encryption.

It might seem that the role of the wide area network is just to transport packets between two locations, which is largely true. The complexity starts to set in when we start factoring in the fact that the WAN bandwidths are much less when compared to the bandwidths available in the campus. Consider the fact that campus or the LAN might have 10G or even 40G backbones, but the WAN links would generally be an order of magnitude lower, primarily due to the cost of the WAN links. This forces the network administrators to ensure that these links are optimally utilized, while providing services to the end users with an acceptable quality. This translates to segregating the traffic and prioritizing the critical traffic from nonbusiness traffic and ensuring that the business-critical traffic takes priority over the WAN links.

Redundancy is an essential element of any network design as discussed in the previous chapters. WAN links are more likely to fail, compared to the links within the campus. Also, any outages on the WAN links generally take more time to be restored. Any outage in a WAN link between two locations would isolate the two locations, and, if the business applications cannot work in a standalone mode, the business would be impacted for the duration of time the WAN links are down. To ensure a high uptime of the network and services, network designers use redundant links or use multiple service providers to provide the WAN connectivity. Some networks might also use the internet as the fallback option. These options are depicted in the following figure:

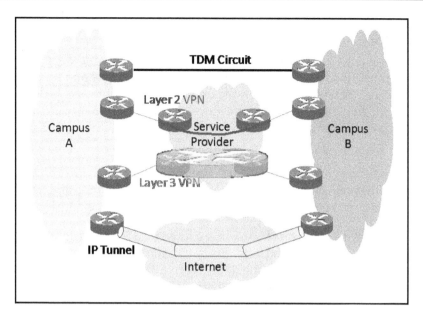

Figure 11: Different options for connecting remote sites

Going overboard with redundancy can become a problem of plenty, as the network designers have to ensure that controls are in place for the network performance and traffic flows to be deterministic. This means that the network design has to be done in a manner such that certain traffic always takes a certain path or link/links as the first preference and only when the primary path/link is down, should the traffic switch to the backup link. This is achieved by defining and configuring the right routing protocols and policies on the WAN links.

The main functions of the WAN block are summarized as follows:

- Providing connectivity between networks at different physical locations
- Providing differentiated services and the right quality of services to the different types of traffic
- Providing enough redundancy and ensuring that the network flows stay deterministic in case of link failures
- Exchanging routes between the locations, or with the SP in case of virtual private networks to direct certain types of traffic on certain links

We will cover these functions and the methods of deploying the different types of WAN connectivity in Chapter 6, *Understanding and Configuring WAN Technologies*.

Data center

Any IT-enabled organization has a large number of applications and data that are crucial for the business operations of the organization. These applications and data can be of multiple types, and different roles within the organization need to access different data and applications. At the same time, these applications and data have to be secure and highly available, as any availability disruption for these systems would mean loss of revenue for the company.

Hence, organizations centralize the data and core applications that are crucial to its business operations in facilities called **data centers**. From a networking standpoint, the data centers are locations with a very high port density and very large compute and storage capacities.

Since the primary function of the data center is to host the IT infrastructure for running the core applications, and storing critical data, the data centers need to be highly available, and secure. Generally, there is more than one data center within an organization. With the advent of cloud computing, some companies are also moving to the cloud for their DC requirements.

A data center is segmented into multiple zones to allow segmentation of the data center infrastructure and provide segregation of traffic from different types of applications from each other. One example of this segmentation could be the segregation of the development databases, and test applications in one zone that is completely segregated from the production application systems and databases.

The data center also hosts the applications such as email, and proxy servers that are used by the company's employees. Such applications need connectivity to the internet. If the DC is hosting the organization's website on a web server, these services would also need connectivity to the internet. These applications that need access from the internet are highly vulnerable to attacks from the internet and are placed in a separate segment or zone within the data center.

Some of the functions of the data center block are as follows:

- Hosting critical IT infrastructure including servers and databases
- Providing segmentation to different types of applications within the DC
- Providing secure network connectivity to the users of the organization that are connected to the campus network to access the application hosted in the DC
- Providing connectivity for the storage networks within the DC and the backup DC, also called the **Disaster Recovery (DR)**
- Providing a network to manage the different IT infrastructure elements within the DC through a secure management network

We will discuss the design of a DC in detail in Chapter 7, *Understanding and Configuring Data Center Technologies* to meet the aforementioned requirements.

Internet edge

The internet is probably the biggest network that one can imagine today. It shouldn't be a surprise then that most IT networks are connected to the internet. There are exceptions to this in case of military networks, and networks that are totally isolated, but this is true in general for organizational IT networks. Even if organizations do not allow internet browsing, connectivity to the internet is required for connectivity of the mail servers.

We are living in an age where the internet is full of security threats to the IT infrastructure. These threats range from infecting machines with viruses and worms to more sophisticated attacks such as ransomware attacks to extort money from organizations. Hence, it is critical that the organizations protect themselves from the internet to prevent any loss to business continuity.

Most organizations centralize the internet access for their employees at a limited number of locations, to provide better control over the traffic and provide better security from the internet. This also helps the organization to manage costs in a more effective manner and gain more visibility into the utilization of the internet bandwidth.

The main functions performed at the internet edge are as follows:

- Providing connectivity to the internet for services such as email and web browsing
- Managing redundant links from internet service providers and ensuring the optimal utilization of the links
- Securing the network infrastructure from any attacks from the internet
- Providing an infrastructure for remote access to the corporate network infrastructure in line with the organization's policies
- Hiding the internal IP addresses from the internet and doing **Network Address Translation** (**NAT**) for connecting to the public internet
- Providing information about the internet bandwidth utilization and the type of traffic being carried in the internet links
- Implementing any security controls to block certain types of traffic or websites aligned to the organization's security policy

Most of these functions are performed as a separate segmented zone within the data center. We will discuss the implementation of the aforementioned functions on the internet edge in Chapter 7, Understanding and configuring DC technologies.

Interdependency between the various components

We have discussed the major functional blocks of the IT infrastructure within an organization, with each functional block performing a specific set of functions and providing specific capabilities to the overall network. The capabilities of the network as a whole will be determined by the capabilities of each block, and will depend upon the way the functions are implemented in each block. Since the blocks connect to each other and handover traffic to each other, the end-to-end capabilities of the network will also depend upon the manner in which these functions are handled and if they are compatible with the other blocks in the network.

As an example, the campus access block marked the traffic for providing differentiated services and a certain quality of service to selected applications. If these markings are not coherent across the WAN block, where the bandwidth is the lowest, and the chances of congestion are the highest, then the end-to-end quality of service will not meet user requirements.

Let's consider another example of the interdependencies between the different blocks. If there is a security threat detected by the internet block, and it is found that a particular host or IP address is sending malicious traffic towards the internet because of a possible malware, the host needs to be isolated from the network so that the malware does not spread to other hosts on the network. Hence, the threat is detected at the internet block, but needs to be acted upon at the campus network or network access block.

The end-to-end capabilities of the network will be as desired if, and only if, the network blocks are designed and implemented coherently considering the functions performed at each block.

Let's consider this from a bandwidth sizing perspective. The following figure shows the functional blocks and the traffic flows:

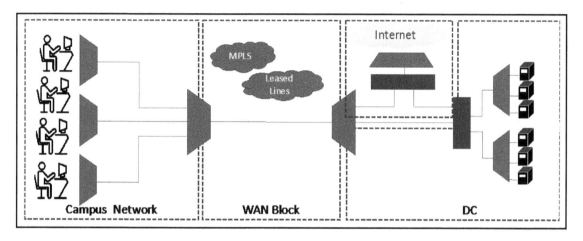

Figure 12: Traffic flows in a typical organization

The campus network provides access to the end users, and the port speeds at the access are typically 1Gbps per port. For a 1000 user network, the total access bandwidth provisioned is 1 * 1000 = 1000 Gbps. It would be impractical to consider 1000 Gbps of bandwidth all the way into the DC. A lot of factors such as oversubscription, the user mix of wired and wireless, and the types of applications need to be factored while designing the network at the access. This sizing would then have implications on the WAN bandwidth that is provisioned to carry the traffic from the campus or branch into the data center. Similarly, the traffic analysis has to be done for the servers in the DC, and the type of traffic that would flow to the end users and between the servers itself, from a data synchronization and replication perspective. All these sizing considerations have to be coherent to ensure an end-to-end user experience. We will get into the details of the sizing as we discuss the design of the various blocks in the subsequent chapters.

Summary

We have discussed the various parts of the IT network. We started with the common devices deployed in the IT network, discussed the hardware and software aspects of the devices and introduced Cisco IOS.

We also progressed to cover the functional blocks in the IT network and detailed the functions performed at each functional block, ending with highlighting the interdependencies between the various functional blocks.

Starting with the next chapter, we will delve deep into each functional block and discuss the technologies and protocols that are used in each functional block.

In the next chapter, we will discuss the various protocols, and technologies used within a building or a campus of the organization.

4
Understanding and Configuring Campus Network Technologies

"I'm not an isolated person. The more I connect to people, the more I have the feeling that things work."

– Raf Simons

We discussed the various elements of the enterprise network in the previous chapter. In this chapter, we will delve deep into the campus network, and the various technologies used in the campus network. A list of the topics discussed in this chapter are as follows:

- Layer 2 technologies used in the campus network, including Ethernet, Spanning Tree protocol, link aggregation, and their configuration
- Various layer 3 technologies used in the campus network, including first hop redundancy protocols and routing protocols
- Configuration guidelines for the various layer 2 and layer 3 technologies
- Campus design considerations

We will adopt a use case approach in the document, and take a sample enterprise as an example to discuss the considerations for designing the network and the protocols and technologies to use.

Before delving into the specifics of configuration, we will describe the various technologies and their working in brief so that the user can comprehend how to use the features on the network.

Campus network technologies

A campus network consists of multiple switches and routers that are interconnected to provide ports for connecting the devices to the network. We will discuss the various technologies that correspond to layer 2 and layer 3 of the OSI model, which are used on the campus network. Ethernet is the de facto standard for layer 2 connectivity for devices, and hence we will focus on the Ethernet technologies during our discussions. We will discuss the wireless technologies used within the campus network in `Chapter 5`, *Understanding and Configuring Wireless Access Technologies*.

Layer 2 technologies

We will start with a brief introduction to Ethernet, describe the linkages between Ethernet and the IP layers, and then discuss link bundling to enhance Ethernet capacity using different protocols. We will also discuss loop prevention mechanisms such as Spanning tree protocols in this section.

Ethernet

Ethernet is the most popular physical layer LAN technology in use today, as it strikes a good balance between speed, cost, and ease of installation. These benefits, combined with the ability to support most layer 3 protocols, make Ethernet an ideal networking technology for most computer users today. Ethernet is defined in the standard IEEE 802.3.

Ethernet is available in a wide range of speeds, using different types of physical cables and connectors. While Ethernet started at a basic speed of 10 Mbps, it is today available at speeds of 10 Mbps, 100 Mbps, 1 Gbps, 10 Gbps, 40 Gbps, and even 100 Gbps, all of which are in use today in the industry. The lower data rates up to 1 Gbps usually have copper interfaces running **Unshielded Twisted Pair** (**UTP**) cables with standard RJ45 connectors. The most common form of cabling standard used in the Ethernet industry is Cat5e that can carry 1 Gbps signals up to a length of 100 m. As the data rates increase, optical cables are used to connect Ethernet ports as there is no electromagnetic interference, and the signals are carried across larger distances. The optical cables connect to the **Small form-factor pluggable** (**SFP**) transceiver that provides a modular interface for the Ethernet port at a physical layer. SFPs available today can safely drive native Ethernet up to a length of 40 kms and beyond. Ethernet interfaces can be half or full duplex, and can autonegotiate speed for multirate interfaces.

Ethernet was developed for a shared medium, and hence any frames transmitted by a node on the Ethernet interface can be received by all other nodes on the same LAN. Ethernet uses **Carrier Sense Multi Access/Collision Detection** (**CSMA/CD**) technology to detect whether the medium is idle. This is important as the medium is shared between all nodes, and the receiver has to ensure that there is no other host transmitting on the physical medium at that point in time. However, there are still some chances of collision as two hosts at the remote ends of the shared medium may start to transmit at the same time. This leads to collisions of frames, and the devices have to backoff as per the protocol standards and wait before retransmitting the frame again. A larger number of hosts on the shared medium increase the chances of collisions and hence reduce the throughput of the link.

An Ethernet frame is as shown in the following figure with the field lengths in bytes given in parentheses for every field:

Destination MAC Address (6)	Source MAC Address (6)	Type (2)	Data (46-1500)	FCS (4)

Figure 1: Ethernet Frame

- The **Destination MAC Address** and **Source MAC Address** are the **Media Access Control** (**MAC**) layer addresses of the interface. These addresses are burnt into the physical Ethernet adapter, also called the **Network Interface Card** (**NIC**).
- The **Type** field denotes the higher layer protocols carried in the Ethernet frame. A common value is 0 x 0800 for IP, and 0 x 0806 for **Address Resolution Protocol** (**ARP**) that we will describe next.
- The **Data** field is the actual payload, which is an IP datagram where the Ethernet is carrying IP datagrams. In this case, the type field is set to the hex value of 0800.
- **Frame Check Sequence** (**FCS**) is a 4-byte field that denotes the check sum to be used to verify whether the frame has been received without errors or needs to be discarded.

Ethernet adds an overhead of 18 bytes to the payload because of the header fields. The maximum frame length that can be transmitted by the Ethernet interface is called the **Maximum Transmission Unit** (**MTU**). Since there is no fragmentation at the Ethernet layer, the maximum size of the IP datagram that can be transmitted is 18 bytes less than the MTU of the Ethernet link for untagged frames. The header length increases with 802.1Q tags, which we will describe in the section on VLANs.

Ethernet switch and MAC-based forwarding

An Ethernet switch has dedicated ports to which hosts are connected using physical cables. Any frame received on a port is not sent to all other hosts, but forwarded only to the hosts for which it is destined. The switch uses the MAC table to identify the port on which the frame should be forwarded. If the switch does not have the destination MAC address in its MAC tables, the switch will send the frame on all ports, resulting in a broadcast. This broadcast also happens if the Ethernet frame is destined for a broadcast MAC address. We will discuss this special case during the discussions on *Address Resolution Protocol (ARP)*.

Hence, Ethernet switches simulate the shared medium, but drastically reduce collisions as the frames from one host are not sent to all other hosts on the network. This allows multiple hosts to transmit at the same time, thereby improving the throughput of the LAN. The throughput also increases because of the use of full-duplex mode of operation, where the transceiver can transmit and receive at the same time.

An Ethernet switch works on the basis of a MAC table that it creates while forwarding traffic. When the switch is powered on, it has an empty MAC table. As the hosts start to send data, the switch keeps populating the MAC table based on the source MAC addresses received on the ports.

A very simple representation of a MAC table is as shown next. The MAC addresses are stored in the MAC table for a set time called the MAC ageing time, after which the address is flushed out to conserve device resources. The ageing timer is reset every time the switch sees the MAC address. So, the MAC entry is flushed only if the MAC is not active for a duration that exceeds the MAC ageing timer. This timer is set to 300s by default, but can be changed using the IOS command `mac address-table aging-time seconds`:

MAC address	Physical Port
00:23:54:76:87:d5	1
00:54:9a:76:e1:75	2
00:b2:0e:f6:3e:a1	3
00:54:65:e6:d2:e3	4
00:85:0c:f2:20:73	4

Figure 2: MAC table

When the switch receives a frame, it sees the source MAC address and populates its MAC table for the port on which the frame was received. The switch then also looks up the MAC table to see if a mapping between the destination MAC address exists for a particular port. If yes, the switch sends the frame only to that port. If there is no such mapping present, the switch broadcasts this frame on all ports other than the one on which it was initially received, thereby simulating the shared medium. The destination host, if connected, receives the frame. And when the destination host sends a frame back, the switch knows the physical port on which that host is connected from the source MAC address of the reply.

Broadcasts are bad for a switch as they interrupt all hosts on the LAN segment and need to be minimized. However, they cannot be eliminated altogether as the switch needs to use broadcast when sending frames to unknown MAC addresses. ARP, that we will discuss later, is another example where the frames have to be broadcast to all hosts on the Ethernet segment.

To minimize broadcasts on a network, network engineers generally limit the number of hosts on an Ethernet segment and create different Ethernet segments. Each segment is a different layer 3 domain, and we need a device with layer 3 functionality to send packets between the hosts in different segments.

Virtual LANs

An Ethernet switch has multiple ports, and not all of them might be required for a LAN segment. As an example, consider that we have a 24-port switch model and we need to create two different LAN segments with 10 hosts in one segment and 12 in the other. Virtual LAN technology allows a switch to be partitioned into multiple virtual switches or Ethernet segments. The MAC table in a switch that allows VLANs has additional information in addition to the one seen earlier. Each VLAN is denoted by a number, and there can be 4094 theoretical VLANs using 12 bits. There are some reserved VLAN numbers for FDDI and token ring, and not all switches will support 4094 VLANs.

The following figure shows a physical switch with 24 ports numbered 1 through 24. The switch can be partitioned into two logical virtual switching domains defined by VLAN 10 and VLAN 20. Note that although we have shown 12 ports in each VLAN, this is purely a logical configuration, and any port can be assigned to any VLAN:

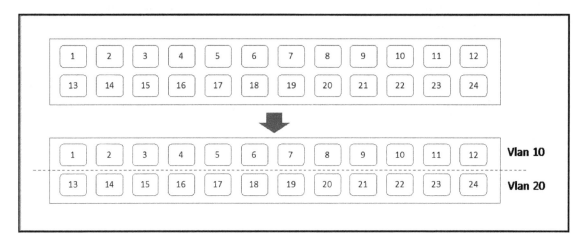

Figure 3: Creating VLANs

When VLANs are created on the switch, all ports in one VLAN are treated as one broadcast domain independent of the other ports on the switch. This helps to limit the number of broadcasts on the switch. The MAC table of the switch gets modified to include additional information, as shown in the table in the following figure:

MAC address	Physical Port	Vlan number
00:23:54:76:87:d5	1	10
00:54:9a:76:e1:75	2	20
00:b2:0e:f6:3e:a1	3	10
	4	10
	5	20
	6	10,20

Figure 4: MAC table with VLANs

Note in the preceding figure that the ports are preconfigured with the VLAN numbers, even though the MAC addresses are not known in advance. Also note that there are certain ports that have more than one VLAN associated with it and are called trunk ports as described next.

Access ports and trunk ports

When two switches having more than one VLAN are connected to each other, they need a way to intimate the other switch about the VLAN number to which a particular frame belongs. The basic Ethernet header described earlier does not have any field to do this. IEEE defines a new specification 802.1Q that defines the use of VLAN, and how to transfer this information across the links that are shared by more than one VLANs. Ports that have only one VLAN are called access ports, and ports that need to connect to hosts in more than one VLAN are termed trunk ports. Generally, the inter switch links and the uplinks are trunk ports, and ports that connect to normal hosts are access ports:

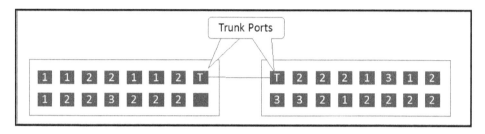

Figure 5: Trunk port

The trunk ports carry tagged frames, as shown next, that have a specific field called the 802.1Q tag. This tag has fields that can be used for identification of the VLAN number and also for the classification of frames with regard to the priority that these frames need when being processed by the devices. We will describe the priority fields when we discuss Quality of Service in `Chapter 9`, *Understanding and Configuring Quality of Service*. An Ethernet frame with an 802.1Q header is as shown the following figure. The field lengths in bits are given in parenthesis:

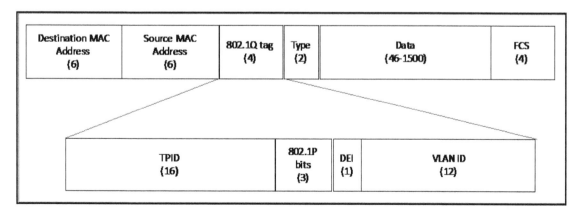

Figure 6: 802.1Q Header

Note in the preceding figure that the TPID value is always set to 8100 (hex) to indicate that this is a tagged frame. The VLAN numbers are carried in the VLAN ID field that is 12 bits long. Note that with the addition of the 802.1Q tag, the Ethernet header increases to 22 bytes.

Spanning Tree Protocols

Consider the Ethernet switching domain as shown in the following figure. For simplicity, let's assume a single VLAN across the Ethernet segment and untagged frames:

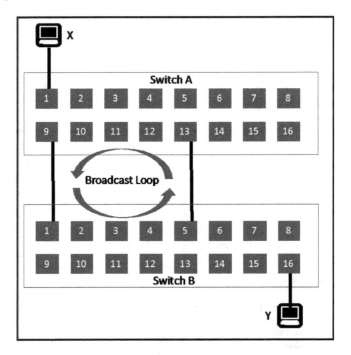

Figure 7: Broadcast Loops in Ethernet

There are two switches A and B with all ports in the same VLAN. The switches are connected to each other with the connections from port A9 to B1 and A13 to B5. Let's consider that the host X connected to port 1 of switch A and called A1 wants to send a frame to host Y. Switch A receives the frame from host X on port A1, and does a lookup of its MAC table to find the port associated with the destination address of the Ethernet frame. Since the switch has an empty MAC table at start up, the switch has to broadcast the frame on all ports. So, switch A broadcasts the frame on ports A2 through A16. The frame exits through port A9, and reaches port B1 on switch B. Switch B also does not have the MAC address of host Y in its MAC table, and hence broadcasts the frame on all ports other than B1. This broadcast reaches port 13 on switch A again through port 5 on switch B, and a loop is formed. Since there is no field that will time out these frames on the switch, there is an endless loop and the magnification effect causes a huge amount of traffic and CPU spikes on the switch and can disrupt the entire switch.

This looping of frames happened because there was a closed physical loop on the Ethernet network. Any Ethernet topology will have problems if there are physical loops in it. One way to solve the problem is to disconnect the second link, but we need that for redundancy purposes. The other way to solve this is to use **Spanning Tree Protocol** (**STP**) that can put some ports in the blocking mode by sending a set of STP packets, and avoiding a loop on the Ethernet. In case the active or forwarding link goes down, the STP recalculates the topology and brings the blocking ports into the forwarding state. Loops can also be created when a switching topology has a physical loop across a set of switches. These loops are also handled by STP to provide a loop-free topology. STP is defined as the IEEE Standard 802.1D.

STP can run on the switch either in a per VLAN mode creating a separate forwarding loop free topology for each VLAN or in a multi-vlan mode, where a forwarding topology is created for a bunch of VLANs that can be defined via configuration. These modes are called **Per-VLAN Spanning Tree** (**PVST**) and **Multiple Spanning Tree** (**MST**) respectively. If there are a large number of VLANs, it is recommended to run MST so that the control packets are minimum and the CPU does not get overloaded due to processing of the STP packets for each VLAN.

STP runs by default on Cisco Ethernet switches in the PVST+ mode. STP sends special packets called **Bridge Protocol Data Units** (**BPDUs**), which are encapsulated within Ethernet headers. These frames are sent periodically and processed by all switches to put certain ports in blocking state, thus creating a loop-free topology. The topology is recalculated if a port state changes on the network thereby ensuring redundancy on the network, by unblocking a port. STP uses a concept called root bridge that is used as the root of the loop-free topology tree that connects all Ethernet segments. A sample Ethernet topology and the resulting STP topology is as shown in the following figure:

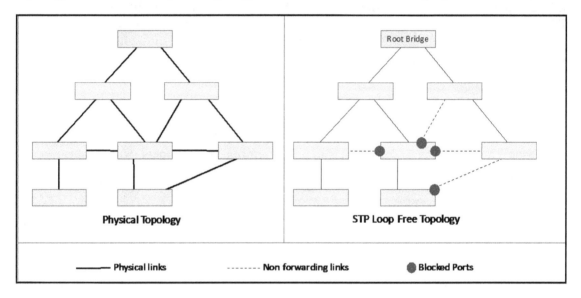

Figure 8: Blocked ports due to STP

The switch that acts like the root bridge is critical. Traffic from hosts on different branches passes through this root bridge. The root bridge should be the device that is the topmost device in the L2 hierarchy. The root bridge is elected through the processing of BPDU messages. The IOS command to configure the switch as the root bridge is `spanning-tree vlan <vlan-id> root primary`.

We will cover the security aspects of the root bridge in `Chapter 8`, *Understanding and Configuring Network Security*.

Link aggregation

Another way to break the loop is to treat the two links between a set of devices as a single logical entity. This is called link bundling or link aggregation and is defined in the specification IEEE 802.3ad.

While running STP puts all alternate links in standby mode and doesn't use the available capacity, aggregating the links allows the network administrator to increase the available capacity between a pair of switches.

Note that 802.3ad link aggregation works on links between a set of switches. This does not help in cases where a switch has two uplinks, each terminated on a different switch. In such scenarios, we can either use first-hop redundancy protocols to achieve load balancing across the uplinks as discussed later in the chapter. Another way to achieve link aggregation across a set of uplink switches is by using virtual port channels, which is used primarily in the data center. We will discuss this in `Chapter 7`, *Understanding and Configuring Data Center Technologies*.

Address Resolution Protocol (ARP)

When a datagram is handed by the layer 3 of the host to the layer 2 of the host, it needs to be encapsulated with the layer 2 headers before it can be transmitted on the physical medium. Recall that an IP datagram at layer 3 has no knowledge of the layer 2 or the MAC address, and layer 2 encapsulation needs the source and the destination MAC addresses for creating the layer 2 headers and trailers. The discovery of the destination MAC address from the destination IP address is done using the ARP.

ARP is a query-response protocol. When the layer 2 host receives the IP datagram, it checks its ARP table to see if it has a MAC entry corresponding to the destination MAC address. If not, the host initiates an ARP query. This ARP query is encapsulated in an Ethernet frame with the destination MAC broadcast address (0xFFFFFFFF), and is received by all hosts on that LAN segment. The hosts on the LAN segment receive this ARP request, which contains a query for the MAC address of the destination IP address. The host which owns the destination MAC address then creates an ARP response with its MAC address as one of the parameters in the response, and sends the ARP response as a MAC unicast reply to the source, which initiated the ARP query.

Let's consider a LAN with five hosts, **A** through **E**. Let the MAC addresses for the devices be represented by **A2**, **B2**, **C2**, **D2**, and **E2** and the corresponding IP addresses be represented as **A3**, **B3**, **C3**, **D3**, and **E3** respectively. The ARP process is shown in the following figure:

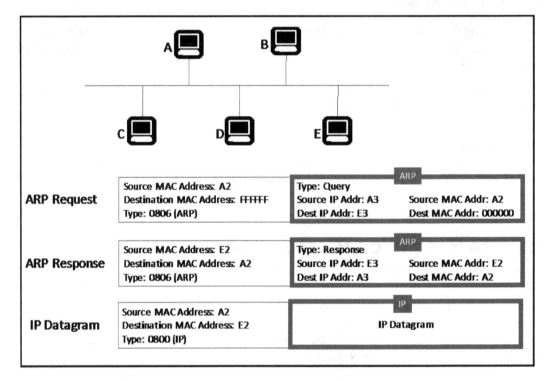

Figure 9: Resolving IP address to MAC address using ARP

Once host **A** has received the MAC address of **E** through an ARP process, it will cache it in its ARP table. The caching is done for a specific time that can be configured on routers, and is generally preconfigured on hosts. Host **A** can then start sending IP packets to host **E**.

ARP entries can be viewed on the switch by using `show arp` or the `show ip arp` commands. The ARP entries also age out like the MAC entries. The default ARP timeout interval is 14400s, and can be changed by using the `arp timeout` command in the interface configuration mode.

Static ARP can be defined for binding an IP address to a specific MAC address by using the commands, as shown next, that statically maps the IP address 10.0.0.1 to the MAC address bbaa:ddcc:8642:

```
Router(config)# arp 10.0.0.1 bbaa.ddcc.8642 arpa
```

Figure 10: Creating a static ARP entry

ARP can be cleared using the clear arp-cache command.

Configuring layer 2 protocols

Let's consider a sample topology, as shown in the following figure, to show a sample configuration for the layer 2 features on the switch. In the sample topology shown in the figure, there are three switches, each having 24 ports. Four ports on each switch are in VLAN 10, and four ports on each switch are in VLAN 20, as defined by the legend in the figure. The remaining ports on each switch are in the default VLAN 1, and we will not use these ports. The switches interconnect with each other and form a STP loop that needs to be broken, and we will run PVST on the switches. Also, we will restrict the interconnect links or trunk links to carry only VLANs 10 and 20. The interconnect between **Switch-A** and **Switch-B** consists of two physical links that form a link bundle:

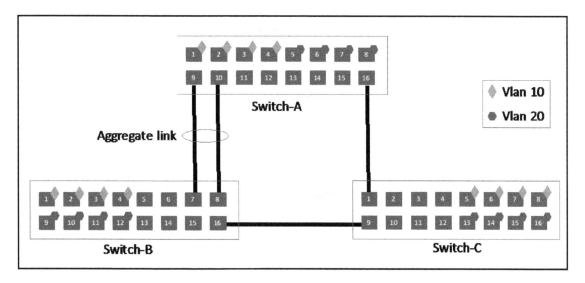

Figure 11: Sample topology for configuration

The configurations for enabling the same on switch A are as shown next. Note the following in the configuration:

- We have used an interface range command to configure a set of interfaces in one command
- We have forced a set of ports to 1Gig speed and full duplex mode to avoid autonegotiation as a best practice
- We bundled two ports into a port channel
- The port channel created port-channel2 was configured to run STP and to carry specific VLANs 10 and 20:

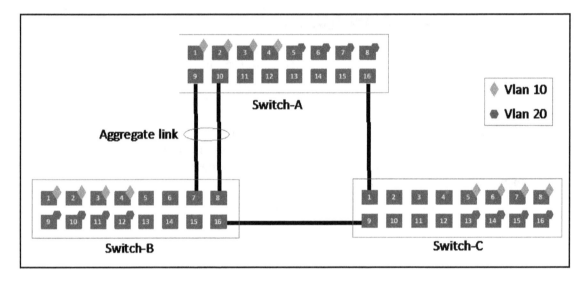

Figure 12: Layer 2 feature configuration

Layer 3 technologies

As discussed in the previous chapters, **Internet Protocol** (**IP**) is a layer 3 protocol. Recall that a primary function of layer 3 is routing of packets across different subnets. Every interface that is connected to the network needs to have an IP address for identification. Since IP addressing design is critical to any network, we will start with a quick recap of IP addressing and then delve into the considerations for IP address planning for networks.

IP addressing

An IP address is a logical identifier for an interface that is connected to the network. Two versions of IP are currently in use: IPv4 and IPv6. We will focus on IPv4 in this book.

IPv4 addresses

An IP address is a 32-bit identifier that uniquely identifies an endpoint on an IP network. Remembering a 32-bit IP address would be a nightmare, so the address is represented as a dotted decimal notation.

Firstly, the 32 bits are grouped into four octets having 8 bits each. Secondly, the IP address is represented in a doted decimal notation, meaning that the four octets are separated by a decimal between them, which is read as a dot while reading the address. Thirdly, the octets are converted into a decimal number for easier identification, and the IP address takes the form A.B.C.D.

The following figure illustrates the steps in converting the 32 bits of an IP address into the familiar dotted decimal notation:

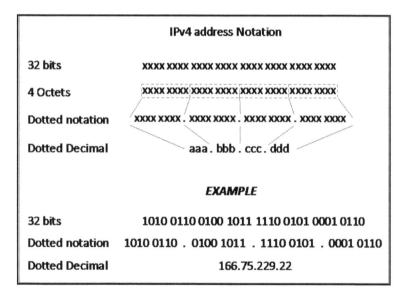

Figure 13: IPv4 address notation

An IP address is a logical address for the network layer of the host connected to the network. Note that each interface of the host has an IP address, and if a host has two interfaces connected to two different networks, it will have two different IP addresses--one for each interface. The host may also have an address for a logical interface, which is different from a physical interface. As an example, most devices on a network will have a logical interface configured as a loopback interface. This is purely a logical interface with no physical interface mapping. This is done to identify the device on the network through the logical interface, as that interface would never go down as long as any one interface on the device is connected to the network and the TCP/IP stack on the device works normally.

Since an IP address is a logical address, it is easy to build a hierarchy in the addressing schema, which is required for routing the packets from one network to another. All interfaces connected on one network have a common network that is a logical identifier for the network. This network number is embedded in the IP address itself, and can be derived from the IP address using the network mask. Another way of looking at the network number being embedded in the IP address is to look at the IP address as a combination of the network number and host number. The 32 bits of the IP address are divided into two parts: the **Network Bits** on the left, and the **Host Bits** on the right:

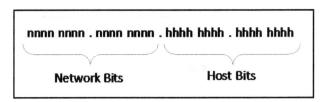

Figure 14: Network and host bits

The number of bits that denote the network bits is represented as a value called the network mask. The network mask is denoted as a number between 1 and 32 after a / sign. This is appended to the IP address in the dotted decimal notation. As an example, since the number of network bits in the preceding example is 16, the IP address will be written as 166.75.229.22 /16. This means that the IP address is 166.75.229.22 and the network mask is a /16.

Sometimes the network mask is also represented in the dotted decimal notation. To get the dotted decimal notation of the network mask, write the first n bits in the 32 bits as 1, and the remaining trailing bits as 0. Then, convert the resultant 32-bit number into the dotted decimal notation. We use the method shown in the following figure to convert the network mask of /16 into the dotted decimal notation:

Network mask is /16
Network Bits = 16
Host Bits = 32-16 = 16
1111 1111 . 1111 1111 . 0000 0000 . 0000 0000
255 . 255 . 0 . 0

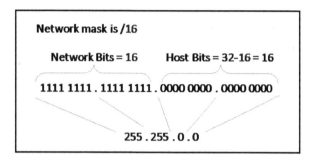

Figure 15: Network mask

If we look only at the network bits and replace all the host bits with a 0, the resultant 32-bit representation is called the network identifier. For the IP address example that we considered earlier, and assuming the network mask is /16, the network identifier is as derived in the following figure:

166.75.229.22 /16
1010 0110 . 0100 1011 . 1110 0101 . 0001 0110
Network Bits =16
Host Bits = 32-16 = 16
Replacing the host bits by a 0, Network identifier is
1010 0110 . 0100 1011 . 0000 0000 . 0000 0000
166.75.0.0

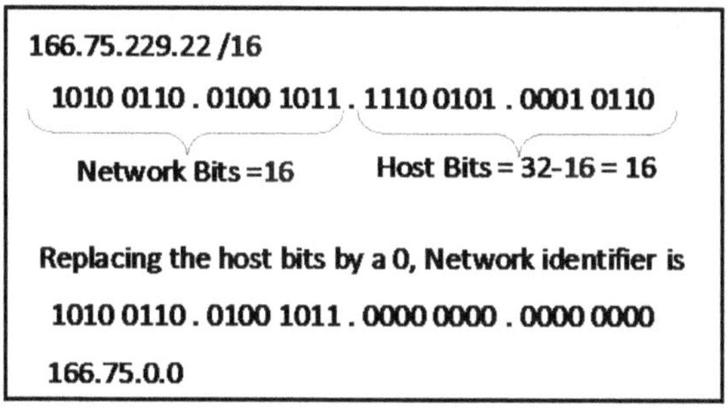

Figure 16: Calculating the network address

The network identifier can also be derived by masking the IP address with the network mask in dotted decimal notation. To mask the IP address with the subnet mask, just do a logical AND operation bit by bit for 32 bits. Note that a logical AND between a binary 1 and binary x is x itself, and the result of the AND operation between a binary 0 and a binary x is always 0. Hence, the logical AND operation for the 32 bits will get us the same result, as shown in the following figure:

IP Address	**166.75.229.22 / 16**
Network mask is /16	
Network mask is 255.255.0.0	
IP Address bits	1010 0110 . 0100 1011 . 1110 0101 . 0001 0110
	AND
Masking bits	1111 1111 . 1111 1111 . 0000 0000 . 0000 0000
Network ID	1010 0110 . 0100 1011 . 0000 0000 . 0000 0000
Network ID	**166.75.0.0**

Figure 17: Masking the host bits

All hosts on the same layer 3 network have the same network number or ID. Therefore, if a network has a mask of /n, the first n bits of the IP address are the network bits. The remaining (32-n) bits out of the 32 bits of the IPv4 address represent the host part of the address. Since the IP addresses are unique, in a subnet the maximum number of host addresses is $2^{(32-n)}$. The first and last addresses of the range have a special purpose. The first address will be where all the host bits are 0 and, as we discussed earlier, this number represents the network identifier for the network. If all the host bits of an IP address are set to 1, we get an address that is called the IP broadcast address or broadcast ID for the network, which represents the collection of all hosts/interfaces on the network. Hence, the maximum number of hosts/interfaces on a subnet is $2^{(32-n)}-2$. The following figure explains this with the IPv4 example:

```
IP Address        166.75.229.22 / 16

IP Address        1010 0110 . 0100 1011 . 1110 0101 . 0001 0110

Subnet Mask       1111 1111 . 1111 1111 . 0000 0000 . 0000 0000

Network ID        1010 0110 . 0100 1011 . 0000 0000 . 0000 0000

Broadcast ID      1010 0110 . 0100 1011 . 1111 1111 . 1111 1111


Network ID        166.75.0.0

Network ID        166.75.255.255

Maximum number of hosts = 2 (32-16) – 2  =  2^16 – 2 = 65536 – 2 = 65534
```

Figure 18: Calculating the number of hosts in a subnet

When IP addresses were formalized, IP addressing was classified into five classes, A through E, as shown in the following figure. Classes A, B, and C were used for user addressing, while class D was used for multicast addressing, and Class E addresses were reserved for experimental use. The identification of the address was based on the higher order bits in the binary representation of the address. If the highest order bit was 0, the address was a class A address. If the highest order 2 bits were 10, the address was a class B address, and if the highest order 3 bits were 110, it was a class C address. Similarly, the highest order 4 bits for class D and class E addresses were 1110 and 1111 respectively.

The rationale was based on the fact that there would be large, medium, and small networks, and hence three different classes of address, namely A, B, and C, were devised accordingly. The class A addresses were for the largest networks, where the number of hosts would be very large. It was assumed that very few networks of such types would exist on the internet. Accordingly, 8 bits were reserved in a class A address for the network bits in a class A address, and the remaining 32 bits were for hosts. Since the first bit was already set to 0, this meant that there could be 128 such networks ($2^{(8-1)}$), and each network could have up to 2^{24} - 2 hosts each. This can also be interpreted as class A networks having a network mask of /8 or 255.0.0.0.

Similarly, the network bits in a class B address for medium networks was 16, leaving 16 bits for the host part. Class C networks had 24 bits reserved for the network and 8 for the hosts:

Class A	0nnn nnnn . hhhh hhhh . hhhh hhhh . hhhh hhhh
Class B	10nn nnnn . nnnn nnnn . hhhh hhhh . hhhh hhhh
Class C	110n nnnn . nnnn nnnn . nnnn nnnn . hhhh hhhh
Class D	1110 xxxx . xxxx xxxx . xxxx xxxx . xxxx xxxx
Class E	1111 xxxx . xxxx xxxx . xxxx xxxx . xxxx xxxx

Figure 19: Classful addresses

The following table summarizes the hosts and networks for the different classes of address:

Class	Network mask	Network Bits	Host bits	Number of networks	Maximum hosts per network
A	255.0.0.0	8	24	2^{8-1}	$2^{24}-2$
B	255.255.0.0	16	16	2^{16-2}	$2^{16}-2$
C	255.255.255.0	24	8	2^{24-3}	$2^{8}-2$

Figure 20: Hosts per address class

The address structure discussed so far is generally referred to as **classful addressing**. This format of addressing had severe limitations as the IP networks expanded rapidly. Since the number of networks were finite, the demand for IP addresses far outnumbered what was available.

Also, the smallest networks had 254 addresses for hosts. However, even if there were 10 hosts on the network, the remaining addresses could not be used anywhere, the network numbers had to be unique, leading to a lot of wastage of the available IP addresses. This wastage of IP addresses became a big cause for concern and the industry started looking at new ways of reducing this wastage and finding efficient ways to use the available IP address space. This led to the introduction of **classless addressing**, wherein the concept of bucketing all networks into small, medium, and large, and hence allocating class C, B, or A addresses was done away with.

In classless addressing, the number of network bits was not fixed like in classful addressing at 8, 16, or 24, but there was flexibility that the number of bits reserved for the network (Network mask) could be any number from 1 to 32. Hence, the networks could be partitioned into smaller networks called subnets, and the utilization of IP addresses improved drastically. This meant that any number of bits could be reserved for the host bits, and the remaining bits would be the network bits. Hence each network could have addresses that were as granular as the power of 2. For example, if the host bits were 4, there could be 2^4 addresses, similarly if the number of host bits were 5, there could be 2^5 addresses. Note that the usable addresses would still be 2 less than the actual number, one each being reserved for the network ID and the broadcast address.

As an example, consider a situation where there were four different LAN segments or networks that had 40 hosts each to be connected. If we had followed classful addressing, we would have assigned a class C address to each of the 4 LAN segments and utilized only 40 addresses out of the 254 available for use in each segment leading to a huge wastage of addresses. In classless addressing, the addressing is done based on the requirement of addresses.

In this example, since we need 40 addresses per network and we can allot addresses in powers of 2 (2, 4, 8, 16, 32, 64, 128, 256, and so on), the minimum number of addresses that would fulfil the requirement of 40 addresses is 64, which requires 6 bits for the hosts. Hence for one class C (/24) network, we can fulfil the requirement of four such networks. Let's assume that the address block 166.75.229.0/24 was allocated to us.

The same address block can be subnetted into four smaller subnets for each subnetwork. Since the address block allocated to us had a subnet mask of /24, the first 24 bits are fixed. Now we need 40 addresses per LAN segment and, as discussed earlier, we need 6 bits as the host bits for each subnetwork. The number of bits that we can use as the subnet bits are 32-24-6 or 2 bits. Using the 2 bits, we can have 2^2 or 4 subnets. This is shown in the following figure for the address block of 166.75.229.0/24. Note that the subnets now have a subnet mask of /26 or 255.255.255.192 because each subnet now has 26 bits that represent the subnet:

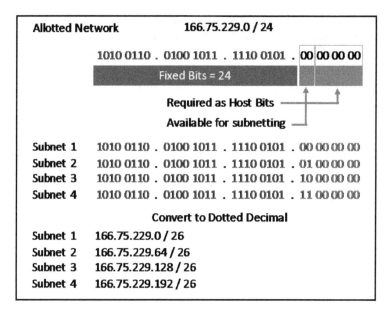

Figure 21: Subnetting beyond classful addressing

Note that in the new scheme of addressing, the subnet mask is not fixed at octet boundaries, but can have any value as long as it can be represented as a continuous string of binary 1 followed by a continuous string of binary 0, and the total number of bits being 32. This concept of splitting subnets for creating smaller subnets, where each subnet can have different subnet masks depending upon the number of addresses required in the subnet is called **Variable Length Subnet Masking (VLSM)**.

The concept of subnetting led to a large number of prefixes on the network. This led to an increase in the resources required for the routing tables that stored these prefixes. To overcome the effect of the increase in the number of prefixes, the standards defined a new concept called **supernetting**, which aggregated smaller prefixes into a fewer number of prefixes with a smaller netmask. We will discuss this later in the routing section.

Routable and private addresses

IP addresses are designed for providing routing functions on the internet. However, some networks can still be private and not connected to the internet. The IP address schema defined IP address pools called private IP address blocks that can be used for organizations to address the hosts within their networks that are isolated from the internet. These addresses are defined in RFC1918 and are sometimes also referred to as RFC 1918 address blocks.

These private address blocks can be reused by different organizations, as these are private and it is expected that these organizations will not communicate with each other, and hence the uniqueness of IP address would be maintained in the respective domains in which they are routable.

If these organizations want to communicate with the external internet, they can use technologies such as **Network Address Translation** (**NAT**). Private addressing is generally done as there is a paucity of routable or public IPv4 addresses. However, this also ensures that not all hosts are reachable from the internet, and hence the security of the hosts can be maintained through effective controls at the NAT gateways. We will address the NAT technology and implications in `Chapter 7`, *Understanding and Configuring Data Center Technologies*.

The private address blocks used in organizations are shown in the following figure:

Class	Private Networks
A	10.0.0.0 / 8
B	172.16.0.0 / 16 to 172.31.0.0 / 16
C	192.168.0.0 / 24 to 192.168.255.0 / 24

Figure 22: Private IP addresses

Sample addressing

Let's apply the concepts studied so far in creating an IP address plan for the sample organization we considered in the previous chapter. Recall that the organization had a headquarters office with a large number of users that also hosted the data center. The applications were hosted in the data center. The organization also had a lot of branches where the employees used to connect to the network for access to the central applications. Let's also assume that the organization will deploy a lot of IoT systems such as sensors and CCTV cameras. The organization accesses the internet from the central location, and has a public IP address pool that is routed on the internet that it uses for internet access.

The basic criteria of IP address design is to classify and segregate the different types of traffic requirements into distinct blocks. This classification could be on the basis of blocks where there is no communication, or the hosts to which access needs to be controlled from other devices. As an example, we classify the IT systems and IoT systems as two distinct blocks, as there will be little or no communication requirements between the IT systems and the IoT systems. This segregation is required to have contiguous blocks of IP addresses for the systems, which will make it easier to identify the devices based on their IP address and will also help in creating effective security policies and enforcing them on the security devices such as the firewalls. We will discuss more about this in Chapter 7, *Understanding and Configuring Data Center Technologies*.

The next step is to drill down into the next level of detail and use the same classification principles and create separate address blocks for the IT users on the network, the servers hosted in the data center, and the infrastructure block, which is a grouping of all network devices that need addresses for interfaces and loopbacks. Finally, the **Network operations center (NOC)** is treated as a functionally different address block, because the NOC needs to be highly secure and the connectivity into the NOC needs to be restricted. A similar hierarchy can be defined for the IoT systems for the NOC and the various remote devices. The classification principles can be drilled down further to contain address blocks for the different locations such as the head office and the different branches. Further, the address blocks can be segregated based on the different user groups within the office if there are multiple user groups such as marketing, development, human resources, and finance. This segregation will help if only selected user groups need to be provided access to a certain set of servers, for example, if the HR servers need to be isolated from non-HR users:

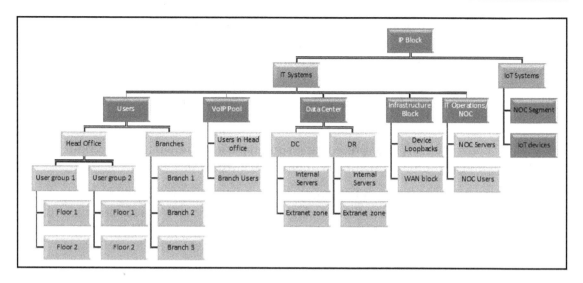

Figure 23: Sample IP address plan

Note that no one size fits all and address assignments can be done differently, but the fundamental principle of classification and segregation is fundamental to the success of an effective addressing plan. Another factor to keep in mind while designing the address plan is scalability to meet the future requirements of the organization. Note that scalability and room for expansion needs to be factored for all areas, including the servers in the DC, the number of users, and the number of branches. It will always be a compromise to keep room for future expansion and manage a limited number of IP addresses, but if the organization uses private IP addresses, adequate room should be kept at the time of initial planning of IP addresses.

Let's make some assumptions on numbers and do the IP address assignment using a 10.0.0.0/8 address block. The assumptions are as summarized here:

- The users involved in development need to be segregated from all other users
- There are two floors in the HQ building; each floor has an area for development users and non-development users
- Each floor has 80-100 development users that can go up to 120 on each floor

- Each floor also has 80 other users that can go up to 100
- There are currently four branches each having 30-40 non-development users; branches might grow to 10 in the near future
- Every employee in HQ and remote branches needs a VoIP phone
- There are two data centers, each having 3-4 zones with each zone having 8-10 servers

A sample IP address plan for the preceding assumptions is as shown in the upcoming figure. The rationale for the subnetting is briefly explained here:

- Each floor will have a subnet for development users and a separate subnet for nondevelopment users. Since each subnet should be able to accommodate 100 hosts, we will need a /25 subnet that has 126 host addresses. This is shown in the figure as pools for development and nondevelopment users for each floor.
- Each branch needs 40 addresses, and hence a /26 subnet that can accommodate 64 host addresses. The address plan allots addresses to four branches and reserves continuous addresses for 12 more branches in the future.
- For VoIP phones, no distinction is made between the users, and /24 pools are reserved per floor for VoIP at the HQ. Similarly, /26 pools are reserved at the branches to cater to the 40 users.
- Each DC and DR needs 3-4 zones with 8-10 servers each. We have reserved /24 for DC and DR. Each zone only needs a /28 for 8-10 servers, and 4 such zones can be accommodated in a /26. Continuous addresses are also reserved for expansion.
- The infrastructure pool is a /24 pool split into two subnets of /25, one for WAN addresses and one for loopback addresses. The /25 WAN pool can accommodate 64 WAN links, which we will describe during configurations.

The IoT block can be taken from another pool such as the 192.168.0.0/16 block for easier identification:

10.0.0.0 /20							
	10.0.0.0 /21 USERS	10.0.0.0 /22 HEAD OFFICE	10.0.0.0 /23 DEVELOPMENT USERS	10.0.0.0 /24	10.0.0.0 /25		Development users Floor 1
					10.0.0.128 /25		Development users Floor 2
				10.0.1.0 /24	10.0.1.0 /25		Spare
					10.0.1.128 /25		Spare
			10.0.2.0 /23 NON-DEVELOPMENT UESRS	10.0.2.0 /24	10.0.2.0 /25		Non-Development users Floor 1
					10.0.2.128 /25		Non-Development users Floor 2
				10.0.3.0 /24	10.0.3.0 /25		Spare
					10.0.3.128 /25		Spare
		10.0.4.0 /22 BRANCHES	10.0.4.0 /23	10.0.4.0 /24	10.0.4.0 /25	10.0.4.0 /26	Users Branch 1
						10.0.4.64 /26	Users Branch 2
					10.0.4.128 /25	10.0.4.128 /26	Users Branch 3
						10.0.4.192 /26	Users Branch 4
				10.0.5.0 /24	10.0.5.0 /25	10.0.5.0 /26	Spare
						10.0.5.64 /26	Spare
					10.0.5.128 /25	10.0.5.128 /26	Spare
						10.0.5.192 /26	Spare
			10.0.6.0 /23	10.0.6.0 /24	10.0.6.0 /25	10.0.6.0 /26	Spare
						10.0.6.64 /26	Spare
					10.0.6.128 /25	10.0.6.128 /26	Spare
						10.0.6.192 /26	Spare
				10.0.7.0 /24	10.0.7.0 /25	10.0.7.0 /26	Spare
						10.0.7.64 /26	Spare
					10.0.7.128 /25	10.0.7.128 /26	Spare
						10.0.7.192 /26	Spare
	10.0.8.0 /21	10.0.8.0 /22 VoIP Pool	10.0.8.0 /23	10.0.8.0 /24			VoIP Pool HQ Floor 1
				10.0.9.0 /24			VoIP Pool HQ Floor 2
			10.0.10.0 /23	10.0.10.0 /24	10.0.10.0 /25	10.0.10.0 /26	VoIP Branch 1
						10.0.10.64 /26	VoIP Branch 2
					10.0.10.128 /25	10.0.10.128 /26	VoIP Branch 3
						10.0.10.192 /26	VoIP Branch 4
				10.0.11.0 /24	10.0.11.0 /25	10.0.11.0 /26	Spare
						10.0.11.64 /26	Spare
					10.0.11.128 /25	10.0.11.128 /26	Spare
						10.0.11.192 /26	Spare
		10.0.12.0 /22	10.0.12.0 /23 DC	10.0.12.0 /24	10.0.12.0 /25	10.0.12.0 /26	DC Server Zones
						10.0.12.64 /26	DC Server Zones
					10.0.12.128 /25	10.0.12.128 /26	Spare
						10.0.12.192 /26	Spare
			10.0.13.0 /24 DR	10.0.13.0 /24	10.0.13.0 /25	10.0.13.0 /26	DR Server Zones
						10.0.13.64 /26	DR Server Zones
				10.0.13.128 /25	10.0.13.128 /26	Spare
						10.0.13.192 /26	Spare
			10.0.14.0 /23 Infra & NOC	10.0.14.0 /24 Infrastructure	10.0.14.0 /25	10.0.14.0 /26	32 WAN Links *
						10.0.14.64 /26	32 WAN Links *
					10.0.14.128 /25	10.0.14.128 /26	64 Loopback Addresses
						10.0.14.192 /26	64 Loopback Addresses
			10.0.15.0 /24 NOC	10.0.15.0 /24	10.0.15.0 /25	10.0.15.0 /26	NOC Users
						10.0.15.64 /26	Spare
				10.0.15.128 /25	10.0.15.128 /26	NOC Servers
						10.0.15.192 /26	Spare

Figure 24: Sample IP address plan

Configuring IP addresses

In this section, we will discuss how to configure an IP address on an interface. Recall from the previous chapter that all configurations are done in the configuration mode of the Cisco IOS. We will follow the following steps to enter into the configuration mode of the IOS.

On normal boot or login into the router, the prompt of the router is the name of the router, also called `hostname` (which we set to `TESTROUTER` in the following figure) followed by a > sign. When we enter the privileged mode by entering the `enable` command, the prompt changes to the `hostname` followed by a # sign. It is in this mode that we can enter into the configuration mode by using the `configure terminal` command. On successfully entering the configuration mode, the prompt would change to the `hostname` followed by the text `(config) #` as shown in the following figure. We can also use unambiguous short forms such as `conf t` for `configure terminal`:

```
Router>
Router> enable
Router#
Router# conf t
Enter configuration commands, one per line. End with CTRL/Z
Router(config)# hostname TESTROUTER
TESTROUTER(config)#
```

Figure 25: Configuring the device hostname

As discussed in the previous chapter, the configuration mode has multiple submodes. To configure an interface, we enter the interface configuration mode by entering the interface name at the configure prompt. The IP address is configured as shown through the commands in the following figure:

```
TESTROUTER(config)#
TESTROUTER(config)# interface ethernet0/0
TESTROUTER(config-if)# ip addr 10.0.0.1 255.255.255.192
TESTROUTER(config-if)# no shut
TESTROUTER(config-if)# end
TESTROUTER#
* Jun 20 17:44:23.754: %SYS-5-CONFIG_I: Configured from console by console
TESTROUTER#
```

Figure 26: Configuring an interface address

The `no shut` command is a short form for no shutdown, which enables the interface and brings it in the active state. To administratively shutdown the interface, the `shutdown` command can be used. After the configuration has been done, the system displays a message that the router was configured from the console. After making the configuration, the running configuration should be copied to the startup configuration and saved to the NVRAM, as shown in the following figure:

```
TESTROUTER#
TESTROUTER# copy running-config startup-config
Destination filename [start-up config]?
Building configuration...
[OK]
TESTROUTER# write mem
Building configuration...
[OK]
TESTROUTER#
```

Figure 27: Saving the configuration

The IP address can be assigned to any layer 3 interface on a router. The interface could be a physical interface or a logical interface such as a VLAN or the loopback interface. The syntax for the IP address assignment would remain the same.

A note about WAN addresses

A WAN link is a point-to-point link that has two end points. Hence, we need two usable IP addresses to configure each endpoint of the WAN link. Recall that in a subnet, the network ID and the broadcast addresses cannot be used, and hence we will need a subnet with four IP addresses for a WAN link. A /30 subnet has four addresses, and hence /30 IP addresses were used to assign IP addresses for WAN links.

When IP addresses started becoming scarce, new ways were devised to save IP addresses. One of these was defined in the RFC 3021 that allowed using /31 IP addresses for WAN links.

Secondary addresses

There can be situations in a campus where an Ethernet domain was originally configured for 30 hosts using a /27 mask. However, if we need to add more hosts to the same network, we ideally have to change the IP address subnet and use a bigger subnet say a /26 that will allow a larger number of hosts. This will mean readdressing all hosts on the subnet.

A workaround for this is to use secondary IP addresses on interfaces. This will allow an interface to have two IP addresses, and hence act like the default gateway for two subnets without having the need to readdress the hosts on the network:

```
Router# conf t
Router(config)# interface gig0/1
Router(config-if)# ip address 10.0.0.1 255.255.255.0
Router(config-if)# ip address 10.2.0.1 255.255.255.0 secondary
Router(config-if)# exit
Router(config)# exit
Router#
```

Figure 28: Configuring a secondary IP address

First Hop Redundancy Protocols (FHRP)

The hosts connect to a LAN switch and can communicate to each other on the LAN without the need for a router. The router is a layer 3 device and is required to route packets across different subnets, and hence is not required for communication with the same subnet that is the case for a LAN. However, when packets have to go to destinations that are outside the subnet/LAN that the source is a part of, the packets are routed through the router. The router acts as the default gateway for all packets that are to be sent outside the subnet.

Let's consider how traffic flows from a host to other devices using a simple network shown next. There are two subnets in the figure with a router connecting the two subnets. The IP addresses and the MAC addresses for each interface of the devices is also shown alongside the devices in the figure. The default gateway configured for hosts **A**, **B**, and **C** is **10.0.0.1** and the default gateway configured for hosts **P**, **Q**, **R**, and **S** is **10.0.1.1**:

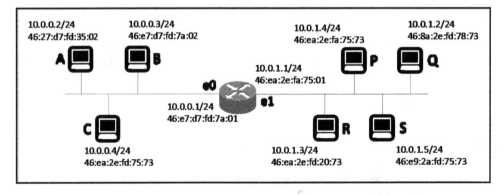

Figure 29: Packet flows across a router

If host **A** wants to send an IP packet to host **C**, the flow of packets is as follows:

- The IP stack at host **A** looks at the destination address and verifies whether the destination IP address is in the same subnet. In this case, the subnet of device **A** is **10.0.0.0/24** and the destination address **10.0.0.4** belongs to the same subnet.
- Next, device **A** checks to see if the MAC address for the IP address of the destination is in the cache. If not, **A** initiates an ARP request to find the MAC address of the IP address **10.0.0.4**.
- Once the ARP process is complete and **A** knows the MAC address of the destination, it frames the Ethernet packet with source and destination addresses as the MAC address of **A** and **C** respectively, and sends the IP packet on the network.

This is the case if the packets were to be sent to the same subnet. If **A** now wants to communicate with **R**, which has an IP address of **10.0.1.3**, the packet flow would be as follows:

- The IP stack at host **A** looks at the destination address (**10.0.1.3**) and verifies whether the destination IP address is in the same subnet. In this case, the subnet of device **A** is **10.0.0.0/24** and the destination address **10.0.1.3**, which belongs to a different subnet.
- Device **A** checks its IP configuration to find the default gateway configured. If it has multiple interfaces, the device will check its routing table to find the next hop IP address. For simplicity, let's assume a single interface and the default gateway being configured as **10.0.0.1**.
- Next, device **A** checks to see if the MAC address for the IP address of the gateway (**10.1.0.1**) is in the cache. If not, **A** initiates an ARP request to find the MAC address of the IP address **10.0.0.1**.
- Once the ARP process is complete and A knows the MAC address of the gateway, it frames the Ethernet packet with source and destination addresses as the MAC address of **A** and **e0** of the router respectively, and sends the IP packet on the network, that is received by the router.
- The router now checks the routing tables to find the next hop for the destination. In this case, the destination address is on a directly connected subnet on the router. The router has this knowledge as it has another network **10.0.1.0/24** on the interface **e1**, and the destination **10.0.1.3** belongs to this subnet.
- The router then forwards this packet to host **R** by framing it in the Ethernet frame, after finding the MAC address of **R** either in the cache or by initiating an ARP request.

If host **A** does not find the IP address of the default gateway or the interface **e0** on the router goes down, host **A** will not be able to communicate with any device outside its own subnet 10.0.0.0/24. The router acts like the first layer 3 hop for communications between hosts on different subnets. If a router for a LAN goes down, the entire subnet is isolated from the outside world. To build redundancy into the network infrastructure, most subnets have more than one router.

The challenge in having two routers on the subnet is that each router has a unique IP address for connecting to the network and the host can have only one address configured as the default gateway. Hence, the two gateways/routers on the subnet need to be able to talk to each other and assume the IP address of the default gateway as its own interface IP address. This enables the host to have one default gateway configured and one of the routers acting like the gateway on the subnet. In case the router goes down, the other router detects this and assumes the default gateway address, and the hosts on the subnet start communicating to the outside world using the second router. All this is transparent to the hosts and they don't even get to know that there is a network outage.

The set of protocols that achieves this is called **First Hop Redundancy Protocols** (**FHRP**). There are three protocols that come under this category, and the following sections discuss the configuration of these protocols.

We will assume a part of the network topology shown in the following figure for the configurations:

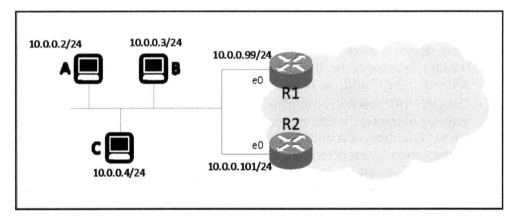

Figure 30: Creating a static ARP entry

HSRP

Hot Standby Router Protocol (**HSRP**) provides high-availability by providing first-hop routing redundancy for IP hosts on networks configured with a default gateway IP address. HSRP is used in a group of routers for selecting an active device and a standby device. Hosts send the packets to the default gateway to the active router and when the active router fails, the standby router takes over transparently.

Most IP hosts have a single IP address configured as the default gateway. This default gateway is a **Virtual IP** (**VIP**) address that is assumed by the active HSRP device on the network. To maintain transparency of the failover mechanism, the HSRP devices also use a virtual MAC address corresponding to this VIP so that the ARP entries on the hosts don't change when HSRP failover happens. Both the virtual MAC address and the virtual IP address are assumed by the currently active device in a group of devices running HSRP. Note that HSRP can work with more than two devices on a subnet and hence survive failures of multiple routers, as long as one of them is up.

HSRP works on a per VLAN basis, and if there are multiple VLANs configured on the physical interfaces, the load can be spread across the devices by making one router active for one VLAN and the other router active for the other VLAN. Each HSRP device is configured with a priority value, and the working device having the highest priority is the active device at any given instant and assumes the virtual IP and MAC addresses. The only deviation from the previous statement is when pre-emption is configured to delay the standby device from becoming active for a considerable amount of time. The default HSRP priority for an interface is 100. In case the devices have the same priority, the IP address is used as the tie-breaker and the device with the higher IP address becomes the active router.

The current version of HSRP is version 2, which provides faster failover compared to HSRP v1, and we will describe the configuration of HSRPv2 in this section. If we have configured 10.0.0.100/24 as the default gateway for all hosts (A, B, and C) in the figure, the Virtual IP should be 10.0.0.100. The configuration of HSRP for the two routers in our example is as shown in the following figure:

```
R1(config)# interface e0
R1(config-if)# ip address 10.0.0.99 255.255.255.0
R1(config-if)# standby version 2
R1(config-if)# standby 1 priority 105
R1(config-if)# standby delay minimum 30 reload 60

R1(config-if)# standby 1 preempt
R1(config-if)# standby 1 ip 10.0.0.100
R1(config-if)# standby 1 authentication md5 key-string C!sc0
R2(config)# interface e0
R2(config-if)# ip address 10.0.0.101 255.255.255.0
R2(config-if)# standby version 2
R2(config-if)# standby 1 priority 95
R2(config-if)# standby delay minimum 30 reload 60

R2(config-if)# standby 1 preempt
R2(config-if)# standby 1 ip 10.0.0.100
R2(config-if)# standby 1 authentication md5 key-string C!sc0
```

Figure 31: Configuring HSRP

In the `standby 1 priority 105` command in the preceding figure, value 1 represents the group number and can be any value from 0 to 4095 for HSRP version 2. 10.0.0.100 is the virtual IP address of the virtual device and should be configured as the default gateway on the end hosts.

HSRP authentication is configured to protect the network from spurious devices attacking the system, by sending HSRP messages with a higher priority. This will force all trusted routers on the network to give up the active role, leading to service disruptions. HSRP messages can be authenticated either using clear text passwords or using encrypted MD5 hash values. It is recommended to use MD5 hash for authentication, as clear text messages can be sniffed to read the password on the network. The `standby 1 authentication md5` command forces the router to use MD5 authentication for the HSRP packet exchanges between them. The key argument in this command is the actual authentication key, and appears as encrypted text in the configuration if the password encryption service is enabled on the router.

The `standby delay` command delays the HSRP groups from initializing for the specified time after the interface comes up. This prevents the router from becoming active for the time specified in the command as it has the risk of the router becoming active after a reload without having the complete routing table.

Consider a campus scenario where there are multiple access points having two different VLANs, and the VLANs are connected to the gateway routers on a trunk port with both VLANs on the same physical interface. In this case, it might be desirable to make one router active for one VLAN and the second router as the active router for the second VLAN:

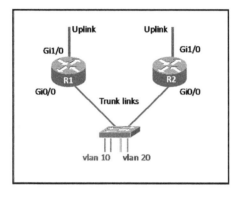

Figure 32: Load balancing across uplinks

For the sample topology shown earlier, the configurations for making **R1** as the active router for **vlan10** and **R2** the active router for **vlan20** are as follows:

```
R1(config)# interface vlan10
R1(config-if)# ip address 10.0.0.99 255.255.255.0
R1(config-if)# standby version 2
R1(config-if)# standby 1 priority 105
R1(config-if)# standby delay minimum 30 reload 60
R1(config-if)# standby 1 preempt
R1(config-if)# standby 1 ip 10.0.0.100
R1(config-if)# standby 1 authentication md5 key-string C!sc0
R1(config-if)# exit
R1(config)# interface vlan20
R1(config-if)# ip address 10.0.1.99 255.255.255.0
R1(config-if)# standby version 2
R1(config-if)# standby 1 priority 95
R1(config-if)# standby delay minimum 30 reload 60
R1(config-if)# standby 1 preempt
R1(config-if)# standby 1 ip 10.0.0.100
R1(config-if)# standby 1 authentication md5 key-string C!sc0
```

Figure 33: Load balancing across routers R1

The corresponding router configuration for router **R2** is as shown in the following figure:

```
R2(config)# interface vlan10
R2(config-if)# ip address 10.0.0.101 255.255.255.0
R2(config-if)# standby version 2
R2(config-if)# standby 1 priority 95
R2(config-if)# standby delay minimum 30 reload 60
R2(config-if)# standby 1 preempt
R2(config-if)# standby 1 ip 10.0.0.100
R2(config-if)# standby 1 authentication md5 key-string C!sc0
R2(config-if)# exit
R2(config)# interface vlan20
R2(config-if)# ip address 10.0.0.101 255.255.255.0
R2(config-if)# standby version 2
R2(config-if)# standby 1 priority 105
R2(config-if)# standby delay minimum 30 reload 60
R2(config-if)# standby 1 preempt
R2(config-if)# standby 1 ip 10.0.0.100
R2(config-if)# standby 1 authentication md5 key-string C!sc0
```

Figure 34: Load balancing across routers R2

The preceding configurations will enable the routers to share the load and hence both the uplinks from the routers will be used to carry traffic. The challenge is when one of the uplinks goes down.

Let's assume that the uplink from the router R1 goes down. The HSRP would still be working on the LAN as the layer 2 connectivity would still be up, and HSRP would be working normally. In this scenario, the traffic will flow to R1, and will be black-holed as there is on active uplink. We use HSRP tracking in such scenarios to ensure that HSRP is active only when the uplink is up. The configurations for this are as shown next. For the sake of brevity, we have assumed a single vlan10 for the configurations and only depict the configurations to track the uplink interface. The configuration can be replicated for all VLANs:

```
R1(config)# track 100 interface gi1/0 ip routing
R1(config)# interface vlan10
R1(config-if)# ip address 10.0.0.99 255.255.255.0
R1(config-if)# standby version 2
R1(config-if)# standby 1 priority 105
R1(config-if)# standby 1 preempt
R1(config-if)# standby 1 track 100 decrement 10
R1(config-if)# standby 1 ip 10.0.0.100
R1(config-if)# exit
R1(config)#
```

Figure 35: Tracking interfaces

The corresponding configurations for R2 are as shown in the following figure:

```
R2(config)# track 100 interface gi1/0 ip routing
R2(config)# interface vlan10
R2(config-if)# ip address 10.0.0.101 255.255.255.0
R2(config-if)# standby version 2
R2(config-if)# standby 1 priority 100
R2(config-if)# standby 1 preempt
R2(config-if)# standby 1 track 100 decrement 10
R2(config-if)# standby 1 ip 10.0.0.100
R2(config-if)# exit
R2(config)#
```

Figure 36: Tracking interfaces

In the preceding configurations, the tracking process is configured to track the IP-routing capability of the interface Gi1/0. HSRP on gigabit Ethernet interface 0/0 then registers with the tracking process to be informed of any changes to the IP-routing state of interface Gi1/0. If the IP state on interface Gi1/0 goes down, the priority of the HSRP group is reduced by 10 from the original value of 105 to 95, which is less than the priority configured on R2. Hence if the uplink on R1 goes down, R2 will become the active HSRP router for the vlan10.

VRRP

Virtual Router Redundancy Protocol (**VRRP**) is another FHRP that dynamically assigns the IP addresses of the default gateway to one of the physical routers on an Ethernet link.

A VRRP router is configured to run the VRRP protocol with one or more other routers on the LAN. One router is elected as the virtual router master, with the other routers acting as backups in case the virtual router master fails. VRRP enables a group of routers to form a single virtual router. The LAN clients can then be configured with the virtual router as their default gateway. The virtual router, representing a group of routers, is also known as a VRRP group. VRRP provides the same benefits as HSRP like redundancy, load-sharing, multiple virtual routers on an interface, pre-emption, authentication, and object tracking.

The device that would become the logical router can be controlled by defining the priority of the VRRP router. Priority also determines whether a VRRP router functions as a virtual router backup and the order of ascendancy to becoming a virtual router master if the virtual router master fails. The priority on the router can be configured by using the VRRP priority command. The router with the highest priority becomes the master for the VRRP group. In case of a tie, the IP address acts as the tie breaker and the higher IP address wins.

We can disable a newly configured router from becoming the master router even if it has a higher priority using the negative form of the pre-emption command.

Next, we will describe the configurations on the routers to enable redundancy using VRRP for a sample topology, as shown in the following diagram:

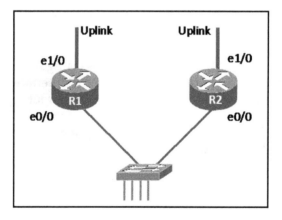

Figure 37: Sample topology for VRRP

Let's configure the devices with the subnet 10.0.0.0/24. One advantage of VRRP is that it allows us to load balance between the hosts on the same subnet. To do this, we will configure half the hosts connected to the LAN with a default gateway of 10.0.0.1, and the other half with the default gateway of 10.0.0.2. We will have to create two VRRP groups now, and there will be two virtual routers: one having the address 10.0.0.1 and the other having the virtual address 10.0.0.2 for forwarding. The two physical routers R1 and R2 will provide failover for each other:

```
R1(config)# track 100 interface e1/0 ip routing
R1(config)# interface e0/0
R1(config-if)# ip address 10.0.0.99 255.255.255.0
R1(config-if)# vrrp 1 priority 120
R1(config-if)# vrrp 1 authentication md5 key-string C!sc0
R1(config-if)# vrrp 1 timers advertise 3
R1(config-if)# vrrp 1 timers learn
R1(config-if)# vrrp 1 ip 10.0.0.1
R1(config-if)# vrrp 1 track 100 decrement 15
R1(config-if)# vrrp 2 priority 110
R1(config-if)# vrrp 2 timers learn
R1(config-if)# vrrp 2 ip 10.0.0.2
R1(config-if)# no vrrp 2 preempt
R1(config-if)# vrrp 2 track 100 decrement 15
R1(config-if)# exit
R1(config)#
```

Figure 38: VRRP configuration

The configurations for router R2 are as shown in the following figure:

```
R2(config)# track 100 interface e1/0 ip routing
R2(config)# interface e0/0
R2(config-if)# ip address 10.0.0.101 255.255.255.0
R2(config-if)# vrrp 1 priority 110
R2(config-if)# vrrp 1 authentication md5 key-string C!sc0
R2(config-if)# vrrp 1 timers advertise 3
R2(config-if)# vrrp 1 timers learn
R2(config-if)# vrrp 1 ip 10.0.0.100
R2(config-if)# vrrp 1 track 100 decrement 15
R2(config-if)# vrrp 2 priority 120
R2(config-if)# vrrp 2 timers learn
R2(config-if)# vrrp 2 ip 10.0.0.200
R2(config-if)# no vrrp 2 preempt
R2(config-if)# vrrp 2 track 100 decrement 15
R2(config-if)# exit
R2(config)#
```

Figure 39: VRRP configuration

In the configuration templates shown earlier, we used different timers for the two VRRP groups just to illustrate the commands. In practice, we will have the same timers to allow similar failover experience. The less the timer values, the faster will be the failover, as failover uses the packets sent at specific values for detection of failure of the active node.

GLBP

Gateway Load Balancing Protocol (**GLBP**) is the third protocol that provides first hop redundancy for the gateway router. In HSRP and VRRP, the load balancing can happen for different VLANs or some hosts on the same network using manual configuration of defining separate default gateways on a set of hosts, as described earlier in the VRRP section. GLBP achieves this load sharing between different hosts on the same subnet automatically. GLBP provides load balancing over multiple gateways using a single virtual IP address and multiple virtual MAC addresses. The forwarding load is shared among all devices in a GLBP group rather than being handled by a single device while the other devices stand idle. Each host is configured with the same virtual IP address, and all devices in the virtual device group participate in forwarding packets.

Members of a GLBP group elect one gateway to be the **active virtual gateway** (**AVG**) for that group. Other group members provide backup for the AVG if the AVG becomes unavailable. The AVG assigns a virtual MAC address to each member of the GLBP group. Each gateway assumes responsibility for forwarding packets sent to the virtual MAC address assigned to it by the AVG. These gateways are known as **active virtual forwarders** (**AVFs**) for their virtual MAC address. The AVG answers all ARP requests for the virtual IP address, hence controlling which AVF will be used by which host on the network, thus providing load sharing by sending different MAC addresses to different hosts in response to the ARP requests. GLBP supports up to four AVFs per group.

While the default configuration parameters of GLBP will suffice for normal operation, the parameters can be customized if required. The GLBP group starts operating as soon as it is enabled through configuration. Hence, any customization to the GLBP parameters should be done before enabling GLBP on the interfaces.

GLBP gateway priority determines the role that each GLBP gateway plays and what happens if the AVG fails. Priority also determines if a GLBP device functions as a backup virtual gateway and the order to becoming an AVG if the current AVG fails. The sample network topology and the GLBP configurations on the routers are as shown in the following figure:

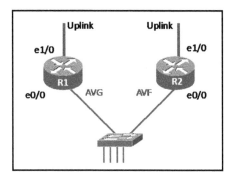

Figure 40: Sample GLBP configuration

The configuration for enabling GLBP on R1 is shown in the following figure:

```
R1(config)# track 100 interface e1/0 ip routing
R1(config)# interface e0/0
R1(config-if)# ip address 10.0.0.99 255.255.255.0
R1(config-if)# glbp 1 priority 120
R1(config-if)# glbp 1 preempt delay minimum 60
R1(config-if)# glbp 1 authentication md5 key-string C!sc0
R1(config-if)# glbp 1 load-balancing host-dependent
R1(config-if)# glbp 1 ip 10.0.0.1
R1(config-if)# glbp 1 weighting 110 lower 95 upper 105
R1(config-if)# glbp 1 weighting track 1 decrement 10
R1(config-if)# glbp 1 forwarder preempt delay minimum 60
R1(config-if)# exit
R1(config)#
```

Figure 41: GLBP configuration

The corresponding configuration on router R2 is as shown in the following figure:

```
R2(config)# track 100 interface e1/0 ip routing
R2(config)# interface e0/0
R2(config-if)# ip address 10.0.0.101 255.255.255.0
R2(config-if)# glbp 1 priority 115
R2(config-if)# glbp 1 preempt delay minimum 60
R2(config-if)# glbp 1 authentication md5 key-string C!sc0
R2(config-if)# glbp 1 load-balancing host-dependent
R2(config-if)# glbp 1 ip 10.0.0.1
R2(config-if)# glbp 1 weighting 110 lower 95 upper 105
R2(config-if)# glbp 1 weighting track 1 decrement 10
R2(config-if)# glbp 1 forwarder preempt delay minimum 60
R2(config-if)# exit
R2(config)#
```

Figure 42: GLBP configuration

Routing protocols

Upto now, we have discussed the communications within the LAN up to the gateway router. In this section, we will discuss the routing of packets beyond the LAN.

Routing table

A router routes and forwards IP packets based on the destination IP address of the received packets. The only exception to this is policy-based routing, where specific policies are built on the ingress interfaces of the router to route packets based on the source IP addresses. The router looks at the destination IP addresses and finds the best route for the destination in the routing table. The routing table is built using manually defined routes, or dynamically using specific routing protocols, that exchange information between the routers.

Each routing entry in the route table at a bare minimum has the following components:

- A prefix that is being routed, including the network mask
- The next hop or the egress interface for this prefix
- A method in which this route was populated in the routing table
- The associated cost or other route metrics for the route
- The protocol-specific information through which the prefix was learned

The prefix in the routing table is an IP prefix or a network that might be a subnet that exists on the network, or an entry that denotes the aggregate of a group of prefixes. Consider the example we discussed in the IP addressing section where we split a single 10.0.0.0 /20 prefix into multiple subnets. These were private IP addresses that are not routable on the internet. However, if we had used public IP addresses for the organization, all these prefixes would be routed on the internet and we would have more than 20 prefixes with the subnet masks as small as a /26. This would lead to a large number of prefixes in the routing tables of the internet. A large number of entries to maintain in the routing tables would require more memory, more processing power on the routers, and would take more time for lookups.

Let's use the analogy of how an international package is delivered to the recipient. The origin collection staff collects the package and takes it to the sorting office. The sorting office looks at the country of destination and sends it to that country without bothering about which city or area or street the destination is. Once the package reaches the destination country, the sorting office then sends it to the city of the recipient with no regard for the area or the street. Once the package reaches the destination city, the local city office delivers it to the package delivery staff of the respective area, who then finally looks at the street address and the house number and delivers the package to the recipient.

The basic idea in the preceding example is that the farther you are from the destination, the less relevent are the finer details. As you get closer to the destination, you need to drill down more and more into the details. The same logic is applied to the processing of IP packets. The only difference being that the complete address is the IP address. If we consider the IP address as consisting of host and network bits, the host bits are the actual identifier on the LAN, and the network bits are the street bits. If we aggregate a number of streets to form the area, we get an aggregate address of a network mask that is smaller in length compared to the original networks. As you go higher and higher in the connection hierarchy on the internet, the mask lengths become smaller. This grouping of smaller IP subnets into a bigger IP prefix is called supernetting.

IP routing works on the basis of the longest prefix match. There could be multiple prefixes in the routing table that will match the destination IP address. The IP routing decision will be based on the longest prefix match. Consider a router with the routing table as shown in the following figure:

Prefix	Next Hop
0.0.0.0/0	1.1.1.1
10.0.0.0/8	1.1.1.2
10.20.0.0/16	1.1.1.3
10.20.30.0/24	1.1.1.4
10.20.30.64/26	1.1.1.5

Figure 41: Understanding the next hop

If the router receives a packet for the destination IP address of 10.20.30.80, this destination matches all five route entries in the table. However, the match that has the longest prefix matching is 10.20.30.64/26, as that has the first 26 bits matching the IP destination address, and hence the packet would be routed to the destination 1.1.1.5.

If a router has multiple next hops for the same network and each next hop has the same cost, the router load balances the traffic across multiple next hops. This is valid if and only if the cost of the two next hops are equal. This feature is called Equal cost multipath. Cisco routers send all packets belonging to one conversation or flow on one link. Hence, if there are two conversations or flows, the flows would be load balanced across the two links. If the flows are not equal in size, which they seldom are, the actual utilization of the two links would not be exactly equal.

As discussed, there are multiple routing protocols that are used to build a routing table such as RIP, OSPF, and ISIS. In addition, the router can be configured statically through configuration for routing entries. The router also would have some connected prefixes, and the same would also appear in the routing table as directly connected route entries. If the routing table has multiple entries with the same prefix length that match the destination, the routing decision is based on the protocol through which the route was learned. Each protocol has a predefined administrative distance, which determines the choice of the routing decision in case of a tie in the longest prefix match. The protocol with a lower administrative distance is preferred over the ones with a higher distance. The administrative distance for common protocols is shown in the following figure:

Route Source	Default Distance
Connected interface	0
Static route	1
Enhanced Interior Gateway Routing Protocol (EIGRP) summary route	5
External Border Gateway Protocol (BGP)	20
Internal EIGRP	90
Interior Gateway Routing Protocol (IGRP)	100
Open Shortest Path First (OSPF)	110
Intermediate System to Intermediate System (IS-IS)	115
Routing Information Protocol (RIP)	120
Exterior Gateway Routing Protocol (EGP)	140
On Demand Routing (ODR)	160
External EIGRP	170
Internal BGP	200
Unknown	255

Figure 44: Default distance for different protocols

A directly connected interface is the one that is configured on the router. The router uses the network ID of the directly connected subnet and populates that as a routing table entry. For example, if a router has an interface configured with the IP address 10.1.2.101/26 as one of its interfaces, the routing table will have an entry for the subnet 10.1.2.64/26 as a directly connected subnet.

We will discuss how to configure other routing protocols in the next sections.

Static routing

Static routing is where the router is explicitly instructed to route packets for specific prefixes to a particular next hop.

A static route is configured by using the `ip route` command, as shown in the following figure. The configuration builds the routing table that was used to explain the longest prefix match:

```
R1(config)# ip route 0.0.0.0 0.0.0.0 1.1.1.1
R1(config)# ip route 10.0.0.0 255.0.0.0 1.1.1.2
R1(config)# ip route 10.20.0.0 255.255.0.0 1.1.1.3
R1(config)# ip route 10.20.30.0 255.255.255.0 1.1.1.4
R1(config)# ip route 10.20.30.64 255.255.255.192 1.1.1.5 tag 10
R1(config)#
```

Figure 41: Configuring static routes

Note that the last route configuration in the preceding example has a specific tag value assigned to it. This value is not relevant for routing purposes, but is used to identify a set of routes in the routing table. This can be used if a subset of the routes needs to be advertised into other routing protocols, which we will discuss during the configuration of dynamic routing protocols.

Configuring static routing is easy and deterministic, but has the disadvantage that when links fail or the network topology changes, the configuration needs to be done all over again, as optimized paths could appear for certain prefixes or certain prefixes might be routed on incorrect interfaces leading to the traffic being black holed.

Dynamic routing

Dynamic routing protocols are a set of protocols that are used to automatically build the routing tables in the routers deployed in a network topology. These protocols define a set of packets that are used to exchange routing information between the routers, and a set of algorithms that are used to build the routing tables from the received packets.

Dynamic routing tables broadly fall under two categories based on the fundamental characteristics of the routing algorithm used. These are Distance Vector protocols and Link State algorithms. We will briefly discuss these protocols with a view on how to configure these protocols on Cisco routers.

Distance vector routing

Distance vector algorithms are also sometimes known as Bellman-Ford algorithms. These algorithms rely on the routing devices periodically advertising copies of their routing tables to their immediate network neighbors. Each recipient then adds a cost or distance value to each route received in the table and forwards it to its immediate neighbors. This process occurs for all connected neighbors. Each router runs the Bellman-Ford algorithm on the received copies and creates a routing table of its own, based on the lowest cost or distance value. When the process is complete, each router has a routing table that is optimized for the lowest distance to each known prefix, but with no visibility of the topology of the network. Note that DV routing protocols are too noisy as they exchange a lot of information on the network and are very slow to converge in case of network topology changes. DV protocols are not suited for large networks.

RIP:

Routing Information Protocol (**RIP**) is an example of a distance vector routing protocol.

We will focus on **RIP Version 2** (**RIPv2**) in this section. It supports authentication (both plain text and MD5), route summarization, **classless interdomain routing** (**CIDR**), and **variable-length subnet masks** (**VLSMs**).

RIP uses messages encapsulated in the UDP protocol to send periodic routing updates to its immediate neighbors. Cisco IOS sends routing information updates every 30 seconds to its neighbors. All entries learned by RIP and the directly connected interfaces that run the RIP protocol are exchanged in the RIP updates, including the default route. The sending of routing updates on specified interfaces can be disabled by configuring the passive-interface command.

RIP uses hop count as the routing metric to measure the distance between the source and the destination network. When a route is received from a neighbor, the receiving router increases the metric value for the prefix by 1, and the sender is indicated as the next hop. RIP devices maintain only the best route (the route with the lowest metric value) to a destination. After updating its routing table, the device immediately begins transmitting RIP routing updates to inform other network devices of the change. These updates are sent independently of the regularly scheduled updates that RIP devices send.

If a router does not receive an update from its neighbor for 180 seconds or more, it considers the neighbor to be down and doesn't use the routes received earlier from this neighbor. After 240 seconds, the router deletes all routes from this neighbor. These timers can be tweaked for achieving faster convergence.

If there are certain parts of the networks where the networks can be summarized at classful boundaries, route summarization can be used in RIP. Summarizing routes improves scalability and efficiency, as all child routes are supressed and only summary routes are advertised across the boundary, thus lowering the size of the routing table. If summary routes are configured on an interface, a summary route would be advertised only if there is at least one child entry for the aggregate route in the RIP database. It may be noted that aggregate routes should have subnet masks of /8, /16, or /24 only. Note that the summarization is configured on an interface, as shown in the figure.

The source IP address for the RIP updates sent by the router is the interface on which the packets are sent out. This means that packets by the same router on different interfaces have a different source address. This can cause problems as RIP validates the source address of the incoming RIP updates and all interface addresses need to be defined on the adjacent routers as neighbors. Cisco IOS uses a command to disable the update source validation as shown in our configuration in the upcoming figure.

A sample RIP configuration showing only RIP-specific commands is given next. The keychain commands are not RIP specific but are shown, as they are referenced in the RIP configuration for authentication:

```
R1(config)# key chain pwd
R1(config-keychain)# key 1
R1(config-keychain-key)# key-string C!sc0
R1(config-keychain-key)# exit
R1(config-keychain)# exit
R1(config)# router rip
R1(config-router)# version 2
R1(config-router)# no auto-summary
R1(config-router)# no validate-update-source
R1(config-router)# network 10.0.0.0
R1(config-router)# neighbor 192.168.1.2
R1(config-router)# timers basic 5 15 20
R1(config-router)# exit
R1(config)# interface e0
R1(config-if)# ip rip authentication mode md5
R1(config-if)# ip rip authentication key-chain pwd
R1(config-if)# ip summary-address rip 10.2.0.0 255.255.0.0
R1(config-if)# exit
R1(config)#
```

Figure 46: Sample RIP configuration

Enhanced Interior Gateway Routing Protocol:

Enhanced Interior Gateway Routing Protocol (EIGRP) is an advanced distance vector routing protocol, which was developed by Cisco, and remained as a Cisco proprietary protocol for a long time before being published as RFC 7868. EIGRP uses an algorithm called **DUAL**, which is a **Diffusing Update Algorithm**. EIGRP also provides MD5 authentication between neighbors. EIGRP uses IP protocol 88, and uses a multicast address of 224.0.0.10 for hellos and routing updates.

The metric used in EIGRP is a composite metric that factors the delay and bandwidth on the network to reach a specific destination. Note that the bandwidth and delay are not measured but configured on the routers for the links.

EIGRP does not send the routes periodically to its neighbors like conventional DV protocols, but maintains a neighbor relationship using hello messages such as OSPF. This reduces the protocol traffic on the network. Routers running EIGRP send hellos to its configured neighbors and receive the routing updates from the neighbors. The router then selects the best route from among the multiple routes learned, and only maintains the neighbor relation post that. In case of a topology change on the network, EIGRP converges much faster in cases of topology changes, as EIGRP maintains a database of the alternate routes in addition to the best route that helps in convergence.

EIGRP can perform unequal cost load balancing between links, as long as the cost on the selected paths is within a range. This is controlled with the `variance` command. In the following example, the variance is 3, which means that all routes that have the metric within three times the lowest metric would be treated as eligible routes for load-balancing.

A sample configuration for enabling EIGRP on a router is as shown in the following figure:

```
Router(Config)# router eigrp 65500
Router(Config-router)# network 192.168.0.0
Router(Config-router)# traffic-share balanced
Router(Config-router)# maximum-paths 5
Router(Config-router)# variance 3
```

Figure 47: Sample EIGRP configuration

The value in the first statement in the preceding configuration is the AS number, which is treated as an identifier of the process. The network statement is used to define that all the interfaces that belong to the subnet 192.168.0.0 will participate in EIGRP.

Link-state routing

Link-state routing protocols use a set of algorithms called **Shortest path first (SPF)** algorithms. These protocols maintain full knowledge of all devices on the network and how they are connected. This knowledge is passed on from routers using a set of **link-state advertisements (LSAs)** and is collectively known as the **link-state database (LSDB)**. The routers then run the SPF algorithm on the LSDB to create the shortest path to each prefix on the network, which results in the routing table. The LSAs are exchanged between devices only during startup of the router and when the network topology changes. This ensures that the protocol traffic is kept to a minimum. However, to keep track of neighboring routers and their health, hello packets are exchanged periodically between the devices.

Open Shortest Path First (OSPF) and **Intermediate System - Intermediate System (IS-IS)** are two examples of link state routing protocols.

Open Shortest Path First (OSPF):

OSPF, as it is commonly called, is a link state protocol commonly used in large networks. The link state information is exchanged through exchange of different types of OSPF LSAs depending upon the type of information being exchanged.

An OSPF network exchanges the link states of all nodes between all devices within a domain. Consider the following figure showing a sample topology of nine routers. All nine routers will exchange the information about the networks that are connected to them with each other. Any link going down will result in the information being exchanged again using LSAs. In a large network, this is not desirable as it causes very remote routers to know about information that might be irrelevant to them. OSPF uses the concept of areas to build a hierarchy of domains in which the information is flooded. In the following sample network, the hierarchy of areas is shown using dotted lines. An area consists of a set of continuous links terminated on routers. It is mandatory to have a backbone area or area 0 that sits on the top of the hierarchy and all other areas are connected to this area.

The routers that connect to area 0 and one or more nonbackbone area are called area border routers. These routers can summarize the information about all networks that are in the nonbackbone area and just advertise that single network prefix towards area 0. In the sample topology, there is an area 0, and three nonbackbone areas. Routers **A**, **B**, and **C** act as area border routers or ABRs:

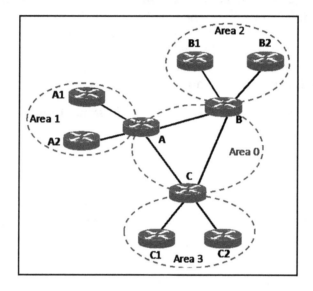

Figure 48: Sample OSPF topology

It is important to plan the IP addressing effectively in order to reap the benefits of the OSPF hierarchy. Consider the IP addressing for the sample network as shown in the following figure:

Area	Infrastructure Prefix Range	User/ LAN Prefix Range
0	10.0.0.0/24	10.0.64.0/20
1	10.0.1.0/24	10.0.80.0/20
2	10.0.2.0/24	10.0.96.0/20
3	10.0.3.0/24	10.0.112.0/20

Figure 49: Sample addressing for OSPF topology

In the sample network, all user networks in Area 1 that are connected to routers A1 and A2 can be summarized into a single prefix 10.0.80.0/20, then the ABR A can advertise only one prefix 10.0.80.0/20 to all routers in area 0. Since router A is connected to Area 1 also, it has more granular visibility of the prefixes connected to routers A1 and A2. When a packet destined for a LAN on router A1 (say 10.0.81.0/24) is to be reached from outside the area, the packet is routed to router A because of the aggregate prefix, and then A can route the packet toward A1 using the more granular link-state database of Area 1. You can relate it to the way IP routing in general works on the principle of being more specific and granular as you reach closer to the destination.

Building a hierarchy of areas also helps in reducing the impact of flooding. If the link between A1 and A goes down, the routers outside area 1 do not need to know about this, as they only have an aggregate prefix advertised from router A. This prevents a lot of SPF computations on the routers outside the area in which the topology has changed.

OSPF also uses a concept of stub areas to reduce the size of the LSDB in the routers. This is generally done to avoid sending all prefixes from area 0, including the ones that are received from other areas into the stub area. In this case, the ABR only advertises a default route into the stub area, and the routers in the stub area use the default route to get to the ABR. The ABR has the LSDB of area 0, and hence has more visibility into the routing topology of the network. All routers in the area need to be configured as a stub area for normal OSPF operation. In our sample topology, since there is only one prefix to go out of each area, we can configure these areas as stub areas.

OSPF is configured on a link-by-link basis. Each link that needs to participate in an OSPF domain needs to be configured. There might be some interfaces, which need to be advertised into OSPF, but there are no other routers on that link, and hence OSPF packets don't need to be sent on these links. Such links are configured as passive interfaces.

With the proposed IP addressing plan we have discussed, the sample address assignment for the routers shown in a subset of the topology is as shown in the following figure:

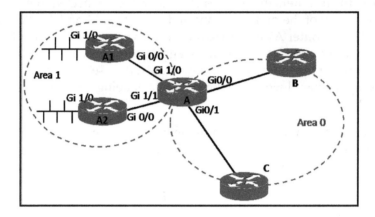

Figure 50: Sample OSPF topology with interfaces

The IP addresses for the various routers in the topology are as given in the following figure:

Router	Loopback	Interface addresses
A	10.0.0.255/32	Gi0/0: 10.0.0.1/30 Gi0/1: 10.0.0.5/30 Gi1/0: 10.0.1.1/30 Gi1/1: 10.0.1.5/30
A1	10.0.1.254/32	Gi0/0: 10.0.1.2/30 Gi1/0: 10.0.81.0/24
A2	10.0.1.253/32	Gi 0/0: 10.0.1.6/30 Gi1/0: 10.0.82.0/24

Figure 51: Sample OSPF topology interface addressing

Note that we have taken the IP addresses for the loopback of the ABR, router A, from the area 0 infrastructure pool, and the loopback addresses for A1 and A2 from the infrastructure pool for area 1. Also, the link addresses for the links on router A that lie in area 0 have been taken from the pool of infrastructure addresses for area 0, and the link addresses for the links that lie in area 1 have been taken from the infrastructure pool for area 1. The user LAN segments for routers A1 and A2 have been taken from the user pool for area 1. With these assignments, the OSPF configurations on the three routers is as shown in the following figure:

```
A(config)# router ospf 100
A(config-router)# router-id 10.0.0.255
A(config-router)# network 10.0.0.0 0.0.0.255 area 0
A(config-router)# network 10.0.64.0 0.0.15.255 area 0
A(config-router)# network 10.0.1.0 0.0.0.255 area 1
A(config-router)# network 10.0.80.0 0.0.15.255 area 1
A(config-router)# area 1 stub no-summary
A(config-router)# area 0 authentication
A(config-router)# area 0 range 10.0.0.0 255.255.255.0
A(config-router)# area 0 range 10.0.64.0 255.255.240.0
A(config-router)# area 1 range 10.0.1.0 255.255.255.0
A(config-router)# area 1 range 10.0.80.0 255.255.240.0
A(config-router)# exit
A(config)#
A(config)# interface Gi0/0
A(config-if)# no shut
A(config-if)# description "To router B in area 0"
A(config-if)# ip address 10.0.0.1 255.255.255.252
A(config-if)# ip ospf cost 10
A(config-if)# ip ospf message-digest-key 1 md5 C!sc0
A(config-if)# exit
A(config)#
```

Figure 52: Sample OSPF configuration

The configuration to enable OSPF on router A1 is as shown in the following figure:

```
A1(config)# router ospf 100
A1(config-router)# router-id 10.0.1.254
A1(config-router)# network 10.0.1.0 0.0.0.255 area 1
A1(config-router)# network 10.0.80.0 0.0.15.255 area 1
A1(config-router)# area 1 stub no-summary
A1(config-router)# passive-interface Gi1/0
A1(config-router)# exit
A1(config)#
```

Figure 53: Sample OSPF configuration

Note in the preceding configurations that the configuration on the internal routers (non-ABR) like A1 is only about enabling the OSPF process and assigning interfaces to the OSPF. The interfaces are assigned to OSPF by using the network-area command, and all interfaces that have the network address that match start running OSPF in the specified area. If the IP addressing hierarchy is defined properly, we can enable OSPF on the complete range, and all interfaces would start to participate in OSPF when they are configured with an IP address. We have configured area 1 as a stub area with no summary LSAs and hence only a default route would be advertised into area 1 by the ABR, which is router A.

The area range commands are to be configured only on the ABR, that will suppress the specific prefixes from being advertised out of the area, and only the aggregate prefixes defined in these commands will be advertised for the specific areas.

We have also forced the router ID to use the loopback 0 address of the router for ease of identification of the messages that will be advertised by this router.

There are more advanced features of OSPF, such as virtual links, that are beyond the scope of the current book as they will not be used in campus networks.

IS-IS:

IS-IS is a part of the **Open System Interconnection** (**OSI**) suite of protocols. The OSI suite uses **Connectionless Network Service** (**CLNS**) to provide connectionless delivery of data, and the actual layer 3 protocol is **Connectionless Network Protocol** (**CLNP**). IS-IS uses CLNS addresses to identify routers and to build the link-state database. IS-IS protocol was extended to enable the routing of IP and the protocol was called Integrated IS-IS or Dual IS-IS that is defined in RFC 1195 and ISO 10589, which supports routing for both OSI protocols and IP.

IS-IS is a dynamic link-state protocol, which provides fast convergence, high stability with efficient use for bandwidth, memory, and CPU. Like OSPF, the routing domain in IS-IS can also be divided into a hierarchical manner for scalability. Each subdomain is called an area and is defined by an area address or a NET address. The backbone area similar to area 0 in OSPF is called L2 domain in IS-IS. The nonbackbone equivalent of OSPF is the L1 routing domain.

Since IS-IS is based on CLNP, it uses NSAP addresses from the OSI realm. For the purposes of our discussion, let's just consider an NSAP address as a number with the following format:

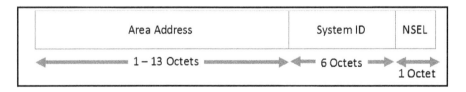

Figure 54: NSAP address pattern

In the preceding figure, the **Area Address** denotes the IS-IS area ID and the system ID represents the node ID within the area. NSEL is always set to 00. Like in OSPF, all devices within the same area should have the same area address. The **System ID** has to be unique within the area to uniquely describe a node. When using IS-IS for IP routing, we generally embed the IS-IS address in the system ID field for easier identification.

IS-IS also sends hellos, called IS-IS Hello or IIH, to maintain relationships with neighboring routers that are running IS-IS. The database information is exchanged using **Link State Packets** (**LSPs**), which can be thought of as analogous to LSAs in OSPF.

The difference between IS-IS and OSPF is that in OSPF, the area boundaries run through the routers and the interfaces are in area, while in IS-IS, the area boundaries don't run through the routers. The entire router is in one area and the area boundary falls on the links. IS-IS routing takes place at two levels as follows:

- **Level 1 (L1) routing within an IS-IS area (intra-area routing)**: All devices in a L1 routing area have the same area address. Intra-area routing is accomplished by looking at the locally significant address portion (system ID) and choosing the lowest-cost path.
- **Level 2 (L2) routing between IS-IS areas (inter-area routing)**: If the destination address has a different area address, the L1 router sends the traffic to the closest L1/L2 area border router (ABR).

In a multiple-area IS-IS setup, IS-IS routers are classified as follows:

- **Level 1**: L1 routers learn about paths within areas they connect to (intra-area paths). L1 routers store **L1 link-state database** (**L1 LSDB**). L1 routers use L1/L2 routers (ABRs) to reach inter-area routes. This is done via a default route injected by the ABR into L1 area.
- **Level 2**: L2 routers learn about paths among areas (inter-area paths). L2 routers store L2 link-state database (L2 LSDB).
- **Level 1/Level 2 (like an OSPF ABR)**: L1/L2 routers learn about paths both within and between areas. L1/L2 routers store both L1 and L2 databases (L1 and L2 LSDBs). L1/L2 routers act as the gateway for L1 routers to reach inter-area routes.

By default, all Cisco IS-IS routers are level 1/level 2 routers, which enables them to carry both L1 and L2 link state databases. The type of link-state information exchanged between two IS-IS routers is dependent on the adjacency type formed. L1 adjacency routers exchange L1 link-state information. L2 adjacency routers exchange L2 link-state information. L1/L2 adjacency routers can exchange both L1 and L2 link state information.

A sample topology for IS-IS is shown in the following figure:

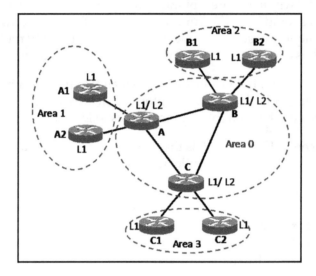

Figure 55: Sample IS-IS topology

The router configuration to enable IS-IS is shown in the following figure:

```
A(config)# key chain ISIS-KEY
A(config-keychain)# key 1
A(config-keychain-key)# key-string C!sc0
A(config-keychain-key)# exit
A(config-keychain)# exit
A(config)#
A(config)# router isis XYZ_ent
A(config-isis)# net 49.0000.0100.0000.0255.00
A(config-isis)# exit
A(config)#
A(config)# interface Gi0/0
A(config-if)# circuit-type level-1-2
A(config-if)# ip router isis XYZ_ent
A(config-if)# exit
A(config)# interface Gi1/0
A(config-if)# circuit-type level-1
A(config-if)# ip router isis XYZ_ent
A(config-if)# authentication mode md5 level-2
A(config-if)# authentication key-chain ISIS-KEY level-2
A(config-if)# exit
A(config)#
```

Figure 56: Sample IS-IS configuration

The configuration for the router A1 is as shown in the following figure:

```
A1(config)#
A1(config)# router isis XYZ_ent
A1(config-isis)# net 49.0001.0100.0000.1254.00
A1(config-isis)# exit
A1(config)#
```

Figure 57: Sample router A1 configuration

Note how the loopback address of the routers has been embedded into the net ID for routers A and A1. Most enterprise networks use the basic forms of OSPF and IS-IS or even static routing, and hence we have not delved deep into tuning of the protocols for timers, and so on.

External routing

The protocols we have studied so far are the protocols that are used for exchanging the routing information within the organization or a domain within a single administrative control. These protocols exchange a whole lot of information between the devices. When it comes to exchanging routing between two different organizations, or two networks under different administrative domains, we use a different set of protocols that are called Exterior Gateway Protocols. **Border Gateway Protocol** (**BGP**) is one such protocol that is used when ISPs connect to each other or the organization connects to the internet. We will describe the use cases and BGP configurations in `Chapter 7`, *Understanding and Configuring Data Center Technologies*.

Route redistribution

We have discussed multiple ways of building a routing table using different protocols such as static routing, RIP, OSPF, and IS-IS. Although each type of protocol creates entries in a routing table for the prefixes in the domains that run the specific protocols, the protocols do not, however, take the routes from the routing table that were populated by other means and advertise them. As an example, consider the upcoming figure, where we use static routing within one domain of the network and OSPF in another domain.

The routing table for router **RA** would have the prefixes in the network **10.0.0.0/21** from domain **A** as they are learned by OSPF. Router **RA** also has a static router pointed toward router **RD** for the prefix **10.0.12.0/23**, which exists in domain **B**. Router **RD** will be configured for a static default route towards **RA**. Hence, all the packets from domain **B** if they have to go to a destination in domain **A**, will be routed to **RA**, which will route them to the desired destination as it has complete visibility of the prefixes in domain **B**. However, for the return routing to happen, routers **R1**, **R2**, **R3**, and **R4** should have a route for the prefix **10.0.12.0/23**, but that is not there as router **RD** is not participating in OSPF. It is only **RA** that knows about this prefix and that too through a static route configuration:

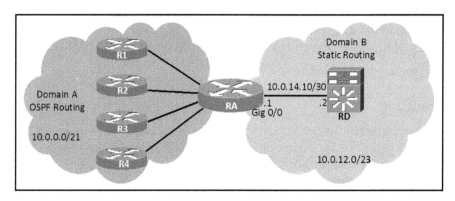

Figure 52: Topology for route redistribution

In such cases, there is a need to redistribute routes from one routing protocol to another, for providing end-to-end connectivity across the entire network. This is called route redistribution and occurs in all dynamic routing protocols. The routes that need to be redistributed can be selected based on the source protocol of the route, or other parameters supported by configuration. As an example, if there are ten static routes on router **RA**, only selected routes can be redistributed into OSPF. This selection can be done using access lists or tags as the filter for redistribution. The configuration for redistribution of routes into OSPF and IS-IS is as shown in the following figure. Note that the redistribution is required only at the boundary router where the two domains converge and not at other routers. **RA** will insert the static prefixes into OSPF, and the OSPF LSAs will propagate these prefixes to the entire domain:

```
RA(config)#
RA(config)# router ospf 1
RA(config-router)# redistribute static tag 10 subnets
RA(config-router)# redistribute connected subnets
RA(config-router)# redistribute rip subnets
RA(config-router)# redistribute isis subnets
```

Figure 59: Route redistribution into OSPF

The same set of commands can be used to redistribute prefixes into IS-IS under the IS-IS hierarchy.

Routing table segmentation

The previous section described how the routes can be merged from one routing domain into another. In this section, we will consider how to segment the routing table into virtual routing tables.

Let's consider a very simple network topology where two VLANs are configured on a router/switch:

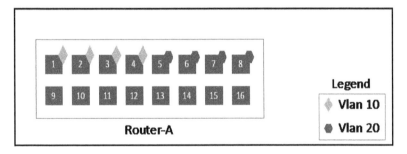

Figure 60: Creating logical routing tables

The sample configuration for the device is as shown in the following figure:

```
RouterA(config)#
RouterA(config)# interface range gig0/1 - 4
RouterA(config-if-range)# switchport mode access
RouterA(config-if-range)# switchport access vlan 10
RouterA(config-if-range)# exit
RouterA(config)# interface range gig0/5 - 8
RouterA(config-if-range)# switchport mode access
RouterA(config-if-range)# switchport access vlan 20
RouterA(config-if-range)# exit
RouterA(config)# interface vlan10
RouterA(config-if)# ip addr 10.0.0.1 255.255.255.0
RouterA(config-if)# exit
RouterA(config)# interface vlan20
RouterA(config-if)# ip addr 10.0.1.1 255.255.255.0
RouterA(config-if)# exit
RouterA(config)#
```

Figure 61: Creating VLANs on a Layer 3 switch

With the preceding configuration, if host X is connected to port 1 with an IP address of 10.0.0.2 and host Y is connected to port 5 with an IP address of 10.0.1.2 with the right default gateways, then host X would be able to ping host Y.

Since the device is a layer 3 device, it will have a single routing table and all packets will look up that routing table.

Cisco technologies use the concept of **Virtual Routing and Forwarding**, called **VRF** or **VRF-Lite**, where the routing table can be partitioned and only packets coming in from one interface will be able to access the routing table assigned to that interface. When using VRF-Lite, interfaces are assigned to specific VRF names, and packets from the interface will have visibility only to the routes that are in that VRF table and will not have any visibility into other VRF routing tables.

If we want to segregate the two VLANs in the preceding routing device, we can disable IP routing on the device. However, this will mean that the device will not do any IP routing at all, irrespective of the interfaces. If we want `vlan10` to use a default route for a specific host, and `vlan20` to use a separate default route, we will use VRF-Lite configurations as shown in the following figure:

```
RouterA(config)#
RouterA(config)# interface range gig0/1 - 4
RouterA(config-if-range)# switchport mode access
RouterA(config-if-range)# switchport access vlan 10
RouterA(config-if-range)# exit
RouterA(config)# interface range gig0/5 - 8
RouterA(config-if-range)# switchport mode access
RouterA(config-if-range)# switchport access vlan 20
RouterA(config-if-range)# exit
RouterA(config)# interface vlan10
RouterA(config-if)# ip vrf Domain-1
RouterA(config-if)# ip addr 10.0.0.1 255.255.255.0
RouterA(config-if)# exit
RouterA(config)# interface vlan20
uterA(config-if)# ip vrf Domain-2
RouterA(config-if)# ip addr 10.0.1.1 255.255.255.0
RouterA(config-if)# exit
RouterA(config)# ip route vrf Domain-1 0.0.0.0 0.0.0.0 10.0.0.100
RouterA(config)# ip route vrf Domain-2 0.0.0.0 0.0.0.0 10.0.1.100
RouterA(config)#
```

Figure 62: Creating logical routing tables

We have discussed various routing protocols and different layer 2 and layer 3 technologies used in the campus. The next sections will focus on the design considerations and when to configure these technologies.

Campus LAN design considerations

A campus LAN is the most important part of the network, as it is the place where most of the users connect to the network to access services and applications. This is also the part of the network where senior executives and the core team of the organization will connect, and any unavailability on this network will result in a loss of revenue and management time.

Like any other network, the design of a campus LAN starts with the gathering of customer requirements. The requirements from a campus network are broadly stated as follows:

- Connecting users to the network
- Providing connectivity to wireless access points
- Providing connectivity to IP phones
- Providing connectivity to IoT systems such as CCTV
- Ensuring proper access control of the network

Let's describe a sample hierarchical campus design and the rationale behind choosing the specific features on the network.

A typical campus design would be a hierarchical network design with a typical three-tier or a two-tier design. A three-tier design consists of a core, distribution, and access layer, while a two-tier design has the core and distribution functions on a single device. Sample network topologies are shown in the following figure:

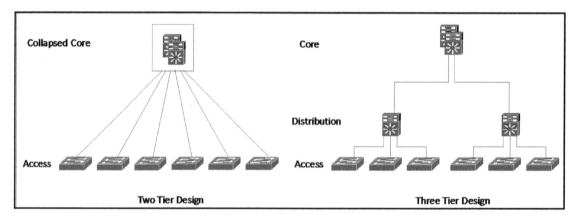

Figure 63: Two-tier versus a three-tier design

In a three-tier design, the access layer provides connectivity to the end systems and enforces the network access policy, and has the function of classifying and marking the different types of traffic for defining how the traffic will be treated on the rest of the network. These functions are done at the edge of the network because this is where we get to see the traffic in the most granular manner. As we go toward the core of the network, traffic gets aggregated and we lose the granularity required to perform specific functions, such as classification and marking.

The distribution tier of the network aggregates different types of traffic that comes in from various access layers. The primary function of the distribution layer is to aggregate the various layer 2 broadcast domains and act as the first layer 3 hop for the user traffic. This layer also provides high availability to the network by providing redundant devices and deploying protocols such as FHRP to ensure a high-service uptime.

The core layer of the network is the aggregator for all types of users and traffic and acts as the central point for connecting the users, data center, and the remote sites connecting over the WAN to the rest of the network.

Some organizations might deploy separate access layers for user networks, and IoT networks, and aggregate them at the distribution layer, while certain network designers might want to keep that isolation all the way into the DC. The choice is primarily a matter of the security perception of the organization from the various IoT technologies that are being deployed on the network. We will consider the segregation of the IoT traffic as a different routing domain itself in the distribution layer and converge the traffic at the core.

Topology choices

Network topology is the layout of the connectivity of the various devices in the network. This represents how the devices are connected together on a network. The topology may be physical or logical. While physical topology shows the connectivity of the various links, the logical topology describes the actual flow of traffic and the protocols. The logical topology may be different from the physical topology.

Ring and star topologies

The two most common topologies seen in the campus network are the ring and the star topologies. Ring topologies are more common in manufacturing plants where multiple small buildings need to be connected, and the physical fiber topology is a closed loop. In an enterprise network, the star topology is the preferred topology. The two topologies are shown in the following figure for the access layer of the network:

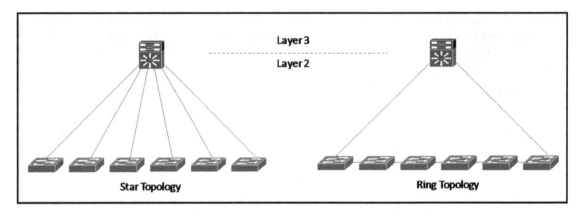

Figure 64: Star and ring topologies

Generally, the access layer is purely a layer 2 domain, and the layer 3 boundary is at the distribution device, as shown in the preceding figure. In this case, the star topology provides dedicated bandwidth to each access switch up to the distribution device. In a ring topology, however, the bandwidth is shared between the various access switches that form a part of the ring. Also recall from the spanning tree section that Ethernet loops are not allowed in a broadcast domain, and a ring topology forms a physical loop. Hence, some ports of the ring will be blocked by the STP protocols running on the Ethernet segment.

Physical versus logical topology

Let's consider the ring topology in the previous section. Let's assume that each switch has a group of users that all belong to the same VLAN and each switch has a separate VLAN. Since the VLANs terminate at layer 3 on the distribution switch, the trunk links that connect the various access switches just act like the physical medium for carrying traffic up to the core. From a logical layer 3 perspective, the topology will become like a star topology, as all access switches are logically connected to the distribution switch. It is important to understand this distinction between the physical and logical topology as this helps visualize the traffic as it flows across the different segments of the network. A layer 3 logical topology for the physical ring topology is shown in the following figure:

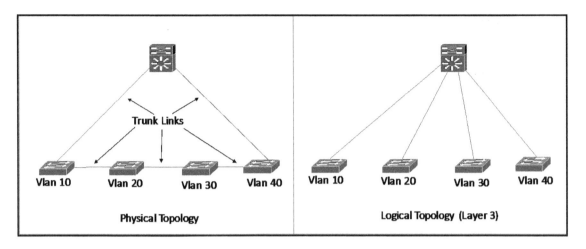

Figure 65: Physical and logical topologies

Naming convention

Each network could have hundreds of network devices. Each device needs to be manged and will send traps to the NMS systems. It is important to adopt a systematic naming convention for the hostname of each device on the network. There are multiple benefits of having an intuitive naming convention:

- A network operator will log in to multiple devices during troubleshooting. An intuitive hostname will make it easier to identify each device from the CLI prompt on the console.
- The network devices will send alerts and syslog messages to the NMS systems, which can quickly overwhelm the storage with thousands of log messages. If you are using structured hostnames, you can easily identify the important devices and parse the logs using scripts easily.
- Structured hostnames will also help network engineers to identify the role and model of the device easily as it can be embedded into the hostname.
- A good hostname naming plan should be able to identify the geographical location at which the device is installed, the facility within the city/location, the type and role of the device, and preferably the model of the device as well for easier identification.

- A sample hostname naming plan that uses 12 characters for each hostname is shown in the following figure. The organization can standardize the location names as three-digit codes, and use them from a central GIS system, or the airport codes for the city. If the organization has multiple facilities within the city, some characters can be used to code that in the hostname to identify the facility at which the device is installed. Some organizations go a step further and reserve additional characters to encode the floor and the rack in which the device is installed as well. It is always a compromise between the length of the hostname and the information that one can code into the hostname:

Field Name	Length (Characters)	Example Codes
Location City	3	MUM: Mumbai DEL: Delhi LON: London BGL: Bangalore
Facility	3	XXX
Type	1	R: Router S: Switch F: Firewall
Function	1	C: Core D: Distribution A: Access I: Internet
Device Model	2	2: Cat 2960 3: Cat 3000
Number	2	01, 02 etc.

Figure 66: Sample naming convention

Layer 2 versus layer 3 boundaries

One of the most important design aspects within a campus is to locate the layer 3 boundary. If the layer 3 boundary is too close to the access, the number of prefixes increases rapidly, adding to an increase in the size of the routing tables. If the layer 2 boundary is very far from the access, the broadcast domain gets bigger, thus impacting throughput and performance.

The important decisive factor in determining the layer 3 boundary is taken as the mobility considerations for the users. In conventional networks, if a user belongs to a particular group, he is always assigned to a particular VLAN, so that he always gets the same IP address from the DHCP server when he connects his laptop to the network. Some organizations have fixed seats for each employee, and in this case, there is no flexibility of movement across seats. This can lead to inefficient utilization of real estate if the average in-office attendance is low for the job roles.

Some organizations reserve a pool of seats for user departments, and the users from that department can sit anywhere within the area. If the user has to get the same IP address from the same pool every time he logs in, the VLAN has to be extended across the entire area in which mobility is allowed. This can make the layer 2 broadcast domain too large. There are technologies such as **Software Defined Access** (**SDA**) that have been launched by Cisco to provide seamless mobility using advanced techniques and protocols that are beyond the scope of this book. However, smaller and mid-size organizations will continue to use the legacy technologies as they are well understood from an operations perspective and are more cost effective than the new upcoming technologies.

Typically, the distribution layer will act as the layer 3 boundary in a campus network, and all VLANs will come and terminate at the distribution switch. Geographically, a pair of distribution switches will typically be deployed for a building with multiple floors, and access switches or a stack of switches will cater to each floor of the building. The network designer can choose whether to span the VLANs from one floor to the other. Keeping the layer 3 boundary at the distribution will provide the flexibility to span the VLANs to the other floors, if required at a later date.

Sizing the campus network

The campus network has to be sized as per the user requirements. Typically, the users are connected to a VoIP phone, and the VoIP phone has an inbuilt switch that can be used to connect the desktop/laptop on a wired connection. Access points are also connected to the access switches for the uplink bandwidth.

The network has to be sized keeping in mind the services to be delivered on the network, the bandwidth requirements for each type of service, the number of users provisioned for these services, and the concurrency ratio of users.

Let's start with the port requirements. Typically, we will reserve one port for each user for wired connectivity. Some organizations reserve two ports per user for redundancy purposes, but that could be a waste of resources from a cabling perspective. The wired port generally connects to the VoIP desk phone, which provides a physical Ethernet port for PC connectivity. So as a rule of thumb, we will take one port per user with spare ports to cater for expansion at a later date. Let's assume we need 100 ports per floor. Typically, the port count on a typical standalone switch used at the access layer is 24 ports. Plain mathematics would tell us that we need five switches to cater to the 100 users. This can increase the number of active devices that need to be managed as each switch would need to be configured and operated during the operations phase. Certain models of Cisco switches allow multiple switches to be stacked together using special cables, and be treated as a single logical entity from a configuration perspective. It is recommended to use up to six switches in a stacked mode from a physical port connectivity perspective.

Next, let's look at the bandwidth required for each user. A typical organization will have voice, video, business critical applications, and internet connectivity as the main bandwidth-consuming applications. Further, there will be different types of users who will need different amounts of bandwidth. Let's categorize the types of users into three broad categories as follows:

- Heavy users that consist of the executives and the people with a lot of market research work
- Medium users who use the bandwidth but are not too dependent on emails
- Light users who are normal office staff, who don't use emails too often

Each organization will have its own classification, and its own assessments about the amount of bandwidth required per user. As a benchmark, a good benchmark to start the network planning process is to consider an average bandwidth consumption of 150 kbps, 100 kbps, and 60 kbps for heavy, medium, and light users respectively. These numbers can be used to size the bandwidth requirements for the uplinks on a number of ports. Note that this does not mean that the heavy users will get only 150 kbps of bandwidth, as not all users would be using the available bandwidth at a given instant. This is only a statistical average, and since data is bursty in nature, the users can burst to very high speeds for short intervals of time. The benchmarks are only starting guidelines and can be refined specific to an organization.

As an example, if we calculate the bandwidth from a switch stack consisting of 100 users with a 20:60:20 mix, the bandwidth requirements toward the distribution switches will be about 10 Mbps. This will increase significantly as we keep adding real-time video and other collaboration capabilities on the network. Assuming a 10 percent concurrency for IP voice calls, we will have 10 percent of 100 or 10 users making a voice call on their IP phone. Let's factor in 200 kbps of bandwidth per voice call, the total voice bandwidth will be 2 Mbps. The heaviest contribution to bandwidth comes from video. Assuming real-time video conferencing on the desktop at a 3 Mbps bandwidth, 100 users would need 30 Mbps of bandwidth for a 10 percent concurrency. Conference rooms will need a much higher bandwidth (~4 Mbps) and the network designer should not factor any concurrency for the conference rooms and assume that they will be occupied full time. All these considerations would lead us to the total uplink bandwidth required, which would be about 1 Gbps only. However, 10 G Ethernet is cheap and is available on most switches, the uplink ports from the access to the distribution are generally 10 G links within the campus to keep headroom for scalability and traffic bursts.

Stacking switches

A switch stack is a set of up to eight stacking-capable switches connected through their stack ports. A switch stack has up to eight stack members connected through their stack ports. A switch stack always has one stack master. The stack master controls the operation of the switch stack and is the single point of stack-wide management.

A switch stack is created by connecting the special ports called stack ports on the switch in a specified manner. A switch stack should have all the switches of the same model and should run the same IOS version.

All configurations to the stack are made from the stack master. The stack member number (1 to 8) identifies each member in the switch stack. This number also determines the interface-level configuration that a stack member uses.

When there are multiple switches in a stack, one of them becomes the master. The switch with the higher priority value for a stack member becomes the stack master on election. The priority value can be 1 to 15, the default being 1.

The MAC address of the stack master determines the stack MAC address. When the stack initializes, the MAC address of the stack master determines the bridge ID that identifies the stack in the network. If the stack master changes, the MAC address of the new stack master determines the new bridge ID and stack MAC address. The stack should be configured with the MAC persistency feature so that the stack MAC address does not change to the new master MAC address.

A configuration for a stack is as shown in the following figure:

```
Switch# configure terminal
Switch(config)# stack-mac persistent timer 0
Switch(config)# switch 1 priority 15
Switch(config)# switch 5 priority 14
Switch(config)# end
Switch# copy running-config startup-config
Switch#
```

Figure 67: Configuration for a switch stack

Note in the preceding configuration that we have increased the priority of switches 1 and 5 to 15 and 14 respectively. This is assuming that the two uplinks are connected on switches 1 and 5.

A sample network

Finally, let's consider the sample network for the sample organization discussed earlier. The design assumptions are as follows:

- There are two floors in the campus. Each floor has an area for development users and nondevelopment users. Development and nondevelopment users have to be separated from each other.
- Each floor has 80-100 development users that can go up to 120 on each floor.
- Each floor has 30 nondevelopment users that can go up to 50 on each floor.

The campus design for this will look similar to the following figure:

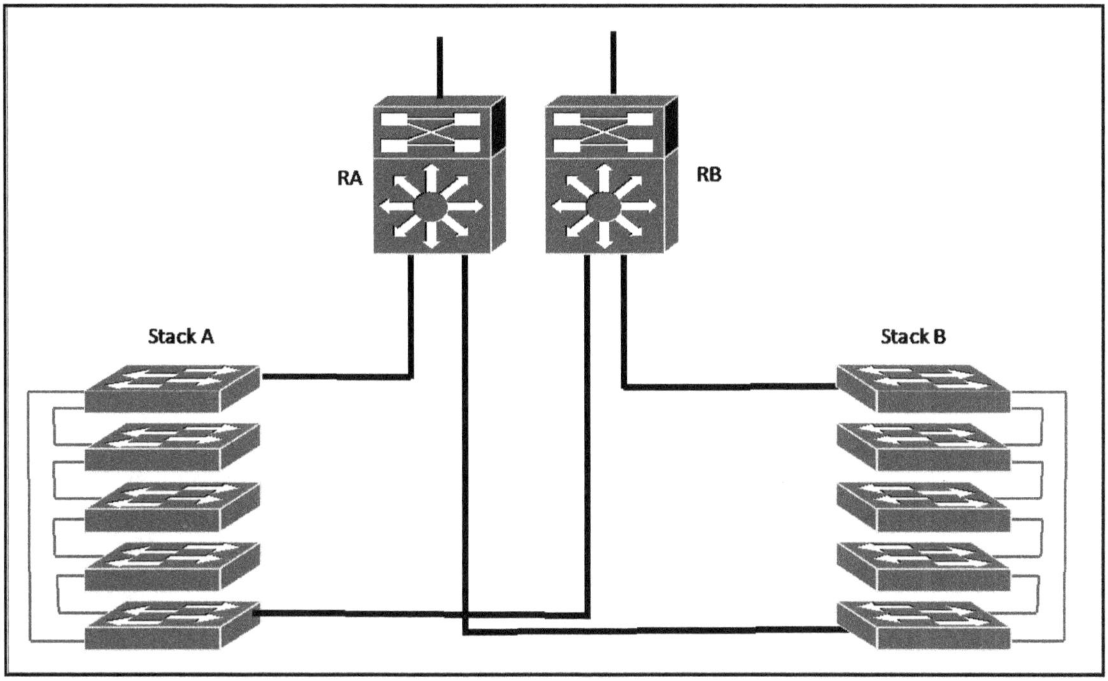

Figure 68: Connecting multiple switches in a stack

Some of the important observations about the design are as follows:

- Stack 1 caters to the users on floor 1 and stack 2 caters to users on floor 2.
- Stack A has some ports configured in VLAN 10 for development users and VLAN 20 for nondevelopment users.
- Stack B has some ports configured in VLAN 11 for development users and VLAN 21 for nondevelopment users.
- The ports connecting to the users on stack A and B are configured as access ports.
- The ports connecting stack A to the collapsed core devices RA and RB are trunk ports carrying VLANs 10 and 20.
- The ports connecting stack B to the collapsed core devices RA and RB are trunk ports carrying VLANs 11 and 21.
- RA and RB run HSRP for VLANSs 10, 11, 20, and 21. RA is the HSRP active router for VLANs 10 and 20, and RB is the HSRP active router for VLANs 20 and 21. This has been done to ensure load balancing across the routers.

- HSRP active is using the state of the physical ports that connect to the downstream stack routers and the uplink port before becoming the HSRP master.
- RA and RB have uplinks toward the firewall that will enforce the policy and allow only traffic that is explicitly defined as per policy.
- The uplink port of RA is a trunk port with VLANs 100 and 101. The uplink port of RB is a trunk port with VLANs 200 and 201.
- The VLANs 10, 20, and 100 on RA are in a vrf-lite instance named dev. The VLANs 11, 21, and 101 are in the vrf-lite instance non-dev. This has been done to prevent any interval routing at RA and prevent development users talking to nondevelopment users through the device RA. Similar configurations are done at RB with VLANs 200 and 201 instead of 100 and 101.
- Since this is a small setup, we will use static routing. Static routing has been defined at RA and RB with default route pointing to the upstream firewall.

These guidelines will allow the devices to ensure what has been listed as the user requirements for the campus. If the company grows and more floors are added, switch stacks can be added at each new floor and configurations can be replicated for the new floors. If the campus becomes large enough and expands to multiple buildings, the same setup can be replicated for each building, and a new core layer can be introduced to aggregate the distribution nodes at each building.

Summary

We have covered layer 2 and layer 3 technologies used in a campus network, and provided configuration guidelines and templates on how to configure Cisco routers with the required features. We have also discussed various considerations in designing a campus network, and finally put everything learned thus far in the chapter to build a small campus network.

In the next chapter, we will discuss how wireless access can be added to the network to provide user mobility.

5

Understanding and Configuring Wireless Access Technologies

"Birds have wings; they're free; they can fly where they want when they want. They have the kind of mobility many people envy."

– Roger Tory Peterson

As the computing devices became smaller, the users felt the need to carry them along. This led to the evolution of wireless technologies in the access, where the networked devices communicated using radio waves over the air interface. The adoption of wireless technology has increased considerably over the last couple of years, and the number of devices that use Wi-Fi as the access mechanism has far outnumbered the wired devices.

In this chapter, we will cover the following topics:

- Benefits of wireless technologies
- Fundamental principles of wireless access technologies
- Wireless standards
- Design considerations for a wireless network
- Configuration guidelines for setting a wireless network in a campus

Benefits of wireless networks

IT organizations are challenged by businesses today for improving the agility of the networks, maximizing the return on investment, and faster rollout of services among other tasks. The emergence of **wireless local area networks** (**WLANs**) helps the IT organizations achieve some of these objectives within the organization. The ways in which WLANs can help the overall business goals are as follows:

- **Mobility**: WLANs allow users to be mobile and move anywhere within the coverage area of the WLAN and be productive even within meeting rooms and cafeteria.
- **Agility**: WLANs allow the users to send time-sensitive data directly from the location with the WLAN coverage using handheld terminals without having the need to shuttle between the site where data is generated and the terminal that has a wired connectivity to the network. This helps the organization in their digitization efforts and streamlines their business processes.
- **Faster network rollout**: WLANs help faster rollouts of networks, without the need for pervasive cabling to all desks within the organization. This helps new sites to be commissioned faster and also allows interim ad hoc expansion of users if required. Further, WLANs can be used in areas which are hard to wire such as old buildings that do not have the required cabling infrastructure or the shop floor in the manufacturing plant where cables cannot be drawn.
- **Flexibility**: WLANs also allow the physical infrastructure teams to remodel the existing layouts of the office without having to worry about the Wi-Fi deployment within the enterprise, providing more flexibility to meet the changing needs of a workspace.
- **Improving network availability**: Most faults that occur in the IT infrastructures are attributed to physical layer faults, such as a faulty crimping on the RJ45 connector, broken or damaged cable due to accidental stretching, or wrong patching to the port of the switch from the user port. WLANs minimize the need for cabling up to the end user location, thus minimizing the scope for such faults, helping improve network and service uptimes.
- **Induction of new services**: WLANs also enable the induction of new services that can be deployed in certain sectors. Location-based service is an example of one such set of services that use WLAN as a technology to identify the user through his wireless device and track the user in real time. This data can be used for analytics and even track the movement of users/ devices within the organization enabling new use cases that were hitherto not possible.

Wireless fundamentals

We will begin the chapter by describing the basic terminology used in wireless networks to set up the context for better understanding of wireless technologies. Though these might not be directly related to the configuration of the devices, an understanding of the basic wireless technology and terminology will enable you to interpret the output from the RF devices and communicate better with the RF engineer who will typically conduct a site survey for wireless deployment or troubleshooting.

An RF signal

A radio wave is an electromagnetic wave that is designed to carry information through the air over relatively long distances. These waves have a broad frequency range and are used in different areas depending upon the use of these waves. The use of these waves is regulated in each country depending upon the technology availability and the frequencies used by different communication mechanisms within strategic areas such as defense and telecommunications.

Radio waves, also known as **radio frequency** (**RF**) signals, oscillate at a very high frequency that allows the waves to travel through the air. As a thumb rule, lower the frequency, further, the wave will travel in the air.

Signal strength

The signal strength of an RF wave is the amount of power that is available in the wave. As the wave travels further from the source, the energy is spread out in all directions and the power of the signal decreases. The signal strength reduces as we go further away from the source.

Power is generally measured in Watts or milliWatts (mW). However, the strength of an RF signal is generally measured in dBm. Power in Watts can be converted into dBm using the following formula:

$$dBm = 10 \log (P)$$

$$where\ P = Power\ in\ milliWatts\ (mW)$$

Figure 1: Converting absolute power to dB

Hence, 1 mW power will be equal to 0 dBm, 10 mW of power is 10 dBm, and 0.1 mW of power is -10 dBm. As a general reference, power below 1 mW is negative and power above 1 is positive when measured in dBm. Every 3 dBm decrease in power reduces the power in Watts to half and vice versa.

The typical dBm values for a wireless access point depend upon the geography in which the power is being radiated, the general range is around 30 dBm that corresponds to 1 W. The typical receive power at which a device can work effectively should be better than -70 dBm.

Modulation

Modulation is the process in which a normal RF wave is modified in terms of its characteristics, namely amplitude and phase, to encode the signals that it is supposed to carry. There are different types of modulation used in WLANs, such as DSSS, OFDM, BPSK, QPSK, and QAM.

Signal to Noise Ratio (SNR)

There are multiple sources of radiation around us. These include electronic devices, a spark in electrical circuits or clouds, thermal devices, and even signals from the stars and clouds. These unwanted signals are called noise and they distort the original modulated signal that was transmitted by the RF source. Noise causes the signal to degrade and makes it difficult for the receiver to decipher the information from the modulated wave once it is received.

The ratio of ambient noise is typically measured as a ratio of the signal power received at a point to the power of the noise signals. The signal to noise ratio, also known as SNR, is also expressed in dB as a unit, as follows:

$$SNR = 10 \log\left(\frac{P_s}{P_n}\right)$$

$$\text{where } P_s = \text{Power of Signal (mW)}$$
$$P_n = \text{Power of Noise (mW)}$$

Figure 2: Calculating SNR

SNR and the received signal strength collectively determine the ability of the receiver to interpret the signals effectively. The acceptable SNR values should be typically higher than 25 dB for WLANs carrying voice traffic.

Frequency bands

There are two frequency bands in which most WLAN equipment operates. These fall in the 2.4 GHz and 5 GHz frequency bands. The actual channels allowed for use within these bands might be different in different countries, depending on the regulation. Different standards mandate the use of different bands, which we will discuss later in this chapter.

Channels

A band is a range of frequencies that are used for a specific purpose. The use of frequency bands varies from country to country and is licensed by the regulation within the area or country. Within a band, specific frequencies are used to radiate the modulated signal. Modulation changes the frequency characteristics of the carrier, and even though the RF carrier wave is of a specific frequency, it is seldom a single frequency and the power is spread across a small range of frequencies above and below the carrier frequency. This leads to the concept of channel bandwidth, where each carrier can spread above and below the center frequency and radiate. In the 2.4 GHz band, this range is 20 MHz.

A typical 2.4 GHz band is shown in the following figure. The entire band is split into multiple channels of 20 MHz each. The channels available in the 2.4 GHz band are as shown in the following figure:

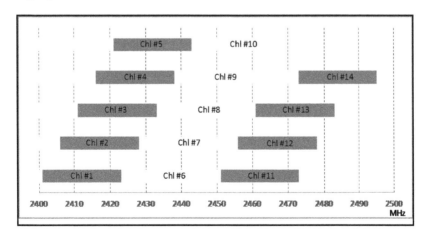

Figure 3: 2.4 GHz Wi-Fi bands

When a wireless access point is radiating, there are other APs around it. If they radiate in the same channel, there is a lot of interference in the areas where the coverage of the two APs overlaps. Hence to avoid interference, different APs that are adjacent to each other use different channels that are not overlapping. A maximum of three non-overlapping channels can be found in the 2.4 GHz band, which are {1,6,11} or {2,7,12}, {3,8,13}, {4,9,14}, {5,10,14}, {1,7,13}, and so on.

A sample deployment in an area with the channels 1, 6, and 11 are as shown in the following figure:

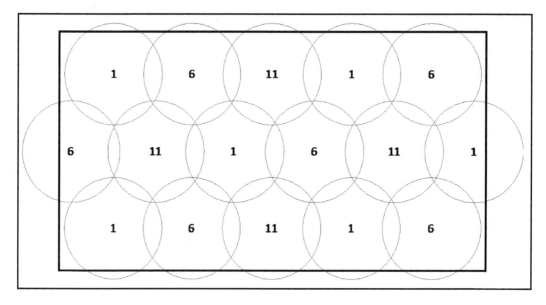

Figure 4: Providing Wi-Fi coverage with three channels

The 5 GHz band has a number of channels that can be used by the WLAN systems. A table of different channels in the 5 GHz band is shown in the following figure for the US:

Channel Number	Center Frequency (GHz)	Channel Number	Center Frequency (GHz)
U-NII 1 Band			
36	5.180	44	5.220
40	5.200	48	5.240
U-NII 2 Band			
52	5.260	60	5.300
56	5.280	64	5.320
U-NII 2 Extended Band			
100	5.500	132	5.660
104	5.520	136	5.680
108	5.540	140	5.700
112	5.560	144	5.720
116	5.580		
U-NII 3 Band			
149	5.745	161	5.805
153	5.765	165	5.825
157	5.785		

Figure 5: 5 GHz Wi-Fi bands

MIMO

Traditional WLANs communicate using a single antenna to radiate and receive the RF signals. Since the WLAN functioning is half-duplex, the same antenna will radiate and receive signals at different times. If we have multiple antennas, both at the transmitting and the receiving stations, we can send multiple data streams from the sender to the receiver through each antenna, thereby increasing the effective bandwidth between the two systems. This is referred to as **Multiple-Input multiple-output** and is abbreviated as **MIMO**. A MIMO configuration is generally denoted as $n \times m$, where n is the number of transmitting streams and m is the number of receiving streams.

The following figure shows a 2 x 2 MIMO configuration as an illustration:

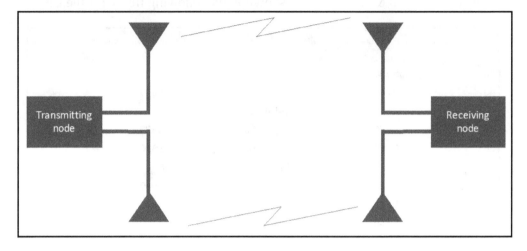

Figure 6: A 2 x 2 MIMO system

The preceding figure depicted the same set of antennae being used between a single set of transmitter and receiver. This is called **Single-user MIMO** or **SU-MIMO**. If the transmitter can split the antennas to communicate with more numbers of users as shown in the following figure, this is called **Multi-user MIMO** or **MU-MIMO**:

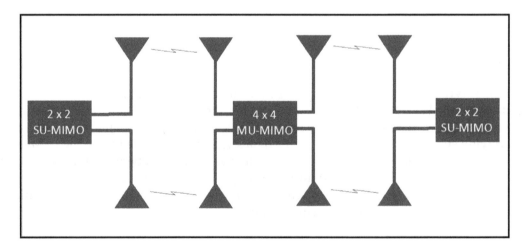

Figure 7: A 4 x 4 MIMO system

Channel bonding

Legacy WLANs operate using 20-MHz channels. This limits the amount of data bandwidth that can be transmitted using these narrow channels. Newer standards allow the Wi-Fi systems to use two channels in a bundle and increase the channel bandwidth to 40 MHz. This enables the same RF channel to provide double bandwidth. In practice, the bandwidth of a double channel is slightly more than double. When two adjacent channels are bundled together, we also use the guard band that separates two consecutive channels and hence the bandwidth is slightly more than double.

Channel bonding is best if done in the 5-GHz band because the 2.4-GHz band has a limited number of channels (14), and if the channels are bundled, we get only one channel bundle.

Antenna characteristics

The RF signals are transmitted using an antenna that converts the electrical signals into RF waves in the air. An ideal antenna will radiate in all directions and the radiation pattern will be a sphere. Such an antenna is called an isotropic antenna.

In a WLAN deployment, the clients are located in one plane, and hence the antenna needs to radiate in one plane only. The antenna that radiates and receives signals from all directions in one plane is called an **omnidirectional antenna**. These antennae are generally used for indoor WLAN deployments. A dipole is the most common form of an omnidirectional antenna that has a radiation pattern that is 360 degrees in the horizontal plane and 75 degrees in the vertical plane, assuming a vertical dipole. The increase in power as compared to an isotropic antenna is called the gain of the antenna. It is measured in dBi, the *i* in the unit implies that the reference is an isotropic antenna. The gain of the dipole antenna is typically 2.14 dBi as compared to an isotropic antenna.

Sometimes, there is a need to radiate the signal in a specific direction rather than spreading the signal in all directions even within one plane. This could be because the clients will be only on one side of the antenna and hence, any power radiated on the other side will be wasted. Special antennae are used in such cases that radiate the power in a given direction. Such an antenna is called a directional antenna.

Directional antennas concentrate the RF signal in a certain area, which is called a sector and is defined by the angle in which it radiates. The antenna does not add power to the signal, but because it radiates the same power in a smaller sector, the signals travel further in that sector. A 90-degree antenna will be more directional than a 120-degree antenna, as it concentrates the power in a smaller area and hence has a greater gain. Directional antennas are placed in corners or near the walls to radiate within the room. Other uses of directional antennas could be to direct the RF beam within corridors or to direct a beam toward another building and use the RF link for backhaul of traffic from another building.

Typical radiation patterns of the omnidirectional and a directional antenna in the horizontal plane are shown in the following figure:

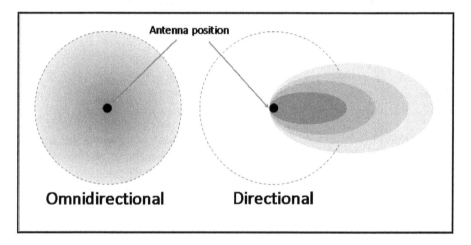

Figure 8: Directional antenna

Wireless standards

Wireless access in campus deployment is based on IEEE 802.11 standard. This standard defines multiple physical layers and **Media access control** (**MAC**) layer specifications for implementing wireless local area networks. Since its first release in 1997, the standard has been revised and multiple additions have been made to enhance the speed that can be delivered using these specifications.

IEEE 802.11

The 802.11 family consists of different modulation techniques of the RF waves over the air interface working in half-duplex mode. Although 802.11 was the basic specification defined, the specification allowed speeds of only up to 2 Mbps in the 2.4 GHz band.

IEEE 802.11a

IEEE created an extension of the IEEE 802.11 specification, which was subsequently named 802.11a that could offer higher speeds of up to 54 Mbps. However, this standard used the 5 GHz frequency band, that was a licensed band and hence the adoption of 802.11a was low due to the higher cost.

IEEE 802.11b

Parallelly, IEEE also created an extension of the original specification that came to be known as IEEE 802.11b that used the unlicensed 2.4 GHz spectrum band and hence was much cheaper. This standard provided speeds of up to 11 Mbps and hence was comparable to the use of 10Mbps Ethernet at the time and thus became much more acceptable.

IEEE 802.11g

Later standard enhancement led to IEEE 802.11g that could support bandwidths of up to 54 Mbps on the unlicensed 2.4 GHz band. This technology was also backward compatible with 802.11b that operated in the same frequency band.

IEEE 802.11n

In the year 2009, IEEE standardized IEEE 802.11n that introduced the **MIMO** technology. MIMO allowed a single device to have multiple wireless antennas, and the antennas could send streams that were received by the antenna at the receiving node. The maximum number of spatial streams allowed is 4. This increased the speed that could be delivered using the 802.11n, being the aggregate of multiple streams. This specification also allowed the use of channel bonding. A typical wireless channel is 20 MHz wide, thus limiting the bandwidth that can be transmitted using this limited wireless spectrum. 802.11n could use two 20 MHz channels, thus increasing the effective channel to 40 MHz and hence increasing the data rate. Note that the channel bonding is best utilized in the 5 GHz band, as the number of channels in the 2.4 GHz band is limited to 3 non-overlapping channels, while the 5GHz band provides a lot more channels in each region that can be bonded together.

802.11n can provide data speeds of up to 600 Mbps using 40 MHz channels and shorter (400 ns) guard intervals.

A guard interval is a duration between consecutive signals during which there is no transmission so that any reflected signals can fade down and do not interfere with the next signals. Having longer guard interval increases the error handling capacity of signals, as there is less interference but leads to longer idle times of the medium, thus lowering the throughput. The previous 802.11 specifications had an 800ns guard interval, while the 802.11n added an option of having a smaller guard interval of 400 ns to enhance throughput.

IEEE 802.11n could theoretically go up to 300 Mbps of network bandwidth over the air interface, while the actual throughput is in the range of 100-150 Mbps depending upon several factors such as client density, signal strength, interference patterns, and the capabilities of the end devices among other factors. The 802.11n standard could operate in either of the two frequency bands 2.4 GHz and 5 GHz and hence is backward compatible with the 802.11b and g standards.

IEEE 802.11ac

The latest generation of Wi-Fi signaling is based on the IEEE 802.11ac standard that works in the 5 GHz Wi-Fi band. This standard extends the maximum number of MIMO streams to 8 and provides support for MU-MIMO that allows the multiple streams to be used for different users rather than a set of transmitting and receiving user pair. 802.11ac also offers backward compatibility to 802.11b/g/n and can provide bandwidth up to 1.3 Gbps on the 5 GHz band. 802.11ac also allows the use of 80 MHz channels (mandatory as per specification) and 160 MHz (optional). This increases the data rates available and hence the bandwidth over 802.11ac. The specification also allows the use of bonding two non-contiguous 80 MHz channels to form a single 160 MHz channel.

Mixed mode operation/interoperability

The choice of the frequency band to use for the WLAN deployment in the organization depends upon multiple factors and might be influenced by the following factors:

- **Deployment location**: Some countries might not allow the use of 5 GHz band for WLANs and hence the only option is to use 2.4 GHz band and thus use 802.11n.
- **Performance considerations**: 5 GHz band provides much wider channels and hence greater bandwidth. 5 GHz is the choice if you want peak performance.

- **Existing device base**: Since a lot of legacy devices will support 802.b/g devices that operate only in the 2.4 GHz band, one might be forced to defer the use of 802.11ac that operates only in the 5 GHz range. The network designer might also consider deploying a hybrid environment using both bands; peak performance devices using 5 GHz on 802.11ac and legacy devices using 2.4 GHz.

- **Coverage area**: Range of RF waves decreases as the frequency increases. Hence, 5 GHz will attenuate more rapidly than the 2.4 GHz RF signals. Using 5 GHz APs might require a larger number of APs for the same coverage area. The actual number of APs will depend upon a lot of other factors such as the walls, material of construction, and the location of APs and can be arrived at only after a thorough site survey.

- **Interference**: Many industrial and electronic devices can cause high interference in the 2.4 GHz range causing disruptions. Microwave ovens, cordless phone, and Bluetooth devices can all cause interference in the 2.4 GHz range, while the 5GHz band is immune to interference from these devices. High interference levels will limit the coverage area of an AP and hence have an impact on the overall cost of deployment.

In most organizations, some of the devices will be legacy 802.11a/b/g devices that operate in the 2.4 GHz band, and hence 802.11n is a good choice for the WLAN, as it operates in both 2.4 GHz and 5 GHz bands. However, to achieve peak performance for newer devices that support 802.11ac, WLANs need to be deployed in the 5 GHz band. Most organizations will end up deploying dual networks for legacy devices running 802.11 b/g/n in the 2.4 GHz range and 802.11ac in the 5 GHz range.

Configuring the WLAN

A WLAN consists of Wireless Access Points as discussed in `Chapter 2`, *Networks for Digital Enterprises*. These **access points** (**APs**) provide the layer 1 and layer 2 functionality of the OSI stack. An AP is a self-sufficient layer 2 device that provides connectivity back to the network. The upstream connectivity from the AP is generally through an Ethernet port on the AP. Sometimes, the APs are used in a mesh mode or as repeaters and the uplink connectivity might also be through a wireless medium. We will consider the APs connected directly to a switch port, which is the most common form of enterprise deployment in this book.

All 802.11 WLANs use a **service set identifier**, abbreviated as **SSID**, which is a unique identifier that the wireless clients use to identify and join networks. APs can broadcast this SSID so that it is visible to other users. Some SSIDs might also be hidden and not broadcast, and such networks can be joined by the clients only if they have prior knowledge of SSID. APs might use different SSIDs to broadcast two different WLANs on the same frequency band to segregate two networks. It is analogous to having two different VLANs in an Ethernet domain, as this provides segregation between the clients on the two WLANs. Each SSID may be secured using different security mechanisms such as **Wired Equivalent Privacy** (**WEP**) and **Wi-Fi Protected Access** (**WPA**). Additional security can be built in through authentication of users through AAA servers.

Cisco mobility express

The earlier models of the Cisco APs supported a mode called the **autonomous mode** of deployment. This mode enabled each AP to be configured individually, either using the console port CLI or an inbuilt GUI.

As the number of wireless APs increased in the organization, administrators found it challenging to manage multiple devices, and a need was felt to find alternative means of configuring the access points without having the need to configure each AP independently. This led to a new network element known as a **Wireless LAN controller** (**WLC**) that provides a centralized means of managing the APs that are under its control.

In this new mode of deployment, the APs do not need to be configured individually but are configured through a controller based on a centralized configuration policy. This reduces the configuration time for the APs and also ensures consistent policy across the APs lowering the chances of manual errors in configurations. This makes the WLAN scalable and flexible.

One will find at least a few APs in even a small organization. In a standalone mode, the APs don't communicate with each other and hence have no knowledge of any client associations on the neighboring APs. Hence, when a client moves from the coverage area of one AP to another, the client has to initiate a fresh connection request to the wireless network and get authenticated with the new AP. This is against the spirit of mobility within the enterprise. In a controller-based deployment, the WLC handles the **roaming** function and hence there is no re-authentication of the clients when clients move across the coverage zone of APs that are managed by the same controller. This feature was not available in the autonomous mode, as there was no controller in the deployment.

Cisco, in an attempt to overcome these challenges of mobility and to ensure a consistent deployment and user experience, embedded the WLC code inside the new generation 802.11ac wave 2 Access Points. The inbuilt WLC feature is known as **Cisco Mobility Express (CME)**. The autonomous mode has since been deprecated from the Cisco IOS for these new devices. The older devices still provide for configuration using the autonomous mode with GUI or CLI. With CME, even small deployments can use one of the APs as the controller and use this controller to configure the other deployed APs within the organization. Large organizations will need a WLC, as mobility express limits the number of APs that can be controlled to 25 at present.

Wireless LAN controller and CAPWAP

A WLC is a network element that manages the configuration and management of the APs in a domain. As discussed earlier, the WLAN APs provide a **Media Access Control** (**MAC**) function of the OSI stack. In a WLC-based deployment, the MAC functions are split between the AP and WLC. The functions that are time sensitive are managed by the AP, while the functions that can be centralized and are not very time sensitive, for example, authentication are handled by the WLC. The communication between the AP and WLC is done using a new protocol called **Control and Provisioning of Wireless Access Points** (**CAPWAP**).

CAPWAP is the standardized version of its predecessor **Lightweight access point protocol** (**LWAPP**) and is defined in the RFC 5415. CAPWAP provides the configuration and management of APs and WLANs. It also defines the encapsulation and forwarding of WLAN client traffic between an AP and a WLAN controller. CAPWAP operates over UDP ports 5246 for control and 5247 for data traffic. It is important to know these ports so that if the WLC and the APs have a firewall in the data path, the firewall should allow traffic on these UDP ports.

Since CAPWAP provides for split operation meaning, the data plane traffic and control plane traffic are encrypted in different tunnels to the WLC. In this case, only a subset of the functions is handled by the AP, and hence it uses a smaller IOS image and is called a **Lightweight AP**, sometimes written as **LWAP**.

CAPWAP protocol provides the discovery and configuration of the APs in a centralized deployment. In a WLC-based deployment, the AP connects to the WLC using the UDP protocol over IP. The AP is configured with an IP address, which can be done dynamically using DHCP.

The AP establishes a CAPWAP tunnel to the WLC on the IP address of the WLC. The IP address of the WLC is known to the AP either through manual configuration or using `Option 43` in DHCP. The AP can also find the address through DNS resolution to the domain name within the domain of the organization; for example, if the organization domain is `xyz.com`, then the AP does a DNS query for `host cisco-capwap-controller.xyz.com`. If the WLC is on the same LAN segment as the AP, the AP does IP multicast or broadcast to connect to the WLC. The DNS server of the enterprise needs to be configured to resolve `host cisco-capwap-controller.xyz.com` to the IP address of the WLC.

The Cisco Mobility Express feature is meant for small wireless deployments and requires all APs to be in the same broadcast domain. The IP-based deployments are for large WLC-based deployments.

We will use the following figure as a reference for the configuration of an AP in a small deployment using the Cisco Mobility Express feature:

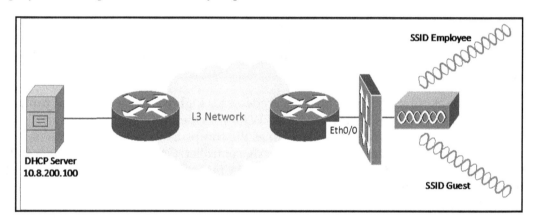

Figure 9: Reference diagram for a small Wi-Fi deployment

The AP is connected to the Ethernet switch and it radiates two SSIDs names: **Employee** and **Guest**. The guest traffic needs to be separated from the Employee traffic within an enterprise, as separate security policies are required for the two types of traffic. This is done by bridging the guest traffic and the employee traffic on two separate VLANs by the AP. The uplink router port needs to be configured as a trunk port in our example since there are two VLANs on the air interface. We have used VLAN 50 for employee traffic and VLAN 70 for guest traffic. The AP will be managed using the native VLAN that is mapped to VLAN 1. Note that the management VLAN is always the native VLAN, as the AP will receive untagged packets for the management interface. The router port configuration will be as shown in the following figure:

```
Router# configure terminal
Router(config)# interface Eth0/0
Router(config-if)# no ip address
Router(config-subif)# interface Eth0/0.1
Router(config-subif)# description VLAN#1-Mgmt
Router(config-subif)# encapsulation dot1q 1 native
Router(config-subif)# ip address 192.168.0.1 255.255.255.0
Router(config-if)# interface Eth0/0.50
Router(config-subif)# description VLAN#50-Employee
Router(config-subif)# encapsulation dot1q 50
Router(config-subif)# ip address 192.168.1.1 255.255.255.0
Router(config-subif)# interface Eth0/0.70
Router(config-subif)# description VLAN#70-Guest
Router(config-subif)# encapsulation dot1q 70
Router(config-subif)# ip address 192.168.2.1 255.255.255.0
Router(config-subif)# exit
Router(config-if)# exit
Router(config)#
```

Figure 10: Configuring the upstream router

The switch configuration in the preceding example will be to use the ports connecting the AP and the router as trunk ports, allowing VLANs 1, 50, and 70 on these trunk ports. Note that the VLAN1 should be the native VLAN for all ports. Note that these VLANs have to be carried on all ports on the switch, where additional APs will be connected.

Also, note the change in syntax for the router port configuration. Since the router has routed ports instead of the switched ports that are available on a switch, the configuration of VLANs is different on the router. In the router configuration, sub-interfaces are created instead of VLAN interfaces that need to be configured with the IP address and another layer 3 details.

The default behavior of the AP on bootup is to send DHCP messages to get an IP address. **DHCP** is an acronym for **Dynamic Host Configuration Protocol**, which is used to allocate user IP address, DNS server information, and another vendor-specific information, using DHCP options to the hosts when they boot up and send DHCP requests. This helps the network administrators in terms of managing a large number of hosts and assigning IP addresses dynamically rather than statically configuring addresses.

In most organizations, there is a central DHCP server, which assigns configuration parameters to hosts in multiple subnets. Hence, it is not practical to deploy a dedicated DHCP server per subnet. In such cases, **DHCP forwarding** is used, where the router on the subnet acts as a mediator, collects the DHCP messages on the subnet, and sends them to the DHCP server.

In our topology, we will use the DHCP address with the IP address as 10.8.200.100 for the Guest VLAN, which is VLAN 70. Hence, this interface needs to be configured with the `ip helper-address` as follows. Similar configurations can be performed for the Employee VLAN or VLAN 50 also.

```
Router(config)# interface Eth0/0.70
Router(config-subif)# ip helper-address 100.8.200.100
```

Figure 11: Configuring the router for DHCP forwarding

Configuring AP using Cisco Mobility Express

Cisco Mobility Express (**CME**) uses one of the APs to act the WLC for the Wi-Fi LAN. The other APs join this controller as normal APs, using the CAPWAP protocol. The APs in this deployment can act as either a CME capable AP or a normal AP in the CAPWAP mode.

The `show version` command from the console port of the AP is used to find out the current mode of the AP. The output of the command is shown in the following figure:

```
cisco AIR-AP1852E-UXK9 ARMv7 Processor rev 0 (v71) with 997184/525160K bytes of memory.
Processor board ID RFDP2BCR021
AP Running Image : 8.2.100.0
Primary Boot Image : 8.2.100.0
Backup Boot Image : 8.1.106.33
AP Image type : MOBILITY EXPRESS IMAGE       1
AP Configuration : MOBILITY EXPRESS CAPABLE   2
0 Gigabit Ethernet interfaces
```

Figure 12: Checking for Cisco Mobility Express image

In the preceding figure, if the fields in the rectangle marked by 1 and 2 are not present, it means that the AP is running in a CAPWAP mode. The code on the device needs to be changed to enable the Mobility Express features. The show version command output as shown in the following figure implies that although the AP image is mobility express capable, the AP is not allowed to function as the controller in the deployment:

```
cisco AI R-AP1852E-UXK9 ARMv7 Processor rev 0 (v7I) with 997184/726252K bytes of memory.
Processor board ID RFDP2BCR021
AP Running Image : 8.2.101.0
Primary Boot Image : 8.2.100.0
Backup Boot Image : 8.1.106.33
AP Image type : MOBILITY EXPRESS IMAGE        1
AP Configuration : NOT MOBILITY EXPRESS CAPABLE   2
```

Figure 13: A Cisco Mobility Express Controller image

In case the AP image does not support mobility express, the AP image can be upgraded to a mobility express image enabling the mobility express mode using a tftp server as follows:

```
AP# ap-type mobility-express tftp://10.8.1.10/ AIR-AP3800-K9-8-3-102-0.tar
```

Figure 14: Upgrading the AP image

You should verify the tftp server address and the image name in the preceding command for the AP that you are trying to change.

If the AP is to be used in a conventional controller-based deployment, the AP needs to have a CAPWAP image and this can be done by executing the ap-type capwap command on the AP CLI.

Once the APs have the right mobility express image on them, the network operator should start the configuration with the AP that will function as the master controller on the network. When the AP is powered on, it will radiate a SSID that can be used to connect to the AP and configure this.

The laptop to be used for configuration should connect to the `CiscoAirProvision` SSID using the `default` password. The laptop should be configured to get an IP address through DHCP and the AP will assign an IP address. All subsequent configurations can be done using the GUI of the in-built WLC that can be accessed using a browser and opening `http://192.168.1.1`. All subsequent configurations are done from this page:

Figure 15: Cisco Mobility Express GUI

The preceding screen allows the user to set the username and password for the controller. Pressing the **Start** button allows the network administrator to configure the system name, time, NTP server, and other parameters of the system. Note that all APs will get an IP address from the management network DHCP pool configured on this page and the gateway address should be an address of the router on the same broadcast domain:

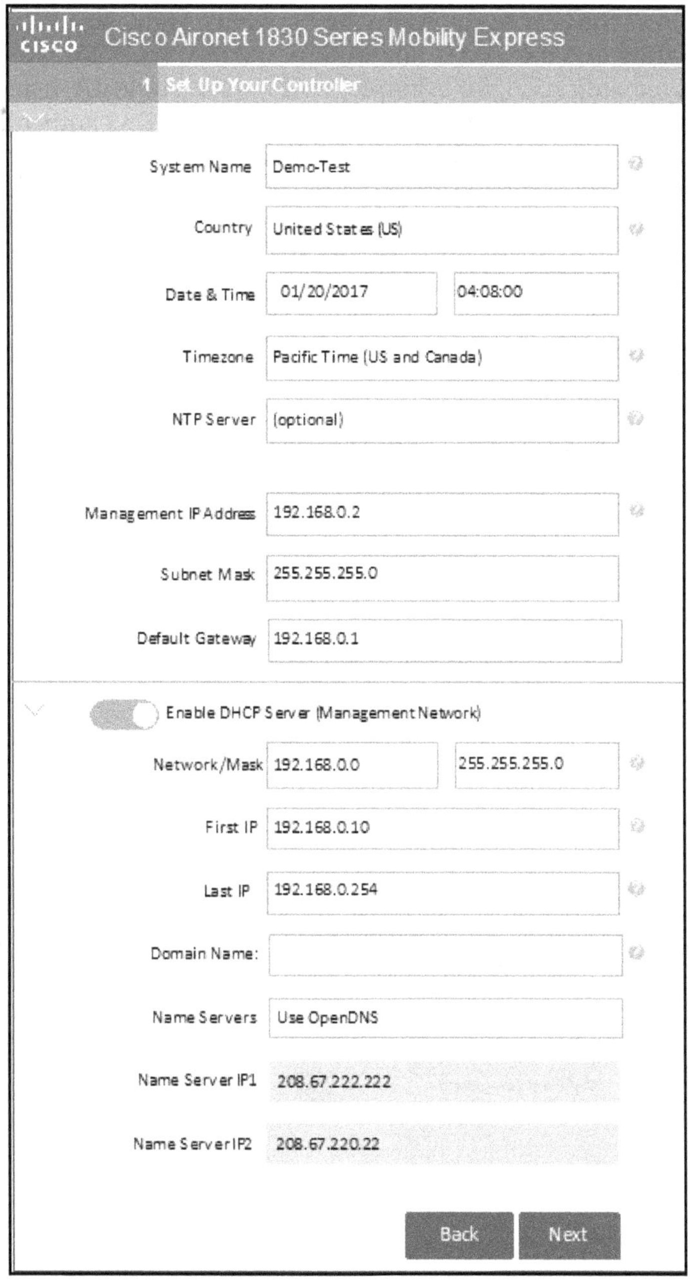

Figure 16: Configuring Cisco Mobility Express Controller

The next screen allows the user to configure the Employee and Guest WLANs and configure their security and the VLAN numbers. A number of options are allowed for employee WLAN authentication, for example, WEP, WPA2, or WPA, using an external RADIUS server. Similarly, the guest WLAN also allows for WPA2 authentication. The Mobility Express also provides an inbuilt captive portal and can be integrated with an external web server for the portal for guest access. A sample screen for configuring the employee VLAN is as shown in the following screenshot. On this screen, the VLAN number for the Employee VLAN should be set to 50, and the IP address should be set to 192.168.1.2/24 with a gateway of 192.168.1.1. The DHCP server address is 100.8.200.100.

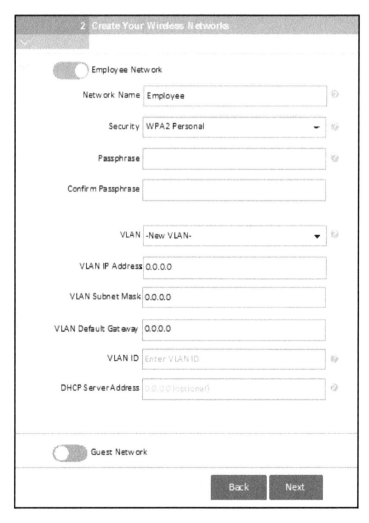

Figure 17: Configuring WLANs using Cisco Mobility Express

The following screen allows the network operator to use predefined RF parameters for standard deployments and these should be good enough for small deployments:

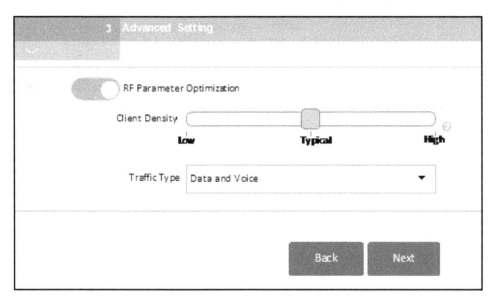

Figure 18: Optimizing WLANs using Cisco Mobility Express

The next screen displays the summary of what has been configured and allows the network admin to verify and save the configurations on the AP, and the AP will reboot and start up with the saved configurations.

Note that the same set of configurations can also be done using the startup wizard from the CLI, although GUI makes it more user-friendly.

The network admin can login into GUI again after the AP is up and use it to monitor the network.

When more APs are added to the Mobility Express domain, they should have the right IOS version. If the new AP does not have the right iOS version, the master AP will download the image from the Cisco support site, and the credentials have to be configured on the system on the master AP page under the **management** I **Software Update** tab on the GUI.

As a final note on Mobility Express, note that the solution provides for redundancy, and if the master controller AP fails, another working AP that is Mobility Express capable will take over the functions of the controller and provide redundancy for configuration and administration of the APs in the domain.

Configuration using the WLC

Mobility Express is designed for small deployments and does not support more than 25 APs. Also, it requires the APs to be on the same broadcast domain, which is not possible in large deployments. Hence, large deployments use an external dedicated WLC that does not have these scalability limitations.

We will describe the deployment method for a large Wi-Fi deployment using a dedicated Cisco 2500 series WLC.

As discussed earlier, the CAPWAP protocol provides the discovery and configuration of the APs in a centralized deployment. Hence, the only configuration required on the APs is an IP address and the WLC IP address so that they can establish the CAPWAP tunnel. This is done using DHCP and DHCP options as discussed earlier. Alternatively, if DHCP options are not available, the DNS server in the enterprise needs to be configured with an entry for the host cisco-capwap-controller.xyz.com in the DNS server with the management IP address of the WLC.

An AP can be configured with up to three WLCs, and the AP will connect them in the order primary, secondary, and tertiary WLC. This enables redundancy in case the WLCs become unavailable.

A sample topology of the centralized deployment using a WLC and 2 APs radiating two separate SSIDs each is shown in the following figure:

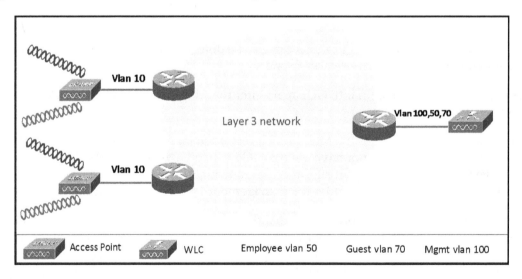

Figure 19: Centralized Wireless LAN Controller

In the preceding figure, there are two LWAPs that are radiating two SSIDs in two different geographical areas: Employee and Guest. Note that there is only one VLAN for the AP to the upstream router, which is the management VLAN. The AP forms a CAPWAP tunnel on this interface and sends all traffic to the WLC. The VLAN number on the uplink port to which the AP is connected could be configured with any VLAN number as long as that VLAN is the native VLAN and sends untagged packets to the AP. We have chosen VLAN 10 for the AP ports in the example. This VLAN could be different at the WLC as the VLAN is a layer 2 technology. We have used VLAN 100 as the management interface for the WLC connectivity and configured this as the native port on the switch interface connecting to the WLC.

Also note that even though the traffic is coming from two different APs at the WLC, there is a single VLAN 50 for Employee traffic, and a single VLAN for Guest traffic, where the traffic from both APs is transmitted back to the network. Since all traffic from the wireless users spread across different APs is centralized at a common place, a consistent policy can be enforced at this common point rather than at different places in the network, simplifying the network configurations and operations.

WLC redundancy

Since a WLC manages multiple APs, the redundancy of the WLC becomes critical for ensuring Wi-Fi service availability. The WLC redundancy is provided in the ways as follows:

- **N+1 WLC redundancy**: In this deployment, a separate WLC is deployed, and all APs are mapped to the WLCs in such a manner that the outage of one AP still ensures that the APs have a redundant configured as a secondary or a tertiary AP. Note that in this deployment, all WLCs are actively managing some APs at a given point in time.
- **N+1 HA WLC redundancy**: This type of deployment ensures a single WLC that is configured as a backup WLC for all APs on the network, with the remaining N WLCs working as the primary WLC for the active APs. Note that the configuration of the backup WLC is not automatic but needs to be managed independently. The advantage of this deployment over the previous one is that in this case, no licenses are needed for the backup WLC.

The two types of deployment are shown in the following figure:

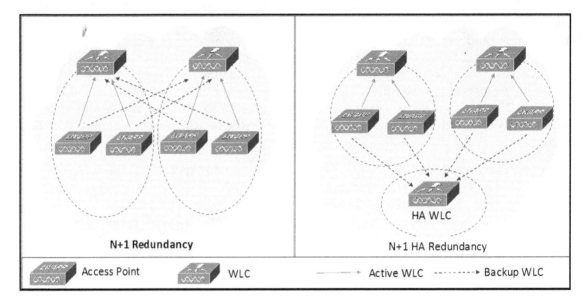

Figure 20: WLC redundancy modes

HA stateful switchover

In the deployments previously discussed, the services will switch over to the backup WLC if the primary or active WLC fails. However, the clients connected to the APs will be disconnected and have to be authenticated again before getting connected once the WLC switchover happens, as there is no synchronization of the state between the WLCs and they work independently of each other. In the HA stateful mode, two WLCs are connected through an onboard redundancy port and they synchronize the working state over this link. Hence, when one of the WLC fails, the APs switch over to the backup WLC without any service disruption. The RPs need to be connected to a layer 2 network, either through a back-to-back cable or on the same wired LAN segment.

The following figure shows the deployment mode of an HA deployment for a WLC:

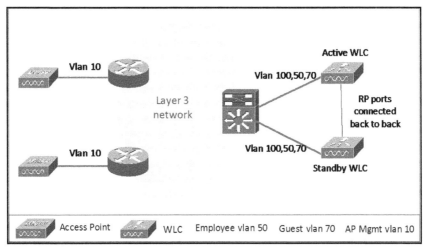

Figure 21: Deploying a WLC for HA

Note in the preceding figure that redundancy ports of the two WLCs are connected back to back. They can also be connected through the switch in this case since there is a common switch. However, this switch can be a point of failure for the entire wireless services. If two switches are available at that location, we can use the two switches in the FHRP mode discussed in the previous chapter and use VLANs as shown in the following figure:

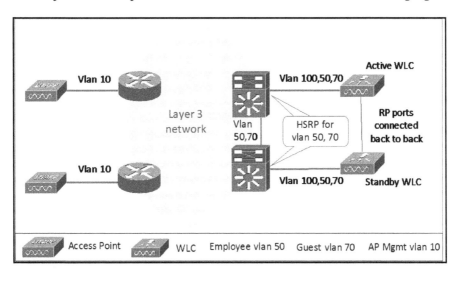

Figure 22: Deploying a WLC for HA using 2 routers

Configuring the WLC deployment

As discussed previously, all the APs are configured through the WLAN controller. The APs in our example will obtain the IP address using DHCP and obtain the WLC address using DHCP options. The APs will establish a CAPWAP tunnel to the controller and will be configured by the WLC with the defined configuration. The WLC will also push the right IOS image to the APs before pushing the configuration.

The switch port to which the AP connects should be configured as an access port in VLAN 10. The default router on that VLAN also has the DHCP forwarding configured to enable the DHCP server to provide the management IP address and the WLC address to the AP.

The WLC configurations can be done using the inbuilt GUI. However, to access the GUI, the WLC needs some basic configuration.

The controller can be configured via the startup utility called **Cisco WLAN Express** that provides step-by-step instructions for configuring the WLC. The WLC can also be configured by CLI by the advanced user or can be configured using the WLC GUI setup wizard. To access the WLAN Express GUI, connect a laptop to any port on the WLC and get the IP address using DHCP. Then, browse to `http://192.168.1.1/` to access the Cisco WLAN Express GUI. Some of the steps to be followed on the GUI are captured in the following figure. The WLAN Express GUI is very similar to the CME GUI described previously for the initial setup:

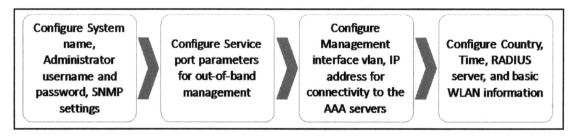

Figure 23: Configuration steps for Wi-Fi deployment using WLC

Once the basic configuration has been done, the WLC will reboot and the WLC console will now be accessed using a different GUI. If the management interface was configured as 92.168.0.200, the GUI can be accessed by opening the browser on a PC connected to the network and opening http://192.168.0.200. This URL opens the monitoring GUI, which can be changed to the configuration GUI by clicking on the **Advanced** link on the top-right of the screen to access the GUI as follows.

Once the advanced GUI comes up, the admin configures the VLANs to be used for the user traffic. These are VLANs 50 and 70 in our case. This is done by configuring the interfaces on the WLC. Navigate to the **Controller | Interfaces** tab to view the active interfaces. Then, click on the **New...** button on the right as highlighted in the following figure:

Figure 24: Create a new WLC interface

The **Interface Name** and **VLAN Identifier** are defined on this page as shown in the following screenshot. These are configured as **VLAN Id**50 for **Employee** and **VLAN Id**70 for **Guest** traffic:

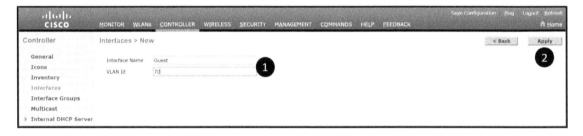

Figure 25: Define a new WLC interface

Once the configuration is applied and the interface is created, the system goes back to the main **Interfaces** tab. The admin has to navigate to the **Edit** interfaces tab by clicking on the name of the interface created to define the IP address of this interface and other configurations such as the DHCP server. This is shown in the following figure :

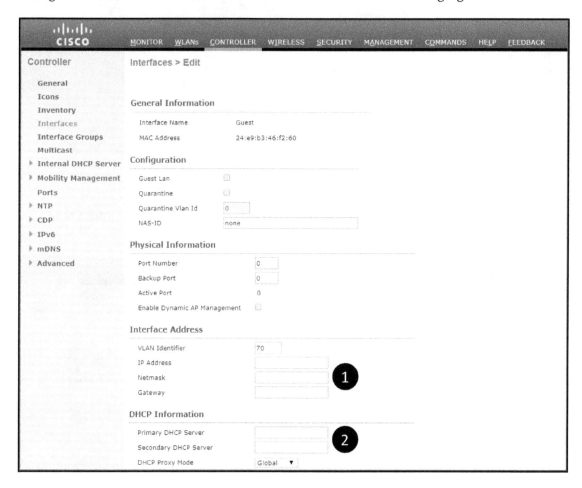

Figure 26: Configure the WLC interface

Note that the IP addresses of the interfaces have to correspond to the VLAN numbers and IP addresses defined on the switch port to which the WLC is connected. Once the interfaces have been created, the WLANs need to be created and mapped to these interfaces to carry data traffic in the native form (de-encapsulated from the CAPWAP tunnels) back to the network. Navigate to the **WLANs** page and the screen changes to one shown as follows, where all configured WLANs are displayed. Create a new WLAN by clicking on the highlighted **Go** button in the following figure:

Figure 27: Create a new WLAN

On a new page, fill in the WLAN details such as the **Profile Name** and the SSID, as shown in the following figure::

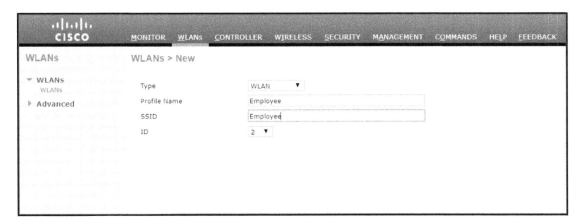

Figure 27: Define the new WLAN

Once the WLAN is created by clicking on the **Apply** button previously, the main WLAN page is displayed. The admin then maps the WLAN to the interface created before on the screen, as shown in the following figure and enables this SSID:

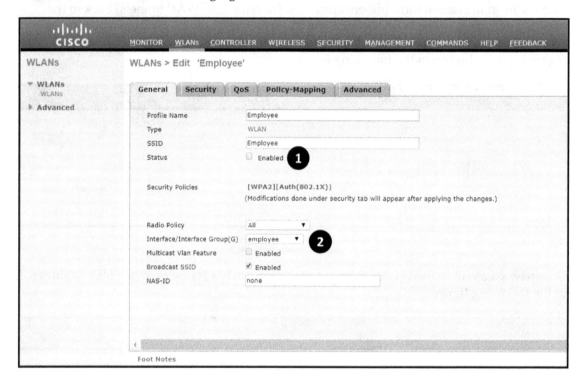

Figure 29: Configure the WLAN

We had already created the `Employee` interface that was mapped to VLAN 50. Hence, the WLAN named `Employee` is applied to the `Employee` interface as shown in the preceding figure:

Additional security parameters for the WLAN are also set on this page by moving to the **Security** tab, as follows:

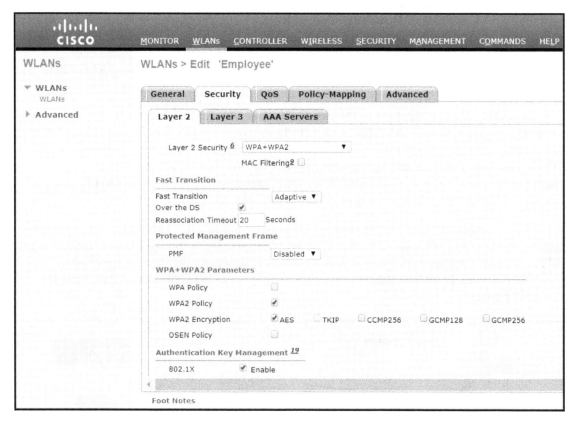

Figure 30: Edit the WLAN security

The remaining parameters can be left at default for the initial phase of deployment.

If you are using a redundant controller, ensure that it has the similar configuration applied and saved to prevent any erroneous behavior.

FlexConnect mode

In the centralized mode, the traffic from the wireless users is tunneled to the data center, where the WLC is located. However, some of the services are delivered locally at the branch office in an enterprise. Tunnelling traffic to a central site will mean that the traffic will have to come back to the branch for local services over the WAN, thus causing artificial congestion on the WAN link and also degrading user experience by causing additional latency.

The FlexConnect mode does away the need to tunnel all traffic and provides the ability to switch traffic from certain WLANs locally at the AP uplink while continuing to provide the AP management functions through the centralized WLC. In a FlexConnect deployment, a WLC is not required at each branch, and the APs use the central WLC for their configuration and control traffic. The FlexConnect mode can be configured to provide services at the branch office even though the WAN link has gone down.

A sample deployment in which certain traffic is switched locally is shown in the following figure, where traffic for local servers can be switched locally at the AP like an autonomous AP, and traffic for the central services in the DC can be sent to the WLC through the CAPWAP tunnel. Note that the control traffic between the WLC and the AP will use the CAPWAP tunnel:

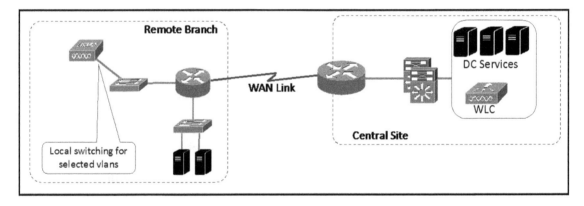

Figure 31: Switching locally at the branch

FlexConnect APs are capable of supporting the following switching modes concurrently, on a per-WLAN basis:

- **Local switched**: Locally-switched WLANs map wireless user traffic to discrete VLANs via 802.1Q trunking to the uplink router or switch. All control traffic is sent to the WLC through the CAPWAP tunnel.
- **Central switched**: Central switched WLANs tunnel both the wireless user traffic and all control traffic via CAPWAP to the centralized WLC.

A practical scenario will be where only the Guest traffic is tunneled to the central site for enforcing internet policy and all Employee traffic is treated at par with the other wired traffic.

The recommended link characteristics of the WAN link between the branch and the WLC location for efficient operation of a FlexConnect deployment are as follows:

- Latency less than 100 ms
- A bandwidth of at least 128 kbps for up to eight APs at the branch
- Link MTU set to a minimum of 500 bytes

Configuring the APs in FlexConnect mode

It is a common practice to allow the Guest VLAN come to the central site but use the Employee VLAN in a FlexConnect mode. We will describe the process to allow the Employee WLAN traffic to be switched on VLAN 50 on the AP interface connecting to the upstream switch. The control traffic and the Guest WLAN traffic will continue to reach the WLC.

The WLANs that need to be enabled for FlexConnect switching should have the **Flexconnect Local Switching** box checked during the creation of the WLAN in the **Advanced** tab. This box is highlighted in the following screenshot. In our case, this has to be done for the WLAN named **Employee**:

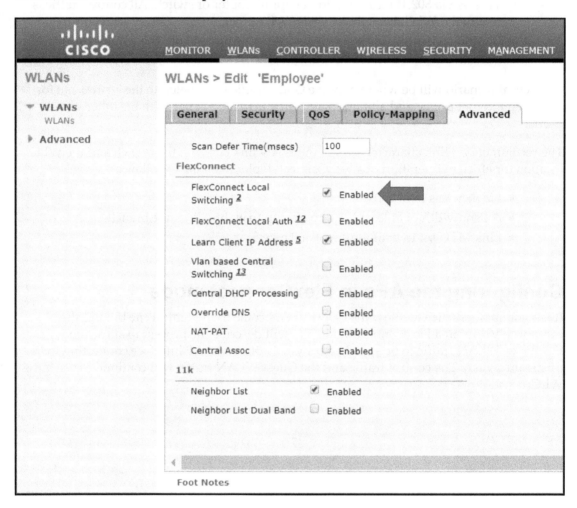

Figure 32: Configuring the WLAN for FlexConnect

As a next step, all the APs that need to be enabled for FlexConnect, which will be the APs in the remote branch should have the mode as FlexConnect:

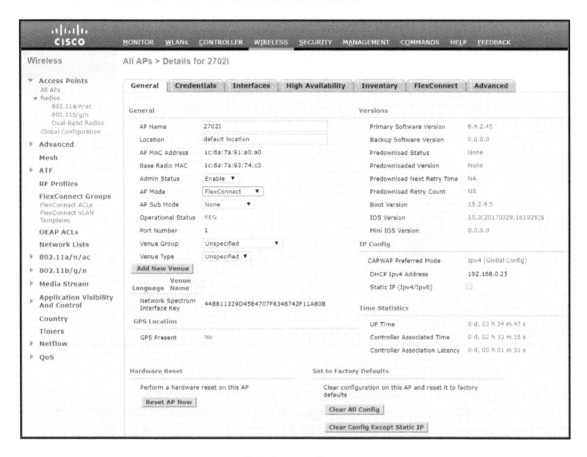

Figure 33: Configuring the AP for FlexConnect

Also, the branch APs should have the VLANs defined in the **FlexConnect** tab as shown in the following figure. The management VLAN should be mapped as the native VLAN. The other VLANs are mapped by clicking on the VLAN mappings button where you need to assign VLAN numbers to the WLANs that need to be switched out locally at the branch:

Figure 34: Configuring the AP FlexConnect features

As a final step, if you need a large deployment, create a Flexconnect group and add the APs to this group. The page is accessed by navigating through **Wireless** | **Flexconnect Groups** | **Add New**. Once a new group is added, it can be edited by clicking on the name of the group as shown in the following screenshot. New APs can be added to this FlexConnect group using the **Flexconnect AP** link in the screenshot and adding new APs from the dropdowns:

Figure 35: Creating FlexConnect groups

It is a good practice to keep the employee VLAN locally switched in the branches so that the traffic does not hairpin across the WAN and the branch users can access the local services even in case of WAN link failures.

We covered three different modes of deployment of Wi-Fi networks in the enterprise, including the Cisco Mobility Express, WLC mode, and FlexConnect mode. As a general recommendation for deploying Wi-Fi network, it is recommended to use the centralized mode, where the number of APs is more than 10. Also, if there are remote branches that are large in size and have a large number of APs, it is recommended to deploy a separate WLC at the branch office. This prevents the traffic from the branches from coming to the central site WLC over the WAN, thereby reducing network delays. Alternatively, the network designer can think of deploying the FlexConnect mode of deployment.

Summary

We discussed in this chapter about the basic concepts of wireless networks and the various terminologies used in the RF domain that will help the network designer and operator communicate effectively with the RF engineers who generally do the RF site surveys for WLAN deployments.

We also discussed the different Wi-Fi standards and discussed the considerations for using 802.11 ac and 802.11n networks in dual bands for better performance. The chapter finally discussed the different modes of deployment of the APs in the enterprise. Even though the centralized mode of deployment requires additional network element in the form of a WLC, there are multiple advantages of using the centralized mode of deployment that justify the cost of the additional WLCs.

The next chapter will focus on the different WAN technologies deployed in an enterprise network.

6
Understanding and Configuring WAN Technologies

"Eventually everything connects - people, ideas, objects. The quality of the connections is the key to quality per se."

- Charles Eames

Organizations have a **Local Area Network** (**LAN**) at each office. These networks need to be connected to each other to form a single network where every endpoint on the network can communicate with every other endpoint, irrespective of the physical location, within the confines of the security policy of the organization. These LANs are connected by wide area links, and are known as **Wide Area Networks** (**WANs**).

This chapter will discuss the following topics:

- Different types of WAN technologies
- Virtual Private Networks (VPNs)
- The internet as the WAN
- Design considerations for choosing a WAN technology

The chapter also introduces **Wide Area Acceleration Services** (**WAAS**), used for WAN connectivity optimization.

Considerations for a WAN design

A WAN is a network that connects other networks over large distances. A WAN is typically owned by a service provider, and organizations pay the lease rentals or usage charges to use these links. The WAN could be a dedicated link between two sites, or might be a shared network that is used to provide connectivity between networks of an organization at different geographical locations.

Each type of WAN link has its own advantages and disadvantages. Thus, choosing the right technology for a WAN link is fundamental to obtaining a balance between the cost incurred on the connectivity, and the business benefits this connectivity provides to the organization. Some of the main factors to be considered for the WAN design are as follows:

- **Cost**: The fundamental question to be answered for any business is the capital required for a project, and the benefits that investment would provide. The cost of a WAN link varies drastically with the type of the WAN technology being deployed, and therefore it is one of the primary considerations for choosing the WAN technology.
- **Permanency**: Another factor to be considered for choosing the WAN technology is the duration for which the link is required. Some links in the organization would be static and permanent, while some other links might just be required for specific purposes; for example, providing connectivity from an exhibition center back to the corporate network for sales demonstrations. Permanent links can justify more investment compared to links that are transient.
- **Type of data**: Another factor that has a lot of bearing on the choice of the WAN technology is the type of data that will be carried on the link. A link that carries voice or video data needs to be very stable, with very stringent requirements on latency, jitter, and packet loss, while links that carry just email traffic don't have these stringent requirements. Another way of looking at the type of data that is to be transported on the link is the value of that data from a security perspective. If the data to be carried is confidential or of high value to the organization, the links have to be private and not shared, while less sensitive data can be carried over shared infrastructures. Alternatively, encryption of links can be a potential technology choice for the network designer.
- **Resiliency requirements**: This refers to the value of the link and the cost of downtime that the organization would incur if the link went down. If the link is core to the business operations, and the connectivity failure would result in business disruptions, the link should be highly available, and redundancy needs to be built in for this connectivity.

- **Type of connectivity required**: The type of connectivity refers to the topology that would be built over the WAN link. Some WAN technologies provide a point-to-point connectivity between two sites, while some other WAN technologies are capable of providing point-to-multipoint connectivity across the WAN to multiple sites.
- **Operational aspects**: The choice of the WAN technology also depends upon the operational aspects of the technology being used. Every organization would want to have clearly defined roles and responsibilities between the internal IT team and the provider of the WAN link. This can further be extended to SLAs that each type of link, and the service provider, can offer. A clear demarcation point for troubleshooting and SLA management influences the choice of WAN technologies used by the enterprises.

The choice of WAN technology would always be a choice between the conflicting requirements as shown in the following figure:

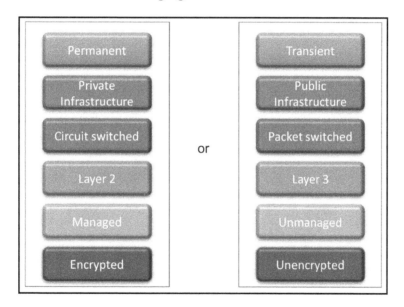

Figure 1: Considerations for a WAN

We will discuss the different types of WAN technologies, with the preceding factors as a reference, to evaluate their suitability within an organization.

WAN technology choices

Conventional WAN technologies operate at the physical and data link layers of the OSI stack. This means that the WAN service provider does not take part in IP routing, but just carries IP packets from the source to the destination for the WAN that connects IP networks. The WAN infrastructure could be built using a private infrastructure or using a public infrastructure. It needs to be emphasized that although the WAN infrastructure is owned by the **service providers** (**SPs**), the SP operates at different layers of the OSI stack for different types of WAN. It is only a part of the infrastructure that is given to an enterprise for the right to use against a fee.

As an example, consider a transmission network infrastructure of a national service provider. That transmission infrastructure would consist of a large number of optical devices and multiplexers that would groom several small data pipes into a larger data pipes that would be carried across the SP infrastructure and split into its constituent data pipes, to be handed over to the end users. The following figure shows a simplistic view of a small part of the transmission network:

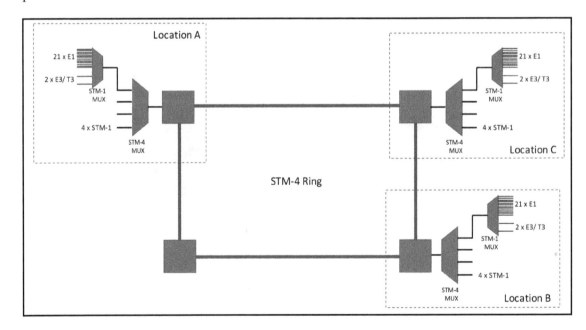

Figure 2: Sample transmission network

An organization takes **E1** bandwidths (2 Mbps) from **Location A** to **Location B**, and **Location A** to **Location C**. The SP would groom the E1s of the customer with multiple other E1 links of other customers but carry them in a **Time Division Multiplexed** (**TDM**) stream, an STM-4 link in the example, over the transmission backbone. Even though the link was shared across physical links and devices on the network, this is dedicated bandwidth that is provisioned on the SP network. Such links are called **leased lines**, and are the most common form of WAN links besides dark fiber connectivity that is generally used within small distances as the last mile.

Another form of WAN connectivity is where the bandwidth is not dedicated, but is available on demand, and a channel is created to send data from the source to the destination. One can compare this to a telephone hotline which is always connected to a normal **Public Switched Telephone Network** (**PSTN**), where a channel is created only when you dial the destination number. In such types of connectivity, the user signals to the service provider, and the service provider blocks a channel to the destination for the duration of the conversation, and the channel is freed after the source signals that the conversation is over. These types of connections can be PSTN or ISDN dial-up connections using modems, where two devices use the PSTN network for communications. Note that these connections are limited to very low speeds and are generally used below 128 Kbps.

We have discussed permanent and signaled connections that were multiplexed in the time domain, and called TDM technologies, the switching in TDM being referred to as circuit switching. Circuit switching is inherently inefficient for data usage. This is because in circuit switching, a certain channel with a predefined data capacity is blocked for a user for the duration of the call, regardless of the fact that the user is sending data at a given point in time or not. Data traffic is *bursty* in nature and is seldom continuous (other than some sort of continuous bit rate streaming). Thus, there was a need for a technology that would use **statistical multiplexing** and switch packets rather than time slots. This led to the evolution of packet-switched backbones, such as **Frame Relay** (**FR**) and **Asynchronous Transfer Mode** (**ATM**), where the user could send traffic to the destination, without having a dedicated bandwidth at all times. Technologies such as FR and ATM established a connection between the source and the destination by signaling through the service provider network about the nature of traffic that would be sent on the connection so that the network can reserve the resources to allow this data transfer. These are called connection-oriented packet-switched technologies. These technologies were prevalent till the last decade but are fading away slowly. These technologies were called **packet-switching technologies**.

Packet-switching technologies, such as ATM and FR, used logical circuit identifiers unlike physical circuit identifiers, for PSTN connections at the last mile. The last mile connection carried analog signals to the SP network in the case of PSTN, or digital signals for ISDN, FR, and ATM. Digital signals could be used to create sub-channels on the physical circuit, similar to the use of VLANs on a single RJ45 cable. This gave the users the advantage of using a single last mile physical cable to carry multiple connections, while allowing the user to burst up to the maximum bandwidth supported by the physical medium on each channel. This is depicted in the following figure, where the rectangles in the graphs denote units of data for each channel/circuit. Note that in the circuit switching example, a circuit was unutilized if there was no data to be sent on that circuit, while in the packet-switched example on the right, each circuit could burst up to the maximum available link bandwidth, and utilize the unused bandwidth:

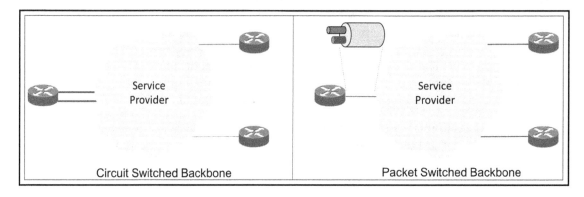

Figure 3: Circuit switching versus packet switching

Lastly, some organizations can also use the internet as a WAN link either to connect to the internet directly, or as an overlay creating a GRE tunnel using the internet backbone simulating a point-to-point link. A summary of the different WAN technologies is shown in the following figure:

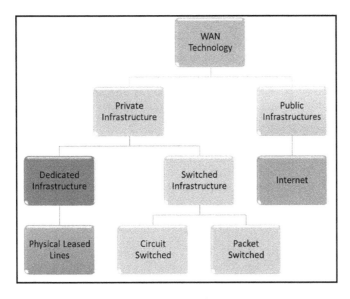

Figure 4: Types of WAN

Configuring WAN serial links

WAN links are generally used on serial interfaces and use different data link layer encapsulations depending on the type of the SP backbone. We will consider two types of encapsulations in this section: an encapsulation used for a 1:1 mapping of a physical to a logical link, and another for multiplexing multiple logical links into a single physical link.

Serial links with PPP/HDLC encapsulation

A WAN link is generally a serial link, which means that the data is transmitted serially on the wire as electrical or optical signals depending upon the media type, and there is no contention as in Ethernet to set the channel to avoid any collision of frames.

The default data link encapsulation on a serial interface for a Cisco router is the **High-Level Data Link Control** (**HDLC**) protocol, which is a Cisco proprietary protocol for sending data on synchronous serial links. Cisco HDLC also provides a simple control protocol called **Serial Line Address Resolution Protocol** (**SLARP**) to maintain serial link keepalives, which helps in detecting the link state as being up or down.

Each router sends periodic keepalives to the router at the remote end of the serial link at a frequency that can be configured using the CLI. The link is declared down after loss of three keepalive messages.

The most common form of serial link is an **E1** port that can also be a channelized card. This means that the **E1** bit rate can be split into 32 time slots. The **E1** frame consists of 32 timeslots of 64 kbps each, and the time slots are numbered 0 through 31. Time slot 0 is reserved for the delimiter and serves to identify the beginning of the timeslots. Thus, 31 of the timeslots can be used in an **E1** to carry 31 independent bit streams in a time division multiplexed manner. Each timeslot can be used independently of the others, and each of the timeslots is treated as a separate interface.

If there is no need to identify different streams, then the delimiter in timeslot 0 is not required, as the bit stream is a continuous bit stream, and thus all 32 timeslots are used as one single whole. This is called the unframed structure of an **E1**, as opposed to the framed structure that carries timeslot 0 with the delimiter. This is configured on the interface using the CLI commands.

The following figure shows the configuration of the **E1** port on a router:

```
Router# configure terminal
Router(config)# controller e1 2/0/0
Router(config-controller)# clock source line
Router(config-controller)# linecode hdb3
Router(config-controller)# channel-group 0 unframed
Router(config-controller)# exit
Router(config)# interface serial 2/0/0:0
Router(config-if)# encapsulation hdlc
Router(config-if)# ip address 10.1.1.1 255.255.255.252
Router(config-if)# exit
Router(config)# exit
Router#
```

Figure 5: Configuration sample for an E1 port

In the preceding example, we had the channelized e1 card at slot 2/0, and we configured port 0 of the card as an unframed e1, meaning all 32 timeslots can be used with an effective line rate of *32 * 64 kbps = 2048kbps*. We used HDLC encapsulation for the serial link.

To configure the controller into smaller data rates, we have to use individual timeslots, as shown in the following figure:

```
Router# configure terminal
Router(config)# controller e1 2/0/0
Router(config-controller)# clock source line
Router(config-controller)# linecode hdb3
Router(config-controller)# channel-group 1 timeslots 1
Router(config-controller)# exit
Router(config)# interface serial 2/0/0:1
Router(config-if)# encapsulation ppp
Router(config-if)# ip address 10.1.1.1 255.255.255.252
Router(config-if)# exit
Router(config)# exit
Router#
```

Figure 6: Configuration sample for using sub-E1 speeds

In the preceding example, we used only one timeslot, timeslot 1, which is a 64 kbps channel, to create an interface. Since the channel group number was 1, the interface is numbered as serial 2/0/0:1, and this is a 64 kbps interface. We used PPP encapsulation for this interface in the configuration.

The most common form of encapsulation used on serial interfaces is the **Point-to-Point protocol** (**PPP**). This is an IETF standard and defined in RFC 1661. PPP is a standard protocol used to send data over synchronous serial links. PPP also provides a family of protocols, such as the **Link Control Protocol** (**LCP**), for negotiating properties of the link, and **Internet Protocol Control Protocol** (**IPCP**) to negotiate the properties of the IP payload to be carried on the link. To configure a serial interface on a router, we need to configure the encapsulation as PPP, and define the IP address on the link. The routing protocols to run on the WAN links have already been discussed in Chapter 4, *Understanding and Configuring Campus Network Technologies*.

If the reader uses PPP encapsulation, the loss of five keepalives causes the interface to go down. The frequency of the keepalives is configured using the keepalive command in the interface configuration mode, and the default frequency of the keepalive messages is 10 seconds.

PPP also supports authentication at layer 2, and would allow the data link to be operational only after authentication of the peer at the remote end of the link. PPP supports three protocols for authentication:

- **Password Authentication Protocol** (**PAP**): PAP authentication uses a clear text username and password to authenticate the peer

- **Challenge Handshake Authentication Protocol (CHAP)**: CHAP authentication is a three-way handshake, and the node is challenged to send a password in an encrypted form upon being challenged by the peer
- **Microsoft Challenge Handshake Authentication Protocol (MS-CHAP)**: MS-CHAP is the Microsoft version of CHAP

The PPP authentication is configured using the PPP authentication command in the interface configuration mode.

FR encapsulation

FR encapsulation is different from the framed **E1** encapsulation. We have seen in the previous section that we can create separate 64 kbps links on a single controller. The point to note is that these channels are multiplexed in time, and if one channel is not being utilized by the user, that bandwidth is still reserved, and cannot be used by another user who is using another channel. Frame relay encapsulation creates logical channels and allows the use of spare bandwidth on the free channels. Each logical circuit on an FR interface is identified by a **Data Link Channel Identifier (DLCI)** number. The FR encapsulation is configured on a router, as shown in the following figure:

```
Router(config)# interface Serial0/0
Router(config-if)# encapsulation frame-relay
Router(config-if)# interface Serial0/0.2 point-to-point
Router(config-subif)# ip address 10.10.10.1 255.255.255.252
Router(config-subif)# frame-relay interface-dlci 50
Router(config-subif)# interface Serial0/0.3 point-to-point
Router(config-subif)# ip address 10.10.12.1 255.255.255.252
Router(config-subif)# frame-relay interface-dlci 70
Router(config-subif)# interface Serial0/0.4 point-to-point
Router(config-subif)# exit
```

Figure 7: Configuration sample for a FR interface

In the preceding example, we configured a single serial interface serial 0/0 into two sub-interfaces using frame relay encapsulation, and treated them as two different point-to-point links.

FR encapsulation is generally used when multiple branches are terminating at a single router to minimize the number of physical links, and to utilize the unused bandwidth from other logical links.

Multilink PPP

Multilink PPP (**MLPPP**) is used to create a bundle of links, and treat them as a single link at the network layer. This helps reduce the number of interfaces that have to be configured at the network layer and reduces the protocol state on the router. MLPPP performs the fragmenting, reassembling, and sequencing of datagrams across multiple PPP links, and creates a single bundle with $n*2$ Mbps bandwidth. MLPPP is the opposite of FR encapsulation, as shown in the following figure:

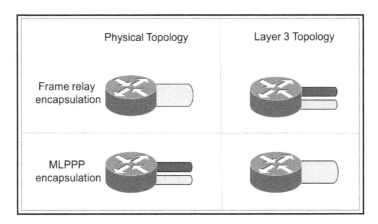

Figure 8: Multilink and FR encapsulation

An MLPPP link is configured as per the following code block:

```
Router(config)# interface multilink 10
Router(config-if)# ip address 10.0.2.1 255.255.255.252
Router(config-if)# ppp multilink
Router(config-if)# ppp multilink group 10
Router(config-if)# ppp multilink min-links 2 mandatory
Router(config-if)# exit
Router(config)# interface serial 0/0
Router(config-if)# encapsulation ppp
Router(config-if)# ppp multilink
Router(config-if)# ppp multilink group 10
Router(config)# interface serial 0/1
Router(config-if)# encapsulation ppp
Router(config-if)# ppp multilink
Router(config-if)# ppp multilink group 10
```

Figure 9: Configuration sample for a multilink interface

In the preceding configuration, two serial links are configured into a single multilink bundle, and that bundle is assigned an IP address. Also, the multilink is configured for a configuration that if the number of links in the bundle goes below 2, the bundle would be deactivated. This is useful in situations where it is better to shut down a link rather than give degraded performance on a lower bandwidth than required by the applications.

Configuring overlay P2P links

Sometimes the internet is used as the network to create a point-to-point link as an overlay. This is done using technologies such as **Generic Routing Encapsulation** (**GRE**), where an IP packet is used as the payload and is encapsulated within another IP header to be transported from the source to the destination. The outer IP header transports the actual IP packet payload from the source to the destination on the basis of the source and destination address fields of the outer header. This is used to create overlay circuits over routed networks such as the internet. The payload packet is "tunneled" through the layer 3 network, and hence this is also known as tunneling, with the interface so created referred to as a tunnel interface. A tunnel can be treated as a single hop, and can be used to run other routing protocols over this tunnel like any other interface. It is best to avoid tunnels, except in extreme cases, and use static routing as the preferred mode of routing over the tunnel interface.

A tunnel interface needs to be defined on the routers at each end of the tunnel. The tunnel interface has a source and destination interfaces that are the IP addresses of any interface on the source and the destination routers. The tunnels have to be configured on both the source and the destination routers for traffic to flow across the tunnel.

Keepalive packets can be sent over the tunnels to maintain the status of the tunnel, and declare the tunnel down on the loss of a predefined number of keepalives. Let us consider a sample topology, as shown in the following figure. Routers **R1** and **R2** are the default gateways for their respective LANs and have the loopback addresses, as shown in the figure. Also, the loopback addresses are routed over the WAN cloud and reachable from each router:

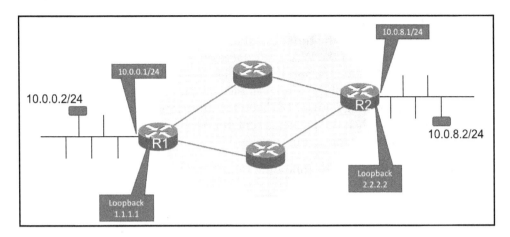

Figure 10: Sample network requiring a tunnel

Since the LAN networks have private IP addresses, they will not be routed over the public cloud. Hence, a tunnel is created over the cloud using the configurations, as shown in the following figure:

```
R1(config)# interface tunnel 0
R1(config-if)# bandwidth 1000
R1(config-if)# keepalive 3 7
R1(config-if)# tunnel source 1.1.1.1
R1(config-if)# tunnel destination 2.2.2.2
R1(config-if)# tunnel key 1000
R1(config-if)# tunnel mode gre ip
R1(config-if)# ip mtu 1400
R1(config-if)# ip address 10.0.1.1 255.255.255.252
R1(config-if)# exit
R1(config)# ip route 10.0.8.0 255.255.255.0 10.0.1.2

R2(config)# interface tunnel 10
R2(config-if)# bandwidth 1000
R2(config-if)# keepalive 3 7
R2(config-if)# tunnel source 2.2.2.2
R2(config-if)# tunnel destination 1.1.1.1
R2(config-if)# tunnel key 1000
R2(config-if)# tunnel mode gre ip
R2(config-if)# ip mtu 1400
R2(config-if)# ip address 10.0.1.2 255.255.255.252
R2(config-if)# exit
R2(config)# ip route 10.0.0.0 255.255.255.0 10.0.1.1
```

Figure 11: Configuration sample for creating an IP tunnel

Note in the preceding configuration that we have used the loopback interfaces as the source and the destination interfaces of the tunnel, as that interface will always be up and reachable as long as even one of the WAN interfaces on the router is up. The tunnel interface is also given an IP address, and the tunnel is treated as an interface on the router. We have also defined the MTU of the tunnel as 1400, as the GRE encapsulation will add some overheads, and by setting a lower MTU on the tunnel interface, the packet length will be within the MTU limits when the packet is sent out on the physical interface. This will avoid any fragmentation of the packet in the cloud.

The logical topology is shown in the following figure:

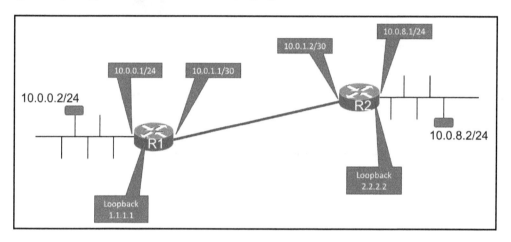

Figure 12: Logical topology after tunnel creation

The following figure shows the additional encapsulation that is added by the routers to transport the network when an IP packet is sent from the host **10.0.0.2** to **10.0.8.2**:

	Overlay IP Header		IP Header	
Source host to R1			SA: 10.0.0.2 DA: 10.0.8.2	IP Payload
R1 to R2	SA: 1.1.1.1 DA: 2.2.2.2	GRE Header	SA: 10.0.0.2 DA: 10.0.8.2	IP Payload
R2 to Destination host			SA: 10.0.0.2 DA: 10.0.8.2	IP Payload

Figure 13: Tunnel encapsulation and overheads

Note from the preceding figure that any additional encapsulation increases the size of the packet to be carried on the network. Therefore, if the MTU on the SP network is limited, the original payload should be restricted so that the total packet size with the additional headers is within the SP MTU.

Virtual private networks

Organizations build networks to meet their IT networking needs. Each network carries data and applications that are specific to that organization only. Hence, the networks so built are private to that extent. Building a network that is restricted to a campus is manageable from a cost perspective, as the distances are small, and fiber can be laid to connect the various buildings within a campus. The challenge is when the connectivity is required over long distances. Every organization cannot set up a private network covering such large distances, as it is very capital intensive. Thus, the organizations use the services of a service provider who provides connectivity services. The services so provided are such that the SP infrastructure is logically partitioned into small blocks that are dedicated to each organization. Such networks, though built on public infrastructures, are virtually private, and are known as VPNs.

The simplest form of such a case is where an organization leases a pair of fibers from a number of fiber pairs in an optical fiber cable. This is generally called **fiber leasing**, and is not the preferred approach for smaller organizations, purely because of cost implications. This is because the capacity of a pair of fiber runs can scale up to multiples of Gbps, using technologies such as **Dense Wavelength Division Multiplexing** (**DWDM**), and an organization would be using that fiber to a limited capacity.

An alternative to this is what we discussed during our discussions in the previous sections on how smaller bandwidths are provisioned by an SP over its transmission network. This can be done by the SP, either using **Time Division Multiplexing** (**TDM**) techniques, such as the build-up of an E1 or a STM-1 link over large distances, or by using DWDM by providing a wavelength from the multiple wavelengths used by the SP on the core network. Smaller organizations generally take TDM circuits, and very large global organizations would opt for a DWDM wavelength.

SPs also offer VPN services that are in the packet-switching domain. For example, at the data link layer, SPs offer layer 2 VPN services, and at the network layer, SPs offer layer 3 VPN services to their customers. Some SPs also offer services such as dial backup services. **Multi Protocol Label Switching** (**MPLS**) is a technology used by SPs to offer a lot of these services, and we will discuss these services in more detail.

A fundamental feature of the VPN services at layer 2 and preceding is that there is an underlay network of the service provider, and the SP or the organization builds an overlay network topology using specific protocols and technologies to simulate a VPN. The P2P GRE links discussed earlier are an example of how an overlay P2P link is built over an underlying routed layer 3 network of the service provider.

Layer 2 VPNs

A layer 2 VPN, as the name suggests, is a link where layer 2 frames are carried transparently from one end to the other. This means that the layer 2 frames are tunneled across the service provider backbone network, by using additional encapsulation headers, and the native layer 2 frames of the user are handed back at the other end of the link. As an example, consider the network shown in the following figure. The cloud comprises a number of networking devices of the service provider network, which are interconnected. The layer 2 frames handed over to the SP at point **A** on the network are transported over the SP network and handed over to the user at point **B**:

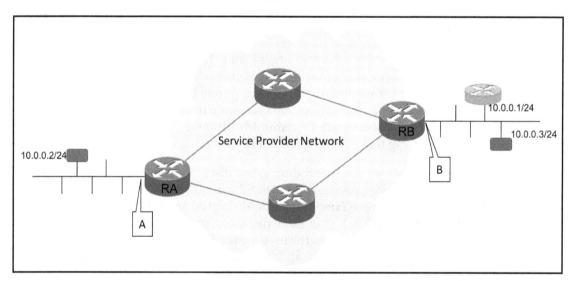

Figure 14: Sample topology requiring a layer 2 VPN

In the preceding figure, point **A** is an interface on the router **RA**, which is a service provider device. Similarly, point **B** is an interface on the SP router **RB**. If we consider an Ethernet LAN at both ends of the layer 2 VPN provided by the SP, the hosts at location **A** can have a default gateway router at location **B**, as all frames including ARP and layer 2 broadcast frames would be transported transparently by the SP. Also note that the interfaces on the routers don't have an IP address, as they operate only at layer 2. This layer 2 VPN simulates a LAN that is extending beyond geographic locations.

Note that a layer 2 VPN can be between the same type of interface only at both ends, as layer 2 frames are specific to the interface type. However, there are some parameters that can be changed between the two ends. As an example, the port at point **A** might be a fast Ethernet port while the port at point **B** could be a GigE port. Similarly, the physical ports could be fiber at one end and copper at the other.

More so, if we create a layer 2 VPN using VLANs, and treat the links at point **A** and **B** as trunk ports, we can create an L2 VPN on one specific VLAN, say VLAN 100 at point **A**, and carry the frames transparently as vlan 200 to the LAN at location **B**, which is also assumed to be a trunk port. The other VLANs can be handled differently on the routers **RA** and **RB**, as each VLAN processing is different. This is called **Ethernet Relay Service (ERS)** by the service provider.

Another form of this service is called **Ethernet Wire Service (EWS)**, where all VLANs within the trunk port handed over to the router **RA** are carried transparently to **RB** and handed out to the user again as a trunk port. In this case, there is no VLAN translation, as the entire port is treated as a single entity.

We have discussed the L2 VPNs in which we carried layer 2 frames from one point to another, and simulated a point-to-point link across the SP backbone. These are called **Point-to-Point (P2P)** services. There is another layer 2 VPN service, where we use the SP network to simulate a LAN switch. In this case, we can have multiple endpoints of the L2 VPN, and all ports behave as though they are connected to a single physical Ethernet switch. These services are called **Point-to-Multi Point (P2MP)** services. The vlan translation can still happen over the SP network, as discussed. These services are called Point-to-multipoint VPNs, and are delivered by using **Virtual Private LAN Service (VPLS)** over MPLS SP backbones.

The following figure shows the comparison of the P2P and P2MP types of services:

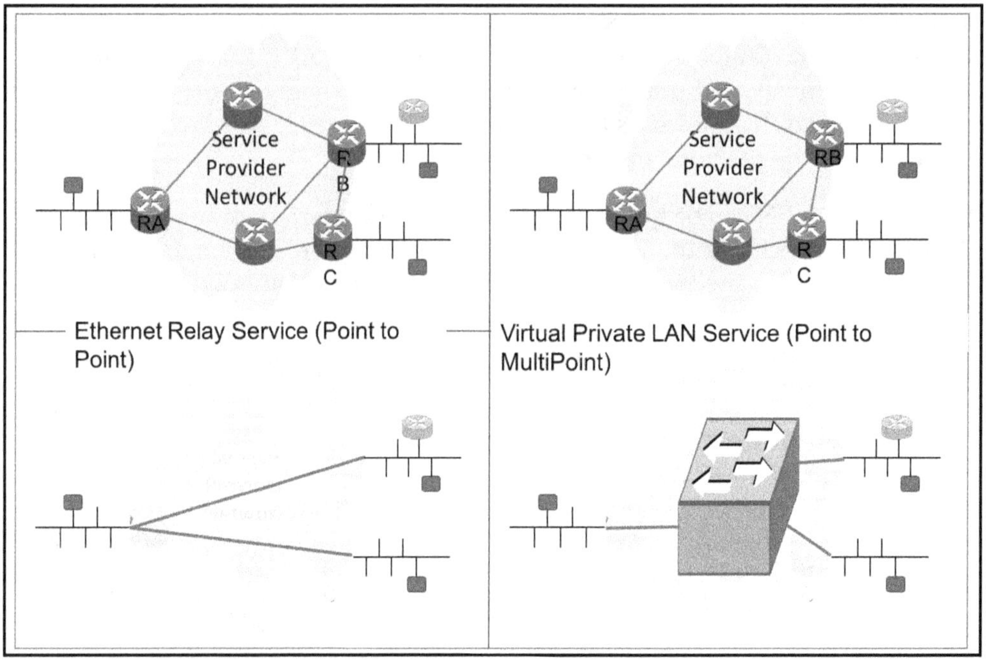

Figure 15: P2P and P2MP L2 VPNs

The service providers also offer other forms of P2P services called **L2 interworking services**, in which the layer 2 data link is different at the two endpoints. As an example, an interworking service could be where there is an Ethernet port at one end, and a serial port at the other end of the P2P link. In this case, the IP frames are carried over to the other end of the P2P link with the compatible layer 2 encapsulation, but without any layer 3 processing. So, even though the data link encapsulation changed, and the L2 frames were not transparent at the two ends of the link, there was still no layer 3 processing by the SP.

Service providers offer additional forms of layer 2 VPN services on dial-up circuits also, where the SP dial-up termination devices, also known as **Remote Access Servers** (**RAS**), are used by the user, but instead of terminating the session at the RAS, the frames are tunneled by the SP network to another network device that could be owned by the SP or the user. These services are delivered using the **L2 Tunnelling Protocol** (**L2TP**) by the SP, and the devices at the two ends of the L2 circuit are called the **L2TP Access Concentrator** (**LAC**) and the **L2TP Network Server** (**LNS**). These services are used by some organizations to provide remote dial-up access for their mobile employees into the corporate network using the SP backbone, without the SP performing any Layer 3 functions.

The users get a layer 2 VPN service that is a replacement of a leased line that the user would have had to buy. The leased line is a point-to-point link, and the protection in that link is limited. However, since the L2 VPNs use the SP network as an underlay network to provide the service, and the PS networks are very robust with lots of redundancy built in in terms of devices and links, the L2 VPNs provide a much higher uptime compared to a dedicated leased line.

We have described a lot of layer 2 services, but did not talk about the configuration of these devices. This is because from an end user perspective, these are standard layer 2 interfaces, and all the configurations required to create the virtual circuit are done by the service provider. The only important thing that the user should be aware of is that since we are sending layer 2 frames across the SP backbone, and there are additional headers that would be added on top of the layer 2 frames, the end-to-end MTU of the link should be verified and adjusted accordingly at the user devices on the ends of layer 2 VPNs.

Layer 3 VPNs

Layer 3 VPNs are overlay networks that are built on the underlay service provider networks, with the SP network providing layer 3 services to the end users. The overlay network created using P2P tunnels is a type of a layer 3 VPN, where the underlay SP network provides transport of IP packets from one end to another. In addition, the network also provides routing functionality, and the routers R1 and R2 provide IP routing functionality and routed packets into the tunnels.

Another form of layer 3 VPN is an MPLS L3 VPN service that is offered by MPLS SPs. In an MPLS layer 3 VPN, the network acts like one big router, and all interfaces of the VPN behave like they are connected to that virtual router directly. Consider the network shown in the following figure as an example:

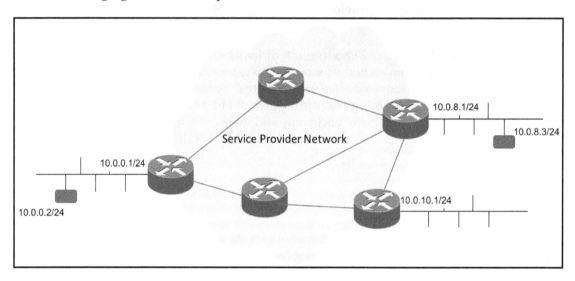

Figure 16: Sample network requiring a layer 3 VPN

The sample user network has three different locations to be connected, each location having a separate IP subnet. The SP routers at each location act like the default gateways for the co-located LANs. If an MPLS L3 VPN is created, the network would behave as if all the three locations were directly connected to one single router, and that router was routing packets between the three LAN segments. The logical overlay network topology from the user view would be as shown in the following figure:

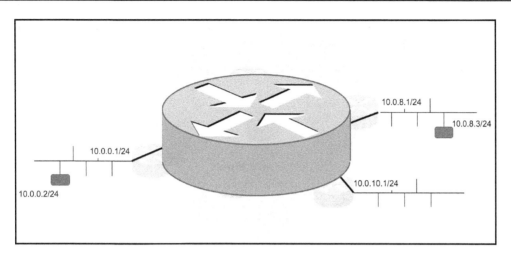

Figure 17: Logical topology for a layer 3 VPN

The logical virtual router so created would have routes only from the user for which this router was created. This enables the service provider to create as many such L3 VPNs with the different users having their own IP addresses in the same address space.

We considered a very simplistic view of a layer 3 VPN in the example. In practice, the SPs don't allow the LAN to be directly connected to the SP router, and the user needs to have a router located at his premises. This is called the **Customer Premises Equipment** (**CPE**) router. The CPE and the SP router, called the **Provider Edge** (**PE**) router, exchange routes using any standard IP routing protocol. The MPLS L3 VPN on the SP network then uses these routing tables to route IP packets and send them to the proper destination.

The routing protocol used between the CPE and the PE router is called the CE-PE routing protocol. This routing protocol can be different at different locations. As an example, let us assume we use **Static Routing** at location **A** and **OSPF** at locations **B** and **C** in the sample topology. Since the routing has to be continuous, the static routes on the **PE** router at location **A** would be injected by the SP network at locations **B** and **C** into the CPE routers at these locations. The SP network uses BGP as the protocol to transfer these routes from one location to another between the PE routers.

Thus, the routes would be injected at locations **B** and **C** CPE routers through the OSPF protocol, but as **OSPF** external routes:

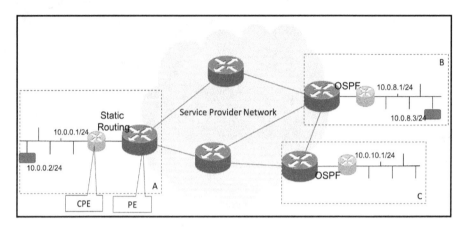

Figure 18: CE-PE routing location independence

Note that, as in layer 2 VPNs, the only configuration required on the CPE routers is normal routing functions to exchange routes with the PE routers. The logical router within the SP is created through configurations on the PE routers that are the SP's responsibility.

The service provider can control the routing between the different PE devices, and therefore between the CE devices percolating through the PEs, by tweaking configurations at the PE routers. This helps create multiple topologies in the MPLS VPN. As an example, if the MPLS VPN is created as a full mesh VPN, all routes are exchanged from all PEs to all other PEs. This is a good use case deployment where we are connecting multiple offices, and the offices need to talk to each other. However, there are cases where there are multiple branch offices, and they need to talk only to the data center. In such a case, it is better to deploy a hub and spoke VPN, where the data center CPE would act as the hub, and the branches would act as the spokes. Thus, the branch routers would only have a route that is injected from the data center location, and the data center CPE router would have the routes for all branches. This would minimize the number of routes that are present in the CPE router at the spoke locations, and avoid unnecessary loading of the router.

Similar to the L2 VPNs, the MPLS L3 VPNs provide very high uptimes, as they utilize the high redundancy and robust underlay network of the MPLS SP.

VRF-Lite

Sometimes layer 3 VPNs are also created within organizations by creating multiple routing tables within a single router. This is done by using a feature in Cisco IOS called VRF-Lite, where **VRF** stands for **Virtual Routing and Forwarding**. This is done to create small routing domains within an enterprise, where two LAN networks need to be isolated from each other, and the routing should happen only with a device at a higher layer.

Let us consider the topology in the following figure. We have two different entities, **A** and **B**, with separate networks in parts of the networks. However, the servers for the two entities are co-located and are terminated on the same router. If we don't do any specific configurations for isolating the networks, a server in the network 10.0.7.0/ 24 would be able to communicate with the server in the network 10.0.0.0 /24 through the common router, as both entries would be present in the single routing table:

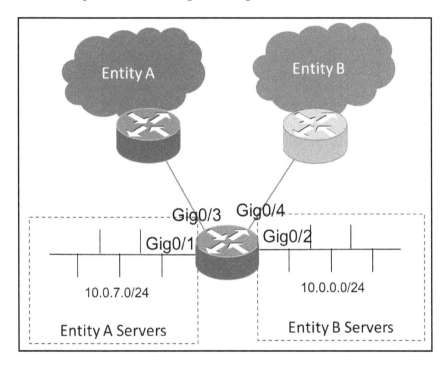

Figure 19: Creating virtual routers

To prevent the two networks from communicating with each other, network admins can either use **Access Control Lists** (**ACLs**), which look at each packet and are like firewall rules that define permitted and restricted communications. However, this loads the routers, as the decisions are taken on a per packet basis. An alternative is to segment the router into two logical routers, by using VRF-Lite. The configuration for this is shown in the following figure:

```
Router(config)# ip vrf Entity-A
Router(config-vrf)# rd 100:1
Router(config-vrf)# exit
Router(config)# ip vrf Entity-B
Router(config-vrf)# rd 100:2
Router(config-vrf)# exit
Router(config)# interface gig0/1
Router(config-if)# ip vrf forwarding Entity-A
Router(config-if)# ip addr 10.0.7.1 255.255.255.0
Router(config-if)# exit
Router(config)# interface gig0/2
Router(config-if)# ip vrf forwarding Entity-B
Router(config-if)# ip addr 10.0.0.1 255.255.255.0
Router(config-if)# exit
Router(config)# interface gig0/3
Router(config-if)# ip vrf forwarding Entity-A
Router(config-if)# ip addr 10.1.7.1 255.255.255.252
Router(config-if)# exit
Router(config)# interface gig0/4
Router(config-if)# ip vrf forwarding Entity-B
Router(config-if)# ip addr 10.1.0.1 255.255.255.252
Router(config-if)# exit
Router(config)# ip route vrf Entity-A 0.0.0.0 0.0.0.0 10.1.7.2
Router(config)# ip route vrf Entity-B 0.0.0.0 0.0.0.0 10.1.0.2
```

Figure 20: Sample configuration for VRF-Lite

The configuration consists of three major parts. In the first step, we create separate routing tables or VRFs by using the `ip vrf` command. In the example, we have created two such VRFs. Each VRF is associated with a **route distinguisher** (**RD**), which is an MPLS terminology, but is required to complete the creation of a VRF. The RD has to be unique for each VRF and is of the form a:b. In the second step, we assign interfaces to be a part of that logical router by using the command `ip vrf forwarding`. In the example, we have assigned the LAN and the uplink interfaces of each logical router to the two VRFs. As a final step, we have created static routes within the VRFs by using the `ip route vrf` commands within the configuration shown in the preceding figure for the two VRFs.

Remote access VPNs

MPLS service providers provide L3 VPN services with different types of access links. The last mile CE-PE link could be a serial link with PPP/ HDLC or even FR encapsulation, or an Ethernet port which could be native or a trunk port with a specific VLAN being a part of the Layer 3 VPN. These circuits are dedicated circuits. For remote users, the SP also provides remote access to VPN services called RA-VPN services. The RA-VPN services allow mobile users to dial into one of the access servers of the service provider, and after authentication, the user becomes a part of the layer 3 VPN. These services are used by large enterprises for providing access to their mobile workers. All configuration at the routers and remote access servers is done by the SP, as these are SP devices. The user only needs a dial-up client to dial into the RAS and provide the authentication details.

Managed versus unmanaged services

When an organization subscribes to a MPLS VPN service from the service provider, there needs to be close interaction between the user IT department which manages the CPE routers, and the service provider who manages the PE routers, as the CPE and PE routers form routing peering relationships, and any change in the routing parameters can lead to loss of connectivity.

These two sets of people also need to coordinate for troubleshooting purposes. If something goes wrong in the SP network, and there is loss of connectivity, it becomes important to pinpoint the problem and resolve that. This leads to contention between the two IT teams, with one team blaming it on the other for any outages. This in invariably the case where the CPE routers are managed by the customer IT teams in an unmanaged services model.

Some SPs provide managed services, where the CPE router is also managed by the SP. This provides the end user organization with the benefit of a highly skilled team of the SP that manages the routers at the customer premises. Further, the CPE routers are being polled by the **network management system** (**NMS**) of the SP to check for any issues. This provides real-time monitoring and reporting of the SLAs and the uptime of the devices and connectivity to the end users.

Connecting to the internet

The internet has become a central part of all businesses. All organizations connect to the internet for web connectivity, email connectivity, and, more recently, moving to cloud service providers, for meeting their data center requirements. Therefore, the links that connect the organization to the internet are a critical part of the WAN infrastructure and are being handled as a separate section.

The internet WAN links carry the traffic from the organization to the **World Wide Web (WWW)**, and vice versa. These links are also sometimes used to create overlay point-to-point tunnels that can be used as backups for important primary links, or even as secure connectivity to smaller branch locations.

The internet WAN link connects the organization to the upstream **Internet Service providers (ISPs)** that provide internet connectivity. The organization needs public IP addresses to connect to the internet as the addresses on the internet are unique. Given the fact that the world is short of IPv4 addresses, and organizations use private IPv4 addresses for their internal networks, we use **network address translation (NAT)** technologies to connect the private IP addresses to public IP addresses at the internet edge of the organization. We will describe the configuration of NAT in Chapter 7, *Understanding and Configuring Data Center Technologies*.

For the purposes of this chapter, let us assume that the organization has a public IP address block that it uses to connect to the internet. This public IP address block could be provided by its upstream ISP or might be procured by large organizations from their regional IP address registries, such as the **Asia Pacific Network Information Centre (APNIC)**, **American Registry for Internet Numbers (ARIN)**, **Latin America and Caribbean Network Information Centre (LACNIC)**, **African Network Information Center (AFRINIC)**, and **Réseaux IP Européens (RIPE)**.

If the organization has the IP addresses assigned by an upstream service provider, it can connect only to that upstream provider, as the IP address would be assigned to the upstream ISP in the internet routing tables. The organization can still have multiple links to the same ISP for redundancy purposes. However, if the organization has its own IP address block, it can peer with multiple upstream providers, and exchange routing information with the upstream ISPs using the **border gateway protocol (BGP)**.

Routing at the internet edge

An organization can use two different types of routing protocols on the internet WAN: static routing or BGP. We will discuss the configuration of the two types of routing on the internet WAN in the next sections.

Static routing

Static routing is generally used when the organization has a prefix that is assigned by the upstream ISP, and the organization has a single upstream ISP. Consider the organization shown in the following figure, which has an IP pool of **200.100.80.0/24** allocated by its ISP. This **/24** prefix would be a part of the larger address block that is owned by the ISP, and would be advertised on the internet. The organization only has the option of pointing a default route to the internet on the internet WAN, and the ISP in turn points a route for the 200.100.80.0/24 prefix back to the organization:

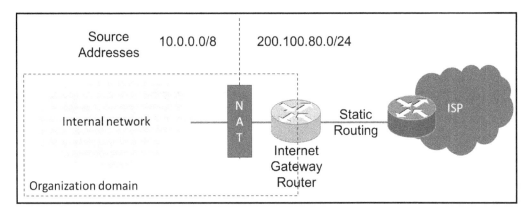

Figure 21: Connecting to the internet

Note that the organization might have a large number of hosts internally using private IP addresses. These hosts would be able to access the internet using NAT at the internet gateway location, as shown in the preceding figure. The internet gateway router would have a static default route to the internet. Note that the public IP address of the organization would be location dependent. If the organization has multiple connections to the internet, it would have multiple pools of addresses to use for NAT translations for each location. The incoming traffic would be controlled by the upstream ISP and all traffic for that prefix would be received at the location where the public IP prefix is allocated.

BGP

Large organizations have pubic IP address blocks assigned to them from their regional address registries. Such organizations also have something known as an **Autonomous Number**, commonly known as **ASN**, which they use as their identifier to the internet.

Assume an organization that has an IP address block of 200.80.80.0/22 allocated to it, and has an ASN of 1000. This organization can connect to two or more upstream providers using BGP as the routing protocol, and can advertise the /22 prefix to any of the upstream providers. The advertisement of the prefix would control the incoming traffic from the upstream ISP into the organization. The internet generally takes the shortest number of AS hops from source to the destination, and therefore the incoming traffic would generally be distributed between the two uplink providers. The organization can get granular in the prefix advertisements, and can force all traffic for more specific prefixes from certain ISPs, and the traffic for other IP addresses in its address block from the ISP to which it advertises the aggregate prefix. Tweaking the incoming traffic is not very deterministic, as the source of traffic is not known beyond the organization boundary. However, the ISP has full control over which ISP it would use for outgoing traffic. This is done by manipulating a parameter called the Local Preference in the BGP routing table.

Let us consider the organization as shown in the following figure:

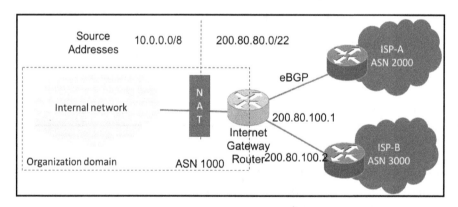

Figure 22: Connecting to multiple internet service providers

A sample BGP configuration for a gateway router without manipulating any parameters is given in the following figure:

```
Router(config)# router bgp 1000
Router(config-router)# router-id 200.80.80.1
Router(config-router)# neighbor 200.80.100.2 remote-as 3000
Router(config-router)# network 200.80.80.0 mask 255.255.252.0
```

Figure 23: Sample configuration for advertising routes into BGP

We have assumed in the preceding configuration that the router loopback for the internet gateway router is 200.80.80.1. The value against the command router bgp is the local ASN, and the remote ASN is defined in the neighbor x.x.x.x remote-as z command. The network command is used to let BGP know what prefixes to advertise to the BGP peer. In our example, we have advertised a single aggregate /22 prefix. As discussed, we could send a more specific prefix on different neighbors to achieve granularity in incoming traffic.

Encrypting and securing the WAN

One of the considerations of choosing a WAN circuit is security, and the type of data that is being transmitted over that WAN link. If the data is very confidential, it should not be transmitted over public infrastructures, as it is vulnerable to be exploited.

MPLS VPNs were launched in early 2000, and even though it was highly secure from a transport perspective, a lot of organizations were skeptical about using the shared infrastructure of the SP for their internal IT environments. But they saw the huge benefits in cost savings with regard to building their own dedicated infrastructures using TDM links from SPs, and the availability benefits the users realized due to the redundant infrastructure of the MPLS SP. Also, the services could scale up and scale down by just changing the access port bandwidth of an Ethernet port, and thus made the networks much more agile, and flexible. To get the best of both worlds, such organizations started to use the MPLS backbone for their VPNs, and started to use encryption on top of the VPN created by the MPLS SP.

Encryption is also used when overlay links are created using GRE over the public internet. It is a matter of judgment and perception of the end user using the link on whether they would like to use encryption or not. Encryption adds overheads to the traffic, and also loads the routers to a large extent, as cryptography uses a lot of resources on routers in terms of CPU and memory.

A sample configuration of an L3 VPN with encryption on top of the MPLS VPN is as shown in the following figure. Note the change in the overlay network created each time a functionality is added:

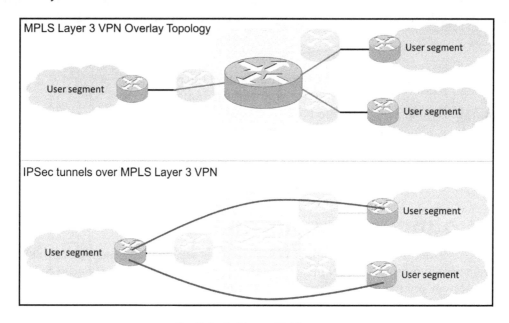

Figure 24: Securing links over public infrastructures

Note that the tunnels are created as point-to-point tunnels, and only the loopback addresses of the CPE routers are advertised over the MPLS L3 VPN of the SP. The tunnel can also be formed on the CE-PE address on the CPE router if there is only one MPLS SP. If there are multiple links or SPs, then the tunnel should be created on the loopback address.

Once the connectivity is established between the loopbacks of the CPEs, point-to-point tunnels are created from one router to another, and are encrypted using IPSec. These encrypted tunnels are then used as P2P logical links to route the user traffic from the user segments at the various locations over the shared infrastructure of the MPLS VPN SP. This ensures that neither the user routes are visible on the SP network, and the data that flows on the MPLS SP network is also encrypted. The following figure shows the parameters between a pair of sites in the preceding topology:

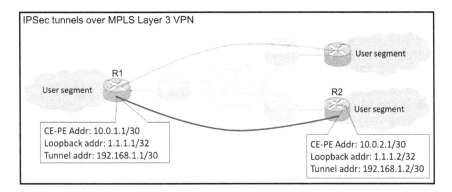

Figure 25: Securing VPNs using tunnels

In the preceding topology, the loopback address of the CPE routers is used to create GRE tunnels that are encrypted using IPSec. To complete the routing from an underlay perspective, let us assume that all the loopback addresses of the CPE routers are in the 1.1.1.0/24 range. Thus, to ensure IP reachability to the loopback addresses over the MPLS L3 VPN, the range has to be pointed on the CPE routers towards the PE router. This has to be done on all CPE routers. This would ensure that all CPE loopbacks are reachable from all other CPE routers for the tunnels to come up.

The sample configurations for creating the IPSec encrypted tunnels on the routers R1 and R2 are as shown in the following figure:

```
R1(config)# interface Tunnel0
R1(config-if)# ip address 192.168.1.1 255.255.255.252
R1(config-if)# ip mtu 1400
R1(config-if)# ip tcp adjust-mss 1360
R1(config-if)# tunnel source 1.1.1.1
R1(config-if)# tunnel destination 1.1.1.2

R1(config)# crypto isakmp policy 1
R1(config-isakmp)# encr 3des
R1(config-isakmp)# hash md5
R1(config-isakmp)# authentication pre-share
R1(config-isakmp)# group 2
R1(config-isakmp)# lifetime 86400

R1(config)# crypto isakmp key C!sc0123 address 1.1.1.2
R1(config)# crypto ipsec transform-set TS esp-3des esp-md5-hmac
R1(config)# crypto ipsec profile protect-gre
R1(ipsec-profile)# set security-association lifetime seconds 86400
R1(ipsec-profile)# set transform-set TS

R1(config)# interface Tunnel0
R1(config-if)# tunnel protection ipsec profile protect-gre

R1(config)# ip route 10.8.100.0 255.255.255.0 192.168.1.2
```

Figure 26: Sample configuration for creating tunnels over MPLS

The preceding configuration creates a tunnel interface, as discussed earlier, and sets the MSS to 1360, which translates to a MTU of 1,400 bytes. The next section of the configuration defines the policy parameters and encryption parameters for the IPSec tunnel. In the last section, we apply the IPSec encryption to the tunnel interface, and then route the user subnets into the IPSec encrypted tunnels. We have assumed the user network at site R2 has a user prefix of 10.0.100.0/24. The configurations on the router R2 are similar to the the peer addresses changed.

Configuring P2P IPSec tunnels is a tedious process, and large organizations might use **Dynamic Multipoint VPN (DMVPN)** that simplifies the configuration for a large number of tunnels by using group encryption techniques and using a hub and spoke topology of tunnels. DMVPN is out of the scope of this book, but has been mentioned for the sake of completeness.

Optimizing the WAN

A WAN link is a critical part of the network, as this is the network segment that is most prone to failures, adds the maximum amount of latency in communications, and is bandwidth constrained. WAN links are generally the choke points on the network from an end-to-end bandwidth perspective. WAN bandwidth is expensive, and hence organizations tend to optimize the WAN utilization.

Most of the communication on the WAN link is TCP/IP. TCP uses a flow control mechanism that restricts the rate at which users can send data on the network. Any loss of packets on the link leads to retransmission of TCP segments, therefore wasting bandwidth. The loss of packets is sensed by the receiving host when the acknowledgment for a given segment doesn't arrive within a specified time duration. This can happen due to link congestion, and it is possible that even though the transmission was received by the receiver, the transmitting node retransmits the packets. This can cause artificial congestion on the WAN links.

There are products that provide **Wide Area Acceleration Services (WAAS)** devices from Cisco that can help mitigate these issues by using techniques such as compressing the data being sent over a WAN link, and reducing the unnecessary retransmissions over a WAN link by sending local acknowledgements. The induction of these devices on the network causes the WAN performance to improve considerably. WAAS deployment requires a pair of devices to be used at each end of the link and the traffic goes through a compression-decompression cycle for each link. Since there is a cost of equipment and operations associated with the induction of WAAS services, organizations can evaluate the business case for deployment of these services on their networks with regard to upgrading the WAN bandwidth.

Summary

We discussed the various aspects of WAN design in this chapter. We also discussed the different WAN technologies that can be used by organizations, and the factors that influence the choice of one technology over the other. We delved deep into the different types of VPN services provided by different service providers, and the pros and cons of using each type of VPN. We also evaluated the use of public infrastructures to create secure WAN links using encryption techniques, and introduced some of the advanced concepts that can be evaluated as the WAN requirement grows in an organization.

In the next chapter, we will discuss the various technologies used in a data center.

7
Understanding and Configuring Data Center Technologies

"Users ultimately want to get at data quickly and easily. They don't care as much about attractive sites and pretty design."

- Tim Berners-Lee

A **data center** (**DC**) is a facility where an organization hosts all of its data and applications. This facility provides a means of centralizing the applications, thus providing better control over the management of the applications and the server infrastructure. Centralizing the important data and applications also simplifies the security of data and applications as the network administrators can focus on a single facility rather than discrete servers spread across the organization. The DC has evolved from the early days of computing to become highly flexible and scalable. The emergence of the cloud has also influenced the DC design and scale. In this chapter, we will discuss the following topics:

- The evolution of the data center
- Design principles of the data center
- Planning redundancy for the DC
- Securing the data center infrastructure

Functions of a data center

A DC is the core of the enterprise network. Most enterprise network communications have one end of the communications within the DC. This is because the DC hosts most of the enterprise applications that are accessed by a majority of the users. These applications could be core business applications, or business supporting applications such as email applications.

The DC also hosts the major databases within the organization. Most of the organizational data is stored in databases such as SQL, RDBMS, Oracle, and so on. These databases require large computing and storage resources and skills to manage and maintain the databases. Centralizing these databases helps to contain the operational costs of the organization.

If an organization deploys some IoT applications, the servers and the central processing of those applications also happens within the DC. Any CCTV feeds are also captured and stored within the data center infrastructure.

An organization also relies on the internet for some of the services. These could be connectivity to the **World Wide Web** (**WWW**) for research and browsing, connectivity for email, and so on. If the organization uses cloud services from cloud service providers, such as Amazon, Google, Microsoft Azure, and so on, then the internet connectivity to these services also flows through the data center.

Some organizations also host some services, such as their own websites, locally rather than on public hosting platforms. These services are also hosted within the data center.

Since most services are provided out of the data center, and the internet connectivity is also provided through the DC, the DC becomes an important point where security can be enforced to protect the organization's IT infrastructure form the internet threats, and also to protect the IT assets from any internal threats from the users on the internal LAN.

Evolution of the DC

Data centers have evolved significantly in recent years, adopting technologies such as virtualization, software defined storage, and the cloud to optimize resource utilization and increase IT agility and flexibility.

A data center hosts a lot of IT equipment from servers, to storage, to network equipment. All of this equipment has undergone a lot of change with the evolution of technology. We will explore some of the evolution that has happened in recent years in the DC technologies in the following section.

Network

Traditional data centers were built using a three-tier architecture with core, aggregation, and access layers, or a two-tier collapsed core with the aggregation and core layers combined into one layer, as shown in the following figure. This architecture provides optimal packet forwarding when the data flow follows a north-south traffic pattern, where one end of the traffic flow is outside the DC (the WAN link or the campus network) and the other end is the servers hosted within the DC. This was the common type of traffic in client server applications:

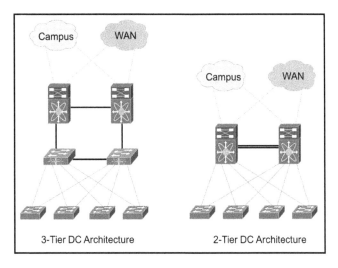

Figure 1: DC tiered architecture

As we have seen in the earlier chapters, traffic coming in from the WAN locations is constrained by the amount of WAN bandwidth available, and hence we can have some over subscription at the access layer within the data center. If the traffic comes in from the campus network, the traffic comes in through a firewall and the throughput of the firewall provides the same choking effect as the WAN. These types of communications are efficiently supported by conventional DC designs.

We have also seen in `Chapter 4`, *Understanding and Configuring Campus Network Technologies*, that we need to restrict loops in a layer 2 network. These loops are restricted by using protocols such as **Spanning Tree Protocols** (**STP**). Running these protocols put some links in the physical topology of the network in blocking or non-forwarding modes, and hence led to the inability to use all available bandwidth on the network. Network administrators looked at alternate means of augmenting capacity and used techniques like link aggregation protocols.

These technologies worked well as long as the two links connected the same pair of devices, as shown in the following figure:

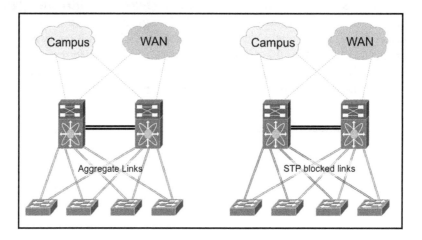

Figure 2: Aggregate links and spanning tree

In order to build redundancy within the DC, there are invariably two core switches or distribution switches. The uplinks from the access switches are to two different uplinks, and there is a need to utilize both the uplinks in active-active mode. This is done by using technologies such as **virtual PortChannel** (**vPC**). We will describe the configuration of the vPC in the subsequent sections.

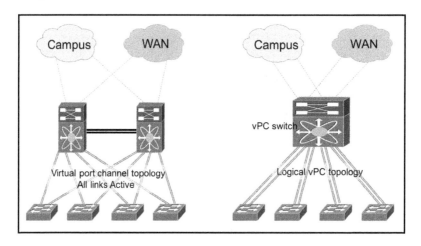

Figure 3: Enabling port channels across devices using virtual port channels

Most applications in the DC need to communicate a lot with each other rather than to end hosts. This is typical of a lot of multi-tiered applications, and also analytical applications that use a lot of inter-application communications within the data center. This leads to a change in the DC traffic patterns from the typical north-south traffic pattern in a traditional DC to an east-west traffic in newer data centers. As the traffic pattern in the DC moves to east-west traffic, there is a need to minimize the number of hops from one server to another, and optimize the packet forwarding. This is achieved through a spine leaf architecture, as shown in the following figure:

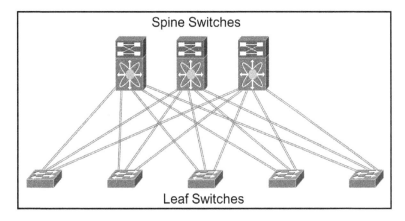

Figure 4: Optimizing east-west traffic using spine-leaf architecture

Spine-leaf architecture is typically deployed as two layers:

- **Spine layer**: This is similar to an aggregation layer. The spine switches are used to connect to all leaf switches and serve as a backbone interconnect for leaf switches. The spine switches are typically deployed at the end or middle of the row in the DC.
- **Leaf layer**: This is analogous to the access layer. The leaf switches provide devices access and are typically deployed at the top of the rack.

Spine-leaf topologies provide high-bandwidth, low-latency, non-blocking server-to-server connectivity. All devices connected to the fabric are an equal number of hops away from one another. This delivers predictable latency and high bandwidth between servers.

With the advent of **Software Defined Networking** (**SDN**), Cisco provides a DC architecture based on a spine-leaf architecture and managed through a central controller. This is called the **Application Centric Infrastructure** (**ACI**) and uses the underlying spine-leaf networking fabric. Details on ACI are beyond the scope of this book.

Computers

Computers have evolved in size and computing power ever since they were first invented by Charles Babbage. "Computing power doubles every couple of years" is a popular rephrasing of Moore's law. This has held true for over 50 years and humans have found means and applications to use that enhanced computing capacity.

Computers have also become better in terms of their form factors, from mainframes occupying huge rooms, to the modern day personal computers and servers with much more computing capacity in much smaller form factors.

We have seen the introduction of blade servers, where servers are shipped out as blades that fit into a chassis with an inbuilt switch. The Cisco blade server chassis provides up to eight servers in a chassis that occupies just 6U rackspace in a standard 19" rack. The other major revolution in the computing domain has been a technology known as **Fiber Channel over Ethernet (FCoE)**. A computer has an ethernet port for connecting to the data network, and a separate **Fiber Channel (FC)** port to connect to the storage area networks. The FCoE technology enhances Ethernet to data center grade and uses a single Ethernet cable to carry both user data and FC data over a converged network adapter. A typical DC layout with Cisco UCS servers is shown in the following figure, showing the Cisco platforms of the Cisco **Unified Computing Servers (UCS)** chassis, the Nexus switches for Ethernet switching, and Cisco MDS switches for **Storage Area Networks (SAN)**:

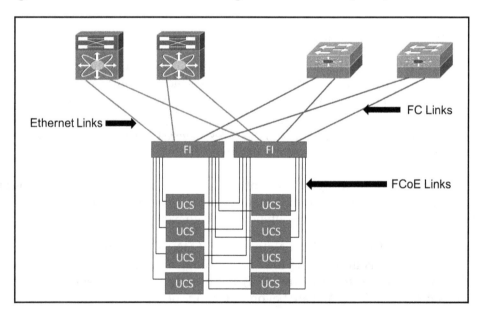

Figure 5: A sample FCoE topology using Cisco Unified Computing Systems

While most of the features in the preceding figure have led to form factor reduction and some power savings in terms of cabling costs due to the reduction in the number of cables, the single most important disruptive change in the server domain has been the introduction of virtualization technology.

Virtualization

Typical servers run at an average CPU utilization of about 20% in the DC. Each server consumed a lot of power, and administrators were looking at ways to improve the utilization of the IT infrastructure. This led the server administrators to run multiple applications on the same server, and hence achieve better utilization of the CPU cycles of the servers. This approach led to the extinction of boundaries between different applications, as they were running on the same hardware. Any single application malfunction leading to changes at the OS level meant that all applications running on the server would be impacted as they were running on the same OS. The pre-virtualization method of increasing server utilization is shown in the following figure:

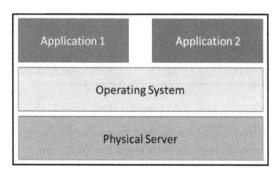

Figure 6: Multiple applications on a server (pre-virtualization)

Virtualization introduced hypervisors that were pieces of code that would abstract the underlying hardware and present the hardware as individual pieces of hardware to the servers running on top of the hypervisor. The servers running on top of the hypervisors are called virtual machines or VMs. There are two types of hypervisors: type-1 and type-2 hypervisors.

A type-1 hypervisor runs directly on the bare metal server. This hypervisor then abstracts the underlying hardware and provides virtual interfaces to access the hardware resources of the underlying compute infrastructure. The operating systems use the virtual interfaces as though they were communicating directly with the physical server. The applications then run on top of the operating system.

In contrast to the type-1 hypervisor, a type-2 hypervisor runs on top of an operating system and not the physical hardware directly. This hypervisor uses the underlying operating system and presents multiple interfaces for the network interfaces, CPU cycles, and memory to the virtual machines, so that each VM runs as though it is running on a dedicated hardware of its own. The OS for the different VMs runs on top of the type-2 hypervisor. The difference between the two types of hypervisors is shown in the following figure:

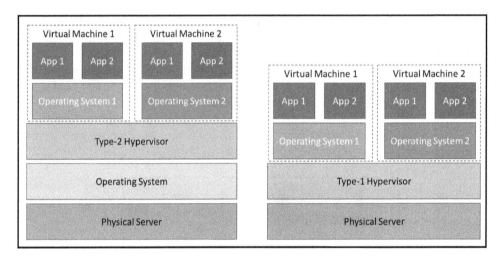

Figure 6: Types of hypervisors

The VMs were image files that could be moved from one hypervisor to another, and hence bringing up a new server was as easy as moving a file from one machine to another. This also provided features such as auto scaling where the administrators could bring up more machines during peak load time and bring the machines down during slack hours, leading to huge operational efficiencies in terms of power and server admin costs and also made the DC infrastructure more agile and responsive to the business needs. Virtualization technology is the fundamental technology enabling the cloud services.

Type-1 hypervisors are the most commonly depoyed hypervisors today. Some of the type-1 hypervisor vendors are KVM (Open-source), RedHat Enterprise Virtualization (RHEV from RedHat), Xen (Citrix), Hyper-V (Microsoft), and ESXi (VMWare).

Storage

Each organization needs storage capacity to store business data, be it emails, intellectual property, sales data, HR data, or business critical information. In the past, this was done through hard disks within computers, till the industry moved to networked storage in the form of **Network Attached Storage** (**NAS**) and **Storage Area Networks** (**SAN**).

These traditional forms of storage had vendor dependency and the storage software and hardware were tightly coupled together. The next wave of virtualization came in the storage space and led to **Software Defined Storage** (**SDS**), where an intelligent software layer abstracts the underlying storage hardware into a single, logical pool of cost-effective, scale-out storage resources. SDS enables the storage capacity to scale independently of the compute capacity, providing more flexibility to the end users, and bringing down the overall cost of operations.

Cisco has a hyper-converged solution that is based on the Unified Computing Servers, and the common management platform that provides these features. Detailed discussion on the SDS is beyond the scope of this book.

Cloud computing

Cloud computing is a form of network computing that uses a physical infrastructure to provide virtual computing resources in the form of VMs on demand. This helps the users to optimize the utilization of the available infrastructure and realign resources when required between the various users. Large enterprises use this within their data center exclusively; this is called a **private cloud**.

There are also multiple service providers in the market that offer the computing capacity on demand. These are called **cloud service providers**, and since these infrastructures are public, and shared between multiple customers, these are called **public clouds**.

Some organizations use both private clouds and public clouds to provide better scaling and use cheaper public clouds to host workloads that don't need a high level of security or compliance and can be hosted on the public infrastructure. These clouds are called **hybrid clouds**.

The cloud service providers provide a variety of services, broadly classified into three major buckets:

- **Infrastructure as a Service (IaaS)**: IaaS **cloud service providers** (**CSPs**) provide on-demand computing, storage, and associated networking infrastructure to the end users. IaaS consists of highly scalable compute, storage, and networking infrastructure that is automated for flexible and agile provisioning, monitoring, and reporting, using customer-friendly frontend web portals to order new services or making changes to existing services. The services are provisioned automatically as soon as the user requests them on the portal and the requisite authorizations have been done using the automated workflow systems. The shared infrastructure is carved into virtual data centers that contain the compute, storage, and networking resources as requested by the end users, and the entire provisioning is done using scripts or other coordinated management tools.
- **Platform as a Service (PaaS)**: PaaS functions at a lower higher than IaaS, and provides the associated OS, and the platform on which the software can be deployed; for example, web platforms such as Apache, or database applications that can be used directly by the end users. Thus, the user is not exposed to the physical servers, or the operating systems, or even the application platforms, making them ready to be consumed by the users for development or deployment of applications.
- **Software as a Service (SaaS)**: SaaS services are a level higher than PaaS and the complete software application is offered as a service to the end user. It is very similar to a client-server model, where the users use the web browser as the client, and the application is hosted on the SaaS CSP. Typical SaaS services include Salesforce, Google apps, and Dropbox.

Some of the major cloud service providers include Amazon Web Services, the Google cloud platform, Citrix cloud, Microsoft Azure, and Rackspace, amongst a host of others including the telcos in each geographic area.

Management systems

The management systems used in the data center have also undergone a drastic change because of the evolution of the underlying networking, compute, and storage systems, as well as the move to virtualization and the need for agility and flexibility. The hitherto discrete systems and manual scripts became more integrated with the focus not on discrete systems but the machine as a whole, and a lot more focus on reporting, and automation of complete workflows within the data center.

Design of a DC

A data center networking design is primarily centered around providing access to the various computing resources in the data center and ensuring optimal traffic flows between them in the north-south and east-west directions. Another important aspect of the DC design is around security of the overall DC infrastructure and segregating coherent groups of servers into single domains and isolating them from the other resources that have a different security requirement.

The DC design is a hierarchical two or three tier design. The two-tier design is the most commonly used design in mid-sized organizations. Even larger organizations with a large number of servers with a lot of east-west traffic have started moving to two-tier spine leaf architectures.

A fundamental question to be answered in a DC design is the placement of the layer 3 boundary. Recall from `Chapter 4`, *Understanding and Configuring Campus Network Technologies*, that a layer 2 domain extends the broadcast domain, and needs to be minimized. The DC has a different challenge from a layer 2 perspective. Since the IP address subnet changes from one broadcast domain to another, and servers need to have the same IP address for business continuity, the layer 2 domain in a DC needs to be as large as possible, so that servers can be physically moved across the DC and connected to any port in case more computing power is required. This poses an inherent conflict between the server team and the networking teams that try to limit the Layer 2 domains. The comparison of having a layer 3 boundary at the access nodes against having this boundary at the collapsed core switch in a traditional DC is shown in the following figure:

Consideration	Layer 3 at Core	Layer 3 at Access
Multiple uplinks between access and core switches	Only one active link per VLAN	Load balancing allows multiple L3 links
Spanning Tree Loops	STP runs on the links between access and core switches, preventing the ports from forwarding to prevent loops.	No STP between access and core switches.
Layer 2 domains	Larger L2 domain allowing more flexibility for machine movement and clustering	Layer 2 domains limited to the access layer switch
Convergence time	Slow convergence in case of link failures due to L2 protocols	Faster convergence due to L3 routing protocols.

Figure 8: Factors affecting the choice of layer 3 boundary in a DC

The use of vPC has led to efficient designs overcoming the problems of non-forwarding ports. We will use the vPC based design as a reference for the purposes of this book and discuss the configuration in detail in the next sections.

Application hierarchy

We build the network to support the applications, and hence it is important to understand the application requirements from the underlying network infrastructure so that the network can deliver what is being asked if it. While we will not go too deep within the applications, it is important to understand the traffic flows between various applications as they relate to the network and the traffic they generate on the network.

We discussed the importance of modularity in Chapter 2, *Networks for Digital Enterprises*, as it decouples the different functions of a network and allows the network to scale independently of the other components. Similar concepts are applied to the application design. An application consists of a frontend, the software that implements the actual business logic, and the software that integrates with the database. Each function of the application is implemented in a different tier, providing the required modularity to the application. These tiers are called the web, application, and database tiers of the application.

The web tier of the application architecture provides an efficient, user-friendly interface to the clients who access the application. This tier usually consists of a web server that has the necessary user interfaces to enhance the client's experience.

The application tier comprises of the most important part of the application, where the business logic for the application is coded. This layer takes data from the web tier and data from the database tier and runs the business logic on top of the data, then returns the required data to the web or the database tier.

The third tier of the application is the database tier, which consists of the various database systems that store the huge amounts of data within the organization. This data is confidential and sensitive and only selected parts of this data need to be exposed to the users on request. Hence it is important to secure this database directly from the end users. It is only the application tier that talks to the database tier, thus providing an additional layer of security beyond usernames and passwords for databases.

The three tiers of the application are shown in the following figure:

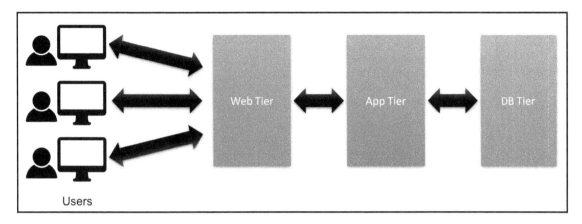

Figure 9: A three-tier application

The modular structure of the application ensures that any tier can scale independently of the other tiers if it becomes a chokepoint for the overall user experience. In addition, the tiered model of the applications ensures security, as the only traffic flows allowed are the ones depicted in the preceding figure with the arrows. As an example, the DB tier of the application can be totally isolated from the end users by blocking all direct communications between the users and the DB tier.

Zoning of the data center

It can be seen from the previous discussion on application design that there are different types of servers in the DC that have different connectivity requirements. All servers with similar types of connectivity and security requirements are grouped together in a "zone" within the DC. Hence, we would have three different zones in the DC from the previous discussion, as follows:

- **Demilitarized zone** (**DMZ**), that hosts all the web servers, and other internet facing servers
- Secure app zone, where we host all the app servers
- Secure DB zone, where all database servers are hosted

Additionally, if there are multiple units within an organization, for example marketing and development, and the applications of one unit should not be accessed by the users of the other units, we would have additional zones within the DC.

Zones are security areas where we block specific communication between various devices depending upon layer 3 and layer 4 information of the OSI stack. Zones are typically implemented using firewalls within a data center. Each zone has a trust level, which is defined by a numeric value on the firewall. The firewall acts like a packet filter looking at TCP and IP information in the packets flowing through the interfaces to allow any communication from a zone with a higher trust level to a lower trust level, but blocking all communication from a lower trust level zone to a higher trust level zone. We will look at the configuration of the zones in the subsequent sections.

Types of networks in a DC

A data center has multiple types of traffic and thus multiple networks for each traffic type. The different traffic types in the data center are:

- **User traffic**: This is the business data traffic that is the actual traffic from the users, applications, or the database servers on the user plane.
- **Management traffic**: This consists of the traffic used by the network operations teams to monitor and maintain the network infrastructure. This traffic could also be on Ethernet links, but these links are generally separated from the user traffic links, so that the devices can be accessed through the management network even if the user plane is flooded or malfunctioning.
- **Fiber channel traffic**: This is the FC traffic that goes from the servers to the storage devices through the storage area networks within the data center over dedicated FC or FCoE links.

Each server typically has three ports that connect to each of the networks. Some servers might have only two ports that use FCoE and use separate VLANs to carry FC traffic over different VLANs over the same physical interface. The Ethernet **Network Interface Card** (**NIC**) is used to terminate the Ethernet interfaces that carry user traffic or the FCoE traffic. Dedicated adapters used for fiber channel traffic are terminated on **Host Bus Adapters** (HBAs). The interfaces that use FCoE, and carry both data traffic and storage traffic over the same Ethernet link are known as **Converged Network Adapter** (**CNA**) ports. The three different network types from a server perspective are shown in the following figure:

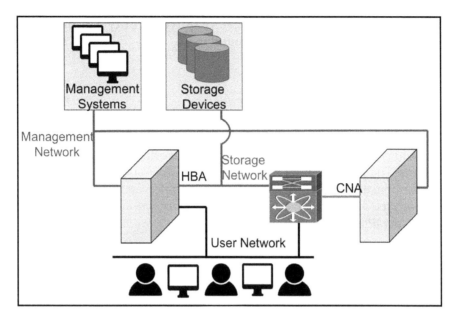

Figure 10: Servers connecting to the data, storage, and management networks

While designing the DC network, three separate networks have to be designed. These networks can be over the same physical infrastructure or share the same physical devices, and just be logically partitioned from each other. While the SAN is beyond the scope of the book, we will discuss a sample design and configuration of the user and management networks in subsequent sections.

Introduction to firewalls

A firewall is a device that protects networks from unauthorized access by users from other networks. The networks are assigned to **security zones** and policies are configured to explicitly allow or block communications between the different networks. An organization would place the internet facing servers in a zone that connects to the internet, allowing traffic for specific applications, and the remaining servers would typically be placed in zones that are not accessible from the internet. The zone that connects to the internet is typically called a demilitarized zone or a DMZ. The other zones depend upon the security design of the organization. Typical names used for the other zones are the application zone, the database zone, and the internal zones.

The Cisco portfolio has a firewall known as the **Adaptive Security Appliance** (**ASA**). The ASA firewall can operate in two different modes:

- Routed mode
- Transparent mode

In the routed mode, the ASA acts like a firewall function that operates on top of a router which is a layer 3 device. Hence, the interfaces of the firewall would have an IP address and the firewall would participate in the routing on the network in addition to performing firewall functions. The different interfaces on the firewall would belong to different IP subnets. In this mode, the firewall acts like the default gateway for the hosts on the subnet that is being protected and a `traceroute` on the network would show the firewall interfaces as distinct IP hops on the network.

In the transparent mode, the ASA acts like a *bump in the wire* and the firewall functions operate on top of the wire. Since the ASA is a bump in the wire, the inside and outside interfaces are on the same network that are bridged. In this mode, the firewall is invisible to the attackers.

Since the firewall has multiple security zones, and each zone has a security level that is a number between 1 and 100, with 100 being the most secure zone. By default, the ASA allows traffic to flow freely from a higher security level to a lower security level network. A security policy can be configured to define which traffic is allowed to pass through the firewall to access another network.

Firewall inspection

All traffic that goes through the ASA is inspected using the Adaptive Security Algorithm and is either allowed through or dropped. Although we can use ACLs on a router interface that can check the source IP address, destination IP address, the protocol and source and destination ports; these are not the main functions of the router. The five fields are commonly called the **tuple**.

The firewall does a far deeper inspection of the packets, as it is a dedicated device to perform the security functions.

Some firewalls monitor the traffic in each direction without maintaining any state of the TCP connections, but monitoring traffic as per the defined security policies. Such firewalls are called stateless firewalls.

The other type of firewall is a stateful firewall, with Cisco ASA being in that category. The stateful firewall monitors the state of each TCP connection from the time the first TCP connection initiation request is sent using a SYN packet, and tracking the state of the connection like the packet sequence and TCP flags looking for any deviations or anomalies in the TCP connection state and blocking them.

Although a TCP connection is a bi-directional connection, the stateful firewall keeps track of the initiator of the TCP connection, thus adding directionality to a TCP connection. A stateful firewall allows connections in one direction (for example, TCP destination port 80 for a web server) only by default and maintains a state table that also records the random TCP source port used by the client, as a part of the connection state. Such firewalls that treat the bi-directional communications of a TCP connection as a single connection and maintain the current state of connections are called **stateful firewalls**.

There are many ways in which a firewall inspects traffic and provides security to the protected networks. These techniques are briefly discussed next.

Basic access control

These are access rules that are configured on the firewall to be applied to the traffic between the various security zones of the firewall. By default, the ASA allows traffic to flow freely from an inside network (higher security level) to an outside network (lower security level). These rules can limit traffic from inside to outside, or allow traffic from outside to inside, based on the tuple value (source address and port, destination address and port, and protocol). Next generation firewalls, commonly known as NGFW, allow IP addresses to be linked to the DHCP servers, **Active Directory** (**AD**) servers, and so on, to allow the creation of the tuples based on hostnames rather than IP addresses.

Protecting from IP fragments

A common attack on the devices with a limited amount of resources is by sending a large number of fragments to the device. Recall from earlier chapters that IPv4 packets are allowed to be fragmented and the destination node reassembles the fragments to form the complete datagram and extract the payload that is then passed on to the upper layer protocol. If a large number of fragments are sent to the host, with one missing fragment from the entire set of fragments, the host would continue to store the fragments, consuming memory, and also CPU in processing these fragments, till some timers expire, and the host discards all fragments to clear memory. This can lead to a security attack on the host.

The ASA provides IP fragment protection, by performing a full reassembly of all ICMP error messages and virtual reassembly of the remaining IP fragments that are routed through the ASA. Fragments that fail the security check are dropped and logged.

Application inspection

There are some protocols that embed IP addressing information within the payload. For example, voice packets where voice control packets connect to the central server with a phone number and the called number's IP address is returned by the call control server. This communication happens in the payload. The client now starts to send packets to the new IP address. If the packets are going through the firewall, the firewall should be aware that a new IP stream would flow between the IP addresses of the calling phone and the called phone. This requires the firewall to look deep into the application payloads to analyze this information. ASA firewalls support application inspection for a variety of protocols such as HTTP, FTP, **Trivial File Transfer Protocol (TFTP)**, **Session Initiation Protocol (SIP)**, and many more.

ASA firewalls also have the ability to integrate with a variety of web proxy servers to block traffic to certain Uniform Resource Locators, more commonly known as URLs. This feature is generally called HTTP, HTTPS, or FTP Filtering.

Applying connection limits and TCP normalization

Hackers have another common method of attacking servers. This is called the SYN attack. In this attack, the attacker sends multiple TCP packets with the SYN flag on random source ports to the server to be attacked. The server sends a TCP packet in response to this connection request with the SYN and an ACK flag and waits for the returned ACK from the client, as TCP is a three-way handshake process. However, since the client was an attacker, the return ACK never comes and the server exhausts its resources waiting for the packets. This is called a SYN attack. If a number of hosts send TCP SYN packets to the attacked machine, unknowingly because a malware was installed on the attacking machines, the machine can be made unavailable due to resource exhaustion.

A TCP SYN attack is a type of **Denial-of-Service (DoS)** attack that can be amplified by using unknowing hosts who become a part of the attack through malware injection, resulting in a **Distributed Denial of Service (DDoS)** attack.

The firewalls can prevent these types of attacks by limiting the number of TCP connections that can be opened for a host or a group of machines simultaneously.

Enabling threat detection

The ASA engine on the firewall analyzes the packets flowing through the firewall and can detect activities such as a port scan flowing through the firewall device. The ASA firewall uses analytics and data algorithms to detect port scans and other advanced threats and sends alerts or initiates other mechanisms such as sandboxing to prevent any security risks to the protected networks.

Firewall security context

An ASA firewall can be partitioned into multiple logical firewalls that are called security contexts. Each context acts like an independent firewall, having its own security policy, interfaces, and administrators. Note that some if the features of a firewall might not be supported in a logical firewall.

Scaling the firewall

Recall from the previous chapters that stacking switches provide a greater number of ports to connect with and the ease of having a single console to manage the element switches within the cluster. Similar to switch clustering, specific ASA firewalls provide the firewall clustering capability.

Clustering allows the network administrator to group multiple ASAs together and treat them like a single logical device from a management perspective while increasing the throughput and providing the redundancy due to multiple devices in the cluster.

Connecting the DC to the internet

The connectivity to the internet is a very important element of every organization's IT infrastructure. This connectivity may be provided at a central location or in a distributed manner from each branch, as has been discussed in `Chapter 6`, *Understanding and Configuring WAN Technologies*. While providing internet access directly from the branches has the advantage that traffic need not come to the central location, helping reduce latency to the internet, it has its own disadvantages.

Some organizations want to control the internet traffic and have certain restrictions on the websites that the employees can access from the office internet connection. Also, organizations need a central internet to monitor and control the costs of the internet connection and have a central skill to manage the routing to the internet. Most organizations are short public IPv4 addresses to connect to the internet and they use techniques such as address translation to connect to the internet. A centralized internet infrastructure ensures that the necessary skills for managing address translation and internet access control are not scattered across locations, but available in the central location.

Network Address Translation

Network Address Translation (**NAT**) is done to conserve public IP addresses within an organization. This allows users with private IP addresses to access the public internet. A NAT gateway translates the source IP address of the outgoing packets from private to public IP addresses and keeps a track of the private to public IP address mapping. This mapping is then used to translate back the incoming packets where the destination IP address is converted from the mapped public IP address to the original private IP address, thereby allowing bi-directional flow of packets.

If a public IP address is reserved for every private address, this is called a 1:1 static mapping. This is a good way to hide the internal addressees from the internet. However, the number of public addresses required in this case is equal to the number of private IP addresses that are being translated. To overcome this, dynamic mapping is used for NAT. In dynamic mapping, a pool of public IP addresses is reserved for network address translation, and the NAT gateway uses this pool for address translation. In this case, if there is a 1 to 1 translation based on IP addresses alone, the number of public IP addresses required is equal to the number of concurrent hosts trying to create connections to the public internet. The following figure shows the change in packets as they flow through the NAT gateway configured with 1:1 NAT:

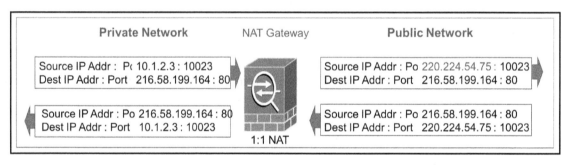

Figure 11: 1:1 Network Address Translation

1:1 dynamic NAT does not provide an efficient address conservation. To improve the address conservation, we use a 1:N translation, sometimes called a **NAT overload**. In a 1:N translation, the source IP address and the source TCP port are used in combination with a public IP address and a separate TCP port that is used as the source port. The destination TCP port is not changed as the connection is to a well-known TCP port number. Since this uses TCP ports in combination with IP addresses, this is also referred to as **Port Address Translation** (**PAT**), even though the correct technical name is **Network Address Translation-Port Translation** (**NAT-PT**). The following figure shows the change in packets as they pass through the NAT device for PAT:

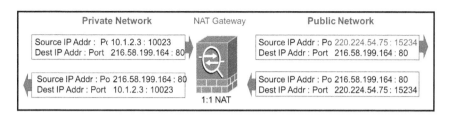

Figure 12: 1:N Network Address Translation

NAT is also sometimes used to convert IPv4 addresses into IPv6 addresses in combination with DNS servers that map the IPv4. A records to IPv6 AAAA records. This type of NAT is called NAT64. A detailed explanation of this is beyond the scope of the current book.

Some of the benefits of NAT are:

- **Address conservation**: The network administrator can use private addresses on the internal networks
- **Security**: NAT hides the local addresses from other networks, so the attackers don't have any knowledge about the real address of the host.
- **Support for overlapping addresses**: In case organizations have overlapping addresses at locations, primarily due to mergers and acquisitions, the hosts can communicate using NAT
- **Enabling IPv6 connectivity**: NAT64 can be used in conjunction with DNS64 to enable IPv4 hosts to communicate with IPv6 networks

We will discuss the configuration of NAT on the ASA firewall in a later section in this chapter.

Designing a sample DC

We will describe a sample DC in this section to show the actual use of the technologies discussed in the preceding sections.

A data center is the most crucial part in an organization's IT network. All services in the organization's IT environment, including business critical databases and applications, are hosted within the data center. Any outage in these services or applications can lead to a loss of revenue for the organization and therefore building redundancy into the overall data center design is paramount. This redundancy has to be built to cater to all failure scenarios including network failure, firewall failure, server failure, and so on. We will discuss the various techniques and designs used to build redundancy in the DC in the sample DC configurations.

A sample DC design from a physical topology perspective is shown in the following figure:

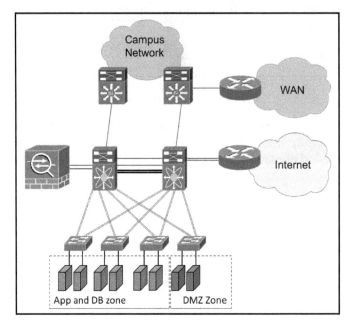

Figure 13: A sample DC design

The preceding figure depicts the physical topology of the network only from a user traffic perspective. The storage networks, and the management networks are not shown in the figure. The management network is generally a flat layer 2 network with the management ports of all devices including the servers, firewalls, and the networking devices connected to it with a gateway router connecting the management network to the Network Operations Center.

Although the figure shows the physical topology of the network, we want the traffic flows to be different and it would be a good idea for the network engineers to build a logical topology of the network as well that shows the elements traversed from a traffic flow perspective. The logical topology for the DC topology shown previously for our sample DC is shown in the following figure:

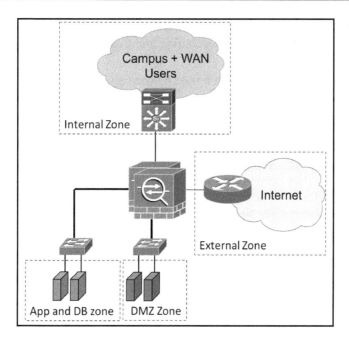

Figure 14: Logical view of the data center

We will describe the configuration of the various elements in the following sections to build the functionality in our sample DC.

Network design

A sample DC network configuration for the DC network using a vPC topology is shown in the following figure. This topology has multiple uplinks from the access to the core, and the uplinks are distributed on the uplink core switches. HSRP can be configured on the devices that act like the default gateways for the LAN segments. Since all segments would typically terminate on the firewall for security, the firewall would act as the default gateway for the LAN segments, and hence the gateway redundancy has to be built on the firewall.

The network is the underlying transport infrastructure for all packets on the network. Any failure on the network without a redundant path can lead to outages. There are a number of techniques useed to build redundancy in the DC network. Some of them include:

- Using dual core or spine switches
- Having multiple uplinks from the leaf or access switches to the core or spine switches
- Distributing the uplinks from the access on both the core switches

- Using first hop redundancy protocols such as HSRP, VRRP, and GLBP, as discussed in Chapter 4, *Understanding and Configuring Campus Network Technologies*.
- Having multiple links between the DC core and campus network and the DC core to the internet routers

The virtual port channel or vPC technology meets all these requirements. A vPC allows links that are physically connected to two different Cisco Nexus series devices to appear as a single port channel by a third device as shown in the figure. The third device can be a switch, server, or any other networking device that supports standard port channels. vPC allows multi-pathing, thus allowing you to build redundancy in terms of physical ports at the layer 2 level, and use both of them for forwarding.

The two devices, which act like a single logical unit, are called vPC peer devices. The combined port channel between the peer devices and the downstream device is called the virtual port channel. The two vPC peer devices are connected through Ethernet links that are used for special purposes. These links are called the vPC peer link and vPC peer-keepalive link.

The peer-keepalive link monitors the state of the peer device by sending periodic keepalive messages between vPC peer devices. The vPC peer link is used to synchronize states between the vPC peer devices and carries much more traffic than the peer-keepalive link. The following figure shows the terminology used for vPC:

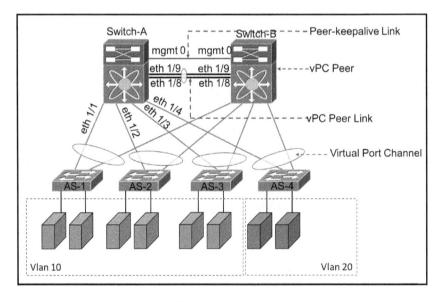

Figure 15: Virtual port channel terminology

The configuration of the vPC on the switches is described next. We have deliberately configured VLANs 1 through 50 in the configuration, so that the addition of new VLANs within this range don't need additional vPC configuration on the peer links.

The first step is to enable the vPC and link aggregation features on the switch using the commands, as shown in the following figure:

```
Switch-A# configure terminal
Switch-A(config)# feature vPC
Switch-A(config)# feature lacp
```

Figure 16: Enabling the vPC feature

In the next step, we configure the management interface as the keepalive link and assign an IP address to the interface. Further, the interface is a part of the management VRF on the Nexus device. The next section creates a vPC domain and defines the other end of the keepalive link within the domain. Finally, we create VLANs 1 through 50 on the switch:

```
Switch-A(config)# interface mgmt 0
Switch-A(config-if)# vrf member management
Switch-A(config-if)# ip address 100.23.45.66/24
Switch-A(config-if)# no shutdown
Switch-A(config-if)# exit

Switch-A(config)# vpc domain 1
Switch-A(config-vpc-domain)# peer-keepalive destination 100.23.45.65
source 100.23.45.66 vrf peer-keepalive
Switch-A(config-vpc-domain)# exit

Switch-A(config)# vlan 1-50
Switch-A(config-vlan)# no shutdown
Switch-A(config-vlan)# exit
```

Figure 17: Creating a vPC domain

In the next step of the configuration, we configure the interfaces for the peer link between the two devices. We configure the ports eth 1/8 and ethernet 1/9 as a port channel for redundancy and then configure the port-channel 10 as the vPC peer link. Note that we have configured the vPC peer link as a trunk port and have allowed all VLANs on the switch on the vPC peer link:

```
Switch-A(config)# interface ethernet 1/8-9
Switch-A(config-if)# description ***vPC Peer-Link member ***
Switch-A(config-if)# channel-group 10 mode active
Switch-A(config-if)# exit

Switch-A(config)# interface port-channel 10
Switch-A(config-if)# description ***vPC Peer-Link ***
Switch-A(config-if)# switchport
Switch-A(config-if)# switchport mode trunk
Switch-A(config-if)# switchport trunk allowed vlan 1-50
Switch-A(config-if)# vpc peer-link
Switch-A(config-if)# exit
Switch-A(config)#
```

Figure 18: Configuring the vPC peer link

Next, we configure the downlink ports that will form the vPCs. This configuration is as shown the following figure for the ports eth 1/1. Note that, although we have only one VLAN on the port channel going towards the access switch connected to the port eth 1/1, which is VLAN 10 in our case, we have still allowed VLANs 1 through 50 for ensuring that any further VLAN addition on the access switches does not need configuration changes on the vPC peer switches. The same configuration needs to be done for the other access switches on ports eth 1/2 through eth 1/4, using different vPC numbers.

```
Switch-A(config)# interface ethernet 1/1
Switch-A(config-if)# channel-group 1 mode active
Switch-A(config-if)# switchport
Switch-A(config-if)# switchport mode trunk
Switch-A(config-if)# switchport trunk allowed vlan 1-50
Switch-A(config-if)# exit
Switch-A(config)# interface port-channel 1
Switch-A(config-if)# vpc 1
Switch-A(config-if)# exit
```

Figure 19: Assigning ports to the vPC

This completes the configuration on the Switch-A. A similar configuration needs to be applied on Switch-B with the change in IP address of the mgmt. port and the vPC is complete. The only configuration required on the four access switches (AS-1 through AS-4) is to create a port channel for the uplink ports and configure the server-facing ports in the access mode and assign them to the specific VLANs, as has been discussed in `Chapter 6,` *Understanding and Configuring Campus WAN Technologies.*

This configuration would provide the redundancy for the packet forwarding infrastructure in the data center. Next, we will look at the firewall configurations within the DC. Note that the ports connecting to the firewalls will also need to be configured on the Nexus switches as layer 2 ports with specific VLANs so that the traffic from the hosts can reach the firewall that acts as the default gateway for the servers. The ports connecting to the internet routers and the campus core switch also need to be configured as access ports with the relevant VLAN numbers.

Firewall design

We have discussed previously that, from a security perspective, we need to restrict the traffic flows in the DC based on the application traffic flow requirements. Let us also assume that all internet users in the organization need access to the internet, and the addresses need to undergo a NAT at the firewall to go to the internet. Note that some organizations might not want to use NAT to access the internet, as it allows all users direct access to the internet. Such organizations force the users through a proxy server for internet access and use two separate firewalls for the external and internal zones. The recommended layout in a real enterprise would be similar to the one shown in the following figure:

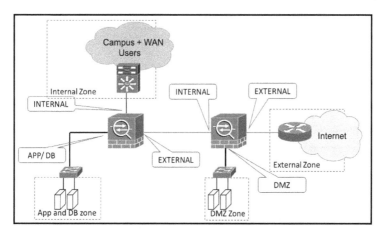

Figure 20: Zones in a sample network

The preceding approach is generally deployed by the enterprise with the two firewalls being from two different OEMs. This is to ensure that any threat left undetected and unblocked by the first OEM would be detected and blocked by the second firewall. This approach aligns with the "layered security" approach that is used to secure the enterprises, and traffic has to pass through multiple layers of security devices as it reaches the critical parts of the network. Since the internet is the network from where most attacks would emerge, this is treated as the most untrusted network, and the traffic flows through two layers of security to reach the application servers. However, for the internal users to access the same applications, the traffic only traverses a single firewall, as these users are treated as trusted networks.

For the purposes of illustrating the firewall configurations, we will use a single firewall and use the topology as shown in the following figure with the allowed traffic flows. We will consider that the DMZ zone has the mail server and the web hosting server in the DMZ and the application and the databases for the web servers run in the secure zones:

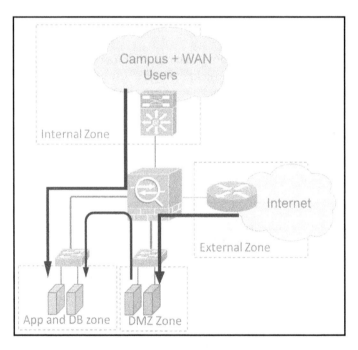

Figure 21: Traffic flows across zones in the sample network

We would need to configure the firewall as follows:

- The firewall needs to have four security zones, with the traffic flows allowed as in the preceding figure
- The firewall would connect to the internet router and have a default route pointing to the internet router
- The firewall would also have a static route for the campus network aggregate prefix pointing to the campus core switch
- The firewall would NAT traffic going from the internal zone to the internet

The configurations for this are done on the ASA firewall that uses the ASA software image. Let us assume that the organization uses the following IP address schema:

Users Pool	10.0.0.0/21
Infrastructure (WAN Links & Loopbacks)	10.0.14.0/24
App and DB Servers	10.0.12.0/26
DMZ Servers	10.0.12.64/26

Figure 22: Sample IP addressing plan

The interfaces on the firewall are configured as layer 3 interfaces with the IP addresses of the WAN links or the LAN segments. Let us also define the various security zones and security levels on the firewall, as shown in the following figure:

Network	Name	Interface	IP address	Security level
Internal Users	inside	ethernet 0/0	10.0.14.1/30	100
App & DB Servers	Secure	ethernet 0/1	10.0.12.1/26	80
DMZ Servers	DMZ	ethernet 0/2	10.0.12.65/26	20
To Internet	External	ethernet 0/3	220.23.45.65/30	0

Figure 23: Sample interface IP addresses

The security policy for the firewall needs to be configured with the following rules:

Source zone	Destination zone	Rule
Outside (0)	DMZ (20)	Allow port 80, SMTP with NAT
	Secure (80)	Block
	Inside (100)	Block
DMZ (20)	Outside (0)	Allow SMTP with NAT
	Secure (80)	Allow only 8080
	Inside (100)	Block
Secure (80)	Outside (0)	Block
	DMZ (20)	Block
	Inside (100)	Block
Inside (100)	Outside (0)	Allow with NAT
	DMZ (20)	Allow only 8080, SMTP & POP
	Secure (80)	Block

Figure 24: Mapping traffic flows into policies

As a first step, the interfaces on the firewall are configured with the corresponding VLANs and IP addresses:

```
ciscoasa(config)# interface ethernet 0/0
ciscoasa(config-if)# nameif inside
ciscoasa(config-if)# security-level 100
ciscoasa(config-if)# ip address 10.0.14.1 255.255.255.252
ciscoasa(config-if)# exit

ciscoasa(config)# interface ethernet 0/1
ciscoasa(config-if)# nameif Secure
ciscoasa(config-if)# security-level 80
ciscoasa(config-if)# ip address 10.0.12.1 255.255.255.192
ciscoasa(config-if)# exit

ciscoasa(config)# interface ethernet 0/2
ciscoasa(config-if)# nameif DMZ
ciscoasa(config-if)# security-level 20
ciscoasa(config-if)# ip address 10.0.12.65 255.255.255.192
ciscoasa(config-if)# exit

ciscoasa(config)# interface ethernet 0/3
ciscoasa(config-if)# nameif External
ciscoasa(config-if)# security-level 0
ciscoasa(config-if)# ip address 220.23.45.65 255.255.255.252
ciscoasa(config-if)# exit
```

Figure 25: Configuring firewall interfaces

As a next step, we define the policies on the firewall to allow only port 80 and port 25 traffic to come in from the internet into the DMZ. Let us also assume that the web server IP address is 10.0.12.66, which is advertised to the external world as a public IP address 220.224.228.232 using NAT on the firewall and the email server IP address is 10.0.12.67, which is advertised as 220.224.228.233 on the internet. This is achieved by the following configuration:

```
asa(config)# object network inside-server1
asa(config)# host 10.0.12.66
asa(config)# nat (DMZ,outside) static 220.224.228.232

asa(config)# object network inside-server2
asa(config)# host 10.0.12.67
asa(config)# nat (DMZ,outside) static 220.224.228.233

asa(config)# access-list outside_access extended permit tcp any object inside-server1 eq www
asa(config)# access-list outside_access extended permit tcp any object inside-server2 eq smtp
asa(config)# access-group outside_access in interface External
```

Figure 26: Configuring NAT on the firewall for incoming traffic

We also allow traffic on TCP ports 8080 from the DMZ zone servers to only the secure zone servers. Also, we allow SMTP traffic for the external to allow outgoing mail. This traffic would go through NAT as defined in the configuration earlier for the mail server:

```
asa(config)# access-list DMZ-in extended permit tcp any interface Secure eq 8080
asa(config)# access-list DMZ-in extended permit tcp any interface Outside eq SMTP
asa(config)# access-group DMZ-in extended deny ip any any
asa(config)# access-group DMZ-in in interface DMZ
```

Figure 27: Creating security policy for inter zone traffic

The following configuration provides dynamic NAT-PT for the internal users to access the internet using the public IP address pool 200.100.80.0/24:

```
asa(config)# object network NatPool
asa(config-network-object)# range 200.100.80.0 200.100.80.255

asa(config)# object network users-net
asa(config-network-object)# subnet 10.0.0.0 255.255.248.0
asa(config-network-object)# nat (inside,External) dynamic pat-pool NatPool
```

Figure 28: Configuring outgoing NAT

The following command configures the routes to the internal user pool towards the campus core router and a default route towards the internet gateway router for allowing the user access to the internet:

```
asa(config)# route inside 10.0.0.0 255.255.248.0 10.0.14.2
asa(config)# route External 0.0.0.0 0.0.0.0 220.23.45.66
```

Figure 29: Creating IP routes on the firewall

The internal zone of the firewall is the most secure zone and will allow us to pass traffic to all other zones. We restrict the traffic from this zone to all other zones using the configuration shown in the following figure. The configuration allows only HTTP traffic on port 80 and DNS queries to the external interface towards the internet after going through a NAT operation. We have also opened port 8080 for traffic going to the DMZ servers. The policy also allows ports 25 for SMTP, and 110 for POP3 to the mail server in the secure zone, and blocks all other traffic from the internal zone. Note that this is only a sample. The network administrators would open all ports required for the specific applications. Also, whenever web browsing is required, port 443 for HTTPS should also be opened along with port 80.

```
asa(config)# access-list frm_ins extended permit tcp any interface External eq www
asa(config)# access-group frm_ins extended permit udp any interface External eq DNS
asa(config)# access-list frm_ins extended permit tcp any interface External eq SMTP

asa(config)# access-list frm_ins extended permit tcp any interface DMZ eq SMTP
asa(config)# access-list frm_ins extended permit tcp any interface DMZ eq POP3
asa(config)# access-list frm_ins extended permit tcp any interface DMZ eq 8080

asa(config)# access-group frm_ins in interface inside
```

Figure 30: Creating interzone firewall policy

Firewall redundancy

Firewalls are generally deployed in a 1+1 redundant mode so that the failure of one device does not lead to service disruption. Two ASA firewalls can operate in active/standby mode, where only one firewall is forwarding at a given instant, or in Active/Active mode, where both firewalls share the load for specific contexts. Note that active/active mode is not supported for a single context firewall. We will limit our discussion to Active/ Standby mode for this discussion.

Failover requires that the two ASA firewalls are identical in terms of the model and the interfaces and software image. Also, there is a requirement for the two ASAs to be connected to each other through dedicated links. The links are:

- Failover link, which is used by the two units in a failover pair to constantly communicate to determine the operating status of each unit. Any unused data interface (physical, redundant, or EtherChannel) can be used as the failover link, as long as it is not configured with a name. The ASA does not support sharing interfaces between user data and the failover link even if different subinterfaces are configured for user data and failover. A separate physical, EtherChannel or redundant interface must be used for the failover link.
- Stateful failover link, which is used to exchange state information for ongoing connections through the active firewall. This link is optional, but having this link would ensure stateful failover in case of failure. If this link is not provisioned, the failover would still happen, but all existing connections would be dropped. Unlike the failover link, the stateful failover link can be shared with other interfaces.

The configuration for the failover for ASA firewalls is as shown in the following figure:

```
asa(config)# failover lan unit primary
asa(config)# failover lan interface folink gigabitethernet0/3
asa(config)# failover interface ip folink 172.27.48.1 255.255.255.0 standby 172.27.48.2
asa(config)# interface gigabitethernet 0/3
asa(config-ifc)# no shutdown
asa(config-ifc)# failover link folink gigabitethernet0/3
asa(config)# failover ipsec pre-shared-key a3rynsun
asa(config)# failover
```

Figure 31: Configuring firewall failover

The same configuration is needed on the other pair. The first line of the configuration needs to be configured only on the firewall that we want to be active. This line would be replaced by the command `failover lan unit secondary` on the standby firewall. Note that, if the firewalls are configured in the active/standby mode, only the active firewall is configured with the IP addresses and policies and the standby firewall is configured automatically after this through the failover link.

The configurations on the interfaces are done using the interface IP addressing commands, as shown im the following figure, on the active firewall:

```
asa(config)# interface gigabitethernet0/1
asa(config)# ip addr 10.1.1.1 255.255.255.0 failover 10.1.1.2
asa(config)# nameif inside
asa(config)# no shut
```

Figure 32: Configuring the standby firewall in a redundant pair

The preceding commands, when executed on the primary firewall, configure the interface gigabitethernet0/1 on the primary firewall with the IP address of 10.1.1.1 and the same interface on the standby firewall as 10.1.1.2.

Once all the interfaces are configured with the right IP addresses, and the policies are configured on the active firewall, they get replicated on the standby firewall and the system works in active/standby mode.

Server redundancy

The applications in the DC run on servers. Any disruption in the server, or the connectivity of the server to the network, can lead to service outages. Some of the mechanisms deployed in the DC for server redundancy are NIC teaming, use of virtualization, or using server load balancers.

NIC teaming

NIC teaming uses multiple NICs on the same server to connect to the network. The ports are used either as an aggregate port to connect to the network or as an active/standby port. The way the NIC teaming would work is configurable on the actual server. NIC teaming provides services redundancy in case of a NIC card failure, or a port/switch failure on the uplink switch where the server is connected.

Virtualization

Virtualization is a revolutionary technology in the DC that allows the applications to run on virtual machines, rather than on physical servers. The virtualization management software keeps track of the virtual machine or the VM that runs a specific application and can bring up the same VM on another physical server if the original VM goes down. This abstracts the actual application from the underlying physical hardware and ensures that the application is up, even though the physical server where the application was running has gone down. Virtualization brings the agility needed in the DC to restore services.

Virtualization can also be used to add more compute capacity during peak hours and shut down some servers and move the workloads across the remaining physical servers to ensure that the compute resources are optimally utilized and power and cooling requirements in the DC are managed by turning off the machines that are not required during off-peak hours.

Server load balancers

A **server load balancer** (**SLB**) is another device that is used to provide redundancy for the application in case the physical or virtual servers go down. A server load balancer is a device that abstracts the actual server pool that runs an application and provides a single logical view of the entire pool to the end users. Note that a basic form of load balancing can also be done using **Domain Name Service** (**DNS**) by resolving the same host to multiple IP addresses at the DNS server.

There are multiple types of SLBs, such as application SLBs and transport SLBs. We will focus on the transport SLBs in this section. A sample deployment using transport SLBs is depicted in the following figure:

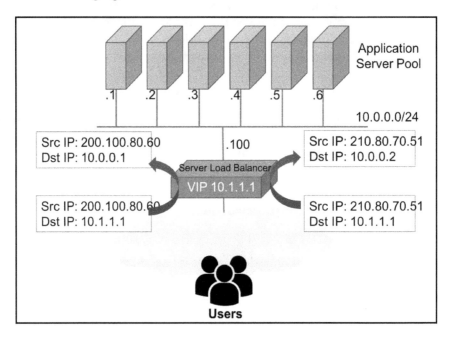

Figure 33: Server load balancers

The six servers in the 10.0.0.0/24 subnet are running the application and the SLB is presenting an IP address of 10.1.1.1 to the end users as the server IP address. The incoming requests are either terminated or NATTED at the SLB to the actual server pool behind the SLB to distribute the load among the servers (the diagram shows the NAT scenario). The choice of the actual server can be done by using multiple algorithms, such as round-robin, least-loaded server, least latency server, and so on. The user is not aware of the SLB, as the SLB transparently performs the functions of the NAT or connection proxy. Any server going down in the server pool is also not visible to the end user, as the SLB monitors the server health, and would stop routing traffic to that IP address, thus making the failover invisible to the end user.

Planning a disaster recovery

A backup data center is another way of providing redundancy to the complete data center in case of a complete DC failure, which could be due to a building collapsing due to a natural calamity such as flood, complete power outage, or connectivity loss or any other reason. A backup DC, generally known as a disaster recovery center, or a DR site, has the infrastructure of the DC at a smaller scale. This would ensure that services can run if there is DC site outage. Typically, the DR is at a geographically different location, and the data is replicated using a Layer 2 link between the DC and the DR to ensure that the DR site always has the current data, and can provide services. Note that, with the emergence of public clouds, some organizations have started using the public cloud as the DR site, or even the primary DC.

Providing remote access to the DC

Organizations generally have remote users who are on the public internet, and are required to access the corporate resources while on the move. This requires the DC to be connected to the internet, and allow the access of the servers in the intranet to the end users.

Although the DC is directly connected to the internet and separate servers can be hosted in the DMZ to allow this access, this would not be secure, as these servers would then be exposed to the complete internet. Such access is provided by bringing the remote users on the internal networks through VPNs, and then treating them as a part of the internal networks. The **remote access VPNs** (**RAVPNs**) are created over IP networks, typically the internet infrastructure and are secured using IPSec. The VPNs are authenticated using the credentials of the users to ensure that only the authorized users of the organization can form a VPN session.

The VPN session is terminated on an ASA device that is placed within the DMZ and that firewall has a separate interface that connects the authenticated users to the internal network. Some organizations might use the same ASA device as the internet firewall device to terminate the VPN sessions. Note that there are certain feature restrictions while using the ASA for VPN termination; for example, the ASA should be in routed mode and should not be running in multi-context mode.

A sample topology for VPN access using a dedicated RAVPN gateway is as shown in the following figure. Note that it has one interface connected to the internet for VPN termination and another for connecting to the internal network:

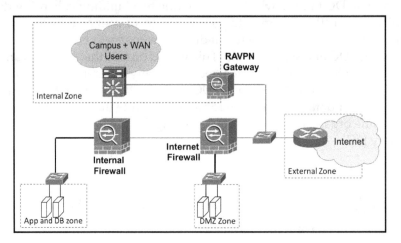

Figure 33: Remote access VPN in a DC

The configuration on the ASA firewall to allow the VPN sessions is shown in the following figure. The users would use a VPN client, such as the Cisco Anyconnect client, to connect to the VPN. The configuration snippet shows only the IPSec VPN related configuration and does not show any routing configuration or policy configuration on the RAVPN gateway:

```
! Configuring the interfaces
ravpn-asa(config)# interface ethernet0
ravpn-asa(config)# ip addr 202.190.80.3 255.255.255.248
ravpn-asa(config)# nameif outside
ravpn-asa(config)# security-level 0
ravpn-asa(config)# interface ethernet1
ravpn-asa(config)# ip addr 10.0.0.2 255.255.255.252
ravpn-asa(config)# nameif inside
ravpn-asa(config)# security-level 100
```

Figure 35: Configuring the VPN zone on the firewall

Once the interfaces have been configured, we configure the ISAMKMP policy and apply it to the outside interface, as shown in the following figure. The ISAKMP policy defines the authentication and the encryption methods to be used. We have used IKEv2 in the example that supports the Cisco Anyconnect client:

```
! Configuring ISAKMP policy and apply on outside interface
ravpn-asa(config)# crypto ikev2 policy 1
ravpn-asa(config-ikev1-policy)# group 2
ravpn-asa(config-ikev1-policy)# integrity sha512
ravpn-asa(config-ikev1-policy)# prf sha512
ravpn-asa(config)# crypto ikev2 enable outside
!
```

Figure 36: Configuring ISAKMP policies

Next, we configure the IP address pool to be used for RAVPN users and configure the user credentials for the RAVPN users. The user authentication can also be done by using the AAA server under the tunnel-group configuration. We also define the IKEv2 proposal set to be used for encryption in phase 2 for data transmission encryption:

```
! Defining pool for RAVPN users.
! This pool needs to be routed on the network towards this gateway
ravpn-asa(config)# ip local pool RA-POOL 192.168.0.10-192.168.0.15 mask 255.255.255.0
!
! Creating user credentials for RAVPN
ravpn-asa(config)# username testuser password 12345678
!
! Configure an IKEv2 proposal set to specify the encryption and hash algorithms.
ravpn-asa(config)# crypto ipsec ikev2 ipsec-proposal secure-AES256-SHA512
hostname(config-ipsec-proposal)# protocol esp encryption aes-256
hostname(config-ipsec-proposal)# protocol esp integrity sha-512
!
```

Figure 37: Configuring RAVPN user pools and credentials

In the next step, we create a tunnel group which allows us to configure the policies to be used for the group including the IP address pool and shared keys. If the enterprise AAA server is to be used for authentication, that is also configured under the tunnel groups. We have used local authentication in our example configuration:

```
! Configure a tunnel group to specify the IP pool to use, and define the group policy.
!
ravpn-asa(config)# tunnel-group RAVPN type remote-access
ravpn-asa(config)# tunnel-group RAVPN general-attributes
ravpn-asa(config-general)# address-pool RA-POOL
ravpn-asa(config)# tunnel-group RAVPN ipsec-attributes
ravpn-asa(config-tunnel-ipsec)# ikev2 local-authentication pre-shared-key C!sc0123
ravpn-asa(config-tunnel-ipsec)# ikev2 remote-authentication pre-shared-key Rem0tek3y
!
```

Figure 38: Configuring tunnel groups

As a final step, we configure a dynamic crypto map that allows remote users with any source IP address to connect to the VPN device:

```
! Create a Dynamic Crypto Map that lets the ASA receive connections from RAVPN users.
!
hostname(config)# crypto dynamic-map DYNMAP 1 set ikev2 ipsec-proposal AES256-SHA512
hostname(config)# crypto dynamic-map DYNMAP 1 set reverse-route
!
! Allow ASA to use the dynamic map to set the parameters of IPsec SAs.
hostname(config)# crypto map CMAP 1 ipsec-isakmp dynamic DYNMAP
hostname(config)# crypto map CMAP interface outside
!
```

Figure 39: Configuring encryption for remote users

The preceding configurations would allow the remote user with the username and password as configured in the configuration to establish a secure connection to the enterprise through the internet.

Summary

In this chapter, we discussed the data center functions and the networking devices used in the DC. We also looked at how the data centers have evolved with time to make them more agile and flexible, with technologies such as virtualization and converged adapters. We discussed the design for the data center, covering networking and security aspects. We finished the chapter with the section on providing access to corporate resources to mobile users.

In the next chapter, we will focus on securing the network infrastructure, and making the network and the applications secure. We will also discuss the different technologies and tools used for security in the next chapter.

8
Understanding and Configuring Network Security

"There are two types of companies: those that have been hacked, and those who don't know they have been hacked."

- John Chambers

Digitization and IT enablement has helped organizations to transform themselves and improve their way they conduct business. IT has enabled improving real-time communications across geographies, helping people collaborate effectively using video over long distances without the need to travel, and significantly reducing the turnaround time for services, making service delivery more efficient and agile. On the other hand, IT has also led to the creation of an infrastructure where everyone can connect to everyone else, creating virtually all information in a digital form that is stored in the data centers, and is accessed by the employees, partners, and customers of the organization. This leads to hitherto unseen issues of data security, where policy enforcement has to go beyond defining roles for people, but also extend the same to networks, application access, and devices.

In this chapter on network security, we will discuss the following topics:

- The evolving threat landscape
- Various facets of enterprise security
- Ways to secure the IT network infrastructure

Security landscape

The security threat landscape has changed drastically over the last few years. The earlier forms of security attacks on the IT assets of an organization were in the form of viruses and worms. Over the years, we have seen blended attacks that use a mix of multiple technologies to attack the victim. There has been an increase in advanced persistent attacks, and targeted attacks that are written specifically for a particular organization. The use of social engineering coupled with the malware that changes forms over time and on different operating systems has made the detection of attacks difficult.

The security landscape has become even more complex because of the increase in the number of devices, some of which are not even organization controlled because of the **Bring Your Own Device (BYOD)** policy in some organizations. The diminishing boundaries of enterprise with the acceptability of cloud technologies and a lot of services being offered on the cloud, coupled with the BYOD polices and users working from home on corporate devices, has also led to the security landscape being more challenging for security administrators.

John Chambers, executive chairman of Cisco Systems, says that the security attacks are so rampant that there is hardly any company that is not impacted by the cyber incidents. The issue of cyber security is also complicated because of the fact that organizations don't even get to know for months and years that they have been hacked and data has been stolen. Sometimes it is only after a detailed forensic trail of an incident that the security team gets to know that they have been hacked.

This changing landscape needs new and innovative security approaches to mitigate and defend against any attacks. These security approaches would be a mix of technology, skills, and processes to ensure that the organization can prevent any attacks from happening, detect any attacks in the case of one happening, respond to such threats to prevent their spread and minimize any loss to the organization, and finally be able to do a retrospective analysis and take steps to bolster the security posture so that the attacks are not repeated.

Elements of enterprise security

The IT security of an enterprise has multiple dimensions, ranging from protecting data, to preventing denial of service attacks, to defending against ransomware attacks and the spread of viruses and worms. All these dimensions need to be taken care of while creating a security architecture for the enterprise. Security is like a complex problem that can be handled if broken into its constituent elements. To this end of breaking the security problem into its elements, we will describe a layered model of the IT assets and what needs to be protected.

The following figure shows a layered model of the enterprise IT assets:

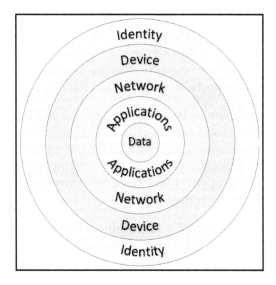

Figure 1: A layered approach to security

The ultimate goal of the organization is to protect its data. This data could be customer data, intellectual property, bank record information, or any other data that is of value to the organization or the loss of which can cause a loss of reputation. Data is protected using technologies on the perimeter systems and end systems, generally called data loss prevention tools. Data loss can also be detected by using technologies such as network behavioral analysis.

The applications are the next set of assets that need to be protected, as the applications going down can mean that the organization cannot conduct its business, leading to loss of revenue and productivity for the organization. Application security has a lot of dependence on the way the application is coded and compiled, and detecting vulnerabilities in the application that can be exploited to launch an attack. Using a Secure Software Development Life Cycle process can help minimize the security risks at the application layer. Routine **Vulnerability and Penetration Testing** (**VAPT**) conducted by the security teams and third parties are a means of detecting any application vulnerabilities and patching them.

The network is the next layer that is the underlying transport infrastructure that carries the data from the source to the destination. The network is also critical for accessing the applications and attacks in the network could manifest themselves in causing the outages to the network by misconfiguring devices, manipulating routing or other configurations on the devices or even sniffing traffic on the network to snoop on the customer data that flows on the network. Network security is ensured by managing access to the network devices and ensuring that the devices behave the way they are supposed to behave. We will describe the network security aspects in detail in this chapter.

Devices are the next set of IT assets that need to be secured, as the devices will connect to the network and can be infected and spread viruses worms/malware and even act on behalf of the unknowing users to carry out certain operations on the network without their knowledge. The devices are generally protected by enforcing strict controls over the operating systems they run, the applications that can be installed on them, and using techniques such as bit encryption on the devices.

Identity is something that can be used for identifying a user on the network. This could be a username/password combination, or a multi-factor authentication system such as a password hash generated randomly and delivered through different channels, such as the network and a mobile network, as a one-time use password. An attacker can try to use the identity of a privileged user on the network and gain access to all the resources on the network that the privileged user has access to. Identity is secured using techniques such as identity management systems and multi-factor authentication systems.

There are a lot of interdependencies between the various layers, as each layer touches the other layers and any attempt of an attack flows through multiple layers. In this chapter, we will discuss the networks security aspects in detail and discuss the security implications from a network perspective where the attack is actually on another layer. A detailed analysis of the other layers is beyond the scope of this book.

Securing network infrastructure

The network infrastructure of an organization consists of a host of network devices such as routers, switches, firewalls, and so on. These devices are vital for the successful conduct of the business of the organization. It is these devices that carry the data of the organization to legitimate users and it is same devices that transport the data to the attacker in the case of a security attack. It is important to ensure that the network devices don't participate directly in any sabotage and are not manipulated to send information to unauthorized users.

To understand the security of the network devices, it is important to dissect the network device into its constituent functional layers, or planes as they are commonly called. All network devices can be thought of as having three functional planes, as shown in the following figure:

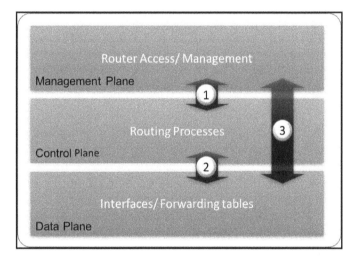

Figure 2: Functional planes of a network device

Let us use a router as an example to discuss the functions of these planes.

As discussed in Chapter 3, *Components of the Enterprise Network,* a router has a set of interfaces that are used to connect the router to the network. These interfaces have forwarding tables, stored in line card memory, that are used to switch/forward data from one interface to another based on the destination addresses of the received packets on the interface. These interfaces that receive the traffic and forward the traffic to the egress interface, based on the information contained in the forwarding tables, constitute the data plane of the router.

Note that the forwarding tables on the interface are populated based on the routing protocols. These routing protocols are algorithms that are run on the routing engine of the device to build a routing table. Copies of the current routing table are then sent to the line cards and stored as forwarding tables, so that the packet switching is faster, and a packet does not have to go through a complete routing table lookup in software, but can be switched in hardware by using the forwarding tables. The routing engine is the main CPU and does a whole lot of other functions that impact the forwarding decisions on the data plane. These components that perform the set of functions to build the information necessary for the actual forwarding of packets constitute the control plane of the router. Note that the control plane has to do much more with the actual CPU, while the forwarding is primarily a hardware switching activity.

The router is a network device that needs to be managed by the network operations team. This includes configuring the device with the right interface addresses and routing protocols and so on, monitoring the device from the **network operations center** (**NOC**), and executing troubleshooting commands on the routers to isolate and rectify any issues on the network. This access is also done to the CPU on the router as that is the element that provides access to the actual router. This plane is called the management plane of the router.

The three planes are functionally separate, but work as a whole for effective router operations. It can be seen from the arrow numbered 1 in the preceding figure that the management plane and the control plane communicate with each other to enable the right configurations and protocol information to be passed on through configuration to the actual routing processes. The arrow marked 2 signifies that the routing plane sends the routing information as forwarding tables to the data plane and that the routing packets from the neighboring devices actually traverse the data plane before they hit the routing engine, which is a part of the control plane. The arrow marked 3 denotes that the management packets (for example, telnet packets from a NOC agent to the router) actually traverse the data plane before they hit the management plane on the router.

Any impact on the control plane would be most disastrous to the functioning of the network, as that has the potential of sabotaging the routing and therefore forwarding to the devices. Any breach of the management plane to provide unauthorized access to the device can lead to the configuration being changed on the device and any attack on the data plane (for example, sending lots of traffic on the interface), can overwhelm the device and starve legitimate traffic to be forwarded by the router.

It is important to secure all three planes of the devices and we shall discuss the techniques used for this in the next sections.

Data plane security

As discussed, the data plane consists of the interfaces and the associated forwarding tables that are used for faster switching of packets. Any attack on the data plane would typically be an attack to push a lot of traffic through the network to try and block the legitimate traffic from being transported across the network.

The access network in an enterprise is typically a layer 2 network. The following figure shows the types of attacks that can happen at the access network at a layer 2 level and the defense mechanisms/features that are used to prevent these attacks:

Attack	Defensive Features/ Actions
MAC attacks	Port Security, Per VLAN MAC limiting
ARP Attacks	Private VLANs, Wire-speed ACLs, Dynamic ARP inspection
VLAN Hopping	Use dedicated VLAN-ID for trunk ports, Set user ports to non-trunking, Avoid VLAN 1, Disable unused ports
Spanning Tree Attacks	BPDU Guard, Root Guard
DHCP Rogue Server Attack	DHCP Snooping
Hijack Management Access	Secure variants of management access protocols, SSH, CoPP

Figure 3: Layer 2 attacks and defense

We will describe these features in the following sections.

Controlling network access

The data plane attacks are the attacks on the forwarding path of the devices. These attacks are best prevented by controlling access to the network from the user side and by managing the traffic coming in from the outside world; for example, the internet. We have discussed internet connectivity in the previous section. In this section, we will focus on controlling access of the users to the network.

Password protection on wireless networks

We mentioned in `Chapter 5`, *Understanding and Configuring Wireless Access Technologies*, that the wireless SSID that is being radiated in the enterprise can be password protected. The SSID can also be hidden, so that only users who know the SSID can connect to the network. As a next level, the SSID is protected using password protection techniques such as **Wired Equivalent Privacy** (**WEP**), **Wi-Fi Protected Access** (**WPA**), and **Wi-Fi Protected Access version 2** (**WPA2**).

Network access control (NAC)

The users connect to the network through wireless networks or wired access ports. Authenticating and authorizing a user at the edge of the network is the most scalable way of managing security, as it allows policy to be enforced on a per user basis even before the user gains access to the network.

The IEEE 802.1x standard is used for authenticating users before they get access to the system and this is enforced by using products such as Cisco's **Network Access Control** (**NAC**). The Cisco NAC solution authenticates the users based on their user credentials and even the device types they are using, as well as the operating system versions, and any antivirus software versions, and so on, before the device is allowed to connect to the network. If some of the checks fail, and the user is using an outdated antivirus version, he can be redirected to an enterprise portal that allows the user to update the software post which the user can connect to the network.

Network Admission Control (**NAC**) solutions allow us to authenticate users accessing the network across both wired and wireless networks and even remote users accessing the enterprise network through a VPN.

The Cisco NAC solution works with other authentication sources, such as a RADIUS, **Lightweight Directory Access Protocol** (**LDAP**), **Active Directory** (**AD**), and so on, to prevent unauthorized network access to protect your information assets, and helps to proactively mitigate threats such as viruses, worms, and spyware by ensuring that the end point protection software, such as AV and OS, are in accordance with the organization's policy. The solution also helps provide detailed audit and compliance reports on the users accessing the network.

Cisco NAC uses 802.1X on the access port to authenticate a user at the time of network access and isolates non-compliant users by passing parameters to the access switches and pushing the user traffic into specific VLANs based on the response received from the authentication servers. These VLANs are pre-configured on the access switches and routing is predefined to allow enterprise VLANs to have access to the entire network and quarantine VLANs to have access only to a specific subnet. A detailed discussion on NAC is beyond the scope of the current book.

Port security and MAC limiting

Any user can connect to the access port if the port is enabled. It is a good practice to keep the ports in a shutdown state and enable them only when a user is provisioned or connected to the network. After a user has connected, an attack can also happen by connecting a hub or an additional switch or by connecting multiple devices to the single switch port. This can be contained by looking at the MAC addresses.

Every decide that connects to the network has a MAC address. Configuring port security restricts a port's ingress traffic by limiting the MAC addresses that are allowed to send traffic into the port. The default number of secure MAC addresses for a port is one, but this can be changed through configuration by using the `switchport port-security maximum` command. Port security restricts the authorized MAC addresses that are allowed to send traffic into the port and helps to mitigate the risk of CAM table overflow, MAC spoofing, and VLAN-hopping-based attacks.

If we want only a specific user to connect to the switchport that is configured as an access port, we can define a static MAC address and only that MAC address will be able to connect to the switch. However, any change in the NIC card would require reconfiguration of the switch, as the MAC address will change with the change in the NIC card. In such cases, it is better to use dynamically learned MAC addresses and restrict them to a limit. There might also be instances where we only want the first device to connect to the switch, and if that device is replaced by a different device, we want to block that device. This is done by using sticky MAC addresses, where the dynamically learned MAC addresses are treated as static MAC addresses and are stored in the memory tables of the device.

Note that if the maximum MAC address limit configured on a switchport is n and we have less than n addresses configured using static MAC mapping, the remaining addresses will be learned dynamically, and these dynamically learned addresses would age with time, and get flushed after the expiry of the MAC timer, and new addresses would take the place of these dynamically learned addresses.

The configuration of the switchport for port security is as shown in the following figure:

```
Switch(config)# interface gig0/1
Switch(config-if)# switchport access vlan 10
Switch(config-if)# switchport port-security
Switch(config-if)# switchport port-security maximum 5
Switch(config-if)# switchport port-security violation restrict
Switch(config-if)# switchport port-security aging time 5
Switch(config-if)# switchport port-security aging type inactivity
```

Figure 4: Protecting the switchport

The `switchport port-security maximum` command sets the maximum number of secure MAC addresses for the interface. If this command is not explicitly configured, the system takes a default value of 1. The `switchport port-security aging time` command is used to set the aging time, which can be set from 0 to 1,440 minutes, with time equal to 0 meaning that aging is disabled for this port.

The command `switchport port-security mac-address sticky` can be used to configure sticky MAC addresses in the preceding example. To configure static MAC addresses, the IOS command is `switchport port-security mac-address <mac_address>`

The IOS command `switchport port-security violation restrict` sets the violation mode and determines the action to be taken when a security violation is detected. In this case, when the number of secure MAC addresses reaches the limit allowed on the port, packets with unknown source addresses are dropped until you remove a sufficient number of secure MAC addresses or increase the number of the maximum allowable addresses. If the keyword `restrict` is replaced with `shutdown`, the port would be shut down for all traffic with security violations and would need to be re-enabled manually using the `no shutdown` command.

Preventing spoofed attacks

Spoofing is a term used when an attacker uses wrong source addresses in the packets that are sent to the target destination. This is generally done so as to prevent any returning traffic and to hide the identity of the attacker. There are multiple ways to detect spoofing and block the traffic from spoofed addresses. The features used to prevent spoofed packet attacks are described in the subsequent sections.

ARP spoofing

An attacker can send a gratuitous ARP packet (an ARP reply sent without first receiving an ARP request) with a spoofed source address, causing the default gateway or another host to learn about it and store it in its ARP table. The ARP protocol (RFC 826) will create an entry for any such malicious host without performing any type of authentication or filtering. This behavior results in vulnerability to spoofing attacks and that lets the attacker receive frames intended for another user. This can be prevented by blocking all user-to-user communication by using the `Switchport protected` command. This allows only the users to talk to the gateway and not talk to each other on the network. We will discuss this in more detail in the Private VLAN section.

Unicast RPF

A router takes a forwarding decision based on the destination address, without any regard for the source of the IP packet. This is used by attackers to send attack packets on the network and using spoofed source addresses.

Cisco IOS software makes it possible to have the router check the source address of the packets before it takes a routing decision. Validating the source address can be a good way of checking that the addresses not in use are not sending packets on the network. This is done by using a feature called **Reverse Path Forwarding** (**RPF**). Since a router uses RPF as a standard mechanism for forwarding multicast packets, the feature when used for unicast packets is called unicast RPF or uRPF.

uRPF can be enabled in two modes:

- **Strict mode**: In the strict mode, the router uses the source address and looks up the routing table to find the interface that it would use to reach the source. If the interface is the same as the one on which the packet is received, the router would forward the received IP packet as a normal IP packet. This mode is generally used when there is a very symmetric routing on the network. However, not all networks are very predictable and some may have asymmetric routing and multiple links between adjacent devices. In such cases, the uRPF check would fail on the router and the packets would be discarded. This can be addresses by using the loose mode, described next.
- **Loose mode**: In the loose mode, the router only verifies that the routing table has a route for the source address. If the router has a route for the source address in the routing table, the router would forward the packet and route it based on the destination address, regardless of the interface as in the strict mode.

The strict uRPF feature can be enabled on the interface using the IOS commands. The IOS CLI syntax for the strict mode uRPF is:

```
ip verify unicast source reachable-via rx [allow-default] [allow-self-ping]
{list}
```

In this case, the rx parameter, meaning receive interface, is the key to configuring the strict mode uRPF. This command is applied within the IOS interface configuration mode. The optional parameters allow for the following:

- `allow-default`: Allows the use of the default route for uRPF verification. Normally, a default route is not considered valid for uRPF verification and source IP addresses found to match only a default route are discarded.
- `allow-self-ping`: Allows a router to ping its own interface(s). Without this option, all packets sourced by the local router and destined to a local router interface enabled for uRPF will fail the uRPF verification check. That is, self-pinging is not allowed by default. The network operator has to ping the interfaces on the router for troubleshooting and self-pinging can be turned on for troubleshooting.
- `list`: Specifies a standard or extended numbered IP ACL to be checked only if a received packet fails the uRPF check. When an ingress packet fails the uRPF verification check, it is then compared against the ACL, if configured, to determine whether the packet should be forwarded (matches a permit statement in the ACL) or dropped (matches a deny statement in the ACL). If no ACL is configured and the packet fails the uRPF check, the packet is dropped.

The IOS CLI syntax for the loose mode uRPF is:

```
ip verify unicast source reachable-via any [allow-default] [allow-self-
ping] {list}
```

In this case, the any parameter, meaning any interface, is the key to configuring the loose mode uRPF. This command is applied within the IOS interface configuration mode. The optional parameters shown are identical to those described for the strict mode uRPF.

IP source guard

IP source guard is a technique available on layer 2 Ethernet switches to prevent IP spoofing. If the hosts on the LAN are supposed to get IP addresses through DHCP, we want only valid users who have a valid DHCP address to transmit on the network. The IP source guard feature helps achieve that functionality by snooping on the DHCP packets and creating a database within the switch on which IP addresses have been assigned by DHCP.

When this feature is initially configured, all IP traffic on the port is blocked except for the DHCP packets that are captured via DHCP snooping. When a client receives a valid IP address from the DHCP server, a **port access control list** (**PACL**) is automatically installed on the LAN port that permits traffic sourced from the DHCP-assigned IP address. This process restricts the client IP traffic to those source IP addresses that are obtained from the DHCP server; any IP traffic with a source IP address other than one in the PACL's permit list is discarded. This filtering limits the ability of a device to spoof itself as another IP address.

DHCP snooping must be enabled on the VLAN to which the port belongs, before IP `source guard` may be enabled. We shall discuss DHCP snooping in a later section. The feature is enabled by using the following command on the switch on the port:

```
set port dhcp-snooping source guard enable
```

Limiting punting to CPU

The forwarding plane of the router performs best when all packets are switched in the hardware. However, there will be instances where some packets have to be forwarded but additional treatment applied to them. As an example, if an IP packet is received with IP options such as source routing, these packets would have to be punted to the CPU and cannot be forwarded by the normal forwarding process. These packets would considerably slow down forwarding as packets would have to forward through software lookups and the hardware based high-speed forwarding advantage is lost. Therefore, it is a good practice to limit the packets that need to be routed to the CPU. Some of the techniques for this are discussed next.

IP options and source routing

IP source routing is enabled by default within Cisco IOS. When IP source routing is enabled, IOS is able to process IP packets with the source-routing headers option.

Allowing the router to use source routing is a potential risk as this can be used to punt packets to the CPU from the normal hardware forwarding plane and even dictate the routers that would process these packets by defining the addresses in the source routing list of the IP packet options.

It is a security best practice to disable IP source routing. This can be done by using the IOS command `no ip source-route` in the global configuration mode.

All IP packets with the IP options present can be dropped by the router using the IOS `ip options drop` command. This command allows a router to filter IP options packets, thereby mitigating the effects of these packets on a router and downstream routers, and perform the following actions:

- Drop all IP options packets that it receives and prevent options from going deeper into the network.
- Ignore IP options packets destined for the router and treat them as if they had no IP options.

For many users, dropping the packets is the best solution. However, there would be specific scenarios (although uncommon in enterprise environments, such as using **Resource Reservation Protocol** (**RSVP**) which would not work without the use of IP options, and in this case, this command should not be used.

ICMP attacks

ICMP is commonly used as an attack vector for data plane DoS attacks. One reason for this is that ICMP processing is often handled at the iOS process level (CPU) of IP routers, and hence, can be leveraged directly from the data plane to attack the same router components that support the control plane.

By default, iOS software enables certain ICMP processing functions in accordance with IETF standards. These default configurations may not conform to security best practices or to security policies you may have for your network. To reduce the impact of ICMP-related data plane DoS attacks within IP network environments, iOS includes interface configuration commands to disable many of these ICMP handling features. These ICMP mitigation techniques are described here:

- `no ip unreachables`: Disables the interface from generating ICMP Destination Unreachable (Type 3) messages, thereby reducing the impact of certain ICMP-based DoS attacks on the router CPU. However, some management applications, such as **Path MTU Discovery** (**PMTUD**), actually use ICMP Destination Unreachable messages. Similarly, messages where an IP packet could not be forwarded because it required fragmentation but the MTU did not allow that also use IP unreachables messages. Configuring `no ip unreachables` would stop these functions on the network. A logical place to apply `no ip unreachables` to mitigate the risk of ICMP Unreachable DoS attacks is at the network edge interfaces, so that the functions still work in the core devices.

- `no ip redirects`: An ICMP redirect message instructs an end node to use a specific router as its path to a particular destination. In a properly functioning IP network, a router will send redirects only to hosts on its own local subnets, no end node will ever send a redirect, and no redirect will ever be traversed more than one network hop. However, an attacker may violate these rules; some attacks are based on this. It is a good idea to filter out incoming ICMP redirects on the router interfaces. This is done by using the interface IOS `no ip redirects` command which disables the interface from generating ICMP Redirect (ICMP Type 5) messages when it is forced to send an IP packet through the same interface on which it was received, and the subnet or network of the source IP address is on the same subnet or network of the next-hop IP address in the Redirect message per RFC 792.

Controlling user traffic

We have discussed techniques to control the access to the network to legitimate users and to prevent any spoofed packets on the network. In this section, we will discuss the features used to control the user traffic.

Rate limiting and storm control

Each user connects to the network on an access port. Given the modern-day switches, the access ports are generally Gigabit Ethernet ports that can pump a lot of traffic on the network. If an attacker starts attacking the network at 1 Gbps of traffic, that can overwhelm the servers. Rate limiting is the easiest way to control the maximum amount of traffic a user can inject on a given port. This limit is without any regard to the type of traffic and all traffic put together is limited to the limit as specified in the rate limiter configuration.

Another way to control the traffic behavior is by using the storm control feature. Using this feature, the traffic can be selectively dropped based on unicast, multicast, or broadcast incoming traffic on an interface.

Excessive LAN traffic may degrade network performance and increase the risk of broadcast storms and bridging loops. Traffic storm control (also called traffic suppression) monitors incoming traffic levels on enabled LAN ports at 1-second intervals and, during each interval, compares the actual traffic level with the port's configured traffic storm control level. The traffic storm control level per LAN port is configured as a percentage of the total available bandwidth of the port.

Within a 1-second interval, if ingress traffic on a LAN port enabled for traffic storm control reaches the configured traffic storm control level, then traffic storm control drops any new traffic received on the LAN port until the traffic storm control 1-second interval ends. Higher thresholds allow more packets to pass through the LAN port.

Note that the broadcast threshold applies only to broadcast traffic. However, the multicast and unicast thresholds apply to all traffic types, including multicast, unicast, and broadcast. When traffic storm control is active for either multicast or unicast and the rising threshold is hit, broadcast, unicast, and multicast frames are all filtered. Traffic storm control may be enabled using the storm control IOS interface configuration command.

The configuration for storm control on a port is as shown in the following figure:

```
Switch(config)# interface GigabitEthernet 0/1
Switch(config-if)# description User_facing_port
Switch(config-if)# storm-control broadcast level 5.00
Switch(config-if)# storm-control unicast level 80.00
Switch(config-if)# storm-control action trap
```

Figure 5: Controlling broadcast traffic bursts

The level value is a percentage of the overall port speed. In the preceding configuration, we have limited the broadcast traffic to 5% of the overall port speed of 1 Gbps and limited the unicast traffic to 800 Mbps. The last command in the example shows the action to be taken in case the threshold is exceeded. We have set the action to send a SNMP trap. If the trap keyword is changed to shutdown, the port can be shut down if the limits are exceeded.

Controlling user to user traffic

The Ethernet protocol was designed to allow direct user-user layer 2 communication, when both users are situated on a common broadcast domain. There might be requirements where, in an untrusted domain, there is a need to prevent the users in the same broadcast domain from communicating with each other. This is achieved using a feature called private VLAN, or PVLAN, sometimes also referred to as protected port feature. This feature effectively disables direct layer 2 communication between protected ports and also VLANs within trunks if the feature is applied to a trunk interface. Only communication is allowed with the router port for the traffic from users to go out of the LAN. PVLAN prevents any sniffing of network traffic between users on the same LAN.

This helps to protect the users against ARP spoofing, as the users cannot see each other. Communication between protected ports can only be achieved by means of another non-protected layer 2 device or layer 3 router. The PVLAN edge feature is deployed on the edge ports of a switch and thus no unprotected layer 2 device will offer direct layer 2 connectivity for users on the same service VLAN—all traffic will flow via the gateway router.

The feature is configured using the interface commands on the switch, as shown in the following figure. Note that the router-facing port on the switch is not configured as a protected port:

```
!
Switch(config)# interface GigabitEthernet 0/9
Switch(config-if)# description User_Port
Switch(config-if)# switchport protected
Switch(config-if)# interface GigabitEthernet 0/1
Switch(config-if)# description To_Router_Gig_0/1
Switch(config-if)#
```

Figure 6: Configuring a protected port

If traffic from one user cannot reach the other users directly, ARP will not work. If we need to allow the communication between the hosts on the same LAN, but prevent them from seeing direct ARP from other hosts, we can use ARP proxy on the router interface as shown in the example. This allows the gateway router to reply with its own MAC address to any ARP message for an IP address that is within the subnet on which it was received. The commands required to configure this function are as shown in the following figure:

```
Router(config)# interface GigabitEthernet 0/1
Router(config-if)# description To_Switch_Gig_0/1
Router(config-if)# ip addr 10.1.1.1 255.255.255.0
Router(config-if)# ip local-proxy arp
```

Figure 7: Configuring proxy ARP

The switchport protected command configures the port as a PVLAN edge port on a switch. If the private VLAN functionality needs to be extended across multiple switches, we have to use PVLANs explicitly, as the PVLAN edge port has only local significance, and configure the ports as one of three types of PVLAN ports: isolated, promiscuous, and community switch ports. Isolated switch ports within a VLAN may communicate only with promiscuous switch ports. Community switch ports may communicate only with promiscuous switch ports and other ports belonging to the same community. Promiscuous switch ports may communicate with any switch port and typically connect to the default gateway IP router.

Access control lists

Access control lists (**ACLs**) are used as additional packet filters to allow and block specific packets from flowing on the network. These ACLs are based on information contained in layer 2, layer 3, and layer 4 headers of the packets. The access list help to classify the traffic based on the specific parameters defined in these ACLs, and deny or permit this traffic. ACLs can also be used to identify specific types of traffic and mark them for priority processing on the network, as we will discuss in detail in Chapter 9, *Understanding and Configuring Quality of Service.*

ACLs on a network can be used to block traffic to/from specific destinations or for certain TCP/UDP ports. An example is where a user might want to allow traffic only for a specific subnet from a user on a specific port. The ACLs can be applied in either the incoming or outgoing direction on an interface, and the source and destination fields should be chosen carefully.

As a practical scenario, let us assume that the user range of addresses is 10.0.0.0/16, and the IP subnet 172.16.0.0/20 is used for infrastructure addresses. The network administrator would not want the users to send packets to the devices on the network, as these can be potential sources of attack. To do this, the administrator can create an access list that would block all traffic from any source IP address to the infrastructure IP address range:

```
Switch(config)# ip access-list extended user-infra
Switch(config-ext-nacl)# deny ip any 172.16.0.0 0.0.15.255
Switch(config-ext-nacl)# permit ip any any
Switch(config-ext-nacl)# exit
Switch(config)# interface gi0/0
Switch(config-if)# access-group user-infra in
```

Figure 8: Using access lists on interfaces

We created an access list named user-infra, and defined that any IP packet with any source address and a destination address in the 172.16.0.0/20 subnet should be denied. Note that there is an additional line permitting IP traffic from any source to any destination after that. This is because there is an implicit deny all statement at the end of an ACL and, unless you define this line, all traffic will be dropped. In the last step, the access list is applied to the interface gi0/0 in the incoming direction, which is the interface to which the user is connected.

ACLs provide a lot of flexibility and can be used with a host of parameters to control different types of traffic based on layer 2 to layer 4 header information. However, ACLs should only be used at the edge of the network where the traffic is limited. ACLs can also be used to do policy based routing, which is enforcing a policy even before the routing table lookup is done and this can allow the packets to be dropped or forwarded to specific interfaces based on source addresses.

Preventing denial of service attacks

Some of the attacks are typically done with the objective of making services unavailable. This can be done by sending a lot of traffic to a destination and choking the link bandwidth to the attacked machine, resulting in a **Denial of Service (DoS)** attack. Sometimes, multiple hosts may be used to attack in a **Distributed Denial of Service (DDoS)** attack. These DoS/DDoS attacks could be pure volumetric attacks to generate a lot of traffic for a particular host and rely on the underlying network infrastructure routing to route packets towards that host and choke the bandwidth to the host or the host itself of the processing resources on the host. Some other attacks attack the actual application, and are called application distributed denial of service attacks. In these attacks, the volume of the traffic might not be large, but the type of traffic being sent to the host would be manipulated to consume a large amount of resources on the attacked host, thus preventing it from delivering services.

Consider an enterprise as shown in the following figure. The enterprise has a pool of servers that are used to do web transactions for the end users. Let us assume that the organization has taken a 1 Gbps internet bandwidth from the upstream internet service provider. If an attacker is able to generate traffic in excess of 1 Gbps towards this pool of servers, the bandwidth of the organization to the internet would be fully choked and legitimate users trying to access the servers would not be able to transact and would experience a lot of traffic congestion, that might lead to application timeouts and hence a denial of service attack:

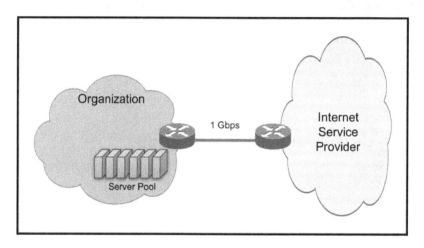

Figure 9: Volumetric DoS attack protection with limited bandwidth

The best way to mitigate such volumetric attacks is at the **internet service provider (ISP)** level, as ISPs have many more resources to manage these attacks compared to individual organizations. Some ISPs offer these services as a managed service, whereby they inspect the traffic coming towards a particular host/subnet that is being protected and they use scrubbing devices that do a deep packet inspection and other techniques, such as proxy for the TCP connection and other proprietary algorithms to send only legitimate traffic on the 1 Gbps link. Note that trying to deal with a volumetric attack within the organization's premises is not useful, because the internet bandwidth is already choked.

The organization can still use application layer DDoS protection techniques that deal with attacks such as half-SYN packets and IP fragments towards the attacked host by using suitable firewalls at the perimeter.

Control plane security

Control plane constitutes the brain of the network device, and controls the forwarding plane. While an attack on the data plane is transient and can bring down a particular host or a port, any attack on the control plane can bring down the entire network node or even the complete network. The attacks on the control plane are more pronounced than the data plane attacks.

The control plane is secured using a variety of IOS features and design techniques, as discussed in the following sections.

Disable unused services

A thumb rule of security is to lock everything that is not in use. The same concepts apply to the security of the network devices. Any services or features that are not required for the normal functioning of the network should be disabled, to limit the attack surface. Some of these services are at a global level and some services are at an interface level.

Disabling unused global services

Many of the built-in services in IOS are not needed in the network. These features should be turned off in the default configuration and only turned on if there are explicit requirements. A configuration to turn off some of these services is as shown in the following figure:

```
Router(config)# no service finger
Router(config)# no service pad
Router(config)# no service udp-small-servers
Router(config)# no service tcp-small-servers
Router(config)# no ip bootp server
Router(config)# no cdp run
Router(config)# no ip http server
```

Figure 10: Disabling unnecessary services on the router

The finger service allows remote users to view the users who have enabled a telnet session on the device. If the service is enabled, the router will respond to a `telnet a.b.c.d finger` command from a remote host and display the users before closing the connection. This can be a potential security issue by revealing all usernames to unauthorized users.

The packet assembler and disassembler service is implemented in Cisco IOS using the PAD service. This is used only if the router is running the X.25 protocol and therefore should be disabled.

The TCP and UDP small services are services such as echo, where the device sends back the received data. Similarly, there are other services such as discard, daytime, and so on that can be exploited by the attacker, and should be disabled.

The preceding configuration also disables the HTTP server for iOS configuration using the in-built HTTP portal and **Cisco Discovery Protocol** (**CDP**). CDP, if running on a network, lets users on adjacent devices know what device they are connected to and on what ports. These services have the potential to reveal unrequired information to unauthorized users and are therefore disabled.

Some of these services will be pre-configured in iOS (depending on the iOS release) to be turned off by default, but the network administrator should ensure that these services are explicitly turned off in the configuration templates used for creating the device configurations.

Disabling interface services

Similar to global services, there are some services that run at an interface level and should be turned off unless explicitly needed by the network administrator as a part of the underlying network design. These services are turned off by using the configuration as shown in the following figure:

```
Router(config)# config term
Router(config)# interface Gig0/3
Router(config-if)# no ip redirects
Router(config-if)# no ip directed-broadcast
Router(config-if)# no ip proxy-arp
Router(config-if)# no cdp enable
```

Figure 11: Disabling interface services

The ip redirects service prevents the device from sending ICMP redirect messages.

Recall from Chapter 4, *Understanding and Configuring Campus Network Technologies*, that each IP subnet has a broadcast address that is not assigned to a specific host. If a router receives an IP packet for the destination address 192.168.10.15 and the router has the subnet 192.168.10.0/28 directly connected, the router will broadcast the IP packet to all hosts on the network. This will cause unnecessary interrupts for all hosts, and is not a normal way of communication. Thus, this service is disabled, and all such broadcasts are blocked, and packets discarded by using the no ip directed-broadcast command.

Proxy ARP is a feature where the router can act like an ARP proxy for all hosts that it has a route to. Therefore, if a device sends an ARP request for hosts not on the network, the router would respond with an ARP reply with its own MAC address, since it can forward the packets to the destination. This has the potential to load the router in sending unnecessary ARP responses, and should therefore be disabled.

Layer 2 control plane security

There are a lot of Layer 2 protocols that run in an enterprise network, including **Spanning Tree Protocol (STP)**, **Dynamic Host Configuration Protocol (DHCP)**, **Address Resolution Protocol (ARP)**, and so on. One needs to protect the device against any attacks that use these protocols as the medium for the attacks.

STP security

Spanning Tree Protocol (STP) is used in networks to prevent Layer 2 loops on the access network. STP may be leveraged by an attacker for a variety of security attacks. To reduce the risk of STP attacks, iOS supports the following security features for STP.

BPDU Guard:

STP uses **Bridge Packet Data Units (BPDUs)** to exchange information across switches to discover the topology and put the ports in forwarding or blocking modes. The BPDUs are exchanged only between devices that participate in the STP domain. An attacker may try to send STP BPDUs from an access port of the switch and try to mislead the network devices by blocking some ports or putting some other ports in a forwarding mode, creating broadcast loops. The BPDUs also influence the choice of the root bridge on the network and can be used to make the access device as the root of the STP domain, thus enabling snooping of all traffic in the layer 2 domain.

An Ethernet switch should receive Bridge PDUs (BPDU) only on interswitch interfaces. Reception of a BPDU on a LAN interface providing connectivity to IP hosts is an STP protocol violation. Only a misconfiguration, software defect, or malicious attack would trigger this error condition.

The BPDU guard feature places the associated port into the error-disabled state if it receives a BPDU. The interface remains in the error-disabled state until you either manually enable error-disabled recovery using the `errdisable recovery bpduguard` global configuration command or enter the `shutdown` and `no shutdown` interface configuration commands. This prevents such access interfaces from participating in the STP protocol and, thereby, mitigates the risk of a misconfiguration, software defect, or STP-based attack sourced from an attached IP host or unauthorized device.

PortFast causes a switch or trunk port to enter the spanning tree forwarding state immediately, bypassing the listening and learning states, thus reducing the convergence time for a switchport for forwarding after it is enabled. The BPDU guard can be applied to all ports on the switch that are in the operational PortFast state by using an IOS global command:

```
spanning-tree portfast bpduguard default
```

BPDU guard can also be enabled on individual interfaces by using the command in an interface mode, which will override the global configuration.

The configuration in the following figure shows the configuration of interfaces for BPDU guard:

```
Switch(config)# configure terminal
! Enable all interfaces configured for PortFast with
! bpduguard by default
!
Switch(config)# spanning-tree portfast bpduguard default
!
! Enable an interface for PortFast
!
Switch(config)# interface GigabitEthernet 0/1
Switch(config-if)# spanning-tree portfast
!
! Interface not configured for PortFast with bpduguard
Switch(config)# interface GigabitEthernet 0/2
Switch(config-if)# spanning-tree bpduguard enable
!
```

Figure 12: Protecting STP using BPDU guard

Enabling BPDU guard will put the port in an error disabled state, and manual intervention is required for bringing the port back into an enabled state. IOS provides another feature called BPDU filter that prevents a port from sending or receiving BPDUs and can be used as an alternative. The configuration for this is as shown in the following figure:

```
Switch(config)# configure terminal
!
! Interface configured for bpdu filter feature
!
Switch(config)# interface GigabitEthernet 0/3
Switch(config-if)# spanning-tree bpdufilter enable
!
```

Figure 13: Enabling BPDU filtering

Root Guard:

STP forwarding paths within a layer 2 switched Ethernet network are calculated based on the elected root bridge. The root bridge is the central element and is the root of the tree formed through the STP protocol. If an attacker becomes the root bridge in an STP domain, it can snoop on all traffic, and traffic across most hosts would traverse through this device depending upon the network topology.

The Root Guard feature provides a way to enforce root bridge selection in the network. When enabled on an interface, the Root Guard feature places the associated port into the root-inconsistent (blocked) state if it receives a superior BPDU from an attached device. This prevents Root Guard-enabled ports from becoming a root port. While in the root-inconsistent state, no traffic passes through the port. Only after the attached device stops sending superior BPDUs is the port unblocked again. Once unblocked, normal STP procedures will transition the port through the listening, learning, and forwarding states.

Root Guard is configured using the `spanning-tree guard root` command within the IOS interface configuration mode. The deployment of Root Guard helps to prevent unauthorized devices from becoming the root bridge due to their spoofed BPDU advertisements.

The following figure shows the commands used to enable BPDU Guard and Root Guard on switch interfaces:

```
Switch(config)# configure terminal
!
! Interface configured for rootguard feature
!
Switch(config)# interface GigabitEthernet 0/3
Switch(config-if)# spanning-tree guard root
!
```

Figure 14: Enabling BPDU Root Guard

Loop Guard:

The fiber links between two switches use two fibers, one for transmitting and one for receiving. There could be instances on a network when only one fiber core is faulty, resulting in unidirectional communications between two devices. This can be prevented by using **UniDirectional Link Detection** (**UDLD**) features in IOS.

An impact of such unidirectional scenarios is that STP would not be able to receive BPDUs, but will keep sending BPDUs, resulting in STP malfunctioning. The network administrator can use loop guard to prevent alternate or root ports from becoming designated ports because of a failure that leads to a unidirectional link. This feature is most effective when it is configured on the entire switched network, and can be configured as shown in the following figure:

```
Switch(config)# configure terminal
!
! Interface configured for loop guard feature
!
Switch(config)# spanning-tree loopguard default
!
```

Figure 15: Enabling BPDU loop guard

DHCP snooping

Organizations use DHCP servers to assign IP addresses to end hosts. The hosts connect to untrusted ports on the access layer. Attackers can use DHCP to attack hosts by running a local DHCP server that is connected on a host connected to an access port. If no safeguards are applied, all hosts on the LAN would get IP addresses from the rogue DHCP server, including the gateway address and other information such as the DNS servers and so on, and the attacker can misguide the hosts on the network to sending packets via routers and DNS servers that can cause additional damage, such as data spoofing, and so on.

The DHCP snooping feature provides a mechanism to differentiate an untrusted switch port connected to an end user from a trusted switch port connected to DHCP server or another switch/router. DHCP snooping acts like a "mini firewall" and blocks all illegitimate DHCP packets received on the access port. These messages could be DHCP messages that spoof the DHCP server, or messages that send invalid information.

DHCP snooping can also rate-limit all DHCP traffic, thus preventing a DoS attack from a data plane perspective. In addition, the DHCP snooping feature is also used to insert additional fields into the DHCP packets, such as Option 82 fields that are used to identify the actual port on which the DHCP request was received when the DHCP server is not on the local LAN, but the network uses DHCP forwarding by using the ip helper-address command. Further, enabling DHCP snooping allows the device to build a database of the IP addresses assigned through the DHCP server, and this can be used for the source guard feature, as discussed previously.

All ports, by default, are untrusted ports for DHCP snooping and the uplink ports/interfaces connected to the network devices should explicitly be configured as trusted ports. If this is not done, the packets coming in from the DHCP server on these ports would be dropped as per the filter policies of DHCP snooping and DHCP will not function. The configuration of the port to the trusted state is also shown in the following figure:

```
Switch(config)# ip dhcp snooping
Switch(config)# ip dhcp snooping vlan10
Switch(Config)# interface Gig0/1
Switch(config-if)# ip dhcp snooping limit rate 100
!
! Defining the network ports as DHCP snooping trusted port
!
Switch(Config)# interface Gig0/23
Switch(config-if)# ip dhcp snooping trust
!
```

Figure 16: Enabling DHCP snooping

Dynamic ARP Inspection (DAI)

ARP provides IP communication within a layer 2 broadcast domain by mapping an IP address to a MAC address. However, because ARP allows a gratuitous reply from a host, even if an ARP request was not received, an ARP spoofing attack and the poisoning of ARP caches can occur. After the attack, all traffic from the device under attack flows through the attacker's computer and then to the router, switch, or host.

To reduce the risk of ARP spoofing and ARP cache poisoning attacks, IOS supports a security feature called **Dynamic ARP Inspection** (**DAI**). The DAI feature behaves very similarly to the DHCP snooping feature, in that it validates all ARP messages received on untrusted interfaces. The DAI function uses the DHCP snooping binding table to validate ARP messages. You can enable the DAI feature on a per VLAN basis by using the `ip arp inspection vlan` command in the IOS global configuration mode.

There might be instances where hosts use static IP addresses, but are still untrusted hosts. The IP to MAC entries would not exist in the DHCP snooping tables for such hosts and configuration is required to create a static entry within the DHCP snooping binding table or to use ARP ACLs to permit or deny ARP messages. This is done by using the `arp access-list <acl-name>` command. Otherwise, DAI will consider all ARP messages sourced from untrusted IP hosts with statically assigned IP addresses as invalid, thereby preventing network connectivity.

The ARP packets can be rate-limited to mitigate the effects of ARP-based DoS attacks that aim to exhaust or poison the ARP cache. This rate limiting is done only on untrusted interfaces and the default rate limit is 15 packets per second. The trusted interfaces are not rate-limited. The rate limit can be changed by using the `ip arp inspection limit rate <pps>` command. When the rate of incoming ARP packets exceeds the configured limit, the switch places the port in the error-disabled state. Manual intervention is needed to bring the port back into the operational state or error disable recovery needs to be enabled.

The ARP-based attacks can also happen by sending a different target/source MAC address in the ARP response packets than the destination/source MAC address in the Ethernet frame header. These checks can be enabled by using the `ip arp inspection validate dst-mac` and `ip arp inspection validate src-mac` commands. ARP messages with invalid source IP addresses can also be dropped using the `ip arp inspection validate ip` command.

Similar to DHCP snooping, the default DAI trust state is untrusted, and interfaces need to be explicitly trusted for the DAI state by using the `ip arp inspection trust` command within IOS interface configuration mode.

The complete configuration for DAI on a switch is as shown in the following figure:

```
Switch(config)# ip dhcp snooping
Switch(config)# ip arp inspection validate src-mac dst-mac ip
Switch(config)# ip dhcp snooping vlan 10
Switch(config)# ip arp inspection vlan 10
!
Switch(Config)# interface Gig0/1
Switch(config-if)# ip arp inspection limit rate 10
!
! Defining the error disabled ports due to DAI to recover after 30s
!
Switch(config-if)# errdisable detect cause arp-inspection
Switch(config-if)# errdisable recovery cause arp-inspection
Switch(config-if)# errdisable recovery interval 30
!
! Defining the network ports as DHCP snooping trusted port
!
Switch(Config)# interface Gig0/23
Switch(config-if)# ip arp inspection trust
!
```

Figure 17: Protecting against ARP spoofing using Dynamic ARP Inspection

Control plane policing

Control plane policing (CoPP) applies a set of rules to selectively block, allow, or rate-limit specific packets that need to be processed by the device for its normal functioning. CoPP is available as specific policer on certain series of high-end routers, such as the Cisco ASR series routers, to limit the packets that get to the CPU on the router. The same policies can be applied on the other series routers by using ACLs, and ensuring that the following functionality is provided:

- Receive packets only from the network interface address range.
- Receive SNMP messages only from the NOC subnet.
- Allow only those protocol packets to reach the router that are explicitly configured. For example, if OSPF is enabled, allow IP protocol 89 packets.
- Rate-limit the amount of SNMP traffic from the NOC.
- Rate-limit all ICMP packets coming into the router.

Protocol security

The control plane can also be manipulated by getting updates from rogue devices. It is recommended to use MD5 authentication for all protocols that are being used on the network wherever supported. If MD5 is not supported, use plain text passwords, but make sure to protect all sessions on the network. This would include authentication for routing protocols, such as RIP, OSPF, BGP, ISIS, and so on, and management protocols, such as **Network Time Protocol (NTP)**.

The protocol security can also be extended to use protocol-specific features and limiting the maximum number of prefixes that are allowed and sending alerts when the limits are exceeded.

In addition, techniques such as dampening should be used in protocols such as BGP, or SPF algorithm delays in OSPF to prevent frequent route changes to increase the CPU load on the device. Dampening can also be used on interfaces to ensure that the link flaps do not affect the routing of packets and interrupt the CPU unless they are considered stable.

Management plane security

The goal of management plane security is to ensure only legitimate users are allowed access to the network devices, and the device is available at all times to be accessed from the NOC.

Some of the best practices to be followed for management plane security are:

- Allow all management traffic to the devices only from the NOC. Organizations should also consider using a jump server to telnet/ssh into the devices and only allow a single device IP address to access the devices.
- Allow SNMP only from the SNMP management servers. Block SNMP attempts from all other IP sources using ACLs.
- Use secure forms of authentication; for example, use ssh instead of telnet to login into devices, wherever possible.
- Use SNMPv3 wherever possible instead of SNMPv2 with specific community strings. The read-only and read-write SNMP strings should be different.
- Create usernames and passwords only on the RADIUS servers and use RADIUS or TACACS for controlling access to the devices.
- Force users to have a password with a minimum length defined in the configuration by using the `security passwords min-length` command.

- Use role-based access to the network devices with only a handful of people who can actually configure the devices, while others can view the configuration and execute the troubleshooting commands. This is done using **role based access control** (**RBAC**).
- Use an **out of band** (**OOB**) management network wherever possible. Some routers have an OOB management port that is not used to route any user traffic but is dedicated for management. This allows the NOC to access the routers even in the case of data plane being flooded with user traffic.
- Use console ports for remote routers and have remote dial-in connectivity to access the devices in case of total outages.
- Use the `service password-encryption` command on the device, so that any passwords are not visible as clear text in the configuration files.
- Disable all unused services on the device.
- Hide all network specific information, such as IP addresses, usernames, and so on, while sending configuration files to people outside the NOC.

For routers that don't support CoPP, some of the functionality, such blocking the traffic to a router from users, can be implemented by using access-lists at all network access ports except the network ports connecting to the NOC to block all traffic destined for the network IP address pool.

We will discuss SNMP and enabling secure user access, and enabling role based access to devices, in `Chapter 10`, *A Systematic Approach to Network Management*.

Security beyond the network devices

Network security is like the proverbial chain. It's only as strong as its weakest link. The organization's IT infrastructure is most secure when every security element works together and threats are contained at every point of entry. A detailed discussion of these systems is beyond the scope of the current book, but this section describes the broad aspects of security beyond the network devices to provide a holistic view to the reader.

Securing the network perimeter

Most of the attacks generally originated from outside the network perimeter. The network perimeter is always treated as the boundary between inside and outside networks. Therefore, it is very important to secure this perimeter. Some of the security devices/technologies used at the network perimeter from a security perspective are firewalls and services protection systems.

Firewalls

We have described firewalls at length in Chapter 7, *Understanding and Configuring Data Center Technologies*. The firewalls act as the first line of defense of the organization and block any traffic that is not explicitly allowed by the security policies. The firewalls also provide a lot of inbuilt security rules that are used to analyze the incoming traffic and block any malicious traffic or any traffic that is not allowed as per the organization's security policies. Firewalls generally work at layer 3 and layer 4 of the OSI stack and can block all traffic based on these policies.

Securing services

The attacks in a modern-day world go far beyond layer 3 and layer 4. We see new protocols being used and the frequently used protocols being used in ingenious ways to attack. As an example, a malware may be sent to the internal users of an organization through an email, which cannot be detected by the firewall. Therefore, it is important to start looking far deeper into the packets as they traverse the network.

Email services

Email is the most commonly used attack medium by attackers. This is because emails cannot be detected by commonly used next generation firewalls as malicious, as they appear on the network as TCP/IP traffic that is allowed as per the organization's security policy.

Devices such as **Email Security Appliance (ESA)** from Cisco are special purpose devices that are tuned to detect any malicious traffic within emails. These devices act like the SMTP relay agents for the mail servers of the organization, and all traffic coming in from the internet and going out to the internet from the mail servers passes through the ESA devices. The ESA device does a deep lookup inside the application headers, including the email contents and the attachments, and runs them through multiple AV engines and rules that help the device infer malicious emails.

Threat intelligence is an important element of security and the ESA receives the threat intelligence from the central servers hosted by the OEM that provide the list of domains/IP addresses that send malicious emails. This can be used to detect any phishing emails.

Certain email security systems also use specific text search within the emails to find if some critical data, such as SSN numbers, credit card information, and so on, is being exchanged through emails, and an alert is triggered if that is in violation of the security policy.

Different OEMs use different threat intelligence sources, different scanning algorithms, and different proprietary techniques to detect any security threats in the email systems. Some OEMs also provide additional plugins on top of the email security systems, such as data loss prevention, advanced malware protection, and so on.

Web security

Users within an organization use the internet and that is another source of attacks. If the users go to malicious sites that are infected, the malware can be downloaded onto the user's system, and that can be used to steal information, or launch ransomware, or data encryption attacks.

Web Security Appliance (**WSA**) from Cisco is an appliance that acts in line for the web traffic from the users to the internet. This device uses the same threat intelligence from the security research organizations that might be OEM specific and also utilizes public security threat intelligence to block specific sites on the web from being accessed by the internal users.

Web security systems also come with additional functionality in the form of plugins, including URL filtering, data loss prevention, and advanced malware protection.

Advanced Malware Protection (AMP)

The threats in the modern cyber world are delivered through multiple channels and as files that might not look suspicious when they enter the network. However, the malware morphs into different forms and becomes active after some time, thus launching an attack.

AMP systems are systems that track any known files using hash values to alert security triggers and prevent the spread of the files and malware. These systems also track unknown files by using a technique called sandboxing where the file is kept in an isolated environment to check if the files morphs and is a security threat. If it does, it is important to block the files from then on, which is done using the hash value for the file. However, an important capability is to track the file on the network using the email and web systems to identify which hosts have accessed the file and have been infected, so as to take remediation measures.

Such systems/services are also heavily dependent on threat intelligence and the ability to communicate with the various security devices on the network to provide a holistic view of security.

Securing the endpoints

Once the network perimeter has been secured, organizations can still not be sure that the network is secured. This is because the endpoints themselves are a potential source of attack. The endpoints have USB ports, which can be used by an employee to transfer a malicious file unknowingly, or the system might be running an older operating system version, which might be susceptible to security attacks.

We have covered NAC briefly under the section on network access earlier in the chapter. In addition, having strong organizational security policies for operating systems and other endpoint protection systems go a long way in securing the overall enterprise.

DNS-based security

Recent advances in security have led to systems that use **Domain Name Services** (**DNS**) to prevent security attacks. All users make a DNS query for a host as the first step when they access any service such as email, web browsing, and so on.

Cisco has an offering called Umbrella where all DNS requests are routed to a DNS server that keeps track of malicious domains and the malicious domains are not resolved in the first place, thus preventing the users from accessing any malicious websites. The Umbrella offering also provides a web proxy service for suspected domains, and ensures that the users are not impacted even if they go to domains which are not confirmed dark domains, but can potentially harm the users.

Securing data in transit

Data in transit is vulnerable to eavesdropping if the network devices are not properly configured. If the users require additional security, they can use IPSec, which provides a means of encrypting and authenticating traffic when the traffic is sent from the source to the destination. We covered the IPSec encryption of the links in Chapter 6, *Understanding and Configuring WAN technologies*. IPSec is also used by remote users when they access the network remotely by logging into the network through a VPN. This configuration was discussed in Chapter 7, *Understanding and Configuring Data Center Technologies*.

Network behavioral analysis

Network behavioral analysis is a technology used to provide indications of any security violations on the network by looking at the traffic flows. Netflow is a protocol that is defined in the IETF standards as RFC 3954, among others, that sends the metadata of all traffic that is traversing the device.

The device on which Netflow is configured looks at the IP packets that are traversing the device on all interfaces and sends a part of the information known as metadata to a central collector. This information contains the layer 3 and layer 4 information, such as the source IP address, destination IP address, protocol, amount of traffic, along with additional information from the device, such as the interface on which the traffic was received, the egress interface, timestamps, and so on. The central collector receives this information from all the devices and does data analytics on top of the raw data to visualize things such as:

- Which IP addresses are talking to which other IP addresses?
- What are the protocols running on the network?
- Who are the top users/clients on my network?
- Which are the top servers on the network?
- How many DNS servers are there on the network?
- This information is then used to build a baseline of the network traffic behavior and used to detect any security incidents, which could manifest as deviations from the baseline traffic behavior, some hosts talking to a group of addresses they should not be talking to, or a new IP address responding to DNS requests and so on.
- Stealthwatch from Cisco is a product that enables the network administrators to get complete visibility into the network from a traffic perspective and also to provide any indicators of security breaches based on network traffic behavior.

Summary

We discussed the overall security approach for an enterprise in this chapter. We started with an overall view of the aspects of IT security and delved deep into securing the network. We discussed the security approaches for the network from a data plane, control plane, and management plane perspective. We ended the discussion with an overall view of securing the organization beyond the network devices.

In the next chapter, we will discuss the need to prioritize certain types of traffic over others, and the features and technologies to do this.

9

Understanding and Configuring Quality of Service

"The worst form of inequality is to try to make unequal things equal."

- Aristotle

The networks in an organization carry multiple types of traffic. Some of this traffic is very critical to business, while some other traffic might just be internet browsing. Furthermore, the traffic on the network could be from an ongoing **Voice over IP** (**VoIP**) call that is real-time traffic, or just an email sent from a user to another, that is not real-time, and can withstand the delays of a store and forward network. Different types of traffic need to be handled differently; treating all traffic equally on the network can cause critical applications to be degraded while noncritical applications choke the network.

In this chapter, we will discuss the concepts related to providing the right quality of service to the different types of traffic on the network, and go on to discuss the design aspects and implementation of the **Quality of Service** (**QoS**) policy on a network built using Cisco devices. The topics to be discussed in this chapter include:

- The need for QoS
- Approaches to implementing QoS
- QoS tools, including classification, marking, and scheduling
- Configuring QoS on Cisco devices
- QoS in a hybrid environment

The need for QoS

We have discussed the different techniques of building an IP-based network in the previous chapters. The enterprise network is fundamentally a packet-based network with the IP packets flowing from the source to the destination. The IP packets would be routed and forwarded from the source to the destination along the best path available from among the various paths available based upon the routing topology.

The network would also carry traffic from multiple users, and the traffic would be of different types. The traffic would consist of business-critical traffic like the one used for business applications such as SAP or other ERP systems, voice traffic for communication between different users on the network, video traffic from video calls between users using dedicated video end points or even soft clients on desktops/laptops, internet traffic for web browsing, email traffic from users within and outside the organization, and might also include a multicast video feed from companywide meetings, and so on.

Even though all the preceding traffic types are encapsulated as IP datagrams, and are transported across the network, not all traffic is equal as each type of traffic has its own tolerance limits and requirements from the network. Streaming video and voice traffic are real-time traffic flows that if delayed by more than a certain time would cause an awful user experience. On the other hand, transferring a large file across the network using **File Transfer Protocol** (**FTP**) would not be as sensitive to the delays caused by the network. However, if some packets on the network get dropped, there would be a lot of retransmission causing more load on the network, and at the same time reducing the actual throughput of the file transfer.

One might argue that if you have enough bandwidth on the network, there is no need for Quality of Service. It might be correct to say that provided what the user considers *enough* is *enough* from an application requirement as well. All of us have seen a video call or a voice call quality degrade on a soft client on the laptop, when the email client starts receiving or sending an email with a large attachment. The point being made is that data traffic is *bursty* in nature, which is too unpredictable. IP networks use this to their advantage by using statistical multiplexing, and store and forward techniques, but the same techniques can also lead to issues with user experience when they use heterogeneous applications on the network.

It is important that the network is designed and configured for different types of traffic that can be injected into the network, and policies defined for how to treat each type of traffic in case of congestion on the network. These policies would include whether to queue and hold the IP packets for a while, or to just drop the traffic, and let the application take care of this. All of this is an integral part of the QoS design of an IP network.

QoS can help prioritize certain types of traffic over other unimportant traffic during times of network congestion. Another misconception among some network engineers is to defer the network capacity upgrades, and let QoS prioritize important traffic. This is the other extreme, and again not a practical approach, as QoS can help only during transient congestion, and cannot create bandwidth. If the total amount of bandwidth required is high over sustained intervals, the network capacity needs to be upgraded, and QoS is not the solution.

QoS on a network needs to be an integral part of the network design, and cannot be taken for granted in networks that are under-utilized or cannot be a panacea for a perpetually congested network.

Let's use an analogy from real life to understand QoS. Let's assume you are going from your house to the airport. The road network acts like the network and links for you to reach the airport. You are the payload and the vehicle you are in is the packet header that encapsulates the payload to create a datagram. The car moves along the roads on the way to the airport, stopping at various manned intersections on the way. Each intersection is analogous to the router, with the person manning the intersection acting like the QoS engine, which holds you in the queue before you are allowed on the road. You reach the airport (destination) traversing the network and the payload is delivered from the source to the destination.

Now, assume that there is a VIP who has a beacon light on his car or a pilot vehicle accompanying him, who is also headed to the airport at the same time. The VIP is the critical payload, his car the packet header, and the beacon light or the pilot vehicle acts like the identifier that this is a critical payload. Every time this important packet reaches the router (traffic intersection), the QoS engine (person manning the intersection) identifies the packet as a priority packet, and he is let on the road to the airport ahead of others. Thus, even though there were two packets from the same source to the same destination, using the same links and routers, one packet reached the destination with a better quality of service.

Network impact on traffic

Having established that a network needs to implement QoS to be able to support different types of traffic on the network, it is also important to understand what impact the network has on application performance. In this section, we will discuss the impact that the network can have on different types of applications, and how we can classify the applications into groups that need to be treated in a similar manner over the network.

Let's start by discussing the impact that the network has on the packets as they travel from source to destination across a series of network devices and links. We have discussed in Chapter 3, *Components of the Enterprise Network*, how a router processes the packets received on the interfaces. We have also discussed additional processing that is done by the router in terms of ACLs in Chapter 8, *Understanding and Configuring Network Security*.

A summary of the high-level actions performed by the router is mentioned in the following list:

- Receive the packet on the ingress interface
- Hold the packet in a queue and wait for its turn to be processed
- Validate the header checksums, and discard the packet if the packet fails the integrity check
- Classify the packet based on any ingress access control lists applied on the interface on which the packet was received, and take the action defined in the ACL
- Perform a routing lookup for the packet, and decide on the egress interface
- Perform the necessary header changes, for example, TTL decrement, and put the packet in a queue on the egress interface
- Validate the packet against any outgoing ACLs applied on the egress interface
- Send the packet out on the interface as a bitstream

We will expand the preceding list and get more specific with the QoS terminology as we go further. The packet is then sent out on the physical link before it reaches the next router or the destination.

The packet might get dropped on the way because of link errors, or link failures, or even getting dropped by a router due to an ACL action. This leads to **packet loss** as seen from the source to destination.

The packet also has to wait in the queues before the packet is serviced based on the router resources, and the link capacity of the egress interface. The packet travels on the physical link and takes a finite amount of time to travel from the source to the destination. This is called **latency**.

Finally, if we send multiple packets from the source to the destination at regular intervals (having equal time intervals between consecutive packets), the packets might arrive out of sequence at the destination. The packets may also arrive at the destination in sequence but with the interpacket gaps that are unequal. This is called **jitter**.

These three characteristics of the network, namely, packet loss, latency, and jitter have a significant impact on the application's performance. The actual impact depends upon the type of application, and the protocol used by the application. Let's describe the impact of these characteristics on the different applications in more detail.

Packet loss

Packet loss is a measure of the packets lost in transit from the source to the destination. It is measured as the percentage of packets that are lost in transit to the total packets sent on the network.

Most applications use TCP as the transport protocol. TCP requires a connection to be established between the end hosts after which the hosts exchange data. The data exchanged between the hosts is acknowledged using the fields in the TCP headers.

TCP protocol uses sequence numbers in the TCP headers to identify the data bytes in the TCP connection. These numbers are baselined at the time of the connection setup. These sequence numbers are used as identifiers to acknowledge the data received by the receiver.

If certain packets are lost in transit, the receiving node requests a retransmission of these packets. The acknowledgement numbers in the TCP header are used by the receiver to inform the transmitter about the packets that have been received. A lack of acknowledgement signifies that the data was lost and needs to be transmitted again. The lost or corrupted data packets need to be retransmitted over the network. Retransmission of packets leads to unproductive use of the available bandwidth.

The sequence numbers are also used to sequence the data bytes received through the TCP segments, if the TCP segments are lost in transit, or arrive out of sequence at the receiving node. The receiving node waits for retransmitted packets to replicate the bit stream of the application layer data before it is passed on to the application layer at the receiving end. Each retransmission due to a packet loss requires the receiving node to hold the packets that were later in the bit stream sequence of the application in the TCP buffer, and hence these packets are delayed for delivery to the application.

Hence, packet loss causes blockage of buffers on the end host as the receiving node cannot pass on the received data to the application, if it is not in sequence. This might not be desirable for certain applications where the packets carry real-time information and are very sensitive to time delays.

Voice packets are one such type of packet, which are sensitive to time delays, and hence don't use TCP as the encapsulating protocol. Voice is carried over UDP, where there is no retransmission, and the packets are passed on to the application in the order they are received, thus ensuring that time-sensitive data is not delayed.

Applications can work well in spite of packet loss, if there is enough redundancy in the information at the application level. To provide a very simplistic example of this information redundancy, let's assume the transmission of voice over IP at 64 kbps, although different codecs use different bandwidths. Voice samples are captured every 125 microseconds and sent over the network. A loss of two consecutive packets would mean that we lost voice for 250 microseconds in a conversation. The listener is still able to make sense of what is being said as 250 microseconds is a short time in the overall conversation span, and the voice syllables before and after the blackout interval of 250 microseconds are enough to decipher the meaning. However, if the packet loss is high, we would not be able to make any sense of the voice call. Different codecs use different bandwidth and different sampling time. As a general rule of thumb, voice can tolerate a packet loss of less than 3%, but the quality of voice is degraded. Real-time video is another application that uses UDP, and is even more susceptible to IP packet loss.

It is clear from the preceding discussion that packet loss needs to be minimized in order to improve throughput in case of TCP applications and to improve the user experience in case of UDP applications.

Latency

Latency is the average time that is taken by a packet to travel from the source to the destination, and for the acknowledgement to travel back from the destination to the source. It is also referred to as **Round Trip Time (RTT)**.

Recall from Chapter 1, *Network Building Essentials,* that the TCP window size is the maximum value of data that can be sent without waiting for an acknowledgement. The sender has to wait to send more data until it gets an acknowledgement of the data sent earlier. So, even for networks without any packet loss, the network is idle until the ACK is received. If the RTT on the network is high, the ACK takes more time to come back, and hence the throughput reduces, as the link is idle for longer durations of time. The TCP throughput reduces for a higher RTT value if the window size remains the same. Hence, the latency on the network needs to be low to improve the TCP throughput on the network.

In case of real-time applications that use UDP as the transport protocol, network latency has no impact on throughput, as the receiver can send as much data as possible. However, a voice conversation is bidirectional at the user experience level. Hence, a high latency would mean that a voice call user starts to hear the other person after a certain time gap from the time that the speaker starts talking. This leads to a degraded user voice experience, similar to a voice call over a satellite link. Note that, in this case, the latency that impacts experience is unidirectional, while in the case of TCP, the latency that impacts throughput is round-trip.

UDP applications, such as videos, which are not bidirectional, are not affected by latency. For example, a video broadcast would not be sensitive to latency, as there is no feedback. On the other hand, a video call over IP would have the same implications of latency as a voice call.

Let's now look at the elements that contribute to latency in the IP packet. An IP packet traverses multiple devices and links on its way from the source to the destination. A subset of the network is shown in the following figure:

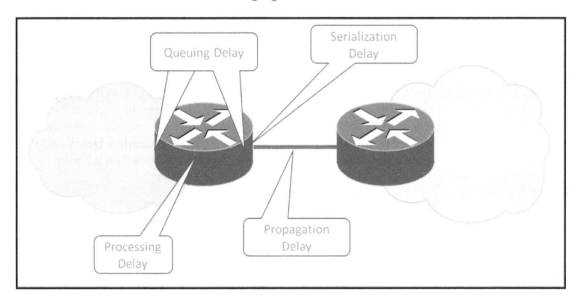

Figure 1: Component of network delay

The router receives a packet and processes the packet to match against any ACLs, routing lookups, and so on. The time taken for this processing is called the **Processing Delay**. This delay is very small given the advancements in the networking hardware processing capabilities. This delay would be of the order of a hundred microseconds or less in most routers. The actual forwarding latency can even be in the nanoseconds range for high-speed switching devices.

Another element of delay is referred to as the **Queuing Delay**. This is when the packet is held in the queue on the ingress interface (input queue) before being taken up for processing, or being held in the queue on the egress interface (output queue) before the packet can be sent out on the medium. Consider a scenario where a router has three links with bandwidths as shown next. Let's also assume that all traffic from links one and two is to be forwarded on link three. There may be instances when the instantaneous rate of packets to be sent out on link three is more than the bandwidth of the link. In such cases, the packets have to be stored in the buffers on the interface, before the packets can be sent out. The holding time of the packets in these buffers leads to queueing delay. The queueing delay is a variable and depends upon the size of the buffers, and the traffic on the link. If the link is not congested, the packets would not be required to be held in queue, and hence the queuing delay is zero. However, if there are moments of instantaneous congestion, we would experience queuing delay, and this would be a variable. Queuing delay is normally of the order of a few milliseconds.

The next element of delay is when the router needs to send the packet out on the physical medium. The network links are serial links, and the packets need to be transmitted on the link as a series of bits. The time taken to send a packet completely on the wire depends on the packet size and the speed of the link. This time is called the **Serialization Delay** and is again variable. For a maximum packet size of 1500 bytes to be transmitted on a 2 Mbps link, the serialization delay is 5.89 ms as calculated in the following figure:

```
IP packet length              : 1500 bytes
PPP header length             : 8 bytes
Total packet size             : 1508 bytes
Total packet size (P)         : 1508*8 bits = 12064 bits
Wire speed (S)                : 2.048 Mbps = 2048 kbps
Serialization delay (D=P/S)   : 12064/2048 ms
                              = 5.89 ms
```

Figure 2: Calculating serialization delay

Note that the serialization delay decreases with the increase in the speed of the link, and should be a cause for concern only over low speed links. In an enterprise network, the speeds within the campus would be Gbps speeds, and the serialization delays would be negligible.

For shared/broadcast type links like Ethernet, the packets are held in the buffers before the transceiver can detect that the link is free, and packets can be transmitted out. This delay is technically a part of the transmission delay and is different from the queuing delay.

The last element of the delay is the time taken by the packet to actually traverse the link from one end of the link to the other. The electrical and even RF signals travel at the speed of light on the electrical/optical cables or even RF medium, in which they travel as electromagnetic waves. But still, the packets have to traverse some physical distance on the physical cable or the point-to-point RF link. In case of a satellite communication, the distance is much longer as the signals have to travel back and forth to a satellite orbiting the earth thousands of kilometers up in the sky. The time taken to travel this distance is called the **Propagation Delay**. The longer the link, the larger the propagation delay. This delay is fixed for a given WAN link and depends on the actual distance. As an example, for a 500 km optical WAN link, the propagation delay would be 2.5 ms, as calculated in the following figure:

Total Link length (L)	: 500 kms
Speed of light in air	: $3 * 10^8$ m/s
Refractive Index of Optical fiber	: 1.5
Speed of light in glass (S)	: $3*10^8/ 1.5$ m/s
	$= 2 * 10^8$ m/s
Propagation delay (D = L/S)	: $(500*1000) / (2 * 10^8)$
	$= 2.5$ ms

Figure 3: Calculating propagation delay

Jitter

Jitter is probably the most important concept that is related to voice and video over IP, and the most confusing as well.

Let's consider a source that is sending packets at a constant rate. The packets experience delays on the network as has been discussed in the previous section. Some of the delays are constant delays, but some of the delays experienced by the packets are variable and depend upon the traffic load and the network state at a given point in time. If all delays were constant, the received packets would be equally spaced. Due to the variable delays, the packets are received with nonuniform gaps between consecutive packets. Jitter is shown pictorially in the following figure as a comparison of the received packets to the transmitted packets. Jitter is defined as the average deviation of the received packets from the normal bitstream:

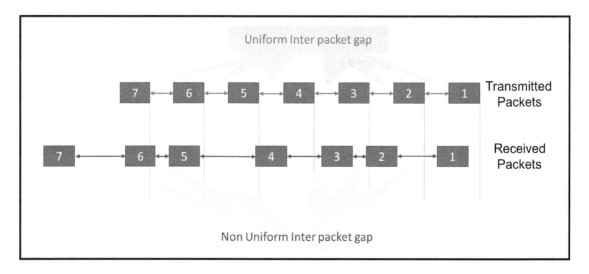

Figure 4: Interpacket gap variations due to jitter

To understand the impact of jitter, it is important to understand how VoIP or video packets are decoded.

Let's use video as the example, as we have all seen video streaming either on IPTV or other video streaming sites. The video packets are sent as a series of equally spaced packets on the network. The receiver receives these packets in the buffer called the de-jitter buffer, and only after a minimum amount of buffer (minimum playout buffer) is full, the buffer starts to send the packets at a constant rate for playback. This allows the decoder to decode and to do a playback of the received packets as though it was a continuous constant rate stream.

Packets may arrive at the receiver out of sequence. If a packet arrives before the turn for that packet to be played, the out of sequence packet is buffered, inserted into the bit stream, and handed out to the decoder in sequence as a part of the continuous bit stream. However, if a packet is lost, or is delayed so that it arrives after its turn, it is simply discarded. The de-jitter buffer is shown in the following figure:

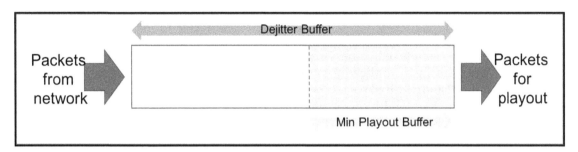

Figure 5: De-jitter buffer in a video device

The packet rate for playout is the same as the rate at which the packets are initially sent by the source. The network causes inter-packet gap variations and packets can come either early or later as shown in the preceding figure. If the packets arrive at the constant rate without any variation (jitter), the decoder would receive the packets from the de-jitter buffer at the same rate at which the packets arrive from the network, and the buffer would always be at a constant level. However, if the packets start to come at a rate less than the playout rate, the buffer levels would start decreasing leading to what is called **buffering**, which degrades the experience. The amount of buffer determines the capacity to hold packets that are out of sequence, and can be held while waiting for the missing packets to arrive in time for their playback. A larger buffer is also required if the delay variation in the received packets is more. The larger the variation of the inter packet variation, the larger will be the de-jitter buffer required on the receiver so that the effects of packet delay variations do not impact the playback. However, a large de-jitter buffer means more memory required at the receiver. It also means that the video would start to playback after the de-jitter buffer reaches its minimum value, resulting in larger delays at startup.

Jitter does not impact the TCP-based applications as much from a user experience perspective and is relevant only for time-sensitive applications with a continuous data stream.

Jitter values are measured in units of time (ms), and jitter should ideally be as low as possible (close to zero) on the network. This would ensure a smooth playback of the voice and video streams.

QoS models

Real-time applications often do not work well across the internet because of variable queueing delays and congestion losses. QoS aims to prioritize critical applications, and minimize the impact of network aberrations. We have seen from the previous discussion that we need to minimize jitter for time-critical traffic, and prioritize the other types of traffic depending upon their criticality to the business needs of the organization. This means that in case of network congestion, the business-critical applications should not be choked for bandwidth, and packets of business-critical applications should not be dropped before the packets of non-business applications are dropped. More realistically, we assign a specific amount of bandwidth to each type of traffic and ensure that the all types of traffic get their fair share of bandwidth on the network. We will discuss this further in the discussion on the QoS tools.

In this section, we will discuss the QoS models that are used for providing quality of service to traffic on Cisco devices.

The integrated services model

The integrated services model, also known as the insert model, was developed as an IETF proposal RFC 1633, to provide quality of services for real-time applications such as remote video, multimedia conferencing, visualization, and virtual reality. The model uses a fine-grained approach to QoS and requires the intermediate routers to maintain a state for the flows that need QoS, and guarantee the bandwidth to these flows.

In this model, the application requests a specific kind of service from the network before sending data. The request is made by explicit signaling; the application informs the network of its traffic profile and requests a particular kind of service that can encompass its bandwidth and delay requirements. The application is expected to send data only after it gets a confirmation from the network. It is also expected to send data that lies within its described traffic profile.

The model uses **resource reservation** and **admission control** mechanisms as key building blocks to establish and maintain QoS by providing explicit admission guarantees based on the available resources as to whether a flow can be guaranteed end-to-end or not. In that sense, the insert model is an end-to-end model for providing QoS.

IntServ uses **Resource Reservation Protocol** (RSVP) to explicitly signal the QoS needs of an application's traffic along the devices in the end-to-end path through the network. If every network device along the path can reserve the necessary bandwidth, the originating application can begin transmitting.

Besides end-to-end signalling, IntServ requires several functions on routers and switches along the path, which are as follows:

- **Admission Control**: This function determines whether a new flow can be granted the requested QoS without impacting existing reservations
- **Classification**: To recognize packets that need particular levels of QoS
- **Policing**: To take specific actions, including possibly dropping packets, when traffic does not conform to its specified characteristics
- **Queuing and Scheduling**: This function is used to queue and forward packets on the links and accord the requisite treatment that is in line with the QoS policy

The IntServ model did not gain much traction in terms of implementation, as it required the flow state to be maintained in the transit nodes, and hence was not very scalable. The IPv6 header still has a flow label that can be used for providing QoS using the IntServ model. A more scalable approach to providing QoS was developed in RFC 2475 called the *differentiated services model*, which is described next.

The differentiated services model

The differentiated services model, more commonly referred to as the DiffServ model, is a more scalable model compared to the IntServ model. This model uses aggregate flows rather than individual flows for prioritizing across the network, and uses a hop-by-hop approach for QoS, rather than an end-to-end approach.

The DiffServ architecture is composed of a number of functional elements implemented in network nodes. These include a small set of per-hop forwarding behaviors, packet classification functions, and traffic conditioning functions, including metering, marking, shaping, and policing. The DiffServ architecture achieves scalability by implementing complex classification and conditioning functions only at network boundary nodes, and by applying per-hop behaviors to aggregates of traffic, which have been appropriately marked using the **Type of Services** (**ToS**) or **Differentiated Services Code Point** (**DSCP**) field in the IP headers. The RFC 2474 defines the new interpretation of the DSCP bits and supersedes the ToS value as defined in the RFC 791. We discussed the DSCP field in `Chapter 1`, *Network Building Essentials*.

The DiffServ model is a source-driven model, where the packets at the ingress are classified and marked with the DSCP values, which are then used to provide the requisite QoS to these packets on the core routers.

The architecture also defines **Per-hop behaviors** (**PHBs**) that are externally observable performance criteria, and does not define the internal implementation mechanisms in the routers. The PHBs permit a reasonably granular means of allocating buffer and bandwidth resources at each node among competing traffic streams. The DiffServ model defines the following PHBs:

- **Default PHB**: The default PHB essentially specifies that a packet marked with a DSCP value of 000000 (recommended) receives the traditional best effort service from a DS-compliant node (that is, a network node that complies with all of the core DiffServ requirements). Also, if a packet arrives at a DS-compliant node, and the DSCP value is not mapped to any other PHB, the packet will get mapped to the default PHB.

- **Class-Selector (CS) PHB**: To preserve backward-compatibility with any IP Precedence scheme currently in use on the network, DiffServ has defined a DSCP value in the form xxx000, where x is either 0 or 1. These DSCP values are called class-selector code points. The DSCP value for a packet with default PHB 000000 is also called the class-selector code point. The PHB associated with a class-selector code point is a class-selector PHB. These class-selector PHBs retain most of the forwarding behavior as nodes that implement IP precedence-based classification and forwarding. For example, packets with a DSCP value of 110000 (the equivalent of the IP precedence-based value of 110) have preferential forwarding treatment (for scheduling, queuing, and so on), as compared to packets with a DSCP value of 100000 (the equivalent of the IP Precedence-based value of 100). These class-selector PHBs ensure that DS-compliant nodes can co-exist with IP precedence-based nodes.

- **Assured Forwarding (AF) PHB**: Assured forwarding PHB defines a method by which **Behavior Aggregates** (**BAs**) can be given different forwarding assurances. The AF PHB is defined as AFxy, with x and y defining the AF class and the **drop precedence** (**dp**) respectively. The AFxy PHB defines four AF classes: AF1, AF2, AF3, and AF4, with each class being assigned a specific amount of buffer space and interface bandwidth, according to the SLA with the service provider. The relative priority of the classes is AF4 > AF3 > AF2 > AF1. Within each class, there are three subclasses defined considering the drop precedence, and a packet with a lower drop precedence would be dropped later as compared to a packet with a higher drop precedence within the same class, for example, a packet marked with AF43 would be dropped before AF41. Using this system, a device would first prioritize traffic by class, then differentiate and prioritize same-class traffic by considering the drop precedence. It is important to note that this standard has not specified a precise definition of low, medium, and high drop percentages. AF PHB is defined in RFC 2597 and RFC 3260.

- **Expedited Forwarding (EF) PHB**: The EF PHB, a key ingredient of DiffServ, provides a robust service by providing low loss, low latency, low jitter, and assured bandwidth service. EF PHB is ideally suited for applications such as VoIP that require low bandwidth, guaranteed bandwidth, low delay, and low jitter. The recommended DSCP value for EF PHB is 101110. EF PHB is defined in RFC 3246 that rendered obsolete RFC 2598.

The following figure is of a table that shows the DSCP markings, the ToS field values, and the corresponding PHBs:

DSCP (Decimal)	TOS	PHB	DSCP (Decimal)	TOS	PHB
111110 (62)	111		011110 (30)	011	AF33
111100 (60)	111		011100 (28)	011	AF32
111010 (58)	111		011010 (26)	011	AF31
111000 (56)	111	CS7	011000 (24)	011	CS3
110110 (54)	110		010110 (22)	010	AF23
110100 (52)	110		010100 (20)	010	AF22
110010 (50)	110		010010 (18)	010	AF21
110000 (48)	110	CS6	010000 (16)	010	CS2
101110 (46)	101	EF	001110 (14)	001	AF13
101100 (44)	101		001100 (12)	001	AF12
101010 (42)	101		001010 (10)	001	AF11
101000 (40)	101	CS5	001000 (8)	001	CS1
100110 (38)	100	AF43	000110 (6)	000	
100100 (36)	100	AF42	000100 (4)	000	
100010 (34)	100	AF41	000010 (2)	000	
100000 (32)	100	CS4	000000 (0)	000	Default

Figure 6: DSCP markings for QoS

Note that in the preceding figure, we have only shown the DSCP bits, where the last of the 6 bits is a binary 0. This is because the standard has reserved the DSCP values with the last bit as a binary 1, and these values are not used currently.

The following figure shows the TOS byte (RFC 791) and the DSCP fields (RFC 2474) in the IPv4 header. In RFC 791, the first 3 bits of the Type of Service field were used for defining precedence, and one bit each was used for delay, throughput, and resiliency:

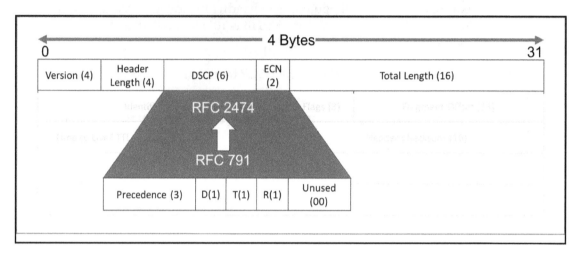

Figure 7: DiffServ code point field in IP header

The following figure is of a table that shows the values for precedence fields and the corresponding traffic class. These classes are mapped using class selector PHBs in the DiffServ architecture to maintain backwards compatibility:

ToS Precedence Value	Description (Class)
0 (000)	Routine
1 (001)	Priority
2 (010)	Immediate
3 (011)	Flash
4 (100)	Flash Override
5 (101)	CRITIC/ ECP
6 (110)	Internet Control
7 (111)	Network Control

Figure 8: ToS values mapped to traffic classes

Nearly all QoS deployment on networks are based on the DiffServ model, due to the scalability and flexibility offered by the model. We will describe the various QoS tools and how to configure them for a DiffServ implementation on Cisco routers next.

QoS tools

We will describe the various QoS tools for implementing the DiffServ QoS model. The following figure depicts these tools as used on a router/switch:

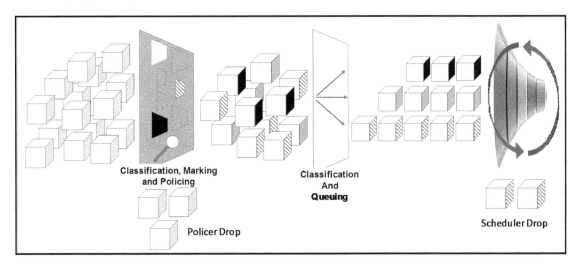

Figure 9: QoS tools

Let's discuss these tools in detail in the upcoming sections.

Traffic conditioning

Traffic conditioning is performed at the edges of a DiffServ domain. Traffic conditioners perform **traffic shaping** and **policing** functions to ensure that traffic entering the DiffServ domain conforms to the rules specified by the **Traffic Conditioning Agreement** (**TCA**) and complies with the service provisioning policy of the domain. Traffic conditioning may range from simple code point re-marking to complex policing and shaping operations.

Policing

This feature allows you to limit the input or output transmission rate of a class of traffic based on user-defined criteria. It also enables the system to mark packets according to a user-defined criterion, such as the IP precedence value, the QoS group, or the DSCP value. Such traffic can then be dropped or transmitted, as desired.

A policer typically drops traffic that is out of profile. For example, the rate-limiting policer either drops the packet or rewrites its IP precedence, resetting the type of service bits in the packet header. Policers can have two or three colors.

A two-color policer lets you identify two types of traffic:

- Conforming traffic (CIR-Committed Information Rate)
- Exceeding traffic (above CIR)

The traffic change when it passes through a two-color policer is as illustrated in the following figure:

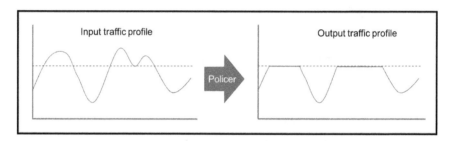

Figure 10: Policing function

The horizontal dotted line in the preceding figure shows the CIR, and any traffic exceeding the CIR is dropped by the policer.

A three-color policer lets you identify three types of traffic:

- Conforming traffic (CIR)
- Exceeding traffic (PIR-Peak Information Rate)
- Violating traffic (above PIR)

Shaping

Traffic shaping *shapes* the flow of traffic by reducing outbound flow traffic to avoid congestion. Traffic shaping constrains traffic to a particular bit rate using a token bucket mechanism.

While a policer simply enforces a rate limit, a shaper smoothens the traffic flow to a specified rate by the use of buffers. A shaper typically delays excess traffic using a buffer or queueing mechanism to hold packets and shape the flow when the data rate of the source is higher than expected. Traffic shaping and policing can work in tandem.

The following figure depicts the input traffic pattern and the output traffic after it passes a traffic shaper. The excess traffic that was dropped by the policer is held back in buffers, and is sent on the link once the bandwidth is free. Note that shaping buffers packets, and hence would lead to additional delays and variable jitters. Also note that there is a limit to the number of packets that can be buffered, and it is possible that if the traffic bursts exceed the CIR by large values, the packets may still be discarded:

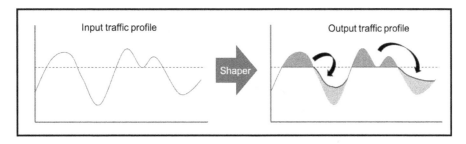

Figure 11: Shaping function

Markdown

There could be instances on the network when the network traffic offered by a user exceeds the designed values for different classes of traffic. As an example, let's assume that the network was designed for the traffic values as shown in the following table:

Traffic Class	Design BW %	Offered BW %
Voice	25%	25%
Gold	25%	40%
Silver	30%	30%
Best Effort	20%	5%

Figure 12: Example bandwidth allocation for QoS

The table also shows the bandwidths offered for each class of traffic at the network ingress. In this case, the gold traffic is exceeding the design parameters by 15%. However, the total bandwidth is still within the overall bandwidth provisioned for the user. In such a case, the network administrator might still allow the traffic that is in excess of the design percentage, and mark the excess traffic with a lower quality of service. This would ensure that, rather than dropping the traffic at the ingress, the traffic can be carried forward on the network as a lower class and be delivered if adequate resources are available. This is called **markdown** where the traffic exceeding the designed/contracted thresholds is marked with a lower QoS marking.

Packet classification

Packet classification uses a traffic descriptor (for example, the DSCP) to categorize a packet within a specific group in order to define that packet. After the packet has been defined (that is, classified), the packet is accessible for QoS handling on the network.

Using packet classification, you can partition network traffic into multiple priority levels or classes of service. When traffic descriptors are used to classify traffic, the source agrees to adhere to the contracted terms and the network promises a QoS. Traffic policers and traffic shapers use the traffic descriptor of the packet (that is, the classification of the packet) to ensure adherence to that agreement.

The classification at the edges of the DiffServ domain is done based on detailed lookups of the packet headers, including layer-3 and layer-4 information using **Access Control Lists (ACL)**. The packets are marked based on this detailed lookup, and a DSCP value is set in the IP header. This enables the devices in the core of the DiffServ domain to classify the packets based only on the DSCP values, making the architecture scalable and flexible.

Any changes to define the traffic class are then done only at the DS domain edge, and the core devices are offloaded with the functions of detailed lookups for classification. The core nodes might still do policing based on the committed rates of traffic streams and rewrite the DSCP values to be used by the downstream nodes in the DSCP domain.

Packet marking

Packet marking is related to packet classification. Packet marking allows you to classify a packet based on a specific traffic descriptor (such as the DSCP value). This classification can then be used to apply user-defined differentiated services to the packet and to associate a packet with a local QoS group.

Associating a packet with a local QoS group allows users to associate a group ID with a packet. The group ID can be used to classify packets into QoS groups based on prefix, autonomous system, and community string. The marking can be done using the DSCP values in the IP header, and also copied onto any layer-2 field if permitted by the underlying layer-2 technology.

As an example, the tagged Ethernet header discussed earlier in Chapter 4, *Understanding and Configuring Campus Network Technologies*, has 3 bits specified for quality of service called the 802.1p bits. These bits can be used in the switching domain to provide quality of service and do the queue management functions as described next.

The following figure shows an example of classification and marking at the edge of the DiffServ domain:

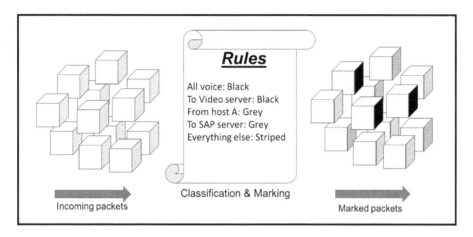

Figure 13: Marking IP packets

Congestion management

Congestion management is required when the traffic to be sent out on an interface is greater than the link bandwidth. Congestion avoidance techniques are used when the traffic to be sent out on an interface is nearing the link bandwidth, so that proactive measures can be taken to prevent congestion. We will describe congestion management techniques in this section, and congestion avoidance techniques in the next section.

The congestion management techniques that help implement a DiffServ model for QoS are **queuing** and **scheduling**.

Queuing

When the number of packets to be sent out through an interface exceeds the capacity of the link, the packets need to be queued so that they can be transmitted on the interface when the bandwidth is available.

In the DiffServ mode, the traffic is classified as discussed in the earlier section, and the different types of traffic are put in different queues on the egress interface. The number of queues on the egress interface depends on the hardware and software capabilities of the device, as the DiffServ architecture only defines the behavior and does not specify the internal implementation.

Queuing for the already-marked packets is shown in the following figure:

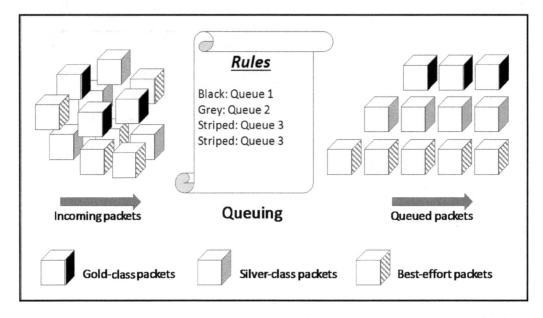

Figure 14: Queuing packets into egress interface queues

The three types of packets are queued in three different queues as shown in the preceding figure.

Note that we could also have two types of packets sharing the same queue, and implement the differential services between the two classes using the packet drop techniques we will discuss in the congestion management section.

Scheduling

Once the packets are lined up for transmission in the different queues, they need to be transmitted out on the link. The process of taking the packets from each queue and putting them on the egress link is called scheduling. Scheduling algorithms determines the queue from which the next packet will be transmitted. By assigning specific weights to the scheduling algorithms, we can process the packets faster and hence provide differentiated services to specific traffic classes. Scheduling is shown in the following figure, where all packets from the topmost (high priority) queue are transmitted on the link, and then the packets from the remaining two queues are transmitted equally:

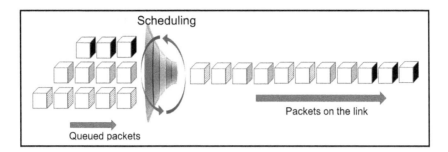

Figure 15: Traffic scheduling

The most commonly used scheduling algorithms are low latency queueing and weighted fair queuing.

Low latency queueing (LLQ)

LLQ is also known as **Priority Queueing** (**PQ**). LLQ allows delay-sensitive data such as voice to be de-queued and sent before packets in other queues are de-queued. In this queuing, all packets from the priority queue are transmitted on the link as soon as they arrive in the queue. The PQ is emptied before the other queues can be served. The gold-class packets in the preceding figure were transmitted ahead of any other packets, illustrating the PQ.

This ensures that the time-sensitive packets do not suffer delays, or variable delays (jitter) by waiting in the output queues. PQ is used for voice traffic as it is the most time sensitive traffic on the network. Note that if too much traffic comes into the PQ, it can starve the other queues, and the packets in other queues would not be served. This can lead to a denial of service for other services. To avoid this, the maximum PQ bandwidth is generally capped at 25% of the overall link bandwidth.

Class-based weighted fair queueing (CBWFQ)

CBWFQ is a scheduling mechanism used to provide a minimum bandwidth guarantee to traffic classes during times of network congestion at an interface. Each of the CBWFQ queues is assigned a weight, and the packets are served from the queues based upon the weight of the queue.

As an example, we considered that the silver-class and the best effort packet queues in our scheduling example had equal weights, and hence two packets were transmitted from each queue. The weights are defined on the basis of the importance of traffic.

CBWFQ ensures that a given **behavioral aggregate (BA)** or traffic class does not exceed the defined bandwidth on a particular link in case of link congestion. However, if there is no congestion, the traffic class can burst up to the unused bandwidth that is left after serving the other queues.

Congestion avoidance

Congestion avoidance techniques monitor network traffic loads in an effort to anticipate and avoid congestion at common network bottlenecks. Congestion avoidance is achieved through packet dropping. The congestion avoidance methods are **tail drop**, **Random Early Detection (RED)**, and **Weighted Random Early Detection (WRED)**.

Tail drop

Tail drop is the default congestion avoidance behavior when WRED is not configured. Tail drop treats all traffic equally and does not differentiate between packet types within the same queue. Queues get filled during periods of traffic congestion. When the output queue is full and tail drop is in effect, packets are dropped from the tail of the queue until the congestion is eliminated and the queue is no longer full.

This dropping of packets in a TCP stream leads to the end nodes reducing their TCP window size, thereby sending less traffic on the network. Packet drops in TCP help control congestion at the source itself. UDP packets on the other hand have no acknowledgement and flow control, and hence are immune to any packet drops, and do not reduce the transmission rates, in case of packet loss on the network.

Though the maximum depth of the queue is configurable, an increase in the queue depth causes an increase in the delay as they are held waiting in the queue. It is recommended to have this depth configured at a value that provides an acceptable delay for packets, and this value of delay is typically 100 ms. Hence, for a 2 Mbps link, the maximum number of packets that the queue can hold is 16, as shown in the following figure:

IP packet length	: 1500 bytes
PPP header length	: 8 bytes
Total packet size	: 1508 bytes
Total packet size (P)	: 1508*8 bits = 12064 bits
Wire speed (S)	: 2.048 Mbps = 2048 kbps
Serialization delay (D=P/S)	: 12064/2048 ms
	= 5.89 ms
Max packets in queue	: 100 / 5.89 = 17

Figure 16: Calculating queue length

Random early detection

The RED mechanism is used to address network congestion in a proactive manner. Implementing RED randomly drops certain packets once a minimum queue threshold is reached. This forces the hosts to temporarily slow down, even before congestion has actually occurred on the network. It is an efficient mechanism to avoid congestion, where most of the traffic is based on TCP.

Packets have a drop probability, which is zero below the minimum queue threshold, and is one when the queue is full. As congestion starts to build up on the network, the queue length starts to increase and the drop probability of the packets increases so that congestion can be avoided proactively.

The drop probability in the RED mechanism is as shown in the following figure:

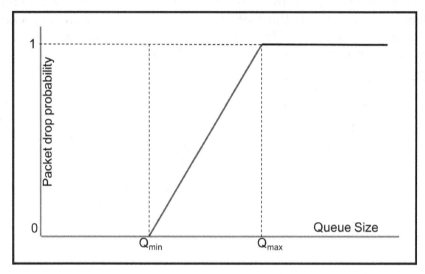

Figure 17: Random Early Detection

Note that if the minimum threshold is too low, packets may be dropped unnecessarily and the transmission link will not be fully used. Hence, the minimum threshold value should be set high enough to maximize the link utilization. The maximum threshold value is after which all packets are dropped, and hence, this is the max queue length after which tail drop starts.

If the difference between the maximum threshold and the minimum threshold is not enough, packets from all flows would start experiencing TCP drops, leading to a situation where all hosts start to reduce their traffic. This is called global synchronization of TCP hosts, and can be avoided if packets from only some flows are dropped, which is done by increasing the difference between Q_{max} and Q_{min}.

Weighted random early detection (WRED)

WRED is a modified version of RED where weights are assigned to multiple classes within the same queue. WRED provides separate thresholds and weights for different IP precedence, allowing the ability to provide different qualities of service in regard to packet dropping for different traffic types. Standard traffic may be dropped more frequently than premium traffic during periods of congestion.

Recall from the discussion on DSCP values that the assured forwarding class has multiple sublevels each with a different drop probability. For example, within the AF4 traffic class, **AF43** has the highest drop probability, followed by **AF42**, and **AF41** has the lowest drop probability. This is implemented by using different queue values for calculating the drop probability within the same output queue as shown in the following figure:

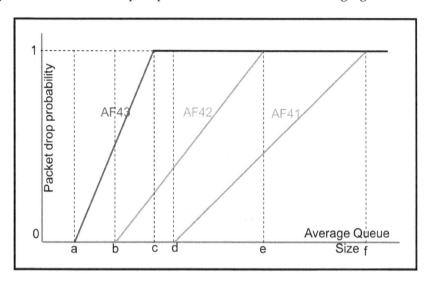

Figure 18: Weighted random early detection

Note in the preceding figure that **AF43** random packet drops start before **AF42**. Also, the **AF43** tail drop starts even before the Random Early Detection packet drops start for **AF41**. These parameters are configurable, and can be tuned to manage the congestion and forwarding behaviors on the network devices.

Modular QoS command-line interface

The MQC provides a CLI structure that allows you to apply QoS features on your network. All the features previously described are implemented using a modular QoS command-line interface that is called MQC. Let's discuss the implementation of the QoS in a sample organization in the next section using the Cisco MQC.

QoS design for an enterprise

Let's now apply the concepts discussed in this chapter to design the DiffServ-based QoS architecture for an enterprise. The steps involved in implementing QOS are as follows:

- Define the trust boundary
- Define traffic types and map them into traffic classes
- Determine the number of QoS classes
- Assess the available hardware deployed and the queuing capabilities
- Estimate the bandwidth required for each traffic class
- Map the traffic classes to queues on devices
- Implement the configurations

We will discuss these steps in detail in the subsequent sections.

Defining the trust boundary

The concept of trust is important and integral to deploying QoS on a network. Recall from the DiffServ architecture that the edge nodes perform the complex functions of classification, policing, and marking, and the core nodes perform the queuing and scheduling functions. Once the edge devices have set DSCP values, the core devices have the option of trusting them. If the device trusts the values, it does not need to do any reclassification; if it does not trust the values, then it must perform reclassification for the appropriate QoS. The core devices trust the DSCP values received from edge devices for efficient scaling of the network.

The notion of trusting or not trusting forms the basis for the trust boundary. The classification should be done as close to the source as possible. The access ports on the edge devices in the control of the network administrator are considered the trust boundary, and all traffic coming in from the end points is classified and treated accordingly. The edge points could be the LAN ports for user connectivity on the access switches, or the access ports for server connectivity in the DC, or even the port to which the internet link is connected.

Defining traffic types

There are multiple types of traffic within the organization's IT network. It is important to identify and classify the traffic so that we can distinguish the critical traffic from noncritical traffic and accord the right QoS treatment to these packets.

The major types of traffic on the network are as shown in the following figure. Note that we have grouped multiple types of traffic into a single class, based on the traffic that needs similar treatment on the network:

Traffic Class	Traffic Characteristics	Types of traffic
Priority	Low Delay, Low Loss, Low jitter, Guaranteed bandwidth, Sequence preservation	Voice traffic Network Control Traffic
Gold Class	Low Delay, Low loss, Jitter tolerant, No oversubscription	Selected Business servers
Silver class	Loss Tolerant, Jitter tolerant, Sequence Preservation, Medium Oversubscription	Email servers, Selected Business servers
Best Effort	Loss tolerant, jitter tolerant, Delay tolerant, High oversubscription	Internet browsing

Figure 19: Example traffic types

We also assign the markings to the various traffic classes for traffic class in terms of the DSCP markings to be used on the network.

Assigning bandwidths

Having classified the traffic into traffic classes or BA, the next step is to assign bandwidths to these traffic classes on each link, and define the scheduling behavior for each traffic class.

From the traffic mapping defined earlier, we would reserve percentage of bandwidth as 25%, 25%, 30%, and 20% on each link, as shown in the following figure. Further, we would map the priority class to the priority queue of LLQ, and the other three classes into a class-based weighted fair queuing scheduler and assign the weights as per the bandwidth allocated to each traffic class:

Traffic Class	DSCP marking	Scheduling	Allocated Bandwidth
Priority	46 (EF)	Low Latency Scheduling	25%
Gold Class	34 (AF 41)	Class Based WFQ	25%
Silver class	26 (AF 31)	Class Based WFQ	30%
Best Effort	0 (Default)	Class Based WFQ	20%

Figure 20: Example bandwidth allotment for various traffic classes

Assessing hardware and assigning classes to queues

Most Cisco hardware used in modern-day networks support at least four output queues for scheduling. If there is legacy hardware that doesn't support four queues, we might need to club two traffic classes into a single queue and use different WRED thresholds. This would ensure that the two traffic classes that are clubbed together still have some differentiation between them.

The hardware queues are generally mentioned as 1p3q, which means that the port has one priority queue and three other queues for output scheduling. If a port queue structure is 1p2t, we would club the silver and best effort traffic classes into one queue, and if the queue structure for a port is 1p5t, we would just use a total of four queues.

Implementing configurations

This section discusses the configurations to be deployed on the devices for classification, marking, and scheduling. The classification and marking are done in the ingress ports at the edge ports. The scheduling is done in the egress direction. Both classification and marking, and scheduling, are done by creating policies and applying them to the ports as discussed next.

The ingress policy

The ingress policy is created to classify traffic depending upon the known parameters at the edge devices. In the example, we create access lists to match traffic based on IP addresses of business-critical servers, and access lists to classify voice traffic based on UDP traffic from any address to the IP address range used within the organization.

These access lists are then called within the class maps, which are referred to within the policy map to set the DSCP values. The following configuration shows the creation of ACLs and class maps:

```
Router(config)# access-list 101 permit udp any 10.0.0.0 255.0.0.0
Router(config)# access-list 102 permit ip any 10.16.32.0 255.255.255.0
Router(config)# access-list 103 permit ip any 10.16.30.0 255.255.255.0
!
Router(config)# class-map match-all voice
Router(config-cmap)# match access-group 101
Router(config-cmap)# exit
!
Router(config)# class-map match-all gold
Router(config-cmap)# match access-group 102
Router(config-cmap)# exit
!
Router(config)# class-map match-all silver
Router(config-cmap)# match access-group 103
Router(config-cmap)# exit
!
```

Figure 21: Configuration for classifying packets

The configuration for building a policy map using the previous class maps is shown in the following figure:

```
Router(config)# policy-map Ingress-Mark
Router(config-pmap)# class voice
Router(config-pmap-c)# set ip dscp 46
Router(config-pmap-c)# exit
Router(config-pmap)# class gold
Router(config-pmap-c)# set ip dscp 34
Router(config-pmap-c)# exit
Router(config-pmap)# class silver
Router(config-pmap-c)# set ip dscp 26
Router(config-pmap-c)# exit
Router(config-pmap)# class class-default
Router(config-pmap-c)# set ip dscp 0
Router(config-pmap-c)# exit
Router(config-pmap)# exit
Router(config)#
!
```

Figure 22: Marking IP packets

Finally, the policy map is applied in the ingress direction on the access ports as shown in the following figure. The configuration commands for applying the policy are as shown here:

```
!
Router(config)# interface gig0/1
Router(config)# service-policy input Ingress-Mark
!
```

Figure 23: Applying policy to an interface

The preceding configuration depicted the marking at the edge devices. The ingress policy on the core devices is not required as they trust the markings done at the DS domain edge by the edge devices.

We can also rate limit and shape certain classes of traffic within the service policy that is applied on the interface. As an example, if we want to rate limit the voice traffic to 25% of the overall link bandwidth, and want to shape the traffic for the silver class to 1 Mbps, we can use additional police and shape commands within the class maps. Note that policing would generally be done for the input service policy and shaping would be done for the output service policy.

A sample configuration for rate limiting voice traffic to 25% of the bandwidth is given in the following figure:

```
Router(config)# policy-map Ingress-Mark
Router(config-pmap)# class voice
Router(config-pmap-c)# police cir percent 25
Router(config-pmap-c)# set ip dscp 46
Router(config-pmap-c)# exit
```

Figure 24: Policing and marking traffic

A sample configuration for shaping the silver traffic in the egress direction is shown in the following figure:

```
Router(config)# policy-map Egress-shape
Router(config-pmap)# class silver
Router(config-pmap-c)# shape average 1000000
Router(config-pmap-c)# set ip dscp 26
Router(config-pmap-c)# exit
Router(config-pmap)# exit
Router(config)#
```

Figure 25: Shaping and marking traffic

The egress policy

The policy on the egress interface is created to classify and match the packets based on the DSCP values as shown next. Note in the following figure that we have matched DSCP values corresponding to CS6 and matched it to the voice class. This is because all packets generated by the network devices have the DSCP value of CS6, and this command marks these packets to get the LLQ treatment. In the absence of this command, the CS6 traffic would be matched to the default class and treated as best effort:

```
Router(config)# class-map voice match-any
Router(config-cmap)# match ip dscp cs6
Router(config-cmap)# match ip dscp 46
Router(config-cmap)# exit
Router(config)# class-map gold
Router(config-cmap)# match ip dscp 34
Router(config-cmap)# exit
Router(config)# class-map silver
Router(config-cmap)# match ip dscp 26
Router(config-cmap)# exit
```

Figure 26: Identifying marked traffic

We need to assign the voice traffic to LLQ, and use CB-WFQ for the remaining three traffic classes. If we assign 25% for voice traffic LLQ, the remaining 75% of bandwidth is split into the gold, silver, and default traffic classes in the ratio of 25%, 30%, and 20% respectively. This means that the percentages of the classes in the remaining bandwidth are 33%, 40%, and 27% respectively, as calculated in the following figure:

Traffic class	Absolute BW %	Queue	Remaining %
Voice	25	LLQ	
Gold	25	CB-WFQ	=25/(25+30+20)= 33%
Silver	30	CB-WFQ	=30/(25+30+20)= 40%
BE	20	CB-WFQ	=20/(25+30+20)= 27%

Figure 27: Calculating bandwidth for Weighted Fair Queuing

These values are used to build the configuration for the CBWFQ weights using the class maps to create a `policy-map` named `Egress-Schedule`, as shown next. We have also used RED detection and drop for the silver and default traffic classes. Further, the RED used for the silver class is used with explicit congestion notification as discussed in `Chapter 1`, *Network Building Essentials*, so that the hosts are informed explicitly about congestion on the network using the ECN bits:

```
Router(config)# policy-map Egress-Schedule
Router(config-pmap)# class voice
Router(config-pmap-c)# priority percent 25
Router(config-pmap-c)# exit
Router(config-pmap)# class gold
Router(config-pmap-c)# bandwidth remaining percent 33
Router(config-pmap-c)# exit
Router(config-pmap)# class silver
Router(config-pmap-c)# bandwidth remaining percent 40
Router(config-pmap-c)# random-detect
Router(config-pmap-c)# random-detect ecn
Router(config-pmap-c)# exit
Router(config-pmap)# class class-default
Router(config-pmap-c)# bandwidth remaining percent 27
Router(config-pmap-c)# fair-queue
Router(config-pmap-c)# exit
Router(config-pmap)# exit
Router(config)#
!
```

Figure 28: Defining a scheduling policy

Finally, the `policy-map` is applied in the output direction to the uplink interface to enable scheduling on the egress interface.

```
!
Router(config)# interface Tengig0/0
Router(config)# service-policy input Egress-Schedule
!
```

Figure 29: Applying scheduling policy to an interface

There are different ways to configure QoS on the network and most of them are device dependent. However, the preceding guidelines would enable the network designer to build the QoS configurations that align to the organization's QoS requirements.

QoS in a hybrid model with service provider WAN

We have discussed the QoS requirements within the enterprise network. The enterprise network also spreads across the WAN, and the WAN can consist of dedicated TDM links, layer-2 links, or even layer-3 VPNs from the service provider.

If the organization's WAN is based on dedicated TDM circuits, there is no need for QoS on the SP backbone. However, if the organization takes a layer-3 VPN from the SP, the packets of the organization would be carried over the SP network that would also carry traffic from other organizations, and can be congested at times, as it is a shared infrastructure.

Hence the organization takes a layer-3 VPN from the SP, with quality of service enabled. This means that the SP would honour the QoS requirements of the organization. Since the SP network has a uniform QoS marking design for its network that is shared across multiple customers, the SP would rewrite the SP markings of the organization if they don't align to the SP QoS markings, so that the SP devices can accord the right priority. The SP then rewrites the QoS markings from the SP specific markings into the organization's original markings, so that when packets are handed over to the enterprise at the remote end, the devices have the right markings that are a part of the organization's QoS design. SPs would generally use a managed CPE to rewrite the QoS markings, or would expect the customer to do these rewrites at the CPE devices, in case of an unmanaged service.

The SP network uses MPLS technology for transport, and MPLS has only 3 bits for QoS. Hence, all DSCP markings would have to be rewritten into the MPLS header using the 3 bits. It is advisable for organizations, while designing their QoS, to use distinct AF classes, and avoid using any subclasses so that the first 3 bits of the DSCP markings align with the CoS markings as shown in the DSCP to the ToS markings table earlier. This would ensure that the mappings are managed easily at the edge routers.

Different MPLS SPs use different numbers of QoS queues, and they manage the customer traffic within these queues on the SP network.

In case of layer-2 VPNs, if the SP can ensure a dedicated bandwidth from one point to another, QoS might not be required. However, if the SP network is congested, QoS would be required for L2 links as well. In this case, the Ethernet frames to be handed over the SP should be tagged frames, so that the QoS markings can be passed on the SP network using the 802.1p bits in the Ethernet headers. This is because the SP does not do any IP lookups when it provides layer-2 VPNs.

Summary

In this chapter, we discussed the difference in characteristics of different types of traffic. We also delved into the impact of the network performance parameters and how these parameters affect different types of traffic. We used these concepts to establish the need for providing differentiated services to the different services on the network.

We discussed the models used for providing QoS on IP networks, and discussed the tools and techniques used for implementing the differentiated services model of QoS. We ended the chapter with configuration samples for implementing QoS in an enterprise network, and also touched upon the impact of a MPLS SP-provided WAN.

In the chapters until now, we have discussed the various technologies used to build an enterprise network. In the next chapter, we will talk about network operations and how they are an important aspect in the overall IT requirements of an organization.

10
A Systematic Approach to Network Management

"We work by wit and not by witchcraft."

- W. Shakespeare

The IT network, in a modern organization, is the lifeline of its business, as this is the infrastructure that helps deliver important communications, business orders, and allows employees to collaborate and be more productive. Any disruption/outage in the network can lead to considerable losses in terms of revenue and productivity. Hence, it is important to ensure that the network is up and services are available on a 24x7 basis.

We discussed the network lifecycle in `Chapter 1`, *Network Building Essentials*, where we talked about the various stages of a network. To recall, the stages are prepare, plan, design, implement, operate, and optimize. We have focused the chapters so far on the design and implement stages. In this chapter, we will talk about the operate phase of the network.

A network is a dynamic entity and it changes with a new port being commissioned, decommissioned, or changed, with a new service being added or removed, with a link or device going down, with a new software image being loaded on one or multiple devices, with traffic flows changing on the network, and so on. It is important to manage these changes and ensure that the services are available and any problems on the network are handled efficiently and effectively. A network problem can be complex and, like any complex problem solving, it helps to break down the problem into its constituents, solve them individually and take a holistic view. It is important to have a systematic approach to network operations rather than having the network operators to take their own decisions for every problem.

In this chapter, we will discuss the following topics:

- The various approaches for network management
- The underlying pillars for effective network operations
- Best practices in different domains of network operations.

Frameworks related to network management

Various approaches have been developed by different organizations and standards bodies toward network management, with each of them focusing on different aspects. Each of the approaches leads to certain best practices that can be followed in the network operations and maintenance of an organization leading to a better service delivery. Each approach has approached the subject of network operations and service delivery with different scopes ranging from strategy, executing the change, and micromanaging the actual implementation and operations.

One of the earliest models for network management is the **FCAPS** model, which is a part of the **Telecommunications Management Network (TMN)** architecture defined by ITU-T. It splits the network management function into five areas: **Fault, Configuration, Accounting, Performance, and Security**. FCAPS is an acronym for these five functions, which are defined in the ITU specification M.3400. The objectives of these functional areas are described as follows:

- **Fault management**: Detect, isolate, notify, and correct any faults in the network
- **Configuration management**: Configure the network devices for addition, deletion, or modification of any services, configuration file, software management, and so on
- **Accounting management**: Collect the usage information of network resources, such as bandwidth on links or ports
- **Performance management**: Monitor and measure various parameters of the SLA, which includes latency, jitter, packet loss, CPU, and memory utilization on devices
- **Security management**: Provide secure access to authorized people to the network devices, resources, and services

The FCAPS model is a precursor to the **Fulfilment, Assurance, and Billing (FAB)** model of operations, as defined in the **enhanced Telecom Operations Map (eTOM)**. eTOM was later renamed to **Business Process Framework**, which is a part of the standard maintained by the **TM Forum**. TMF is a global industry association that drives collaboration and collective problem solving to maximize the business success of communications service providers and their ecosystem of suppliers. The FCAPS functions of TMF are broadly mapped into FAB functions, as follows:

FCAPS	FAB
Fault	Assurance
Configuration	Fulfillment
Accounting	Billing
Performance	Assurance
Security	Fulfillment

Figure 1: Mapping FCAPS and FAB models

Another standard is the **Information Technology Infrastructure Library (ITIL)**, which is a set of IT service management best practices that are developed by the UK government and published by the UK Office of Government Commerce.

The goal of ITIL is to improve how IT delivers and supports business services and provides guidelines around technology management and process management and focuses on improving the capabilities of people, processes, and technology.

ITIL V3 defines multiple processes and functions spread across the following five stages:

- **ITIL Service Strategy**: This focuses on understanding the organizational objectives and customer needs
- **ITIL Service Design**: This focuses on mapping the service strategy with delivering business objectives
- **ITIL Service Transition**: This focuses on developing and improving capabilities for introducing new services in the IT infrastructure
- **ITIL Service Operation**: This focuses on managing the services

- **ITIL Continual Service Improvement**: This focuses to streamline and continuously enhance the operations and processes, as follows:

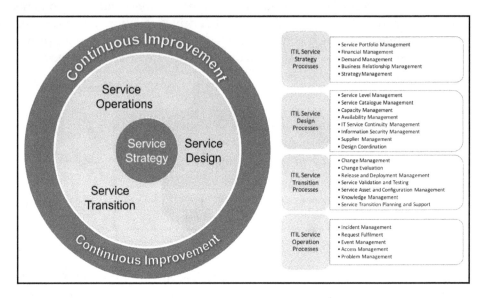

Figure 2: The ITIL framework and processes

The preceding figure shows the ITIL stages of service management and the related processes at each stage.

Information Systems Audit and Control Association (**ISACA**) is an international professional association focused on IT governance that has created another best practices framework for IT governance and management. This framework is known as **COBIT**, which is an acronym for **Control Objectives for Information and Related Technologies**. COBIT is an auditing framework that defines expectations in all IT operations areas, without providing any implementation guidance.

ISACA acquired the CMMI Institute in 2016. It is an organization associated with **Capability Maturity Model Integration** (**CMMI**) that was developed at the **Carnegie Mellon University** (**CMU**). CMMI is a globally adopted capability improvement framework that guides organizations in high-performance operations.

IEC/ISO 20000, developed by the ISO, provides a standard set of specifications for auditing ITIL-based service organizations.

Even though there are multiple frameworks and guidelines, all complementing each other, there is no prescriptive approach for network management and there cannot be one, as each network is unique in terms of design, the services it delivers, and its service objectives. The guidelines, however, provide a framework to create specific processes and practices that are tailored to a specific organization.

Network management planning

The goal of network management is to ensure that services are delivered to the users of the network with the quality of service that the network is designed to deliver. The 'quality of service' needs to be differentiated from the network quality of service that we discussed in Chapter 9, *Understanding and Configuring Quality of Service*. The quality of service from a service perspective will be broader than the network QoS and will include service parameters, such as service uptime, service delivery parameters, and resolution time, in addition to the network delivered parameters with respect to packet loss, latency, and jitter that impact the user application experience.

The network management essentially focusses on ensuring that services are delivered to end customers with the committed SLAs with the users and take proactive actions to avoid any SLA breaches or take reactive measures to restore services if there is a service disruption or degradation. Note that the SLAs will typically be informal within an organization and contractual for external users. Now, let's look at the pillars for effective network management architecture and discuss the deployment aspects for managing Cisco devices.

Pillars of network management

As discussed in Chapter 2, *Networks for Digital Enterprises*, manageability is a key characteristic of the network, and it needs to be factored for at each stage of the network lifecycle. This means that planning needs to be done for network management teams, tools that will be used, and parameters that need to be monitored on the network, to detect any degradation of the SLAs before the services actually go down.

It is important to plan and design the following aspects, among others:

- How will the network be managed?
- What are the tools to be used for monitoring the network?
- What are the parameters that will be managed?

- How will a new service be implemented on the network?
- What are the steps to be followed in case of outages?
- What are the steps to be taken if there are repeat outages?
- What reports are to be provided to the NOC manager, customers, and the top management?

The answers to these questions lie in a combination of the tools deployed on the network, the skills that the people should possess, and the processes to be followed for the operations on the network. An effective combination of these three elements lays the foundation for effective network management.

People

"It is not the gun, but the man behind it"

- John Brown

People are one of the foundational pillars of effective network management. It is their skill that defines how effectively they can use the available technology and tools deployed in the organization for network management and operations.

It is important to hire resources with the right skills to work at different levels within the network management function. It would be highly inefficient for an organization to hire everyone at the same level, as effective network management needs a well-defined hierarchy. An effective NOC team consists of different resources at tier 1 and tier 2 of network operations with general skills in network management, monitoring, and basic troubleshooting. A higher level of troubleshooting skills would be in the tier 3 resources, supported by subject matter experts on specific services or technologies. The organizations' NOC teams would be supported by the vendor support teams through the support services subscribed by the organization.

Processes

"Ability is a wonderful thing, but its value is greatly enhanced by dependability. Ability implies repeatability and accountability."

- Robert A Heinlein

Skilled resources in NOC make the network operations effective. However, each person is different, has different skill sets, and a different temperament. Thus, each individual will behave in a different manner in the same situation. He might still be able to resolve the network problem, but each individual will have an approach of his own. This can lead to problems in situations such as the NOC, where people work in shifts and have to hand over issues to the person on the next shift. This also causes problems for network documentation, as each individual might take different steps and issue a different set of commands to solve the same problem. Having a defined process for most routing activities to be performed on the network make the operations people agnostic and ensure that everyone will perform the same actions in the same situation, actions that have been proven to restore the network effectively and optimally.

Processes can be formal or informal and mature as the organization evolves. The CMM model described earlier has the following levels of process maturity models, and each organization should aspire to go higher on the maturity curve with time, to become more effective:

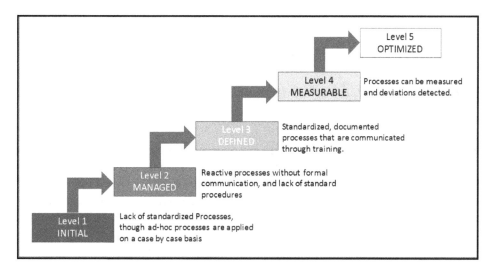

Figure 3: The CMM maturity model

Tools and technologies

"Give ordinary people the right tools, and they will design and build the most extraordinary things."

- Neil Gershenfeld

Tools are required to provide the right type of input to the relevant teams. This input can be extremely helpful in isolating network faults, restoring them quickly, or even providing the input to the planning teams on the performance of various services. Tools go a long way in automating the tasks that the NOC teams perform, thereby freeing the human mind to focus on more powerful and higher goals. These tasks when formalized can be automated again, using new tools, following a continuous improvement cycle.

In an effective network management deployment, consistent tools are deployed that meet business needs for autonomous alerting and reporting and are integrated to exchange data with other tools. There are a variety of tools that are used to monitor the network using **Simple Network Management Protocol** (**SNMP**) that can poll the network devices and provide information on the network parameters, do trending analysis, and provide reports that can be used by other teams and management.

A variety of tools are used in an organization for monitoring, reporting, alerting, and even planning. One of the tools that can be used for network management is the Cisco Prime Infrastructure, which we will cover in a later section.

The importance of metrics

"If you cannot measure it, you cannot improve it."

- Lord Kelvin

We have previously discussed that network management is ensuring delivery of services with the expected service level agreements to end users. Hence, it is obvious that it is important to define and measure the SLA parameters for each service. This will help the organization measure its performance against the stated goals, take corrective steps to improve the operational efficiency, and align the offered SLAs that are closer to what can be delivered.

The service levels for user services are dependent on multiple factors. These include network resiliency, the capacity of the network, and NOC effectiveness in troubleshooting and resolving issues at the very minimum. Each of these individual parameters can be measured and used to pinpoint the areas of improvement that can then be used for taking corrective actions that will help in better service delivery. We will list some of the metrics that can be used in the last section of this chapter.

Network operations systems components

As discussed in the previous section, an effective network management strategy is a combination of people, process, and tools. Since this book is focused on the networking technology, we will cover the network-related aspects that will provide efficient and effective network management in the following sections. We will focus only on the service operations aspects of the network management, as a detailed discussion around the other aspects is beyond the scope of this book.

Simple Network Management Protocol (SNMP)

An important aspect of network operations is to identify network incidents and provide reporting capabilities that will help in proactive problem analysis and root-cause analysis. This requires that specific information be continuously obtained from network devices, such as port status, protocol stats, the traffic load on interfaces, the CPU utilization, and devices. SNMP is a protocol that provides a message format to obtain this information from the network devices.

SNMP is an application-layer protocol that provides a message format for communication between SNMP managers and agents. SNMP provides a standardized framework and a common language used for monitoring and management of devices in a network. The three components of the SNMP framework are the SNMP manager, the SNMP agent, and the MIB:

- **SNMP manager**: The system used to control and monitor the activities of network hosts and the poll-specific information is known as the SNMP manager. This functionality is typically built into the **network management systems** (**NMS**).

- **SNMP agent**: The SNMP agent is the software component within the managed device that maintains the data for the device and reports this data, as needed, to the managing systems. The agent resides on the device that is being managed, for example, a router, switch, or firewall, and sends information to the configured SNMP manager either on request or on hitting specific limits. The information sent in response to the SNMP requests is called SNMP polling and the unsolicited information sent on hitting specific configured parameters is called SNMP traps.

- **Management Information Base** (**MIB**): MIB is a collection of specific parameters that are defined by a specific equipment vendor. Each vendor specifies specific information that the device will store and can be accessed and stores this information in the device memory. This information is arranged in a tree-like hierarchy and each leaf on the tree is called an OID or Object Identifier. The SNMP manager can *Get* or *Set* an OID parameter using SNMP. The MIB has a definite structure and needs to be compiled in the SNMP manager so that the NMS can know the values of the OIDs corresponding to the parameters that it needs to poll:

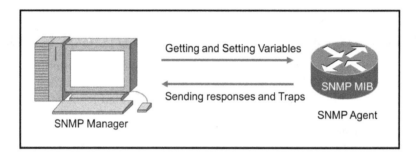

Figure 4: SNMP components

There are three versions of SNMP (v1, v2c, and v3), with SNMPv2 being the most commonly deployed version. However, SNMPv3 supports additional security for authentication and encryption and should be the preferred mode of deployment if both the device and the NMS support SNMPv3.

SNMP traps

Trap operations allow an SNMP agent to send unsolicited notifications that an event has occurred. Traps often termed *fire and forget* are sent on a best effort basis using **User Datagram Protocol (UDP)**. All Cisco devices are capable of generating SNMP traps to notify NMS applications of network events. Cisco routers and switches implement the Cisco syslog MIB as a means of generating SNMP traps in place of or in addition to syslog messages covered in a later section.

Note that SNMP traps are purely reactive, as they are generated in response to an "event" that has already occurred. If the goal is to proactively collect information and ensure that issues are prevented than corrected, we need to collect information from the devices proactively.

SNMP polling

SNMP polling provides a mechanism to proactively collect information about a device's MIB variables. The information obtained through an SNMP MIB query is also far more extensive than the information contained in an SNMP trap, as the trap messages represent only a small subset of the information available through the SNMP MIBs.

SNMPv2 introduced the concept of communities that were used as passwords to authenticate the SNMP requests before the devices could respond to the request and send information. Two types of communities are defined that are **read-only (RO)** and **read-write (RW)**. The RO community allows NMS systems to request information from the device, while the RW community allows NMS systems to set specific parameters and make changes to the device configuration. The communities should be very specific to the organization and should be managed like passwords, so that SNMP cannot be misused to collect information from the network devices by unauthorized sources.

It is also a good practice to have different community strings for RO and RW strings. Further, it is best practice to use different communities for the access layer devices and core layer devices to ensure another layer of "guessing" by the attacker.

An additional layer of security can be added to the SNMP through the use of access control lists to explicitly allow SNMP messages from the SNMP servers only to the device. This can be done using control plane security techniques as discussed in `Chapter 8`, *Understanding and Configuring Network Security*.

SNMP needs to be configured and secured on the Cisco devices using the following configuration:

```
Router(config)# access-list 98 permit 192.168.100.100
Router(config)# access-list 98 permit 192.168.100.101
Router(config)# access-list 98 deny any
Router(config)#
Router(config)# access-list 99 permit 192.168.100.100
Router(config)# access-list 99 permit 192.168.100.101
Router(config)# access-list 99 deny any
Router(config)#
Router(config)# snmp-server contact Admin@001-246-3579
Router(config)# snmp-server location HQ-NOC
Router(config)# snmp-server community C!sc0123 RO 98
Router(config)# snmp-server community C0nf!d3nt!al RW 99
Router(config)#
Router(config)# snmp-server ifindex persist
Router(config)#
```

Figure 5: Configuring and securing SNMP

In the preceding configuration example, two ACLs that allow only the SNMP servers in the NOC to poll the devices are created. The SNMP server contact and location are defined in the configuration, and finally, separate communities are used for RO and RW. The command defined a community C!sc0123 for RO access by SNMP servers that are allowed in the ACL 98. Similarly, the community C0nf!d3nt!al is used for RW access by the SNMP servers defined in ACL 99.

All interfaces on the device are identified in SNMP using a number called **Interface Index** (**ifIndex**). IfIndex is initialized by the device every time the router restarts. Hence, the same interface will have different ifIndex values after a device reboot. This can lead to issues in billing and interface monitoring, as ifIndex needs to be tracked. The last command in the configuration allows the ifindex to have the same values across the router reboot cycles.

The configuration for enabling SNMP traps is as follows:

```
Router(config)# snmp-server enable traps snmp link-status restart env
Router(config)# snmp-server host 192.168.20.11 version 2c public alarms
Router(config)# snmp-server trap-source loopback0
Router(config)#
```

Figure 6: Configuring SNMP traps

The configuration enables specific traps related to SNMP, authentication, restart, and environmental parameters. These traps will be sent to the SNMP server 192.168.20.11 using SNMPv2 and the community public. Further, the traps will be sent only for traps that are of an alarm type as defined in the last keyword in the `snmp-server` host command in the preceding configuration. Lastly, it is a best practice to set the source interface of all locally generated commands to the `loopback0` interface. This makes the messages identifiable on the server using only the loopback address which is always up. If this command is not configured, the source IP address of the messages will be the outgoing interface on the device and, hence, multiple address mappings will have to be done on the SNMP server for the same device.

SNMP can also be used to send alerts on specific events that are configured as a part of the Event MIB. The Event MIB can be configured using SNMP directly from the NMS application. This can be helpful in monitoring specific events, for example, if the CPU of a device hits a 70% threshold or an interface utilization exceeds 80%, the SNMP server will receive the threshold violations as traps that can be used for taking proactive action on the network.

Syslog

Syslog allows a computer or device to deliver messages to another computer or device. Syslog messages are text messages with a particular formatting that associate a facility, severity, and/or priority with a message. The syslog messages have different severity levels, as indicated by the number in the message. These severity levels are essentially a measure of the criticality of a system event. The following image shows the various syslog severity levels and their corresponding meaning:

Severity Level	Level Name	Description
0	Emergencies	System unusable
1	Alerts	Immediate action needed
2	Critical	Critical conditions
3	Errors	Error conditions
4	Warnings	Warning conditions
5	Notifications	Normal but significant conditions
6	Informational	Informational messages only
7	Debugging	Debugging messages

Figure 7: Syslog severity levels

As an example, consider the following syslog message:

```
%SYS-5-RELOAD: Reload Requested
```

This syslog message has a severity level of 5 (notification). This message indicates that a reload or restart was requested, typically issued from the command-line interface (CLI). This message is generated prior to the router resetting. Syslog messages are generally sent to and collected by the NMS server for storage, review, and correlation.

Many network issues involve one or more network devices, often separated by different time zones. Syslog messages are a valuable tool in problem determination and diagnosing chronic problems. It is extremely important to synchronize the timestamps of the devices reporting syslog. In an event, where system log messages do not reach the syslog server(s), having synchronized log files on the reporting devices will aid in the troubleshooting process.

Syslog is configured on the Cisco devices using the following configuration:

```
Router(config)# no logging console
Router(config)# logging buffered 16384
Router(config)# logging trap warnings
Router(config)# logging 192.168.20.11
Router(config)# logging 192.168.20.12
Router(config)#
```

Figure 8: Configuring syslog

Syslog messages are stored in a rolling buffer on the device. The preceding configuration sets the size of this buffer to 16 KB and configures the router not to send the log messages to the console port. This feature has to be turned off during debugging, as the operator will want to see the events, but, during normal operations, it is a good practice to disable logging on the console for better readability of the console screen.

The configuration also sets the logging level to warnings (level 4), which means that the traps for levels 0 through 4 will be sent by the maens of syslog. The last two lines define the IP address to which the device will sent syslog messages over UDP port 514.

Note that SNMP traps can send similar information depending upon the MIBs and the objects contained therein. Syslog in the router buffer, however, is more exhaustive and contains a lot more information than SNMP traps, for troubleshooting.

Network Time Protocol (NTP)

The network is an interconnection of systems and devices. Any change on one device may lead to changes on other devices that might be directly connected or even multiple hops away. As an example, a high CPU on a device can lead to failure routing protocol packets from the neighbors and the routing adjacency going down. This will appear as separate log messages on the two devices.

In order to correlate the different log messages across devices, it is important that the log messages be timestamped, and should have a common time reference. This time reference is provided by **Network Time Protocol** (**NTP**).

In the absence of NTP, all devices will run a clock based on their local clock source that might not be very accurate. Even if the internal clock is accurate on all devices, all devices have to be configured with the precise date and time values so that they have a baseline and start using the internal clock to increment time, which is impractical to do on a large-scale network. Hence, NTP is deployed on networking devices as a best practice to have a common reference for a time across all devices on the network.

The current version of NTP is version 4, which is defined as a standard in RFC 5905. An NTP network usually gets its time from an authoritative time source, such as a radio clock, a **Global Positioning System** (**GPS**) device, or an atomic clock attached to a time server. NTP then distributes this time across the network.

NTP is hierarchical with different time servers maintaining authority levels. This highest authority is stratum 1. Levels of authority then descend from 2 to a maximum of 16. NTP is extremely efficient; no more than one packet per minute is necessary to synchronize two machines to within a millisecond of one another.

It is a good practice to have NTP configured on all devices, with the NTP hierarchy following the network hierarchy. As an example, we can have all core devices on the network derive the clock from central servers at the IP address (say 1.1.1.1 and 1.1.1.2). These devices can then serve as the NTP servers for the devices that are logically parented to these core devices. This hierarchy will ensure that no single device is a source of failure and no single device is overloaded by sending NTP messages to clients.

A sample topology of the NTP hierarchy is as shown in the following image:

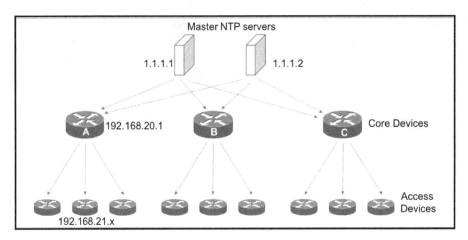

Figure 9: A sample NTP hierarchy

The NTP configuration for the device A is as shown in the following image. In the first section of the configuration, the time zone of the device is defined and NTP is allowed to update the hardware clock of the device. The last line in the configuration makes the hardware clock an authoritative time source for the network to send the NTP information to others:

```
Router-A(config)# clock timezone PST -8
Router-A(config)# ntp update-calendar
Router-A(config)# clock calendar-valid
```

Figure 10: Configuring the device clock

In the next part of the configuration, the source address of all NTP packets is set to the logical interface `loopback0`. Further, NTP is configured to operate in an authentication mode and authentication keys that are trusted are defined. The configuration also receives an NTP time from the NTP servers defined as `1.1.1.1` and `1.1.1.2` using the authentication keys, as follows:

```
Router-A(config)# ntp source loopback0
Router-A(config)# ntp authenticate
Router-A(config)# ntp authentication-key 1 md5 C!sc0123
Router-A(config)# ntp trusted-key 1
Router-A(config)# ntp server 1.1.1.1 version 2 key 1 prefer
Router-A(config)# ntp server 1.1.1.2 version 2 key 1
```

Figure 11: Configuring NTP

Finally, the device is configured to send NTP messages only to the devices that are homed to this core device. This is done to prevent any device to send NTP requests and overload the device. An access list is created for this purpose that contains the IP addresses of the NTP clients and the access list is called in the `ntp access-group` that is used to serve clients:

```
Router-A(config)# ntp access-group serve-only 10
Router-A(config)# access-list 10 permit 192.168.21.1
Router-A(config)# access-list 10 permit 192.168.21.2
Router-A(config)# access-list 10 permit 192.168.21.3
```

Figure 12: Restricting NTP clients using ACLs

If an organization does not have a high-reliability clock, it can use any public NTP servers that are available on the internet if these devices have an NTP reachability. Note that this will expose the devices to the internet and open up security threats, which will need to be managed. Hence, as a best practice, only a handful of devices derive the clock from the public NTP servers and act as NTP servers for the remaining devices in a hierarchical design, as discussed in this section.

Controlling device access using RADIUS

The device can be accessed through Telnet or SSH using virtual terminal lines, known as VTY ports. The recommendation is to use SSH and disable access to Telnet to enhance security. However, in some cases Telnet may be a requirement; therefore the VTYs must be secured.

The use of password protection to control or restrict access to the CLI of your router is one of the fundamental elements of an overall security plan for network devices. Protecting the router from unauthorized remote access, typically Telnet or SSH, is important. At the same time, you should not overlook protecting the router from an unauthorized local access using the console ports. The physical safety of the devices is foremost, before any of the logical security measures can be implemented.

The following configuration creates a radius profile for users to log into the device using the RADIUS server at the IP address `192.168.10.200`:

```
Router(config)# aaa new-model
Router(config)# aaa authentication login default group radius local
Router(config)# radius-server host 192.168.10.200 key C!sc0123 timeout 60
Router(config)# line vty 0 4
Router(config-line)# exec-timeout 5 0
Router(config-line)# transport input telnet ssh
Router(config-line)# transport output none
Router(config-line)# transport preferred none
Router(config-line)# login authentication default
```

Figure 13: Configuring AAA

The following configuration applies an ACL on the VTY ports of the devices to allow only users from a specific subnet, typically the NOC subnet to access the devices. Only the NOC subnet is allowed to log into the devices, as the NOC address prefix is explicitly allowed in the ACL and all other addresses are blocked. We have also created a local user on the device to be able to log into the device if the connectivity to the RADIUS server is lost.:

```
Router(config)# access-list 3 permit 192.168.10.0 0.0.0.255
Router(config)# access-list 3 deny any
Router(config)# line vty 0 4
Router(config-line)# access-class 3 in

Router(config)# username Operator1 password Password
```

Figure 14: Configuring VTY lines

Role-based user access

The discussions so far have focused on logging into the devices. This section focuses on creating user profiles that can be used to allow specific users access to a set of commands and not allow them to make changes to the devices.

Cisco IOS allows different view-profiles that allow users belonging to a certain profile to execute only specific commands. It is necessary to log into the devices in the root view, using the `enable view` command. The configuration for creating a view is as shown in the following image:

```
Router> enable view
Router# configure terminal
Router(config)# parser view OpXYZ
Router(config-view)# secret C!sc0123
Router(config-view)# command exec include show version
Router(config-view)# command exec include all show ip
Router(config-view)# exit
Router(config)#
```

Figure 15: Configuring RBAC

We created a view called OpXYZ, which has the right to execute only the EXEC mode commands as defined in the preceding configuration. Additional views can be created to differentiate users in the operations hierarchy.

When a user is authenticated using RADIUS, an additional custom attribute value pair (av pair) named cli-view-name is passed along with the RADIUS response to associate the user with the configured view.

Role-based access (**RBAC**) is a common way of providing different users with different sets of commands in an organization. This prevents the operators with limited skillets from misconfiguring any devices.

IP Service Level Assurance (IP-SLA)

Cisco IP-SLAs use traffic probes to monitor the performance of the network on the data plane. Using IP-SLA, the network operators can find the actual service levels being delivered to a user, based on the forwarding plane parameters, such as protocol and DSCP bits. IP-SLA provides an actual user experience that is more refined than a ping, which only sends ICMP packets to check reachability.

IP-SLAs send data across the network to measure the performance between multiple network locations or across multiple network paths. It simulates network data and IP services and collects the network performance information in real time. The information collected includes data about response time, one-way latency, jitter (interpacket delay variance), packet loss, voice quality scoring, network resource availability, application performance, and server response time. This data can be used for troubleshooting, problem analysis, and designing network topologies.

The parameters of IP-SLA can be monitored using SNMP and plotted on a real-time basis to show any deviations in the SLAs on the network. The metrics are provided between any two points on the network that may traverse the organizations' own network or even service provider provided networks, such as layer 2 and layer 3 VPNs, thereby providing a complete end-to-end view of the network.

The IP SLAs probe is a feature on the Cisco IOS, where the IP-SLA agent on the Cisco router monitors network performance by measuring response time, network resource availability, application performance, jitter (interpacket delay variance), connect time, throughput, and packet loss. Performance can be measured between any Cisco device that supports this feature and any remote IP host (server), Cisco routing device, or mainframe host.

This is deployed by configuring the IP SLA probes at strategic locations on the network and using the remote routers as responders. As an example, the WAN routers at remote branches in an organization can be configured with the IP SLA probes to check the SLA to the DC gateway routers. The frequency of the probes can be scheduled on the devices, including the number of probes to be sent for each protocol type.

The following image shows the IP SLA configuration on the devices running the IP-SLA agent. We have created two SLA probes, numbered 10 and 20. The first IP-SLA probe numbered 10 is for monitoring UDP jitter to the IP address 10.0.100.2 by sending 20 packets in one go every 180 seconds. The packet size for the UDP packets is 64 bytes, and we have tagged this with a name for easier identification.

The second probe numbered 20 is for finding the response to an HTTP server with the domain name www.xyz.com every 180 seconds.

Finally, we had to schedule the IP-SLA probes, with probe 10 being a never-ending probe and probe 20 being scheduled only for one day (86400 seconds):

```
Router# configure terminal
Router(config)# ip sla 10
Router(config-ip-sla)# udp-jitter 10.8.100.2 num-packets 20
Router(config-ip-sla-jitter)# frequency 180
Router(config-ip-sla-jitter)# request-data-size 64
Router(config-ip-sla-jitter)# tag TO-BRANCH1-ROUTER
Router(config-ip-sla-jitter)# end
Router(config)# ip sla 20
Router(config-ip-sla)# http get http://www.xyz.com
Router(config-ip-sla-http)# frequency 180
Router(config-ip-sla)# end
Router(config)# ip sla schedule 10 life forever start-time now
Router(config)# ip sla schedule 20 life 86400 start-time now
```

Figure 16: Configuring IP SLA probe on a device

There is no configuration needed on the HTTP server, as long as it is a valid HTTP server. However, for the UDP probe, since we are sending the probes to a router address `10.0.100.2`, the remote router should be configured as a responder using the following configuration:

```
Router# configure terminal
Router(config)# ip sla responder
```

Figure 17: Configuring the IPSLA responders

Management network

The management network means the network that will be used by the NMS systems to reach the network devices and vice-versa.

Some organizations build a complete **out-of-band** (**OOB**) management network, which means that the network used to communicate between the network devices and the NMS systems and agents in the **Network Operations Center** (**NOC**) is totally separate from the network used to forward user traffic. This ensures that any outage on the user data plane does not lead to the devices being unmanageable and preventing any corrective action from being taken by the NOC teams. OOB management networks separate the user and management planes on the end-to-end network.

Note that a completely OOB network means that there are two parallel networks, and this adds to the cost of the overall IT infrastructure. Even though the management network is small in terms of capacity or bandwidth of the network, the links are required on a dedicated basis if the devices are being monitored on the OOB network. Some organizations use in-band management, which means that they poll the devices on the same links on which the data traffic is flowing and just have a backup link to the console port or the management port of the devices from the NOC that is activated when there is a need to log into these devices. Other organizations might prefer to do everything in-band and even manage the devices on the user data plane. This type of management is called **in-band management**.

Organizations generally tend to use on OOB network for the core devices that are critical to the overall IT operations and manage the access layer devices in-band.

Cisco Prime Infrastructure

A chapter on network management would be incomplete without a description of a tool that helps in network lifecycle management. Cisco Prime Infrastructure (PI) is a network management system that provides an intuitive and web-based **graphical user interface (GUI)** that provides a complete view of a network use and performance. PI provides a single pane of glass management for all Cisco wired and wireless network elements and can act like an SNMP manager for non-Cisco devices also. The unified GUI helps in service provisioning, service monitoring and assurance, and even changes compliance management:

- **Auto-discover network elements**: Cisco PI can auto-discover the devices on the network based on the inputs provided to the system. PI will use SNMP and login credentials to discover devices and pull the device configurations to create a centralized repository.
- **Grouping of devices**: PI provides the ability to group the discovered or manually added devices based on their location, device type, or any other criteria configured by the user. This grouping can be extremely helpful to push a specific software image to all access switches, for example, on the network.
- **Grouping of ports**: Port grouping helps the user to create groups for the interfaces on the devices. As an example, the WAN interfaces port group is a preconfigured port group and all interfaces in this group will be actively monitored.
- **Visualizing network topology**: PI provides a visual map of the physical topology of the network, including the network devices and the interconnecting links between the devices.
- **Software image management**: PI can be used to push new IOS images to the devices on the network based on their grouping or even individual devices. PI can be used to schedule, download, and monitor the software image update jobs.
- **Configuration archive management**: PI archives and maintains multiple versions of running startup configurations. The system can also be used to compare the configuration of a device against the archived configurations to find any differences to aid troubleshooting.
- **Golden template compliance**: Enterprises generally have a golden configuration template that incorporates the design parameters and best practices and serves as a basis of the configuration for all devices on the network. PI can use the golden network configuration as predefined rules, and perform an audit of the network devices against the actual device configuration to identify any discrepancies on the network. These audits can be scheduled to provide periodic reports to the management.

- **Monitoring, troubleshooting, and reporting**: Running a network requires knowing about the state of the network and the state of individual devices. PI can be used to monitor devices using SNMP against configurable thresholds for defined parameters and generate alarms when the thresholds are violated.
- **Automated deployment**: The Plug and Play feature of PI can help to autoconfigure the device when it is powered up and connected to the network at the time of installation.
- **User monitoring**: PI also provides a list of all users that are active on the network, including their IP addresses and MAC addresses and the ports that they are connected to on the network. The PI system can be integrated with active directory servers to display the usernames.
- **Wireless sitemaps**: Once an image of the physical floorplan and AP deployments has been uploaded into the PI, the system can be used to display the physical locations of network devices, including wireless access points and client devices, such as laptops, tablets, and mobile phones. This helps to visualize wireless network coverage, including heatmap that can help identify the areas of weak Wi-Fi coverage and the locations of RF interferers.
- **Integration with other systems**: PI can be used to integrate with other systems, using the APIs provided by the system.

Implementing the network management strategy

We have discussed the various elements of an effective network management approach. In this section, we will lay out the following guidelines for drafting a network management strategy for effective operations of an organization:

- Identify the network requirements and decide on an in-band approach or an OOB network management.
- Build standard configuration templates for common configuration across all devices on the network such as AAA, IPSLA, syslog, security, and common services. Disable any unnecessary features that are not required on the network devices. Use standard hostname conventions that can be used for effective parsing of the SNMP traps and syslog messages.
- Configure the devices for SNMP and secure the management plane of the devices using the configurations as discussed in the previous sections.

- Identify the parameters that need to be polled and compile the required MIBs on the NMS servers. Start polling the devices at regular intervals.
- Use automation tools and correlation tools to deduplicate the multiple alarms and suppressing the downstream alerts and present only the root cause to the NOC teams. Use automation tools and scripts to parse all log messages at periodic intervals.
- Monitor the network baseline with respect to traffic, a number of login attempts on routers, failed AAA requests, link or network flaps, top devices generating syslog messages, and so on, to find deviations. These deviations will help in proactively preventing outages and detecting any security breach attempts on the network.
- Classify the incidents by severity and take action based on the severity. Use this metric to analyze the NOC performance on turnaround times for issue resolution of various severity levels.
- Group the incidents by hardware types and software types to build a historical database that will help in identifying perpetual problems with the design, hardware failures, or software releases.
- Use IP SLA problems and SNMP threshold violations for proactive steps towards capacity upgrades and improving service levels.
- Create metrics for the NOC operations for each activity that can be monitored. These metrics could consist of parameters such as **mean time between failures** (**MTBF**) for a given service, a number of incidents in the NMS per day, and percentage of the number of incidents reported by users against the total number of incidents. Review the reports and metrics, and evolve the processes for improving the NOC performance.
- Create a training policy within the NOC team to keep them abreast of the new technologies or services being deployed on the network. Ensure that every NOC engineer knows the network well before he is allowed to make any configuration changes on the network. Create processes for day-to-day tasks and common network events, such as link outages and port outages.
- Build processes for communication of incident status to all stakeholders.
- Document all changes on the network and build a configuration management database that has the configuration of all devices backed-up on a daily basis.
- Build a centralized repository for all critical information such as IP addresses, port information, and service flow diagrams, for faster troubleshooting of issues on the network.

- Test all major configuration changes planned to be made on the network and follow a release management approach for device software and new services induction.
- Use consistent software images on the same type of devices on the network as far as possible.

The preceding list is not exhaustive, but will go a long way in making the NOC more effective in an organization.

Summary

In this chapter, we discussed the various approaches to network management that span across the service management lifecycle, with a focus on the network operations. We discussed the various elements of an effective network management and operations strategy and discussed the various configurations required to monitor the network for delivering the services with the designed SLAs. We ended the chapter with a broad list of best practices that can help improve the NOC operations of an organization.

In spite of all the best practices, outages will happen and services will be degraded. In the next chapter, we will discuss the various troubleshooting tools and technologies and provide an approach for troubleshooting common problems in an IT environment.

11
Basic Troubleshooting Skills and Techniques

"Problem solving is hunting. It is savage pleasure and we are born to it."

–Thomas Harris

We have discussed the various aspects of design and configuration of various parts of the enterprise network. We might have done all the right things to build a robust and resilient network, but the fact of the matter is that problems happen. Devices breakdown, software hits bugs, links and ports fail, and people make configuration errors. Any of these can lead to services being down or degraded, requiring troubleshooting.

In this chapter, we will discuss the following topics:

- Define a framework for structured troubleshooting
- Define the techniques used for troubleshooting IP networks
- Discuss common troubleshooting commands

While it is not possible to cover all types of incidents that can occur in an enterprise IP network in one chapter, we will focus on creating an approach that can be used for real-life troubleshooting.

A framework for structured troubleshooting

Every network engineer who has some exposure to networking has found Murphy's Law, *anything that can go wrong will go wrong*, to be true. If a network is delivering services, there is a good chance that it will experience problems at times. The goal of the network engineers is to proactively identify and prevent these incidents from happening. We discussed the details around proactive monitoring in Chapter 10, *A Systematic Approach to Network Operations*. Regardless of the amount of proactive monitoring, things go wrong that cannot be predicted and the network engineer is required to do a lot of network troubleshooting to help resolve issues as quickly as possible. We will cover these aspects of reactive troubleshooting in this chapter.

Divide and rule have always been the driving success factors to solve complex problems. If we can break a complex problem down into its constituent parts and solve them individually, things become manageable. However, it needs to be stressed here that a network is like a Rubik's cube and changing one part of the network will have its impact on the other parts of the network. While it is a good approach to break down a complex problem into its constituents, one should not lose sight of the inter-dependencies between the various components.

While network design could be considered a science and an art at the same time, network troubleshooting is primarily a science. Everything has a reason and, hence, taking a systematic approach helps to identify and correct the issues on the network effectively.

Let's discuss a structured approach as shown in the following figure, which will help the network engineer in troubleshooting the issues on the network. Note that different steps in this approach are carried out by different teams, such as the trouble-ticketing team and the NOC escalation team. What is important is that these steps have to be carried out and information from each step is passed on to the next stage:

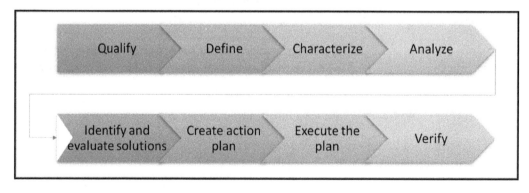

Figure 1: A structured approach to troubleshooting

All **incidents** are either proactively detected or reported to the network engineers. We will use the term incident hereafter in this chapter to define an issue with a network service, as opposed to the word problem, which in the ITIL framework means something that causes recurring incidents on the network.

As a first step, the network engineer has to **qualify** if what has been reported is actually an incident that needs to be addressed. This is because the service degradation could be because of an ongoing activity on the network and will get resolved after the activity is over. Other reasons could be that a user might just be expecting the service to work, while it has not even been provisioned on the network, as the user assumed that this would work on the network. For example, if an organization had a policy of blocking www.youtube.com on the enterprise network, a user reporting *not able to access YouTube* is not an incident. Assumptions are the basis of major issues on the network and all assumptions have to be validated upfront and documented.

This step could also be thought of as a verification that there is something that needs to be addressed and identify the right owner for the action to be taken. Without this step, we might end up *chasing a white whale*.

It is important to emphasize here that networking problems can be transient or intermittent. An issue might exist for some time, fade away and then reoccur after some time. So, the absence of evidence cannot always be treated as an evidence of absence. For example, an internal application running on an overloaded server might be working normally for a user during the time of qualification, but would timeout during periods of congestion.

After having established that there is an incident, the next step is to **Define** what the issue is. This will involve gathering data that is specific to network parameters and not user parameters. This helps to ensure that the issue is defined clearly in networking terms and is not ambiguous. For example, if a user is not able to download mail, the issue definition could be that the mail client is unable to connect to the mail server. The define phase helps collect symptoms of the issue on the network.

The issue also needs to be **Characterized** with respect to getting additional details such as the time of occurrence, the impact of the issue, it's duration, and whether it is permanent or transient. Gathering this data helps the network engineer prioritize the issue based on impact, duration, and so on, and it provides the information about key parameters that would help in analyzing in the next stage. This phase requires collecting a lot of additional information from the users and the network and potentially clubbing multiple events into a common issue such as all users at a particular location not being able to access emails.

For example, the characterization of the email issue could be as follows:

- All mail clients at location ABC first floor were not able to connect to the mail server since yesterday
- The last mail in the inbox of the impacted users was around hh: mm
- The mail server is reachable from the client machines and connectivity was verified using ping

The characterization details include listing down all symptoms of the problem, known historical behavior, known triggers for the symptoms, the timing of the problem, the frequency with which it occurs, and so on.

The next stage is where we **Analyze** the symptoms and the various symptoms collected during the characterization phase. This phase involves correlating the various data collected during the previous phases and collecting and referring to additional data such as historical trends, documentation, research, any other related issues, and the experience of the network engineer.

Having understood the exact nature of the issue and correlating the information from various sources, we **identify potential solutions** that can solve the ongoing issue on the network. These solutions have to be validated against each of the symptoms and analysis findings during the previous stages. Note that the solutions have to be validated against the symptoms observed on the network for the issue at hand and the results of the analysis. There could be multiple potential solutions and the solutions need to be **evaluated** to find the best solution that will solve the issue. The parameters for the best solution could be functionality, time to execute/implement, impacted stakeholders, and so on. Note that if the solution should focus on restoring services and any optimizations for a long-term solution should be deferred to a later stage and implemented only after following a thorough design, solution validation, testing, and change control process.

The evaluated solution then needs to be converted into a **plan of action** that lists down the necessary steps to be performed on the different elements, identifying checkpoints in the plan, and the verification steps that would ensure that the changes being made lead toward the desired results. This step might need testing in a controlled environment if the plan involves introducing additional commands or features than originally designed.

The plan of action is **executed** on the network to make the necessary changes on the network. If, at any checkpoint in the plan of action, the results are different from the desired ones, the plan should indicate a fallback plan and the analysis phase should be re-initiated to validate the solution in light of the changes observed.

After the changes have been made on the network, the network engineer needs to **verify** that the issue has been resolved. The verification steps and parameters should also be a part of the plan of action. Further, the issue details need to be captured in the ticketing system with as much information as possible that would allow the incident to be correlated later to other incidents and help in identifying problems on the network.

Establishing the normal and detecting deviations

There are two scenarios where a network engineer needs to exercise his troubleshooting skills. One, when there is network degradation or an incident detected through proactive monitoring of the network as defined in the previous chapter, and two, when a user reports an issue leading to reactive troubleshooting.

It is important for the network engineer to know what normal behavior on the network is. This normal or expected behavior is referred to as the baseline and any unexplained significant deviations from this baseline would be considered abnormal behavior and should be investigated.

The network baseline

We discussed the importance of monitoring the network in the previous chapter. Monitoring the network for parameters and trending those parameters over time will what is normal for the network. The important parameters that need to be monitored, among others, are as follows:

- Link states of LAN and WAN ports
- User port status for the active ports on the network
- Traffic utilization for links
- Memory and CPU utilization for network devices
- Protocol status for the protocols running on the network

Let's recall from our discussion in Chapter 8, *Understanding and Configuring Network Security*, in which network behavior can be used to baseline user plane traffic as well as using NetFlow. This metadata from the traffic flows can be used to establish what is normal and detect any deviations using **Network Behavioural Analysis and Detection** (**NBAD**) technologies.

The baseline can also be created for various service-level parameters, such as latency, jitter, and packet loss, using IP SLA probes as discussed in Chapter 10, *A Systematic Approach to Network Operations*.

Application baseline

Another aspect of the baseline is the actual application baseline. While IP SLA helps to provide specific parameters across the network, the actual traffic flows for critical applications needs to be documented and provided as a ready reference to the NOC engineers to facilitate troubleshooting. A highest-level sample is shown in the following image:

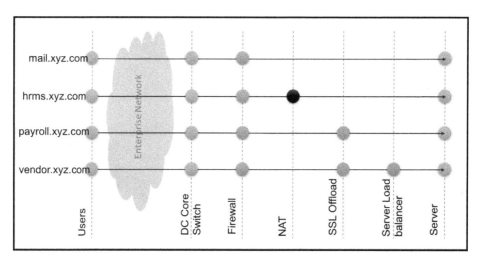

Figure 2: Application flow diagrams

A line diagram like the preceding one will help the network engineers trace the exact path of each application on the network within the DC and bridge the gap between the application and network teams. The next level of details can be built showing the exact port and VLAN information, IP address of the devices, lead balancer IP address pool, and any NAT policies, and so on.

Having the flow diagrams previously is a very ambitious goal, as the applications and network are both dynamic in an organization. However, it is not impossible if strict change control is maintained and processes are followed to make any changes on the network or the applications. Creating such diagrams go a long way not only in troubleshooting but also helping in other areas such as application migration planning.

If the preceding diagrams are not possible in an organization due to the number or complexity of applications, the network engineer has to rely on the design documents, network topology diagrams, and site-specific network diagrams. Hence, it is essential to have updated design documents and precise and accurate network topology diagrams that are maintained religiously.

The preceding documentation coupled with IP Address management tools and historical trends through the NMS portals help the network engineers to restore services faster.

Network troubleshooting commands

A person's efficiency is greatly enhanced if he has the right tools. We have covered some NMS tools earlier, including SNMP, syslogs, and netflow. In this section, we will describe the commands that are used for network troubleshooting.

IOS commands

Cisco IOS provides a variety of commands for monitoring and troubleshooting a network. The commands are clubbed together as the `show` commands. These commands are used to view the various parameters on the devices such as the configuration, interfaces, VLANs, IP addresses, protocols, and routing tables. We will discuss the specific `show` commands in the next section.

The `show` command output can be very long and certain keywords are used within the IOS to parse the information. Some of the keywords and their impact are listed as follows:

- `include`: This option shows the output of the command and includes only the lines that include the text that is passed on as an argument. The syntax for the usage of this option is `show ip interface brief | include up`.
- `begin`: This option shows the output of the `show` command, but starts displaying the text at the point, where the first instance of the passed argument exists in the `show` output. The syntax for the usage of this option is `show running-configuration | begin interface`.

- `exclude`: This option shows the output of the command and does not show the lines that include the text that is passed on as an argument. The syntax for the usage of this option is `show ip interface brief | exclude up`.
- `section`: This option displays the output of the `show` command with only the specific section. For example, if we want to see only the ospf configuration, the syntax is `show running | section ospf`.
- `append`: This option can be used to append the output of the command to a specific file, the location of which is passed as an argument. An example of this usage is `show tech-support | append disk1:showoutput.txt`.
- `redirect`: This option allows the output to be redirected and saved at a defined location. An example of this usage is `show tech | redirect ftp://UNAME:PASSWD@192.168.20.15//outputs/tac/showtech.txt`.

We will use some of these commands as appropriate during the next sections. Note that only a subset of the `show` commands is available in the EXEC mode and the user needs to get into the privileged EXEC mode for advanced commands, including `extended ping`, as follows.

The ping command

The `ping` command is by far the most commonly used command to troubleshoot connectivity issues. This command sends **Internet Control Message Protocol** (**ICMP**) echo messages and verifies connectivity to the destination as it gets the ICMP echo reply messages. ICMP is an integral part of the TCP/IP protocol suite that provides troubleshooting capabilities. ICMP packets are also used in IP SLA probes.

The `ping` command can be used to ping the destination IP address, with a specific number of packets and by specifying the size of the datagrams. The syntax is as follows:

```
ping 172.16.20.39 data ABCD df-bit repeat 1000 size 1472 source 10.8.25.1
```

Figure 3: Pinging a host to verify connectivity

The `ping` response is in the ! ! ! ! ! form, which every engineer generally hopes for. This is because of the ! symbol, which means an echo reply is received. The characters in the `ping` result display can be interpreted using the following image:

Response	Interpretatioin
!	Each exclamation point indicates receipt of a reply.
.	Each period indicates the device timed out while waiting for a reply.
U	A destination unreachable error PDU was received.
Q	Source quench (destination too busy).
M	Fragmentation required but could not fragment
?	Unknown packet type
&	Packet lifetime exceeded.

Figure 4: Interpreting the ping response

In addition to the preceding text, the `ping` result also shows the round-trip travel time intervals for the protocol echo packets, including minimum/average/maximum (in milliseconds).

What is more important for network troubleshooting is the extended ping commands that allow the engineer to set certain additional parameters in the IP packet that encapsulates the ICMP message.

A normal ping message sends out ICMP messages with the source address of the outgoing interface. The interface addresses are not typically advertised outside the organization. Hence, the return packets destined to this interface address would not be able to find their way back. In such cases, ping messages are sent with the source address that is also routed on the external networks. An example of this is the user pool of IP addresses.

The source address to be used should belong to one of the interfaces on the router and, hence, either the loopback address or an address of the user-facing interface is used in the ping packets.

Another example for the usage of extended ping is to test the end-to-end MTU on the network. We have seen that a decrease in the MTU will result in TCP throughput issues and will result in unnecessary IP fragmentation. Extended ping can help identify these issues by sending a packet with a specified MTU and the DF bit set in the IP header, which means that the packets cannot be fragmented.

The usage of this command is as shown in the following image:

```
Router# ping
Protocol [ip]:
Target IP address: 172.16.20.39
Repeat Count [5]: 100
Datagram Size [100]:
Timeout in seconds [2]:
Extended commands [n]: y
Source address or interface: loopback0
Type of service [0]:
Set DF bit in IP header? [no]:
Validate reply data? [no]:
Data pattern [0xABCD]:
Loose, Strict, Record, Timestamp, Verbose [none]:
Sweep range of sizes [n]:
```

Figure 5: Using the extended ping

The argument within the square braces [ ] is the default option. If we input n to the extended commands option, we won't see the subsequent options and the device will send ping packets to the destination.

The datagram size is the actual size of the datagram, including the headers. This is different when you do a ping from a Windows machine, as the ping command on a Windows machine specifies the size of the ICMP payload and we need to add 8 bytes of ICMP and 20 bytes of IP header to find the exact MTU. Hence, a value of 1500 bytes in IOS will correspond to 1472 on a Windows machine.

Validate data reply instructs the router to compare the data received in the echo reply with the data sent in the echo requests. DF bits instruct the router to set the DF bit to check the MTU on the network. The data pattern is the actual data that is sent in the datagram and is used to check any framing errors and clocking issues on the serial links.

The Loose option allows setting loose source routing, while the Strict option forces strict source routing for the IP packet. If you set either the Loose or Strict option, the display will show additional input fields to set the loose/ strict source routing IP addresses.

The `Record` option displays the addresses of up to nine hops that the packet goes through. This can be thought of as a combination of ping and traceroute. Finally, the `Sweep` option allows us to vary the sizes of the echo packets that are sent. This can be used to determine the minimum size of the MTUs configured on the nodes along the path to the destination address.

The traceroute command

The `traceroute` command can be used to trace the exact routing hops and the path that the packets take to the remote destination. The `traceroute` command uses UDP datagrams and uses the TTL field to trace each hop. Since a router sends an ICMP message when TTL expires in transit, packets are sent with incrementing TTL values so that each hop is traced.

 If ICMP unreachables are disabled on an interface along the path, that hop would be shown as a `*`.

Like the `ping` command, the `traceroute` command can also be used in the extended mode. The fields in the extended command are as shown in the following image:

```
Router# traceroute
Protocol [ip]:
Target IP address: 172.16.20.39
Source address: 10.8.25.1
Numeric display [n]:
Timeout in seconds [3]:
Probe count [3]:
Minimum Time to Live [1]:
Maximum Time to Live [30]:
Port Number [33434]:
Loose, Strict, Record, Timestamp, Verbose[none]:
```

Figure 6: Using the extended traceroute

A sample `traceroute` from a router is as shown in the following figure. One might see some * marks instead of the IP addresses of the devices along the path, which implies that there is a hop but traceroute could not get the IP address of the hop. Also, if there is an SP network or an IP tunnel that the packet traverses, there would be IP hops but they might not visible (even as *), as the packet would be encapsulated using additional headers:

```
Router# traceroute 192.168.10.13

Type escape sequence to abort
Tracing the route to 192.168.10.13

    1  172.16.0.2      2 msec     2 msec      2 msec
    2  172.16.1.3     24 msec    16 msec     20 msec
    3  172.16.1.19    42 msec    37 msec     40 msec
Router#
```

Figure 7: A sample traceroute output

Some devices also give the message **Trace complete** to indicate that the destination was reached. The output shows the **Round trip time** (**RTT**) values for each of the three probes sent by the router.

There are times when the destination is not reachable and the packets get into a routing loop, as shown in the following figure. In this case, the command can be terminated using the escape sequence, which is the *CTRL + SHIFT + 6* keys pressed simultaneously.

```
Router# traceroute 192.168.10.13
Type escape sequence to abort
Tracing the route to 192.168.10.13
    1  172.16.0.2      2 msec     2 msec      2 msec
    2  172.16.1.3     10 msec    12 msec     16 msec
    3  172.16.1.19    15 msec    18 msec     21 msec
    4  172.16.1.3     20 msec    23 msec     26 msec
    5  172.16.1.19    26 msec    29 msec     31 msec

!! Press CTRL+SHIFT+6 to abort.

Router#
```

Figure 8: Traceroute output showing a routing loop

The debug commands

The debug commands are a very useful way of troubleshooting. It can help in identifying issues that a human eye can miss. For example, if two connected Cisco routers are configured to run OSPF using the passwords C!sco123 and C!sc0123, the human eye might miss that the letter o is replaced by the numeral 0, thus leading to the protocol not establishing a neighbor relationship.

Running a debug command shows the packets exchanged and also shows messages on the console that can be interpreted to identify the issue.

 Running a debug command can be a CPU consuming process and should be turned on only for troubleshooting.

Various types of debugs can be turned on the route. You can find a complete list by pressing the ? sign after the debug on the IOS console. Some of them, including the syntax, are debug ip bgp, debug ip ospf events, debug ip eigrp, debug spanning-tree events, and debug interface. Note that it is important for the network engineer to understand the working of the protocol in detail before he can use the debug commands effectively. All debug commands running on the network can be disabled using the undebug all or no debug all command. The show debugging command shows all active debugs on the router. Most protocols provide sub-options for debugging, for example, debug ip bgp updates, and they should be used rather than the debugging the complete protocol. This would reduce the load on the device and make the output more readable on the screen.

Troubleshooting the network

Troubleshooting an IP network becomes easier if one follows the networking basics and follows the traffic flow. Troubleshooting typically starts from the user to the application. A methodical approach would help the engineer get to the issue faster. The steps, in this case, are shown as follows:

- Is user able to connect to the network?
- Is the user able to get an IP address through DHCP?
- Is the user able to reach the first layer 3 hop?
- Is the user able to reach the application server?
- Is the user experiencing performance issues?

We will follow the preceding approach and discuss the troubleshooting steps in the following sections. We have taken the command output from the Cisco command reference manuals for most show outputs in the following sections. The engineer can refer to the IOS command references for more commands and the options and detailed explanations for the output.

Troubleshooting user connectivity

The first step in troubleshooting a user issue is to verify if the user has bi-directional connectivity to the network. There are times when a multi-rate interface (such as a 10/100/1000Mbps Ethernet port) is set manually to mismatching speeds.

The show interfaces command is the most frequently used command, as it provides a host of information about the interface. The show interfaces command will show the speed of the interface, the duplex settings and the state of the interface, the protocol status, utilization, MTU, and any errors on the interface among other parameters. A sample output is as shown in the following image:

```
Router# show interfaces ethernet 0

Ethernet 0 is up, line protocol is up
  Hardware is MCI Ethernet, address is 0000.0c00.750c (bia 0000.0c00.750c)
  Internet address is 131.108.28.8, subnet mask is 255.255.255.0
  MTU 1500 bytes, BW 10000 Kbit, DLY 100000 usec, rely 255/255, load 1/255
  Encapsulation ARPA, loopback not set, keepalive set (10 sec)
  ARP type: ARPA, ARP Timeout 4:00:00
  Last input 0:00:00, output 0:00:00, output hang never
  Last clearing of "show interface" counters 0:00:00
  Output queue 0/40, 0 drops; input queue 0/75, 0 drops
  Five minute input rate 0 bits/sec, 0 packets/sec
  Five minute output rate 2000 bits/sec, 4 packets/sec
     1127576 packets input, 447251251 bytes, 0 no buffer
     Received 354125 broadcasts, 0 runts, 0 giants, 57186* throttles
     0 input errors, 0 CRC, 0 frame, 0 overrun, 0 ignored, 0 abort
     5332142 packets output, 496316039 bytes, 0 underruns
     0 output errors, 432 collisions, 0 interface resets, 0 restarts
...
```

Figure 9: Show interfaces output

The preceding figure shows the IP address, the hardware or the MAC address, the MTU, the serialization delay, and the transmit and receive loads as a fraction of the base 255. The last input and output times show when a frame was successfully received or transmitted, which helps to find out when the interface went down. The output also provides information about the traffic rate in each direction in terms of bits per second (bps) and packets per second (pps). The input frame types are also shown as broadcasts (having a broadcast destination address), runts (frames smaller than 64 bytes), and giants (frame larger than 1518 bytes). Throttled frames indicate congestion on the link. CRC errors indicate a noisy link, where CRC checksum has failed. Overruns and ignored frames indicate congestion.

If the port has gone into an `err-disabled` state, the ports need to be shut and no shut to bring it back up. There are options that can be used with the `show interfaces` command to view only a subset of parameters, such as the status option. The output of `show interfaces status` command shows the status of the interface. One can pipe the output using the command `show interface status | inc err-dis` to see only interfaces that are in an `err-disabled` state:

```
Switch# show interfaces gigabitethernet 4/1 status
Port    Name    Status         Vlan    Duplex      Speed   Type
Gi4/1           err-disabled 100.        full        1000    1000BaseSX
Switch#
```

Figure 10: Show interface status

The `show ip interface command` provides a lot of information about the configuration and status of the IP protocol and its services, on all interfaces. The command provides details about IP address and the MTU configured on the interface, along with any access lists that are applied to the interface in either direction. The command also shows the status of IP services on the interface, such as helper-address for DHCP forwarding, ICMP redirects, ICMP unreachable, and local proxy arp. A sample output is as shown as follows, with some of the output lines trimmed for better readability:

```
Router# show ip interface gigabitethernet 0/3
GigabitEthernet0/3 is up, line protocol is up
  Internet address is 10.1.1.1/16
  Broadcast address is 255.255.255.255
  . .
  MTU is 1500 bytes
  Helper address is not set
  . .
  Outgoing access list is not set
  Inbound access list is not set
  Proxy ARP is enabled
  Local Proxy ARP is disabled
  Security level is default
  Split horizon is enabled
  ICMP redirects are always sent
  ICMP unreachables are always sent
  ICMP mask replies are never sent
  . .
  Policy routing is enabled, using route map PBR
  Network address translation is disabled
  . .
```

Figure 11: Show IP interface

A quick way to look at all interfaces on the device and get their IP addresses and status is to use the `show ip interface brief` command. There will be instances where the port has been shut down manually using the `shutdown` command. Such ports will appear with the status administratively down in the output. If nothing is connected to the port or there are physical issues with the cable or the port, the same will appear in the output as the interface status is showing up, but protocol will appear as illustrated in the following image:

```
Router# show ip interface brief | include up
Interface              IP-Address       OK?    Method Status     Protocol
GigabitEthernet0/1     unassigned       YES    unset  up         up
GigabitEthernet0/2     192.168.190.235  YES    unset  up         up
GigabitEthernet0/3     unassigned       YES    unset  up         up
GigabitEthernet0/4     192.168.191.2    YES    unset  up         up
TenGigabitEthernet2/1  unassigned       YES    unset  up         up
TenGigabitEthernet2/2  unassigned       YES    unset  up         up
TenGigabitEthernet2/3  unassigned       YES    unset  up         up
```

Figure 12: Filtering the output

A network engineer can use the filters to see only the interfaces that are enabled on the device using the `show ip interface brief | include up` command.

Troubleshooting layer 2 issues

A switched network at the access could have multiple VLANs. The `show vlan brief` command shows the VLAN database that shows all VLANs configured on the device. This command also shows the VLAN to port mappings. The command also shows the MTU for each VLAN. A trimmed output of the command is as shown in the following image:

```
Switch# show vlan

VLAN   Name               Status      Ports
----   ------------------ ---------   --------------------------
1      default            active      Eth0/0, Eth0/2, Eth1/0, Eth1/1
                                      Eth1/2, Eth1/3, Eth2/0, Eth2/1
                                      Eth2/2, Eth2/3
10     VLAN0010           active      Eth0/1, Eth0/3
20     VLAN0020           active
```

Figure 13: Finding port to VLAN mappings

A VLAN may sometimes need to be tracked all the way up to the first layer 3 device. This can be done using the `show interfaces trunk` command. This will show the trunk ports and VLANs configured on the trunk ports. A sample output is as shown in the following image:

```
Switch# show interfaces trunk

Port        Mode          Encapsulation   Status      Native vlan
Eth3/0      desirable     802.1q          trunking    1

Port        Vlans allowed on trunk
Eth3/0      10,20,30

Port        Vlans allowed and active in management domain
Eth3/0      10,20,30

Port        Vlans in spanning tree forwarding state and not pruned
Eth3/0      10,20,30
```

Figure 14: Display trunk interfaces

The `show interfaces switchport` command can be used to view all ports that are configured as access ports.

The identifier for a layer 2 switching is the MAC address. The MAC addresses can be traced to the physical port on the underlying layer 2 devices using the `show mac-address-table` command. The following command output on a switch shows that the switch has 4 MAC addresses of hosts that are connected to various ports, as shown in the following table. These addresses are not static but dynamically learned and the switch has 41 MAC addresses that it owns because of the interfaces on the switch. One could also use a specific MAC address as an argument to the `show mac-address-table` command to look for a specific MAC address. A very large size of a MAC table will lead to the MAC address table reaching its limit, where no further MAC address can be learned. Such situations will lead to a re-evaluation of the hardware used for the switch:

```
Switch# show mac-address-table

Dynamic Addresses Count:                4
Secure Addresses (User-defined) Count: 0
Static Addresses (User-defined) Count: 0
System Self Addresses Count:            41
Total MAC addresses:                    45
Non-static Address Table:
Destination Address  Address Type   VLAN  Destination Port
-------------------  -----------    ----  --------------------
0010.0de0.e289       Dynamic          1   FastEthernet0/1
0010.7b00.1540       Dynamic          2   FastEthernet0/5
0010.7b00.1545       Dynamic          2   FastEthernet0/5
0060.5cf4.0076       Dynamic          1   FastEthernet0/1
```

Figure 15: Display of the MAC table

The MAC address table for a specific VLAN can be seen using the `show mac-address-table vlan 20` command. To display only the dynamic MAC address table entries, use the `showmac-address-table dynamic` command. The MAC addresses also age from the memory after the expiry of the aging time. This time can be seen using the `show mac-address-table aging-time` command.

There might be instances in a network, where two hosts on a network are incorrectly configured with the same IP address, leading to connectivity problems. If there is a duplicate IP address on a VLAN, it will result as an IP address ARP resolving to two different mac-addresses. Since the router stores ARP as a 1:1 mapping, the ARP table will show the output with one MAC address, which would change the next time the command is executed. This can be verified using the `show arp` command on the router. Note that the command will not show anything on the switch. The two MAC addresses can then be traced to the physical ports using the `show mac-address-table` command.

The output in the following image shows the IP addresses and the corresponding MAC addresses and the physical ports on which the router learned these ARP entries. The age is the time elapsed since this was learned. The ARP entries are cleared from the cache after the expiry of the ARP aging time for the VLAN defined on the device:

```
Router# show arp
Protocol  Address       Age (min)  Hardware Addr   Type   Interface
Internet  10.8.10.2           4    0010.0de0.e289  ARPA   FastEthernet0/0
Internet  10.8.10.13          1    0010.7b00.1545  ARPA   FastEthernet0/0
R2#
```

Figure 16: Display of the ARP table

Sometimes, the MAC address in the ARP table is shown as INCOMPLETE, which points to physical layer issues, as the ARP request was sent but a response was not received.

The hosts typically get an IP address from a DHCP server in an enterprise network. Further, the DHCP server is centralized. If a host is not getting an IP address using DHCP, it needs to be ensured that the `ip helper-address` command is configured on the layer 3 interface, where the DHCP requests are being received. Also, the DHCP server should have the DHCP pool configured with the gateway address that is configured on the layer 3 interface.

One can also use the `debug` commands for finding any unknown DHCP servers on the LAN segment, as the debug would show the DHCP offers from unknown IP addresses that belong to the unauthorized DHCP servers. The command to debug DHCP is `debug ip dhcp`.

The commands that can be used to troubleshoot spanning tree protocol are shown in the following figure:

Command	Purpose
show spanning-tree active	Displays spanning-tree information on active interfaces only.
show spanning-tree detail	Displays a detailed summary of interface information.
show spanning-tree interface interface-id	Displays spanning-tree information for the specified interface.
show spanning-tree summary	Displays a summary of interface states

Figure 17: Spanning tree commands

If **Cisco Discovery Protocol** (**CDP**) is enabled on the devices, we can trace the exact switching path, similar to a ping for an IP packet. The `traceroute mac` command helps to trace the exact switching path showing all switch hops from a source to a destination MAC address. If CDP is enabled, we can also see the Cisco devices that are connected to the device using the `show cdp neighbors` command.

Enabling CDP is not recommended for security reasons and it is better to configure the interface description in the configuration and follow strict processes to keep track of any changes.

Troubleshooting the first hop connectivity

We discussed the use of first hop redundancy protocols to provide redundancy against the default router on the LAN in `Chapter 4`, *Understanding and Configuring Campus Network Technologies*.

Most issues in the protocols appear from the mismatched timers, versions, and passwords, used for authentication between the devices. One can use the various show commands to find out these parameters.

The output of the `show standby` command is given in the following image, where the engineer can verify the state of the active HSRP router, the standby router, and the virtual MAC address that is being used for the HSRP group. The command also shows when the last HSRP failover happened, which was 18 minutes and 4 seconds ago in the following example. If an object is being tracked for HSRP, the same would also be displayed in the `show standby` command output:

```
Router_1# show standby
Vlan10 - Group 10
  Local state is Active, priority 110, may preempt
  Hellotime 3 holdtime 10
  Next hello sent in 00:00:00.216
  Hot standby IP address is 192.168.10.100 configured
  Active router is local
  Standby router is 192.168.10.2 expires in 00:00:08
  Standby virtual mac address is 0000.0c07.ac0a
  8 state changes, last state change 00:18:04
```

Figure 18: Display of HSRP routers information

Similar to the `show standby` command for HSRP, the `show vrrp` command is used to display the parameters for VRRP. A sample output is as shown in the following figure:

```
Router# show vrrp
Ethernet0/1 - Group 1
State is Master
Virtual IP address is 10.21.0.10
Virtual MAC address is 0000.5e00.0101
Advertisement interval is 1.000 sec
Preemption is enabled
 min delay is 0.000 sec
Priority is 100
 Authentication MD5, key-string, timeout 30 secs
Master Router is 10.21.0.1 (local), priority is 100
Master Advertisement interval is 1.000 sec
 .  .  .  .
```

Figure 19: Display of VRRP routers information

Sometimes, there might be a need to debug the protocols and the `debug` commands can be used. A sample output from a `debug` command to troubleshoot authentication failures is shown in the following figure:

```
Router1#: debug vrrp authentication
VRRP: Sent: 21016401FE050000AC1801FE0000000000000000
VRRP: HshC: B861CBF1B9026130DD34AED849BEC8A1
VRRP: Rcvd: 21016401FE050000AC1801FE0000000000000000
VRRP: HshC: B861CBF1B9026130DD34AED849BEC8A1
VRRP: HshR: C5E193C6D84533FDC750F85FCFB051E1
VRRP: Grp 1 Adv from 172.24.1.2 has failed MD5 auth
```

Figure 20: Debugging authentication issues

Troubleshooting routing issues

Routing is fundamental to the forwarding of packets in an IP network, as the routing processes define the path that an IP packet would take at each routed hop. The router builds the routing table using statically defined routes or running routing protocols, such as RIP, OSPF, and ISIS. The routing table defines the next hop for an IP packet with a given destination address.

The routing table on a Cisco device can be seen using the `show ip route` command. A sample output of the command is as shown in the following image:

```
Router# show ip route

Codes: L - local, C - connected, S - static, R - RIP, M - mobile, B - BGP
       D - EIGRP, EX - EIGRP external, O - OSPF, IA - OSPF inter area
       N1 - OSPF NSSA external type 1, N2 - OSPF NSSA external type 2
       E1 - OSPF external type 1, E2 - OSPF external type 2
       i - IS-IS, su - IS-IS summary L1- IS-IS level-1, L2 - IS-IS level-2

--- Output trimmed ----

Gateway of last resort is not set
      1.0.0.0/24 is subnetted, 1 subnets
O E2   1.0.0.0 [110/20] via 10.0.0.1, 0:01:30, Ethernet0/2
      2.0.0.0/24 is subnetted, 1 subnets
S      2.0.0.0 [1/0] via 3.1.1.2
      3.0.0.0/8 is variably subnetted, 2 subnets, 2 masks
C        3.1.1.0/24 is directly connected, Ethernet0/1
L        3.1.1.1/32 is directly connected, Ethernet0/1
      100.0.0.0/24 is subnetted, 1 subnets
O        100.200.9.0 [110/20] via 10.0.0.1, 00:05:37, Ethernet0/2
      192.268.1.2/32 is subnetted, 1 subnets
O        192.168.1.2 [110/11] via 10.0.0.1, 00:05:37, Ethernet0/2
      200.1.0.1/32 is subnetted, 1 subnets
O        200.1.0.1 [110/11] via 10.0.0.1, 00:05:37, Ethernet0/2
```

Figure 21: Display of the IP routing table

The output shows that the routed prefix, the next hop IP address and the interface, and the method a specific prefix, have been added to the routing table. Recall from `Chapter 4,` *Understanding and Configuring Campus Network Technologies,* that there could be multiple protocols that can inject the same prefix in the routing table and the administrative distance is used to find the preferred route.

The output shows the codes used for populating the routes like the preceding output shows routes populated through OSPF (O), local (L), connected (C), and static routes (S). The subnets can be confusing in the show output table, as they reflect the actual mask that is used on the router. If there is only one subnet, the mask of the actual prefix is not displayed as for the prefix 2.0.0.0/24, in the preceding table. However, if the subnet is variably subnetted, the masks are shown along with the prefix in the routing table like the prefix 3.1.1.0/24 and 3.1.1.1/32, in the preceding table. The numbers in the square braces show the administrative distance followed by the metric for the given route. For example, the OSPF learned route 192.168.1.2 has the admin distance of 110 that corresponds to the OSPF protocol and the OSPF metric 11.

Routing takes the most specific route in the routing table, and hence the most specific route entry that the destination address belongs to will used to route the packet. One should look at the /32 address for the host for which troubleshooting is being done to view the actual route rather than aggregate prefixes. Another option that can be used by the network engineer is to use the various options for the `ip route` command such as `show ip route 10.0.0.1 10.0.0.0 longer-prefixes`.

To see the IP routes added by a specific protocol, use the `show ip route protocol` command. For example, to see only BGP routes, use the `show ip route bgp` command, and to view only OSPF routes injected through OSPF process id 10, use the `show ip route ospf 10` command.

Some specific `show` commands for OSPF are as shown in the following image:

Command	Usage
Show ip ospf	Displays the general information about OSPF routing processes.
Show ip ospf interface	Displays the interface specific information related to OSPF including OSPF timers.
Show ip ospf border-routers	Displays the Area Border Routers, and the ASBRs from where any routes are redistributed into OSPF.
Show ip ospf database	Displays the complete OSPF database that the router uses for running the SPF algorithm. This can be filtered using various options for the command.
Show ip ospf neighbor	Displays all OSPF neighbors on a per interface basis for the router.

Figure 22: Commands for troubleshooting OSPF

A sample output for the `show ip ospf neighbor` command is as shown in the following image. Note that the neighbor state should be FULL. If the state is EX-START, it is generally because of MTU mismatch issues and the MTU on either side of the link needs to be checked:

```
Device# show ip ospf neighbor
Neighbor ID      Pri    State          Dead Time    Address         Interface
10.199.199.137   1      FULL/DR         0:00:31     192.168.80.37   Ethernet0
172.16.48.1      1      FULL/DROTHER 0:00:33        172.16.48.1     Ethernet1
172.16.48.200    1      FULL/DROTHER 0:00:33        172.16.48.200   Ethernet1
```

Figure 23: Display of the OSPF neighbor information

Similar `show` commands can be used for other routing protocols such as ISIS, RIP, and BGP. The engineer can see the various commands available by typing the ? key after a part of the complete command. This will provide a complete list of options available in the Cisco IOS for the set of commands that start with the text before the ? sign. The engineer can start at `show ?` and progress on to using commands such as `show isis ?` and `show isis neighbors ?`.

Troubleshooting forwarding plane issues

Forwarding plane is concerned with the forwarding of packets after the routing decisions have been taken. The forwarding of packets can still be blocked due to link congestion, and the application of **access control lists (ACLs)** on any interfaces.

Forwarding plane issues can also manifest themselves as brownouts, where the packets are not totally blocked, but the service is severely degraded due to link congestion or other factors leading to packet loss, excessive latency, or jitter on the network. We shall discuss the brownout scenario in the next section.

Total loss of packets on the forwarding plane can happen due to the wrong use of ACLs on the interface or a firewall blocking certain packets. Note that every ACL has an implicit deny any statement at the end. Hence, if a packet is not explicitly allowed using an ACL, the packets will be discarded by the ACL.

Another reason for the packets to be blocked is when an ACL is applied on an interface in the wrong direction. The in and out direction should be applied with care. An ACL applied in the incoming direction means all packets arriving at an interface would be parsed by that ACL, and an ACL in the out direction means all packets being sent out on that interface would be parsed by the ACL. The direction in which an ACL is applied can be viewed in the running-configuration in the interface section on which the ACL is applied using the `show running-configuration | inc interface | access-group` command, which will list only the lines in the configuration that have the words interface or access-group, making the output easier to read.

The actual entries of the ACL can be viewed using the `show ip access-list` command. A sample output of the command is as shown in the following image. The output of the command also shows the number of packets matched against each line of the access list. If you want to see all access lists, including the non-IP access lists, use the `show access-lists` command. This command will not display any matched packets even for IP access-lists:

```
Router# show ip access-lists
Extended IP access list 150
    10 deny icmp any any (5 matches)
    20 permit ip ay any (8 matches)

Router#
```

Figure 24: Display of IP ACLs

There are also times when a link is not stable, but keeps flapping and goes up and down rapidly. This will lead to frequent triggers to the routing process on the device to bring the link in the routing topology and withdraw it. Such excessive processing will not allow the routing to converge, leading to high CPU and forwarding issues. Such issues can be detected using the `show interface` command and looking for the time that the interface has been up.

Troubleshooting performance issues

Performance issues can occur on the network because of packet loss, latency, and jitter. Packet loss and latency can be measured using the ping commands. However, the ping commands will not take the exact DSCP values and hence the quality of service for these ping packets would be different than the actual application. This can be measured using the extended ping commands.

Performance issues can also be due to MTU issues, where the network has a lower MTU than what the applications are using and hence the routers have to fragment packets. This can be detected with the extended ping commands using the do not fragment option as discussed earlier.

IP SLA probes discussed in Chapter 10, *A Systematic Approach to Network Management*, is a very effective way of measuring and baselining the application performance on a real-time basis.

Performance issues can also happen due to the links that have a lot of bit errors. These errors manifest as CRC errors on the interfaces. These links have to be individually monitored, by seeing the errors on the interfaces using the `show interface` command. The counters can be cleared using the `clear counters interface` command and then running the show interface commands at regular intervals.

Performance issues are generally transient and can be very hard to identify during troubleshooting. They can be effectively handled by monitoring the interfaces over long periods of time using IP SLA scheduling and using scripts that keep monitoring the errors on the link over intervals of time.

Troubleshooting the management plane

Some of the management plane issues can lead to authorization failures or protocols such as NTP and SNMP going down. Most problems arise due to mismatching community or mismatching IP addresses configured for the peer and the actual address that is being sent by the peer. Hence, it is recommended to use the source interface as loopback interface and peer.

The commands that can be used to validate the source address in the management packets are `show run | inc trap-source` and `show run | inc ntp source`.

Further, the ACLs, if any, which are used to control access for SNMP to NOC servers should have the right IP address. This can be seen using the `show access lists` command.

Debugs can also be used to debug any authentication or authorization issues using the `debug accounting` or `debug authorization` commands.

Troubleshooting device level issues

By far the most troublesome issues to detect are the device related issues, where the device behaves erratically and there is no obvious reason.

Device level issues can be attributed to a hardware or software version running on the devices. A hardware-level issue is relatively easy to troubleshoot if the entire line card or a device is faulty. If this happens to be a port amongst a pool of ports on a card, this would still be tricky. A software issue, on the other hand, is the trickiest part, as the software behaving erratically due to a software bug can be transient and might not always provide the right output through show commands to troubleshoot.

Most commands that can help an engineer check and validate the hardware and software health are not publicly available and are available as hidden commands on the IOS. These commands are generally used by the support teams of the vendors to get to the root cause of the issue and declare an issue as hardware or a software issue. Hence, device level issues are generally resolved jointly with the **Cisco Technical Assistance Center** (**TAC**).

Hardware issues

Identifying and diagnosing hardware problems depends on the product being used, as each product has different hardware architecture and can have different slightly commands for troubleshooting.

Some of the commands that can be used to troubleshoot the hardware on Cisco devices are show controllers, show platform, show inventory, and show diag. We are not discussing the output in detail, as this output would be hardware-centric and change from platform to platform.

Software issues

The most commonly used Cisco IOS commands used for diagnosing software level issues are the show processes cpu, show memory, and show interface commands.

The show processes cpu command is issued to view a list of all processes that are running on the router. The output shows the time that these processes have consumed on the CPU since their initiation and the average utilization over the last five second, one minute, and five minute intervals. A sample output of the show processes cpu command is shown in the following image:

```
Router# show processes cpu                    CPU used for switching packets

CPU utilization for five seconds: 0%/0%; one minute: 0%; five minutes: 0%
 PID Runtime(uS)      Invoked    uSecs   5Sec    1Min    5Min TTY Process
   1       4000           67       59   0.00%   0.00%   0.00%   0 Chunk Manager
   2       4000       962255        0   0.00%   0.00%   0.00%   0 Load Meter
   3          0            1        0   0.00%   0.00%   0.00%   0 cpf_process_tp
   4          0            1        0   0.00%   0.00%   0.00%   0 EDDRI_MAIN
   5  586520704       732013     6668   0.00%   0.11%   0.08%   0 Check heaps
   6       4000          991        4   0.00%   0.00%   0.00%   0 Pool Manager
   7          0            1        0   0.00%   0.00%   0.00%   0 DiscardQ Backg
   8          0            2        0   0.00%   0.00%   0.00%   0 Timers
   9          0            2        0   0.00%   0.00%   0.00%   0 ATM AutoVC Per
  10          0            2        0   0.00%   0.00%   0.00%   0 ATM VC Auto Cr
```

Figure 25: Troubleshooting CPU utilization issues

The output on the router also shows the percentage of the CPU cycles that have been spent on switching packets, rather than performing control plane functions. This number is highlighted in the preceding figure. If the time spent in packet switching is high, the configuration needs to be evaluated to avoid punting packets to the CPU. The processes are sorted by process ID by default, but this can be changed using the sorted option. For example, to sort processes by a decreasing utilization in a one minute interval, the command is `show processes cpu sorted 1min`.

The next element on a device is the memory, which is divided into different pools for various uses, including CPU process memory and the input/ output (I/O) pool that is used for packet buffering. There is a finite amount of memory on a device and the utilization can be tracked using the `show memory summary` command. The example output illustrated in the following image shows the processor and the I/O memory utilization. The lowest and the largest values correspond to the minimum and the maximum amount of free memory during the preceding five minute interval. To view the memory used by each process in IOS, the command is `show processes memory`.

```
Router# show memory summary

              Head      Total(b)     Used(b)      Free(b)     Lowest(b)    Largest(b)
Processor   61E379A0   27035232     8089056     18946176     17964108     17963664
      I/O    3800000    8388608     2815088      5573520      5561520      5573472
```

Figure 26: Troubleshooting memory issues

These commands can be used to baseline the values and detect any deviations, which can be used in consultation with the Cisco TAC to identify software bugs.

Summary

Network troubleshooting is an extensive field. It tests not only the engineer's understanding of the fundamental protocol working but also tests his knowledge of the network under his supervision. A good understanding of the preceding information coupled with the skill and experience of the network engineer helps resolve network issues more effectively. Troubleshooting is effective if the engineer follows a systematic approach and correlating various observations before starting to make changes on the network. Lastly, a simple and modular network can go a long way in making troubleshooting easier and efficient.

In this chapter, we covered some of the commands that can be used to identify and diagnose problems on an IP network and provided a systematic approach that can be used by network engineers to troubleshoot issues on the enterprise IP network.

Every network engineer grows in his career based on his dedication and applying the knowledge that he has acquired in other domains and situations. Networking is a vast subject, where an engineer can never get bored. If there are no problems on the network, think of optimizing the network and get back to the drawing board and go after new challenges. I hope that the book has given you enough to think and do on your networking journey. Happy networking!

Index

E

E1 encapsulation 212
egress policy 345, 346, 347
Email Security Appliance (ESA) 308
endpoints
  securing 310
Enhanced Interior Gateway Routing Protocol
  (EIGRP) 138
enhanced Telecom Operations Map (eTOM) 351
enterprise security
  elements 279, 280
Ethernet Relay Service (ERS) 219
Ethernet Wire Service (EWS) 219
Ethernet
  about 92, 93
  access ports 97, 98
  MAC-based forwarding 94, 95
  switch 94, 95
  trunk ports 97, 98
  Virtual LANs 95, 96
Explicit Congestion Notification (ECN) 19

F

Fault, Configuration, Accounting, Performance, and
  Security (FCAPS)
  about 350
  accounting management 350
  fault management 350
  performance management 350
  security management 350
Fiber Channel (FC) 242
Fiber Channel over Ethernet (FCoE) 242
fiber leasing 217
File Transfer Protocol (FTP) 314
firewall design
  about 263
  firewall redundancy 269
firewall
  about 251, 308
  application inspection 254
  basic access control 253
  connection limits, applying 254
  inspection 252
  IP fragments, protecting 253

scaling 255
security context 255
TCP normalization 254
threat detection, enabling 254
first hop connectivity
  troubleshooting 394
First Hop Redundancy Protocols (FHRP) 120,
  121, 122
  GLBP 130
  HSRP 123, 124, 125, 126, 127
  VRRP 128, 129, 130
FlexConnect mode
  about 196, 197
  APs, configuring in FlexConnect mode 197, 198
flexconnect mode
  APs, configuring in FlexConnect mode 199, 200,
  201
FlexConnect mode
  central switched 197
  local switched 197
flexibility 58, 59
forwarding plane issues
  troubleshooting 399
Frame Check Sequence (FCS) 93
Frame Relay (FR) 207
frameworks
  to network management 350, 351, 352, 353
Fulfilment, Assurance, and Billing (FAB) 351
functionality 54

G

Gateway Load Balancing Protocol (GLBP) 130
Generic Routing Encapsulation (GRE) 214
Global Positioning System (GPS) 363
graphical user interface (GUI) 370

H

hardware issues 402
hardware
  assessing 342
high definition (HD) 54
High-Level Data Link Control (HDLC) 209
High-level design (HLD) 34
Host Bus Adapters (HBAs) 250
Hot Standby Router Protocol (HSRP) 123

www.ingramcontent.com/pod-product-compliance
Lightning Source LLC
Chambersburg PA
CBHW060647060326
40690CB00020B/4552